D1172873

ENDORSEMENTS FOR *REVOLUTION IN GENEROSITY*

"Our approach to money and possessions isn't just important—it's central to our spiritual lives. Our giving is a reflexive response to the grace of God in our lives. It comes out of the transforming work of Christ in us. I pray that this book will lead you to a greater understanding and appreciation of this truth."

—RANDY ALCORN, *author of* Money, Possessions and Eternity, *and* The Treasure Principle

"Christians certainly need to become more God-centered in their approach to giving. Wes Willmer has done a marvelous job of providing a rich resource for the church in *Revolution in Generosity*. This is a great opportunity for all of us to learn how to follow a God-centric model of generosity that will transform lives and ministries beyond our wildest dreams."

—KEN BEHR, *President, Evangelical Council for Financial Accountability (ECFA)*

"*Revolution in Generosity* intends to show you how to make genuinely biblical choices in every area of your life, including giving and asking. If the ideas in this book were followed, there would be a revolution in generosity among Christians. This book will be an important resource for those who seek to advance the Kingdom."

—CHARLES COLSON, *Founder, Prison Fellowship*

"The Christian church today needs a revolution in generosity—a revolution that will shape Christians into the image of Christ, a revolution that will spread goodwill and the fragrant aroma of Christ, a revolution that will fuel authentic transformation. Read the book, join the revolution."

—CHUCK BENTLEY, *CEO, Crown Financial Ministries*

"If this book had been available fifty years ago and resources had been handled with the depth of theological insight that *Revolution in Generosity* offers, Christian ministry effectiveness today would be radically improved. Now that the book has arrived, I highly recommend it and suggest that ministries not delay another day in implementing these essential principles to further the Great Commission."

—CLYDE COOK, *President Emeritus, Biola University*

"*Revolution in Generosity* rightly contrasts God-oriented stewardship with human-oriented philanthropy. It underscores the urgency for each of us to be rich toward God. It also includes numerous practical suggestions and referrals. If you're in a position of responsibility in fundraising, whether in a local church or in a parachurch organization, do yourself a favor—read this book."

—FRANKLIN GRAHAM, *President and CEO, Billy Graham Evangelistic Association and Samaritan's Purse*

"This book offers a refreshing and hugely needed biblical perspective so often absent in ministry. It seeks to show that God has given us a much better way: transformation of our hearts and minds that leads to a whole new motive for giving. Churches and parachurch organizations that humbly apply these biblical principles will revolutionize ministry effectiveness—for all the right reasons."

—MARK HOLBROOK, *President/CEO, Evangelical Christian Credit Union (ECCU)*

"Managing money in a God-honoring way is one of the great challenges for every Christ-follower. This book will move people toward a more generous future."

—BILL HYBELS, *Senior Pastor, Willow Creek Community Church*

"At last, a book about money that doesn't dodge the hard questions and doesn't focus on 'fundraising techniques.' This collection of scholars, leaders, and practitioners helps us look at money from God's perspective and teaches us how to 'grow more generous in our hearts' toward God and others. A must for every pastor, ministry leader, or board member!"

—CHIP INGRAM, *President and Teaching Pastor, Living on the Edge*

"Now we have the book written from a biblical worldview with the answers we need. *Revolution in Generosity* is a must read for all of us who want to move to the next level of effectiveness in fundraising by helping donors see the big picture. Thank you, Wes, for putting the goodies down on a shelf low enough for all of us to reach. You have done a great service to God's work in these times."

—MICHAEL D. LITTLE, *President, The Christian Broadcasting Network, Inc.*

"The Christian faith involves all of life. I commend this book to all pastors and parachurch leaders. Focusing on heart transformation is the future for a revolution in generosity for God's work."

—FRANK LOFARO, *President, Christian Management Association (CMA)*

"Wes Willmer has been a pioneer among Christian leaders in encouraging Christians to follow God's plan for money, giving, and asking, which results in a transformed and generous life. This is a great book for any believer serious about his or her faith."

—HUGH O. MACLELLAN, JR., *President, The Maclellan Foundation*

"*Revolution in Generosity* is a compelling vision of 'giving and asking' as they were meant to be done in God's eyes. Every person should read this book . . . you can't afford not to."

—JOSH MCDOWELL, *author of* More than a Carpenter *and* Evidence that Demands a Verdict

"*Revolution in Generosity* offers solid teaching that gets at the heart of giving and asking. It is a helpful resource and a much-needed call to all of us in ministry to be transformed in how we view possessions and spiritual growth."

—ELISA MORGAN, *CEO, Mothers of Preschoolers (MOPS) International*

"Psalm 24 reminds us that God is the ultimate owner of all we are and have. He expects us to be good stewards and invest the resources he has entrusted to us. For Him, returns are measured in eternal values. This book will help you understand the joy of being generous and responsible as you invest and give the resources God has given you."

—BILL POLLARD, *Chairman Emeritus, ServiceMaster Co.*

"An important book devoted to an urgent task: transforming scandalously skimpy Christian giving by nurturing Christians genuinely conformed to the image of Christ. Wise, concrete, practical advice from successful practitioners."

—RONALD J. SIDER, *President, Evangelicals for Social Action*

"If as a believer, my pursuit of true discipleship is reflected by a prayer life that consistently implores, 'Father, what would you have me think, what would you have me say, what would you have me do?' then as a Christian leader I must pursue being informed in godly practices of fund development. *Revolution in Generosity* is a valuable resource in that pursuit."

—KEN SMITHERMAN, *President Association of Christian Schools International*

"The American Church has largely failed the 'test of prosperity' during a century that witnessed the greatest buildup of wealth in the history of man. It's time for a change. Wes Willmer and his collaborative thinkers have given us a book that truly challenges the church and its ministries toward the pursuit of biblical generosity. Stewards awake! May God be glorified through faithful lives poured out for His purposes."

—GREG SPERRY, *National Christian Foundation*

"In the wealthiest nation of Christians in history, the most seldom preached sermon is the one that addresses head-on what we do with our money. If God were to write a letter to the church in America, as He did to the seven churches in Revelation, it would almost certainly challenge our stewardship over the wealth that He has entrusted to us. If we would truly embrace and model the principles set forth by the authors of this important book, I believe that God could use the American church to change the world."

—RICHARD STEARNS, *President, World Vision US*

"There are lots of books about how to get rich, but far too few about becoming rich toward God . . . which, by the way, is far more important! Embrace the wisdom of this book and enjoy true prosperity!"

—JOSEPH STOWELL, *President, Cornerstone University, Grand Rapids, Michigan*

"Convicting, scholarly, and practical—*Revolution in Generosity* is a book that every Christian involved in ministry in Christ's kingdom should read!"

—JONI EARECKSON TADA, *Founder, Joni and Friends*

"This book is countercultural and revolutionary. It is sitting down with the best thinkers in the world of biblically astute financial or development consultants. Who among us as leaders has not cringed at the appeals we receive— and even sent as an organization. As results-driven leaders, we so easily look at the bottom line in financial terms when it is really in the Kingdom lives of people who give and serve with us. Wes Wilmer and his coauthors point us down the road of biblical generosity and true stewardship—a road not easily taken, but so needed in our 'bang for the buck' and 'do whatever it takes' competitive Christian world."

—JERRY WHITE, *President Emeritus, The Navigators*

"Our possessions are an indispensable part of our life in the Kingdom of God. We need to understand how they receive spiritual life by our choices under the direction of the Word and the Spirit. This is not widely appreciated, but Wes Willmer has devoted much of his life to helping people with Kingdom generosity and stewardship. He gives good direction on how to be faithful over little and faithful over much."

—DALLAS WILLARD, *author of* The Divine Conspiracy, The Spirit of the Disciplines, *and* Renovation of the Heart

---

"Money is integral to life. It reflects who we are and what we value. If we are to worship God, this worship must include our finances. Unfortunately, many ministries today overlook this important truth."

—ROBERT WUTHNOW, *Andlinger Professor of Sociology and Director of Center for the Study of Religion, Princeton University*

Revolution in
GENEROSITY

TRANSFORMING STEWARDS
TO BE RICH TOWARD GOD

WESLEY K. WILLMER

GENERAL EDITOR

MOODY PUBLISHERS
CHICAGO

Scripture quotations marked NIV are taken from the *Holy Bible, New International Version*®. NIV®. Copyright © 1973, 1978, 1984 by International Bible Society. Used by permission of Zondervan. All rights reserved.

Scripture quotations marked TNIV are taken from the *Holy Bible, Today's New International Version*. TNIV®. Copyright © 2001, 2005 by International Bible Society. Used by permission of Zondervan. All rights reserved.

Scripture quotations marked ESV are taken from *The Holy Bible, English Standard Version*. Copyright © 2000, 2001 by Crossway Bibles, a division of Good News Publishers. Used by permission. All rights reserved.

Scripture quotations marked RSV are taken from the *Revised Standard Version* of the Bible, copyright 1952 [2nd edition, 1971] by the Division of Christian Education of the National Council of the Churches of Christ in the USA. Used by permission. All rights reserved.

Scripture quotations marked NASB are taken from the *New American Standard Bible*®, Copyright © 1960, 1962, 1963, 1968, 1971, 1972, 1973, 1975, 1977, 1995 by The Lockman Foundation. Used by permission. (www.Lockman.org)

Scripture quotations marked NLT are taken from the *Holy Bible, New Living Translation,* copyright © 1996. Used by permission of Tyndale House Publishers, Inc., Wheaton, Illinois 60189, U.S.A. All rights reserved.

Scripture quotations marked NKJV are taken from the *New King James Version*. Copyright © 1982 by Thomas Nelson, Inc. Used by permission. All rights reserved.

Scripture quotations marked KJV are taken from the King James Version.

All websites and phone numbers listed herein are accurate at the time of publication but may change in the future or cease to exist. The listing of website references and resources does not imply publisher endorsement of the site's entire contents. Groups and organizations are listed for informational purposes, and listing does not imply publisher endorsement of their activities.

Published in association with the literary agency of Mark Sweeney & Associates

Cover Design: UniGlory Studio (www.uniglorystudio.com) Lauren Castady and J. David Schmidt

Interior Design: Smartt Guys design

Editor: Christopher Reese

Library of Congress Cataloging-in-Publication Data
A revolution in generosity : transforming stewards to be rich toward God /
Wesley K. Willmer, general editor.
    p. cm. --
Includes bibliographical references.
ISBN-13: 978-0-8024-6753-9
ISBN-10: 0-8024-6753-9
1. Generosity--Religious aspects--Christianity. 2. Christian giving. 3.
Christians--Charitable contributions. 4. Fund raising. I. Willmer, Wesley
Kenneth.
BV4647.G45R48 2008
248'.6--dc22

2008001626

This book is printed on acid free recycled paper containing 30% PCW (Post Consumer Waste) and manufactured in the United States of America by Sheridan Books, a member of the Green Press Initiative.

We hope you enjoy this book from Moody Publishers. Our goal is to provide high-quality, thought-provoking books and products that connect truth to your real needs and challenges. For more information on other books and products written and produced from a biblical perspective, go to www.moody-publishers.com or write to:

Moody Publishers
820 N. LaSalle Boulevard
Chicago, IL 60610

1 3 5 7 9 10 8 6 4 2

Printed in the United States of America

*Dedicated to Calvin and Lois Howe,
with deep appreciation for their faithful
encouragement for this project.
Cal and Lois desire Christians to experience
the joy of giving generously from a "blessed heart"
as a result of being transformed as stewards
into the image of Christ.*

CONTENTS

INDEX OF CHARTS

FOREWORD

I first became aware of Wes Willmer and his work with parachurch ministries almost twenty-five years ago. More recently, I became aware of this book project because my good friend Calvin Howe (to whom this book is dedicated) suggested that a foundation board, on which we mutually serve, support this effort. As we provided financial support and I became more aware of the significance of people giving from a "blessed heart," the more convinced I have become of the importance of transforming stewards to be rich toward God, as an expression of Christians conforming to the image of Christ.

Our calling as Christians is not only to order our own lives by divine principles, but also to engage the world. Christians see things from an eternal perspective. Everything we do now has eternal significance. When the church is faithful to its calling, it always leads to a reformation of culture. If the ideas in this book were followed, there would be a revolution in generosity among Christians that would be transformational.

Every decision we make reflects our worldview. Every choice, every action either expresses a false worldview and thus contributes to a disordered and broken world, or expresses God's truth and helps build a world that reflects His created order. This book intends to show you how to make genuinely biblical choices in every area of your life, including giving and asking.

Christians are saved not only from something (sin) but also to something (Christ's lordship over all of life). The Christian life begins with spiritual restoration—this is the indispensable beginning, for only the redeemed person is filled with God's Spirit and can genuinely know and fulfill God's plan. All believers receive the power to become children of God, to be transformed and restored to our true nature, people created in the image of God. Having been liberated from sin, we are empowered to help bring Christ's restoration to the entire creation order. This redemptive goal permeates everything we do, for there is no invisible line dividing between sacred and secular, even when it comes to money. We are to bring "all things" under the lordship of Christ, in the home and the school, in the workshop and the corporate boardroom, on the movie screen and the concert stage, in the city council and the legislative chamber, in fundraising and consulting and preaching and giving. If this were to happen, Christians would be giving from a blessed heart, and a revolution in generosity would result.

This book will be an important resource for those who seek to advance the Kingdom.

Charles Colson
FOUNDER, PRISON FELLOWSHIP

INTRODUCTION

Philip Yancey tells the story[1] of how he saved every fundraising appeal he received for one month, and then analyzed the sixty-two items in his collection. His analysis yielded two conclusions: First, the appeals from the Christian organizations employed the same gimmicks as the appeals from everyone else (URGENT! headlines, P.S. underlined in blue, premiums promised, etc.). Second, not a single one focused on Yancey's need as a Christian to honor and obey God with his giving.

The purpose of this book is to equip resource-raising leaders to help Christians become generous by conforming to the image of Christ. The desire of the authors is to reverse the practices Yancey unveiled and rather help Christians grow as stewards who can experience the joy of generosity as they honor and obey God with their giving.

While most Christian resource raising (including in the church) is modeled after secular marketing transactional practices of doing whatever (pressure, gimmicks, etc.) it takes to achieve the financial bottom line, this approach is failing to achieve generous support for ministry. After decades of using all the transactional fundraising techniques imaginable, giving in the Western world averages barely 2 percent per household income. Although Syracuse University researcher Arthur C. Brooks recently confirmed that "religious people give more to everything,"[2] giving among evangelicals (the most generous group) still averages barely 3 to 4 percent per household income.

The authors in this book are proposing that there is a more God-honoring approach of providing resources—focusing on transforming stewards to be rich toward God. It is human nature to be like the rich fool in Luke 12:21, who "lays up treasure for himself and is not rich toward God."[3] John Ortberg hit the nail on the head when he wrote, "The object of life, according to Jesus, is breathtakingly simple: Be rich towards God."[4] The goal of this book is to help people, in concrete and practical ways, to head in the opposite direction, beyond self-seeking ownership and hoarding to embrace stewardship and generous giving, thereby becoming stewards who are rich toward God.

Once a believer understands how God views money and giving, it becomes clear that the asking process for Christian church and parachurch organizations should be drastically different from current secular practice. In contrast, the Christian ministry's priority should be to facilitate the transformation of believers to conform to the image of Christ, to become generous, as Christ is generous; for "in their generosity, believers reflect the character of God, who is the giver of all good things (James 1:17)."[5] John Pearson suggests ministries uphold the statement:

"We believe that extravagant generosity is the Biblical norm, not the exception. We challenge donors to give liberally to kingdom causes. We urge prayerful giving to God's work, not for tax benefits, nor for budget needs. We scrutinize our methodologies against not what works, but against God-honoring principles."[6]

It is out of this paradigm and belief system that this book is written, to assist Christian believers and the Christian resource-raising world to turn off the road they are currently on (focusing solely on the financial needs of the organization) and move onto God's road (motivated to being conformed to the image of Christ).

Transformed Christians will give from their hearts and will truly create a revolution in generosity, in both quantity and quality. This revolution will not come from using more sophisticated marketing techniques or increasing pressure on people by making them feel guilty for not giving. Rather, the revolution will come when churches, parachurch organizations, consultants, fundraisers, financial planners, and other believers focus on facilitating God's work of transforming individuals from self-centered to God-centered, from being greedy to being generous. This whole-life transformation is the supernatural work of God's grace in individual lives, and the money-raising efforts of Christian organizations should conform to the godly approach of raising up stewards to be rich toward God.

To engage this important yet countercultural theme, some of the best scholars and practitioners on the subject have been assembled. Since new territory is being explored, the proposals in this book are pioneering steps forward in what we hope will become a mass migration. To explain how furthering God's transformation of givers' hearts will advance a revolution in generosity, the book is divided into five sections.

1. *God's Plan for Generosity:* This section explores how God views money and giving and, consequently, what asking should look like, and provides a biblical framework for why a revolution in giving will result if raising support focuses on transforming stewards to be rich toward God.

2. *The Church's Role in Transforming Stewards:* Section two outlines the important role of the church in educating and transforming hearts. It introduces the church's role in bringing the topic of stewardship front and center, as well as suggestions for organizing a church stewardship ministry, possible teaching content, and conducting campaigns and special events.

3. *The Asker's Role as a Facilitator of Heart Transformation:* Both churches and parachurch organizations have a responsibility to use God's way of growing givers' hearts when they seek funds. This section presents a Christian worldview of asking for money. It addresses the calling and devotional life of the asker, how to approach asking as discipleship, fundraising centered on transforming stewards, and ways to communicate the message.

4. *The Leader's/Advisor's Role in Raising Up Stewards:* In addition to their frontline responsibilities, church and parachurch leadership have an important role in growing givers' hearts. This section addresses how implementing the ideas of stewardship and transformation becomes the responsibility of the leadership of boards, CEOs, consultants, and financial advisors.

5. *Pitfalls and Potential of Revolutionary Generosity:* This last section looks at ethical and integrity issues, competition, and lessons learned on the journey

of generosity. It concludes with an appendix explaining and drawing implications from the Biblical Principles for Stewardship and Fundraising, articulated by a joint task force of the Christian Stewardship Association (CSA) and the Evangelical Council for Financial Accountability (ECFA), which undergird this book's entire focus.

This book was a team effort over many years. As the table of contents shows, twenty-two authors contributed to this project, and I am grateful to God for the gifts each brought to the task. In addition, six organizations endorsed this effort: the Evangelical Council of Financial Accountability (ECFA), the Christian Stewardship Association (CSA), Crown Financial Ministries, Generous Giving, Kingdom Advisors, and the Christian Management Association (CMA). As of April 2008, CSA and CMA have merged to form the Christian Leadership Alliance.

Two foundations provided financial support. John Bass of the Henry Parsons Crowell and Susan Coleman Crowell Trust was an early proponent of this project, and Paul E. Nelson, executive director of the Crowell Trust, faithfully shepherded this project. A special thanks to all the board members at the time of the decision, including: John Bass, Edwin L. Frizen Jr., Lowell L. Kline, Jane Overstreet, and Jack Robinson. The M. E. Foundation also contributed significantly. Calvin Howe was an early encourager, believing there was a need for a book that encouraged people to give from a blessed heart rather than an obligated heart. He facilitated the support from the M. E. Foundation, including board members Chuck Colson, Sharon Berry, Grace McCrane, and Kelli R. Morris.

On the production side I am grateful to the staff at Moody Publishers, including Greg Thornton, vice president and publisher at Moody Bible Institute, Christopher Reese, Bob Hill, Dave Dewit, Harry Rogers, Tracey Shannon, and Karen Waddles. Mark Sweeney was a helpful and encouraging agent, providing counsel for the book proposal and identifying a publisher. ECFA's vice president Dan Busby and president Ken Behr coordinated the budget for the project. Those involved in facilitating the research and writing over a period of several years include: Andrew Bailey, Rebecca Card, Anne Creamer, Danielle Jorgensen, Christina Maraldo, Hope Rhodes, and Karissa Sywulka. In addition, I am grateful to God for providing meaningful mentors in my life, including David McKenna, Norman Edwards, Clyde Cook, and Barry Corey, who have helped shape my life and thinking.

A personal thanks to my wife, Sharon. Without her patience and understanding of my "hours at the desk" over several years, this book would not have materialized, and her dialogue on the topic helped shape the outcome. Likewise, thanks to my mother, Diantha S. Willmer, who faithfully prayed for this effort and was an encourager when she regularly asked, "How's the book coming?"

Finally, I thank the Lord for allowing me the privilege of being used by Him. My prayer is that this book will draw others into this marvelous understanding of transformation and that God's eternal kingdom will be glorified.

Wesley K. Willmer, Ph.D.
PROJECT LEADER AND EDITOR

1. Philip Yancey, *Finding God in Unexpected Places* (Colorado Springs: WaterBrook, 2005), 263–64.
2. Arthur C. Brooks, *Who Really Cares: The Surprising Truth about Compassionate Conservatism—America's Charity Divide—Who Gives, Who Doesn't, and Why It Matters* (New York: Basic Books, 2006), 34.
3. English Standard Version.
4. John Ortberg, *When the Game Is Over, It All Goes Back in the Box* (Grand Rapids: Zondervan, 2007), 27.
5. Barbara Kois, "Above and Beyond," *Moody* (March/April 2001): 33.
6. John Pearson, *Mastering the Management Buckets: 20 Critical Competencies for Leading Your Business or Nonprofit* (Ventura, CA: Regal Books, 2008).

I.

God's Plan for GENEROSITY

Generosity is the natural outcome of God's transforming work in individuals when they are conformed to the image of Christ and become generous as Christ is generous. The foundation for realizing a revolution in generosity is understanding the biblical view of possessions, giving, and asking for resources. This section sets the stage by exploring this biblical framework and its implications for a Christian view of material stewardship.

Chapter

CREATING A
REVOLUTION in GENEROSITY

BY WESLEY K. WILLMER, *Vice President of*
University Advancement and Professor at Biola University

fter looking at Christianity, India's prime minister Mahatma Gandhi concluded that if all Christians acted like Christ, the whole world would be Christian. He is not alone in his observation. Dallas Willard writes, "This aching world is waiting for the people explicitly identified with Christ to be, through and through, the people he intends them to be."[1] Barna research studies confirm this gap.[2] It seems that most Christians are ignoring their call to be conformed to the image of Christ. Their distinctive faith aside, Christians are acting more and more like the rest of culture, and there is little discernible difference between believers and nonbelievers: from the books they read, to the issues they worry about, to how they use their money.[3] The same is generally true in Christians' giving and asking for resources. Scripture consistently reminds us that if Christ is not first in the use of our money, He is not first in our lives. Our use of possessions demonstrates materially our spiritual status (see Craig Blomberg's chapter). Is it possible that our checkbooks are a better measure of our spiritual condition than the underlining in our Bibles? Is it possible that if biblical stewardship issues ordered Christians' lives, they would be a better reflection of Christ's image to the world?

The last fifty-plus years in American culture have been marked by increasing prosperity and wealth, with a corresponding increase in our obsession with "stuff." Most often, it is hard to tell the difference between believers and nonbelievers by looking at how they view and use the things God has entrusted to them. While wealth among Christians has increased, generosity as a percentage of income has remained fairly static. In their annual report, *The State of Church Giving*, John and Sylvia Ronsvalle explain, "Giving has not kept up with income. . . . In 1933, the depth of the Great Depression, [per capita giving] was 3.2 percent. In 1995 . . . it was still 3 percent. By 2004, when Americans were over 555 percent richer after taxes and inflation than in the Great Depression, Protestants were giving 2.5 percent of their income to churches."[4] Rather than giving back to God as He blesses, Christians are adopting the miserly patterns of the world. While giving by believers is slightly higher than among nonbelievers, the patterns are still very similar. A recent study reported that "the wealth of the world's rich and super rich surged 11.2 percent to $37.2 trillion last year, but the elite group gave less than 1 percent of their net worth to charity."[5] In general, a genuinely generous person is the exception rather than the rule.

Christians are also uncomfortable discussing their possessions, even with other believers. Pastors worry that sermons on giving will sound self-serving or discourage people from attending church, so they often avoid the topic entirely, or only bring it up once a year or when there is a crisis. Similarly, seminaries seldom teach on biblical stewardship.

However, this situation is contrary to God's plan. Scripture is saturated with teaching on possessions: seventeen of the thirty-eight parables of Christ are about possessions. In terms of the number of verses on possessions, this topic is mentioned in Scripture more than any other: three times more than love, seven times more than prayer, and eight times more than belief. About 15 percent of God's Word (2,172 verses) deals with possessions—treasures hidden in a field, pearls, talents, pounds, stables, etc.[6] Most likely this topic is covered so thoroughly in Scripture because God knew His followers would struggle with how to use possessions. Given this emphasis from God, Christians need to seriously consider how their faith and their finances are related. It is easy to copy the habits of those around us, but God has called Christians to greater heights of generosity as we conform to the image of Christ.

This pattern of conforming to the world around us, evident in our giving, is also characteristic of how Christian organizations ask for resources. Christian organizations, including churches, have increasingly adopted secular models of fundraising. For example, supporters are often encouraged to give for what they can get in return (tax deduction, gift, name on a building, etc.) and are not challenged to honor God and be generous as Christ is generous. The common practice of using transactional techniques that emphasize manipulation to motivate giving is contrary to God's Word.

Thankfully there is a more excellent way to view giving and asking, one that turns current notions upside down and places God first; a way that focuses on transforming givers' hearts and lives toward God-focused stewardship. Once a Christian understands how God views money and generosity, it becomes clear that asking should be about facilitating the heart transformation of believers into the image of Christ. As a result they will become generous as Christ is generous, leading to a revolution in generosity, so that God's Kingdom work on this earth will be fully funded.

As described above, we still have a long way to go. Christians have lost their way and are on the wrong road, in both their giving and their asking practices. They are not comfortable with God and money, they are not generous because they have not conformed to the image of Christ, and the asking practices that churches and parachurch organizations have adopted are exacerbating the problem by not encouraging believers toward a genuine godly generosity.

The purpose of this chapter is to set the stage for this book by (1) showing how we have gotten off the godly road, (2) outlining the spiritual process that leads to genuine generosity, and (3) suggesting steps to promote a revolution in generosity.

HOW DID WE GET HERE?

In the beginning, God made and owned all that was. He created humans and entrusted into their care the precious world He had lovingly crafted. These people were His stewards (managers). When the stewards functioned according to their identity and calling, God's created world thrived.

However, over time, God's people became convinced that they owned it all. They became saturated in stuff, greedily surrounding themselves with possessions. They were "stuffocated." They did not want to hear about it in sermons (such talk was always uncomfortable), so the pastors stopped preaching about possessions, and the seminaries stopped teaching the topic. And so, gradually, the system God had established was broken. While God's people have occasionally tried to get back on track, today we are far from acting like responsible stewards in God's economy.

In America, biblical stewardship characterized Christians' approach to resources from 1740 to 1840. John Wesley exhorted his parishioners to "gain all you can, save all you can, and give all you can" because "all that we have is given us by God, and since we have been entrusted with these possessions, we are responsible to use them in ways that bring Him glory."[7] During this period in history, it was acknowledged that the blessings of life were from God; but this mind-set did not last.

Soon stewardship, managing God's resources according to His directives, gave way to "philanthropy," helping others with *our* possessions. In the early 1900s, social Darwinism took ideological root and slowly choked out the biblical vision for the moral community. In his essay "The Gospel of Wealth," Andrew Carnegie presented his own good fortune as evidence of natural selection and survival of the fittest among the human species. With one swift stroke, Carnegie cut the taproot of biblical stewardship and adopted what he called "scientific philanthropy," based on Darwinian theory.[8] He also replaced the ideal of the common good with that of "selective good." He wrote, "The best means of benefiting the community is placing within its reach ladders upon which the aspiring can arise."[9] With these words, Carnegie drew the line of distinction between those who were worthy of charity and those who were not. According to him, the motive for giving ought to be calculated in terms of cost-benefit for continuous economic growth, not a reflection of God's generosity in response to human suffering. Carnegie believed in only helping those who would be of "use" to society, either through their labor or their intellect. The priority of shared responsibility gave way to helping people who were a good business investment. This new venture was termed "philanthropy"—friend of humankind—in contrast to stewardship—servant of God. While being a "friend of humankind" sounds harmless, implicit within the concept of philanthropy is an assumption that we, not God, own our resources and have the sole authority to dispense them. Philanthropy strives to use money to make a prosperous society of the strong and able, while biblical stewardship advocates humans caring for one another as fellow creatures and servants of the God who provides everything we need.

Carnegie's critics claimed that the poor needed more than just money—they needed help emotionally, physically, and spiritually. These Americans believed that newly established voluntary associations—religious and secular—held the solution to the problem. Potential donors were told they could become "agents of change" in society by responding with significant financial support.

These "organized charities" pooled their wisdom and brought further refinements to the scientific model of major gift fundraising. They concluded that religion played only a minor role in influencing generosity and that much more could be gleaned from the business world. The subtle but significant shift in thinking of givers as stewards (servant-managers of God) to viewing them as philanthropists (lovers of humankind) removed faith and God as motives for giving and set up instead a business/sales model of "whatever works."[10]

Charities flooded to consulting firms in hopes that these "experts" could raise large sums of money for their organizations. Interestingly, early records do not suggest that hiring fundraising consultants helped organizations better fulfill their missions.[11] The result was a model of fundraising that emphasized "closing the deal." Borrowing so many principles from sales tactics resulted in a virtual abandonment of biblical fundraising practices, edging the church from center stage to the outskirts of fundraising culture. Major gift programs were keenly intent on "making the sale" and were rarely concerned with the heart of the giver.

As the business community introduced the concept of market segmentation and demographic studies to determine the best ways to get their products into the hands of potential customers, the charitable community followed suit. Databases are now carefully segmented, giving clubs are monitored to move donors toward larger and more frequent gifts, and donor research is conducted to identify those with the greatest potential to give significant gifts. With the help of technology, the scientific model of philanthropy is now the norm. Today's fundraising professionals (including those in church and parachurch organizations) are better informed, prepared, and trained in secular techniques of raising money than ever before. However, generosity (adjusted for inflation) is not increasing per capita among Christians or non-Christians. People give because it makes them feel good, to avoid a sense of guilt, or because they get something in return (tax benefit). Could it be that the use of transactional techniques has run its course, and it is time to look again at God's way that leads to generosity—even a revolution in generosity?

Figure 1–1: The Path to Generosity

UNDERSTANDING THE PROCESS THAT LEADS TO GENEROSITY

Christians by and large are on the wrong road with their giving and are not being generous; so how do we get going down the godly road that should result in at least 10 percent per capita giving? The best way to start both giving and asking correctly is by understanding the process that leads to generosity. Because our motives for giving have been saturated with ideology and methods from the business world, divorced from biblical principles, we need to reorient ourselves by looking through God's eyes at the process of becoming generous. Figure 1–1 shows a five-step process for understanding the Christian's path to generosity. Once we understand this process, believers can change both giving and asking practices to align themselves with God's way, which would lead to a revolution in generosity. Following are five steps on the road leading to generosity.

Acknowledge Our Sinful, Self-centered Nature

Psalm 14:2–3 tells us, "The Lord looks down from heaven on the children of man, to see if there are any who understand, who seek after God. They have all turned aside; together they have become corrupt; there is none who does good, not even one."[12] Giving our hearts over to things other than God is nothing new; material possessions have always been especially alluring. As Israel was moving through the Promised Land, vanquishing enemy after enemy under God's direction, it only took a cloak and one man's greed to bring defeat. Joshua 7 tells us that Achan took a cloak and some silver from the spoils of battle and hid them under his tent. These items did not belong to him, so in taking them he committed theft and brought sin into the camp of Israel.[13] The congregation ended up stoning Achan for this, but the larger point is that this man, who had been through the desert and survived the weeding out of the older, "rebellious" generation, yet fell prey to self-centered desires or, as the apostle John puts it, "the lust of the eyes."[14]

This same tendency continues to this day, as Donald Hinze observes: "Sacred and secular history and literature are replete with examples of the crippling effects of gifts hoarded and unshared. People are not naturally disposed to giving, yet, the life we all prize, filled with joy and spiritual depth, is closely tied to giving generously and with thankful hearts."[15] All of humankind is sinful; and without conscious recognition of the hold sin and selfish attitudes have on our lives and the lives of those around us, we will not be conformed to the image of Christ; nor can we facilitate a revolution in giving.

Accept Christ's Offer of Transformation

Second Corinthians 5:17 is a familiar verse with far-reaching implications: "Therefore, if anyone is in Christ, he is a new creation. The old has passed away; behold, the new has come."[16] Paul is not referring to a cosmetic change, but a heart transformation that occurs at the deepest part of who we are. When we become followers of Christ, our very identity changes, and that should impact everything we do, including how we use our resources. George Barna describes transformation as "any significant and lasting transition in your life wherein you switch from one substantial perspective or practice to something wholly different that genuinely alters you at a very basic level."[17] Dallas Willard writes: "It is love of God flowing through us—not our human attempts at behavior change—that becomes 'a spring of water gushing up to eternal life' (John 4:14, par.)."[18] It is with the decision to follow Christ and be transformed by God that the journey of being generous begins.

Choose God's Eternal Kingdom over the Earthly Kingdom

Even as Christians, we have a choice of two kingdoms. So long as we are on this earth, the earthly kingdom will attempt to claim us for its own. In *Stewards in the Kingdom,* Scott Rodin suggests, "In a very real way the kingdom of the world is never built, but it acts like a black hole constantly demanding more with no hope of ever having enough. The irony of the kingdom of the world is that it does not let us stop long enough to enjoy what we have amassed."[19] Unfortunately the futility of the effort is not enough to dissuade us from grasping for the kingdom of this world. As individuals and communities, we continue to struggle against the desire to "be conformed to this world."[20] The Kingdom of God, on the other hand, beckons us to be transformed to the image of Christ, serving God and others out of love in this world and reigning with Christ to the glory of the Father eternally. When we decide to follow God's eternal Kingdom, we have committed to becoming genuinely generous.

Become Conformed to Christ's Image

Deciding to follow Christ and to pursue God's eternal Kingdom places our two feet on the path to genuine generosity. Once we make these decisions, it is possible to progress down the path by conforming to the image of Christ. The change of our characters is a process of Christ being formed in us, turning us away from sin and toward Him. Mark Allan Powell explains it this way: "The Bible teaches that generosity is a fruit of God's Holy Spirit (Gal. 5:22–23). The way to become generous people, then, involves not quenching God's Spirit (1 Thess. 5:19), but allowing the transforming work of Christ to have its full effect in shaping us to be the people God wants us to be (Rom. 12:2; 2 Cor. 5:17; Gal. 2:20; Phil. 1:6)."[21] Paul says of the church in Galatians 4 that they are "my little children, for whom I am again in the anguish of childbirth until Christ is formed in you!"[22] The image is striking. Paul's care for the Galatians is like that of a mother waiting to give birth, an intense longing for fulfillment. When we are called to Christ, the process of transformation we begin is one that should last our entire lives, one about which God deeply cares.

God is merciful and rarely transforms us overnight; instead, our transformation is, as Barna describes it, "a revolution of character, which proceeds by changing people from the inside through ongoing personal relationship with God and one another. It is a revolution that changes people's ideas, beliefs, feelings and *habits* . . . and generosity."[23] Similarly, Dallas Willard speaks of Jesus drawing apprentices to Himself, and thereby setting in motion a worldwide revolution that will continue until He returns.[24] An apprentice is someone set to learn the master's trade, commonly through imitation. As we continue to grow in our understanding of who God is (through Bible study, prayer, and communion with other saints), our ability to be like Him in practice increases. Our ultimate goal is complete conformity to the image of Christ, including His generosity. We are to shape our inner being "after God's own heart" (1 Sam. 13:14, author's paraphrase).

Implement Genuine Generosity, as Christ Is Generous

Michael Foss writes that "[giving] is the call to reflect the heart of God in our discipline of generosity. We have been created in the image of God. That means, in part, that every human being has within herself or himself a need to give."[25] While there are many facets to Christ's character, generosity is fairly central. Paul describes the very act of resurrection using gift language: "But God, being rich in mercy, because of the great love with which he loved us, even when we were dead in our trespasses, made us alive together with Christ. . . . For by grace you have been saved through faith. And this is not your own doing; it is the gift of God."[26]

As mature Christians, our lives should reflect an ever-deepening understanding of the love and generosity of God. In 1 Peter 4 we are instructed, "As each has received a gift, use it to serve one another, as good stewards of God's varied grace. . . ."[27] The gifts we have—our time, talent, and money—are given us in holy trust, to use as our Master requests. As George Barna concludes in *Revolution*, "I do not give away 10 percent, I surrender 100 percent."[28] By yielding control of our resources to God, we become imitators of Christ, implementing generosity in our lives, as Christ Himself is generous. It is out of this process of becoming generous that believers are able to facilitate opportunities for others to give in a God-honoring way and become rich toward God.

WHAT WOULD IT TAKE TO CREATE A REVOLUTION IN GENEROSITY?

A basic premise of this book is that believers are on the wrong road when it comes to giving and are therefore not generous. Over many decades they have strayed onto the wide path of culture when it comes to their giving and asking practices. We also know there is a more godly way, as illustrated in the Path to Generosity (figure 1–1). The chapters in this book suggest a paradigm shift from merely accomplishing transactions to growing generosity in transformed hearts. So what are the practical steps to facilitate this revolution in generosity? Figure 1–2 illustrates seven important stages.

Acknowledge the Problem

Martin Luther is credited with stating that there are three conversions involved in the Christian life: head, heart, and purse (or wallet). Most Chris-

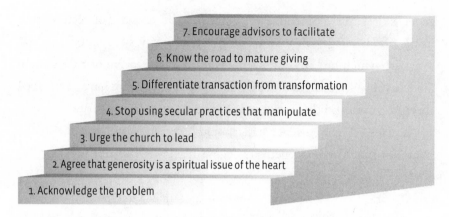

Figure 1–2: Steps to Facilitate Creating a Revolution in Generosity

tians have decided the first two are enough. As you will read throughout this book, Christians as a group are not generous. Per capita giving by denominational affiliation shows that Roman Catholics average 1.5 percent, mainline Protestants 2.8 percent, and evangelicals barely 4 percent.[29] This is certainly well below the benchmark of giving at least 10 percent.

The problem is that Christians, by and large, do not take seriously their faith's relationship to their finances, which would require them to conform to the image of Christ and be generous as Christ is generous. Philip Yancey voices this reluctance when he writes, "Mostly, I wish I did not have to think about money at all. But I must somehow come to terms with the Bible's very strong statements about money."[30] Similarly, Randy Alcorn proclaims, "Large segments of modern evangelicalism have succumbed to the heresy that the present life may be lived selfishly and disobediently without serious effect on the eternal state. . . . Never have so many Christians believed that our monies and possessions are ours to do with as we please."[31] There is a problem; the Christian community needs to recognize it and take steps to remedy the situation.

Agree That Generosity Is a Spiritual Issue of the Heart
The culture in which we live, and often the churches in which we worship,

have convinced us that there is little relationship between our faith and our finances. Believers have come to think that our possessions are ours to do with as we please, and so have taken personal finances into our own hands and left God out of our giving and asking.

Until believers acknowledge the simple truth that "where your treasure is, there will your heart be also,"[32] we will not see believers starting to conform to the image of Christ and become generous like Him. The vital link between our faith and our finances is at the core of the issue. As Scott Rodin writes, "Giving is primarily a spiritual matter . . . an act of obedient worship."[33]

Similarly, Rich Haynie observes, "If God owns it all, spending or giving God's money is a spiritual decision."[34] And former U.S. Senate chaplain Richard Halverson asserts, "Money is an exact index to a [person's] true character. All through Scripture there is an intimate correlation between the development of a [person's] character and . . . money."[35] The revolution in generosity will flood forth when believers realize that generosity is a spiritual issue of the heart and start to allow the Holy Spirit to work this truth out in their lives.

Urge the Church to Lead

The proper place for teaching generosity is the church (see Richard Towner's chapter). If the church were appropriately teaching biblical stewardship, then both giving and asking among Christians would take place within a transformational paradigm.

Princeton University researcher Robert Wuthnow concludes that the topic of finances is the one pastors most avoid and that "there is a kind of mental or emotional gloss to contemporary religious teaching about money that prevents them from having much of an impact on how people actually live their lives."[36]

The Lilly Endowment study of the church's role in finances concluded that today's pastors are, at best, reluctant stewards of their churches' human, physical, and financial resources.[37] This will have to change if the church is to take its proper place in leading the revolution in generosity.

Stop Using Secular Practices That Manipulate

As you will read in this book, true generosity is an act of love that comes from a transformed heart that reflects the image of Christ and is generous because Christ is generous. One of the important steps on the way to facilitating believers' transformation toward generosity is for Christian institutions (both church and parachurch) to abandon resource-generating activities that are not God-centered. One of the major aims of this volume is to provide biblical, transformational alternatives to the dominant secular paradigms. Thus, believers should notice the way God does things, then fall in line—though this eternal Kingdom view may seem like foolish nonsense, as we are reminded in 1 Corinthians 2:14: "The man without the Spirit does not accept the things that come from the Spirit of God, for they are foolishness to him, and he cannot understand them, because they are spiritually discerned."[38]

As outlined in Adam Morris's chapter, Christians should jettison the techniques of the world that restrict or harden the heart of the believer who desires to conform to the image of the generous Christ. Such activities include deceptive or guilt-producing asking; money-raising events that are not ministry focused; rewards for giving (such as premiums or naming opportunities); giving class distinction by amount given; and activities that rob the giver of the joy of giving. One aspect of change is the language we use. For example, if those raising resources are shepherds of God's stewards and look at their work as ministry to people, then maybe our title should be stewardship officer and their clients should be called ministry partners (not donors, prospects, or philanthropists). Consider what other language should accompany your change of heart (see Gary Hoag's chapter).

The focus should be on growing givers' hearts, which will result in God-glorifying use of possessions, joy in giving, contentment, and eternal Kingdom impact.

Differentiate Transaction from Transformation

An important next step is to comprehend that God's way of transformation is different from the transactional money-raising mind-set that churches and other Christian organizations have imported from the business world. It may be peace of mind and blessings that ministers promise in return for monetary contributions, but the implication is still "give to us so you can get something good in return." We have a choice of two roads when asking for support: we can follow the popular path and focus on the number and size of transactions, or we can move down the less-traveled road that places the transformation of hearts at the core of all our activities.

	TRANSACTIONAL MODEL	TRANSFORMATIONAL MODEL
PHILOSOPHICAL UNDERPINNING:	Philanthropy—improving the common good	Stewardship—managers of what God owns
FOCUS:	Raising money through marketing transactions	Facilitate raising stewards to be rich toward God, which results in generosity
ETHICAL FRAMEWORK:	Minimalist—"is it legal?"	Commitment to gospel values of truth, integrity, and love
IDEAL OUTCOMES:	Donor meets organizational need	Giver becomes conformed to the image of Christ and becomes generous, like Christ
SOLICITATION:	Manipulative business sales, technique intensive, hype the need	Present giving opportunity, prayerfully matching call to ministry
MOTIVATOR:	Asker's style, personality	Holy Spirit works to transform heart toward Christlike generosity
FOLLOW-UP:	Pressure and persuade to meet quota, don't take "no" for an answer	Encourage prayer to lay up treasure in heaven and experience godly joy
ACCOUNTABILITY:	To organization, the law	To God, eternal values
PREDICTABLE OUTCOMES:	Success/failure depends on asker. Burnout	Success/failure according to God's calling
REWARDS:	On earth, temporal	Crowns and responsibility in heaven for eternity

Figure 1–3: Comparison of Transactional and Transformational Models

In order to fulfill our calling as disciples, we must shift from this transactional mind-set to a transformational model. If we view giving as an instrument of transformation, we will support our givers through a consistent program of prayer and personal interaction, accepting the fact that it is the Holy Spirit, not our personality, that influences how they give. The change will take time, both for those asking for and those giving funds. But as we embrace the transformational model, the focus shifts from the gift and getting money to seeing God's power work in individual lives. Figure 1-3 outlines the differences between a transactional and a transformational approach.

If we want to embrace the transformational model, the change will take time, both for those asking and those giving funds.

Know the Road to Mature Giving

Citing the New Testament examples of Zaccheus and the rich young ruler, Randy Alcorn notes, "We come to understand that our perspective on and handling of money is a litmus test of our true character. It is an index of our spiritual life."[39] Whether gauging your own faith and generosity or helping others grow in the journey, a good grasp of the benchmarks along the road is essential.

Figure 1-4 outlines six stages of maturity in relation to possessions adapted from James Fowler's research on stages of faith.[40] They provide a framework for us to assess where we are in our use of earthly possessions and the effect that these actions will have on our eternal souls. This assessment can help us see where we are and where we need work as we continue to grow and mature in our faith and in our faithfulness as stewards. Figure 1-4 is a summary of the growth pattern Christian ministries should seek to foster.

Thomas Schmidt observes about the journey of discipleship, "We begin at different points and we move at different rates . . . but the biblical message is clear enough" that the end destination is maturity as followers of Christ.[41] The purpose of this chart is not to become legalistic or to produce

STAGES	FAITH CHARACTERISTICS	EVIDENCE IN USE OF POSSESSIONS
STAGE 1: IMITATOR	Like a child, is marked by imagination and influenced by stories and examples of others.	Is able to mimic the examples of others in giving, when shown or instructed.
STAGE 2: MODELER	Takes beliefs and moral rules literally. Perception of God is largely formed by friends.	Gives sporadically when given an example to follow.
STAGE 3: CONFORMER	Faith becomes a basis for love, acceptance, and identity; involves most aspects of life; and is shaped mainly by relationships. Faith does not yet form a cohesive "philosophy of life."	Gives because it is the thing to do. Likes recognition, tax benefits, and other personal gain from giving.
STAGE 4: INDIVIDUAL	Begins to "own" one's faith. Faith is less defined by others as one becomes able to personally examine and question one's beliefs.	Starts to give in proportion to what God has given. Danger of becoming prideful regarding giving or of giving for the wrong motives. Wonders why others do not give more.
STAGE 5: GENEROUS GIVER	Grasps the main ideas of an individualized faith, as well as individual practices. Becomes interested in developing the faith of others.	Recognizes that all one owns is from God. Begins to give of one's own initiative, rather than obligation or routine. Derives joy from giving.
STAGE 6: MATURE STEWARD	Little regard for self. Focuses on God and then on others. Free from man-made rules.	Recognizes the role of a faithful steward of God's possessions. More concerned with treasures in heaven than on earth. Content with daily provision.

Figure 1–4: Correlation of Soul Maturity and Use of Possessions[42]

guilt, but instead to provide a useful tool to assess where one is in the faith/possession-use journey. It might help to identify the next steps or challenges in the life of faith, and create a vision for where one desires to arrive spiritually. Our spiritual growth has stages, and as we discover where we are and where we want to be, we can form a plan to reach that destination.

While not everyone will pass through every stage, the general flow is useful. Viewing generosity as a growth process with a strong correlation to spiritual maturation helps us focus on individuals, rather than income, as our priority in ministry, moving us back toward a biblical model for fundraising.

Encourage Advisors to Facilitate

The final step in creating a revolution in generosity is for Christian advisors working with Christians and their finances, such as financial planners, fundraisers, and consultants, to become active facilitators of this godly way of generosity. Since the church has by and large abdicated its responsibility to discuss money issues, Christians in advisory roles have more contact and a more visible platform to address these critical issues of faith and finances. "When fundraisers for Christian organizations talk about why people should contribute financial support, they have the opportunity to explain that these works are concrete manifestations of the values and vision of the faith."[43]

As the chapters in this book outline, Christians in each of these professions can make a significant difference in facilitating God's work of creating a revolution in generosity. As citizens of God's Kingdom, we have only a short time to serve as managers for God in this world. We have only a short time and limited resources to prove ourselves faithful. Our time could run out at any point. We should use the stuff we have as stewards to affect people for eternity. The question is not what, or how much, we have; rather, what are we doing with what we have? Are we holding on tightly to the stuff God has entrusted to us, or are we holding it loosely and using it for God, as a tool? Consider R. J. LeTourneau, who was a successful businessman; he lived off 10 percent of his income and gave away the other 90 percent. Donald Whitney issues this challenge: "If you love Christ and the work of His Kingdom more than anything else, your giving will show that. If you are truly submitted to the lordship of Christ, if you are willing to obey Him completely in every area of your life, your giving will reveal it."[44]

As we look to the road ahead, our generosity will bless not just us but also the millions of materially and spiritually needy around the world. The potential is great. Sadly, two out of three senior pastors of Protestant churches believe that their churches are not living up to their giving potential. If members of historically Christian churches in the United States had raised their giving to just 10 percent of their income in 2000, an additional $139 billion a year would have become available for Kingdom work.[45] Our potential is mind-blowing: 80 percent of the world's evangelical wealth is in North America—and the total represents far more than enough to fund the fulfillment of the Great Commission.[46] What might the Lord accomplish through His church if she took the first step of faith on the journey of generosity?

Horace Bushnell writes, "One more revival; only one more is needed; the revival of Christian stewardship; the consecration of the money power of the Church unto God; and when that revival comes the Kingdom of God will come in a day. You can no more prevent it than you can hold back the tides of the ocean."[47] My prayer is that as you read the pages that follow, you will see how God can work in you and through you to transform hearts to be rich toward Him and generate a revolution in generosity. Lord willing, if this revolution of stewardship and discipleship takes hold, then potentially God's Kingdom work will be fully funded and ministries will be saying "give no more," as Moses did in Exodus 36:6.

WESLEY K. WILLMER (Ph.D. State University of New York at Buffalo) is vice president of university advancement and a professor at Biola University. He has been author, coauthor, editor, or editor in chief of twenty-three books and many professional journal publications. Recent books include *God and Your Stuff: The Vital Link Between Possessions and Your Soul*, and *The Prospering Parachurch: Enlarging the Boundaries of God's Kingdom*. He has initiated over $1 million in research grants to study nonprofit management, was chair of the board of the Christian Stewardship Association (CSA), and serves on the board of directors for the Christian Leadership Alliance and the executive committee of the Evangelical Council for Financial Accountability (ECFA). He can be contacted at wes.willmer@biola.edu.

1. Dallas Willard with Don Simpson, *Revolution of Character* (Colorado Springs, CO: NavPress, 2005) 188.

2. George Barna, *Revolution* (Carol Stream, IL: Tyndale House Publishers, 2005), 31–35.

3. Jeffery Sheler, Caroline Hsu, and Angie C. Marek, "Nearer My God to Thee," *US News & World Report* 136, no. 15 (2004); 59.

4. John Ronsvalle and Sylvia Ronsvalle, *The State of Church Giving through 2004: Will We Will?* (Champaign, IL: Empty Tomb, 2006), http://www.emptytomb.org/fig1_05.html.

5. Reuters, "World's Wealth Surges; Giving Doesn't," *Orange County Register*, June 30, 2007.

6. Wesley Willmer, *God and Your Stuff* (Colorado Springs, CO: NavPress, 2002), 9.

7. Frank Baker, ed., *The Bicentennial Edition of the Works of John Wesley*, vol. 2 (Nashville: Abingdon Press, 1985), 268.

8. Andrew Carnegie, *The Gospel of Wealth Essays and Other Writings* (New York: Penguin Classics, 2006).

9. Ibid., 12.

10. Willmer, *God and Your Stuff*, 85–86.

11. A. J. Morris, "The Fund-raising Techniques of Evangelical Parachurch Organizations and God's View of Money and Possessions" (Doctoral diss., Biola University, 2002).

12. Psalm 14:2–3 ESV.

13. Joshua 7:19–26 ESV.

14. 1 John 2:16 KJV.

15. Donald W. Hinze, *To Give and Give Again: A Christian Imperative for Generosity* (New York: Pilgrim, 1990), ix.

16. 2 Corinthians 5:17 ESV.

17. Barna, *Revolution*, 52.

18. Willard and Simpson, *Revolution of Character*, 19.

19. R. Scott Rodin, *Stewards in the Kingdom* (Downers Grove, IL: InterVarsity, 2000), 125.

20. Romans 12:2 ESV.

21. Mark Allan Powell, *Giving to God: The Bible's Good News about Living a Generous Life* (Grand Rapids: Eerdmans, 2006), 4.

22. Galatians 4:1–19 ESV.

23. Barna, *Revolution*, 29.

24. Willard with Simpson, *Revolution of Character*, 13.

25. Michael Foss, *Real Faith for Real Life: Living the Six Marks of Discipleship* (Minneapolis: Augsburg Fortress, 2004), 112.

26. Ephesians 2:4–8 ESV.

27. 1 Peter 4:10 ESV.

28. Barna, *Revolution*, 129.

29. Barna Research Group, "Giving to Churches Rose Substantially in 2003," http://www.barna.org/FlexPage.aspx?Page=BarnaUpdateNarrow&BarnaUpdateID=161.

30. Philip Yancey, *Money: Confronting the Power of a Modern Idol* (Portland, OR: Multnomah, 1985), 3.

31. Randy Alcorn, *Money, Possessions and Eternity* (Wheaton, IL: Tyndale House, 1989), preface.

32. Luke 12:34 ESV.

33. Rodin, *Stewards in the Kingdom*, 209.

34. Rich Haynie, *The Road Less Traveled in Fundraising*, presented at the Christian Stewardship Association 2006 Conference in Denver, CO, available at www.tnetwork.com/Haynie%20Road.doc.

35. Richard Halverson as quoted in *The Compass* (Green Bay, WI: Catholic Diocese of Green Bay, 24 Oct. 2003), http://www.thecompassnews.org/compass/2003-10-24/foundations.html.

36. Robert Wuthnow, *God and Mammon in America* (New York: Free Press, 1994), 151.

37. Daniel Conway, Anita Rook, and Daniel A. Schipp, *The Reluctant Steward Revisited: Preparing Pastors for Administrative and Financial Duties* (Indianapolis and St. Meinrad, IN: Christian Theological Seminary and Saint Meinrad Seminary, 2002), 7.

38. 1 Corinthians 2:14 NIV.

39. Alcorn, *Money, Possessions and Eternity*, 21.

40. James W. Fowler, *Stages of Faith* (San Francisco: HarperCollins, 1995), xii.

41. Thomas Schmidt, "Rich Wisdom: New Testament Teachings on Wealth," (*Christianity Today*), May 12, 1989, 30.

42. Willmer, *God and Your Stuff*, 44–45.

43. Thomas H. Jeavons and Rebekah Burch Basinger, *Growing Givers' Hearts* (San Francisco: Jossey-Bass, 2000), 18.

44. Donald S. Whitney, *Spiritual Disciplines for the Christian Life* (Colorado Springs, CO: NavPress, 1991), 140.

45. John L. Ronsvalle and Sylvia Ronsvalle, *The State of Church Giving through 2000* (Champaign, IL: Empty Tomb, 2002), 51.

46. Ron Blue with Jodie Berndt, *Generous Living: Finding Contentment through Giving* (Grand Rapids: Zondervan, 1997), 201.

47. "Home Problems of Foreign Missions," *The Baptist Missionary Magazine*, American Baptist Missionary Union (1902): 92.

Chapter

GOD AND MONEY:
A BIBLICAL THEOLOGY
OF POSESSIONS

By Craig L. Blomberg, *Distinguished Professor of*
New Testament at Denver Seminary

A s a New Testament scholar who has studied Scripture's teaching on material possessions,[1] I often wonder why Christian ministries that are raising money do not stress the central biblical truths that giving is a part of whole-life transformation, that stewardship and sanctification go together as signs of Christian obedience and maturity, and that God will call us to account for what we do with 100 percent of the possessions He has loaned us. Is it because they would then have to be sure they were modeling these same principles themselves and that their organizations were following suit? Is it because they have tried this approach and it hasn't worked—or does the approach remain unattempted?

I believe that generous giving and wise stewardship are the natural outgrowth of a life devoted to God and Christ, and that it is through God's transformation of a person's heart to reflect the image of Christ that they become generous, as Christ is generous. The focus in raising money, then, should be upon assisting Christians to honor and obey God, not on the needs of the organization. It is out of this understanding that biblical approaches to funding ministry should seek to transform stewards to be rich toward God in every area of their lives and not just when they are giving to the particular organization seeking the funds. A discussion of God's views of money and possessions as described in the New Testament will allow these biblical principles to provide direction to the giving and asking process of funding ministry.

In my two books on material possessions, I begin in Genesis 1 and proceed, with varying degrees of selectivity, throughout the entire biblical canon.

Space obviously precludes such an approach here. I wish instead to move quickly to the five main overarching themes that emerged from my study and illustrate them in thematic rather than canonical order. I have also chosen to limit my comments, for the most part, to New Testament texts. There is more than enough material on our topic in this Testament alone, and fewer complications emerge for the Christian trying to apply the New Testament to today's world than the Old Testament.[2]

Failure to recognize this is, in fact, what has led to the errors of so much of the so-called "prosperity gospel." The covenant that God made with Israel, accounting particularly for a large part of the cyclical history of good times and bad from Deuteronomy through Nehemiah, promised His people material blessings, long life in the land once called Canaan, safety and security from their enemies, and the like (see, e.g., Deut. 11:26–32; 28:1–14; 30:11–20). What is often ignored is that God did not make any comparable covenants with any of the non-Israelite peoples and that the New Testament nowhere suggests that this aspect of old covenant blessing automatically carries over to the new age of the church of Jesus Christ.[3] Indeed, even in Old Testament times, the covenant never guaranteed prosperity to *individual believers*, contingent on sufficient faith and/or obedience. The Psalms and Proverbs are replete with examples of the pious poor, unjust victims of rich exploiters (e.g., Ps. 37:16–17; Prov. 15:16–17; 16:8). The promise was for the *nation*, and even then it represented a broad generalization that as the people as a whole (and the *leaders* in particular) followed Yahweh, more often than not they would prosper. Indeed, that prosperity often continued even after years of disobedience, but God's tolerance would eventually come to an end and judgment would ensue, until the next round of corporate repentance occurred, led by the country's judges or kings.[4]

In the New Testament, the closest one ever comes to legitimate support for a promise of prosperity is in 2 Corinthians 9:11, when Paul assures the church: "You will be made rich in every way so that you can be generous on every occasion, and through us your generosity will result in thanksgiving to God."[5] In context, this generosity must include material provision, though it is by no means limited to this arena. But this same context—Paul is encouraging the Corinthian church to carry through with their pledge to give for the needier congregations in Judea—demonstrates that this is again a collective promise to the church as a whole. When God's people care enough about their fellow believers to give generously to those in need, if it turns out they have given away too much to continue to meet all of their own needs, they can then count on others in the body to care for them.[6]

This same logic accounts for Jesus' command to seek first God's Kingdom and its righteousness and to count on all the basic material needs of life being provided for us (Matt. 6:33)—that is, through His people if we should accidentally overextend ourselves.[7] So, too, Christ's promise that we will receive back one hundredfold houses and fields when we give them up for the Lord accompanies identical guarantees that we will receive an equal number of family members (Mark 10:29–30 pars.). Those new brothers, sisters, and mothers, of course, refer to fellow Christians, so the additional property must refer to access to the material abundance of the church as a whole, as believers share with those in need.[8] Nothing is implied in any of these texts about some principle whereby our donations to a particular Christian ministry guarantee us a supernaturally bestowed hundredfold material blessing in return! What then *does* the New Testament teach about possessions? We may summarize our findings under five headings.

A NEW TESTAMENT THEOLOGY OF POSSESSIONS
The Goodness of Wealth

Although Christians cannot look simply to Old Testament models of rich believers and conclude that God wants *them* to be rich, too, the New Testament still affirms the God-ordained goodness of material possessions. Unlike many religions and philosophies, neither Judaism nor Christianity, when true to its roots, has affirmed the inherent evil of matter.[9] God created this material world *good* (Genesis 1-2), and only subsequently did human sin corrupt it (Genesis 3). Part of redemption involves re-creation, and the last two chapters of the Bible form a marvelous *inclusio* (or "bookend") with the first two. God's original purposes in creation will not be thwarted. The ultimate Christian hope is not to go to heaven after death; that is a better description of what theologians call the intermediate state. Rather, we look forward to the complete resurrection and re-creation of the body and the dissolution of this current universe, to be replaced by new heavens *and a new earth*, with its garden of earthly delights, now fully sanctified for us to enjoy for an eternity (Revelation 21-22).[10] To use the language of modern secular advertising, "we *can* have it all!" *But only on God's terms and in His timing.* He may choose to bless some of His children in this life materially, but worldwide and throughout church history, only a tiny minority of Christians have been so blessed. It borders on blasphemy to blame the suffering of hundreds of millions of believers who have toiled in grinding poverty on their lack of faith![11]

At the same time, a decent standard of living remains something *good*. If it didn't, why would so many biblical texts encourage the alleviation of poverty? Why would Paul go out of his way in 2 Corinthians 8:13-15 to stress that he is not asking the rich to trade places with the poor but to give out of their surplus? Why would Jesus tell a parable, in the two different forms of the pounds (Luke 19:11-27) and the talents (Matt. 25:14-30), in which the good servants invest their master's money and make more? Even if his point cannot be limited to material investment, surely a financial application of his story cannot be excluded. Why would Luke, in the Acts of the Apostles, present as positive models Christians of considerable means, including Cornelius, the family of John Mark, Sergius Paulus, Lydia, the Philippian jailer, Jason, many prominent Greek women in Thessalonica, various Areopagites, Damaris, Aquila and Priscilla, Titius Justus, and Mnason?[12] Why would Jesus Himself adopt an itinerant lifestyle requiring dependence on the charity of wealthy friends, particularly a small group of women, named and described in Luke 8:1–3 as equivalent to what today would be called His "support team"?[13] Why would He elsewhere praise another close female friend and supporter, Mary of Bethany, for her lavishing costly ointment on Him to prepare His body for burial, as it were (Mark 14:9 pars.)? Why would Paul tell Timothy that God "richly provides us with everything for our enjoyment" (1 Tim. 6:17b)?

John Schneider tells the story of enjoying a barbecue on his cedar deck one beautiful summer evening, overlooking his tree-lined backyard, and watching his children play happily in innocence and safety. How horrible, he thought, that some Christians (too many, in his estimation) would criticize his family for enjoying these lovely pleasures of life and enjoin them not to spend nearly so much money on themselves. If we are surrounded by the old-line Calvinists with their sometimes exaggerated, ascetic "Protestant work ethic," unable to relax and enjoy the fruits of their labor, then many of Schneider's emphases in his writings may be just what the doctor is ordering. But in Colorado, and in the other slices of American Christian life I traverse annually in my various speaking engagements, I hardly ever run into such people. Rather, I am far more aware of those who simply take the "luxuries" of large homes, nice neighborhoods, good cars, and ample foodstuffs for granted and never even *ask* the question of whether or not God might be calling them to a simpler lifestyle. For those people, a healthy dose of Ron Sider would seem to be far more needed.[14]

The Seduction of Wealth

Indeed, for every New Testament text that explicitly points to the goodness of wealth, four or five highlight the ways that "mammon" (material possessions as an object of our allegiance or even worship) seduces believers to sin or accounts for why unbelievers remain outside the fold.[15] The seed that falls among the thorns, in the parable of the sower, represents those who "hear the word . . . but the worries of this life, the deceitfulness of wealth and the desires for other things come in and choke the word, making it unfruitful" (Mark 4:18b-19 pars.). The parable of the rich fool describes one who is not rich toward God as a person who takes no thought for anyone else when an unexpected bumper crop is harvested from his fields, but instead merely builds additional storage space so as to preserve his own bounty (Luke 12:16-21). The parable of the rich man and Lazarus portrays a man who has never repented as one who feasts sumptuously every day while refusing to give even the crumbs from his table to the dying, crippled beggar on his doorstep (Luke 16:19-31).[16]

Jesus' three temptations, in fact, epitomize all of human seduction to sin in very material terms (what John would later call "the lust of the flesh and the lust of the eyes and the pride of life"—1 John 2:16 KJV/RSV)—providing food for Himself during His fast, gaining all the kingdoms of the world by worshiping Satan, and showing off how God would save His physical body from harm if He jumped off the portico of the temple (Matt. 4:1-11; Luke 4:1-13). In other texts, the rich young ruler refuses to give up his wealth for the poor and follow Jesus (Mark 10:17-31 pars.), traveling businesspersons aspiring to affluence make their plans a full year ahead of time without any thought for the Lord's will (James 4:13-17), and wealthy landowners exploit the poor Christian migrant workers who harvest their fields, withholding from them their already meager daily wages (James 5:1-6).[17] Ananias and Sapphira's desire to be perceived as more generous than they really were in the giving of their property led to their sudden deaths (Acts 5:1-11). Simon the magician thought that his wealth could enable him to buy the power of the

Holy Spirit (Acts 8:18–23), and attempts to purchase ecclesiastical office have been called "simony" to this day.

A huge body of sociological literature in recent decades has demonstrated how an inordinate number of the problems afflicting the church in Corinth can be attributed to the handful of wealthy church members who hosted house congregations in their homes, functioned as elders, and thought that they could still "call the shots" (even when violating Christian principles) as they no doubt did as patrons and benefactors in their previously pagan lives.[18] For this reason, Paul refuses to accept any money at all from the Corinthians, sensing that it would come with "strings attached," even as he stresses that it is important for congregations to support those who work in full-time ministry (1 Cor. 9:1–18).[19]

Paul will accept money elsewhere, particularly from the Philippians, but apparently never from the community to whom he is currently ministering. The dangers of false accusations or perceptions of how he used such gifts, along with the peril of genuine mismanagement, provided another rationale for his policy and led him to establish elaborate mechanisms of scrupulous accountability. These served to safeguard his integrity as he traveled around the Roman Empire taking up a collection for the impoverished saints in and around Jerusalem (2 Cor. 8:16–24).[20] The deliberate omission of words for "thanks" in his letter to the Philippians (sometimes called his "thankless thank-you") reflects his concern to capture the delicate balance between sounding ungrateful for their support and making him appear inappropriately indebted to them, as though he could not have carried on without them (cf. Phil. 4:10–20).[21]

Church leaders, according to 1 Timothy and 1 Peter, should be neither lovers of money nor pursuing foolish or shameful gain—that is, seeking more than is appropriate in a given setting (1 Tim. 3:3, 8; 1 Peter 5:2).[22] One wonders how often these criteria are seriously scrutinized and applied in the selection of overseers and deacons in local congregations today. We learn precious little about the false teachers lambasted in 2 Peter and Jude except that they are experts in greed (2 Peter 2:14–15; literally, "well trained in covetousness")! Paul, on the other hand, reminds the Ephesian elders, "I have not coveted anyone's silver or gold or clothing. You yourselves know that these hands of mine have supplied my own needs and the needs of my companions. In everything I did, I showed you that by this kind of hard work we must help the weak, remembering the words the Lord Jesus himself said: 'It is more blessed to give than to receive'" (Acts 20:33–35). As I. H. Marshall explains, in context Paul understands Jesus to be saying, "It is better for a person who can do so to give to help others rather than to amass further wealth for himself."[23]

By far the most dramatic picture of the awful potential of riches to lead people away from God comes in Revelation 18. After a chapter that has made it clear that the great, evil, end-times empire of the Antichrist will be both politically influential and religiously idolatrous (Revelation 17), John demonstrates that it will also be the wealthiest superpower of its day.[24] Yet suddenly, in a heartbeat, it is destroyed and all the symbols of its wealth vanish. The laments for the lost cargoes include litanies that read like bills of sale for luxury goods (and staples) imported from the provinces to Rome for the enjoyment of the wealthy there (Rev. 18:11–13). These are enjoyed at the expense of the subjugated peoples who must sell their produce elsewhere in order to make even the barest of livings and who can seldom enjoy the fruit of their own labor.[25] Frightening parallels to contemporary patterns of American self-indulgence at the expense of the Two-Thirds World strike the sensitive reader.[26] Today John might have written that all the real and virtual shopping malls were destroyed, including eBay, and that people lamented that they didn't know how to cope without them!

Generous Giving

How do modern Christians and churches avoid the seductive power of material possessions? How can wealth remain a "good" for their enjoyment rather than leading them further away from God and the priorities of His Kingdom? The recurring answer of both Testaments is through generous giving to others.

It is a shame that conversations about tithing often distract Christians from their real responsibilities. On the one hand, it appears that an unprecedented number of people today think that the word *tithe* is simply a synonym for "gift" or "offering" and have no idea that the word means to give "one-tenth." On the other hand, there are still far too many people who have read neither Testament carefully enough to recognize that, in the New Testament age, no specific percentage is commanded of believers.[27] Instead, generous, even sacrificial, giving is what is enjoined (2 Cor. 8:1–12). For many middle- and upper-class Christians in this country, giving *only* 10 percent hardly qualifies as a genuine sacrifice—that is, going without something that they would deeply desire for themselves that they could have otherwise had. Nor do they notice that the one triennial and two annual tithes in the Old Testament that the faithful Israelite gave to the Lord's work add up to an average of 23 1/3 percent every year.[28] How many of those Christians who think the Old Testament tithing law remains in force (or that Christians should at least give no less than what Jews did) would be happy to discover what the true standard was?

Fortunately, that percentage doesn't matter.[29] What *does* matter is generous, compassionate, loving concern for those in greater need than ourselves, both spiritually and physically, which leads to practical efforts to meet those needs in ways that will make the best long-term difference. While such efforts often require far more than money, in our thoroughly capitalistic world they seldom involve anything less. All other things being equal (which, of course, they often aren't), the person earning $200,000 a year is not making nearly the sacrifice by giving $20,000 to the Lord's work as is the person earning $20,000 and giving $2000.[30] The slogan often applied in capital campaigns— "not equal giving but equal sacrifice"—when applied to Christian stewardship more generally leads to what Ron Sider calls the "graduated tithe."[31] The more money someone makes, the higher percentage they should give away.

That, at least, is the practice our family has adopted over the past twenty-six years—and, to my astonishment, God has blessed us with the ability to give away approximately 50 percent of our adjusted gross income in each of the last four years, and that without abandoning a lifestyle that surely qualifies as enjoying many good gifts that God has richly provided us.

But to whom does the Bible call us to give? The three Israelite tithes were for the temple and its ministrants (Num. 18:8–32), for the numerous annual festivals that took place there (Deut. 14:22–28), and for the needs of the poor and disenfranchised (Deut. 14:29). In the New Testament we read of collections for the poor (Acts 2:42–47; 4:32–35; 6:1–7; 11:27–30; 1 Cor. 16:1–4; 2 Cor. 8–9), of supporting one's spiritual leaders—even though Paul voluntarily renounced his right to "cash in" on this privilege (Luke 10:7 par.; 1 Cor. 9:1–18; 1 Tim. 5:18; Gal. 6:6), and of supporting more itinerant Christian evangelists, preachers, and teachers (Rom. 15:24; Phil. 4:10–20). By far the most commonly stressed of these three themes is help for the poor.[32] Probably the most poignant of Jesus' teachings illustrating this priority is the parable of the great banquet in Luke 14:16–24, preceded by His shorter warnings against seeking places of honor or inviting only those who can invite one back (vv. 7–11, 12–14). (This passage alone should abolish once and for all the idea that "naming gifts" that promise major donors permanent, public recognition for their donations can be harmonized with Christian motivation.[33]) As a sign of his repentance and commitment to follow Christ, Zaccheus promises not only to restore fourfold that which he has defrauded in his work as a chief tax collector, but also to give half of his goods to the poor (Luke 19:8).[34]

James 2:1–7 warns against Christian deference to the rich at the expense of the poor, doubtless in part because of the donations his audience could extract from the more well-to-do. Indeed, using a rhetorical question with the particular adverb that demanded a negative answer in the Greek language (*mē*), James goes on to ask if the kind of faith that sees dire physical need among fellow Christians, is in a position to help and refuses to do so, can even save a person (James 2:14–17). The apostle John puts it no less pointedly: "If any one of you has material possessions and sees a brother or sister in need but has no pity on them, how can the love of God be in you? Dear children, let us not love with words or tongue but with actions and in truth" (1 John 3:17–18). Gary Burge spells out the lesson clearly: "One measure of love is the degree to which people blessed with material wealth distribute that wealth within the community."[35]

Limits on Riches and Poverty

The fourth biblical principle may prove the most controversial, raising what for some is the specter of socialism. But we must remember that even the most recent biblical documents antedate by more than 1,600 years the development of either socialist or capitalist economic philosophy. The principle is simply that there are certain levels of wealth and certain levels of poverty that are inherently immoral.[36] These are never quantified and no doubt change from person to person, place to place, and time to time. But numerous scriptural texts make it clear that there is such a thing as a person having "too much," materially speaking, as well as having too little. Second Corinthians 8:13–15 puts it plainly: "Our desire is not that others might be relieved while you are hard pressed, but that there might be equality. At the present time your plenty will supply what they need, so that in turn their plenty will supply what you need. The goal is equality, as it is written: 'The one who gathered much did not have too much, and the one who gathered little did not have too little.'" The word *equality* is probably not the best translation in this context of the Greek *isōtēs*. "Fairness (of treatment)" might be a better rendering.[37]

That this does not represent what would in modern times be promoted in socialist garb is clear from the context of Paul's quotation of Scripture (Ex. 16:18)—the account of the Israelites collecting manna in the wilderness. Different individuals and different families had varying needs and abilities to gather the supernaturally provided bread. Yet God ensured that no one had "too much" or "too little." Apart from such miracles in the New Testament age, the voluntary sharing of one's surplus goods accomplishes the same thing.[38] The end result is not that all will have the same amount; nor would such complete equality be sustainable even if it could be achieved for one brief moment in the history of the world. Rather, those who have more than an average or median amount of the world's goods generously share with those who have the least, in order to moderate the most extreme disparities between the haves and the have-nots.[39] The Christian vision is one of sharing voluntarily, out of deep compassion.

Spiritual and Material Matters Inextricable

The final principle in our survey involves the way in which spiritual health and material stewardship are intertwined. Jesus heals various people of their spiritual afflictions but typically challenges them to subsequent discipleship. Four times the refrain, "Your faith has saved you," suggests physical and spiritual wholeness simultaneously (Mark 5:34 pars.; 10:52 pars.; Luke 7:50; 17:19).[40] The apostles' encounter with the temple beggar in Acts 3:1–10 proves particularly instructive. Replying to his request for a handout, Peter declares, "Silver or gold I do not have" (v. 6). Strictly speaking, that was false, because in the previous paragraph Luke has highlighted the fledgling church's treasury for the needy. Perhaps Peter means merely that he has no coins with him at that moment, but more likely this is one of the many *relative* contrasts of the Bible couched, in Semitic idiom, as an absolute. Thus, what Peter wanted to give the lame man was far more valuable than money to buy his food for the day; Peter wanted to heal the man of his crippling disease. At the same time, such healing would enable the man to work for a living and support himself. Meanwhile, the healed beggar learns of the spiritual power available to him, as the apostles pronounce his cure "in the name of Jesus Christ." The pronouncement accomplishes its objective as the man accompanies the disciples into the temple courts, "walking and jumping, and praising God" (v. 8).[41] If this praise led to full-orbed discipleship, and his physical healing enabled employment, then he could go on to steward his resources and help others far more than previously.

Of course the most common manifestation of the intertwining of spiritual health and financial matters appears in the numerous accounts where generous giving or wise stewardship is depicted as the natural outgrowth of a life devoted to God or Christ. One thinks of the enigmatic parable of the unjust steward, who is praised not for his injustice but his shrewdness in his uses of the material goods of this world (Luke 16:1–8). Likewise, Jesus' followers are to use their money to make friends who will welcome them into heaven, presumably because they came to faith or Christian maturity through the giving of previous faithful stewards (v. 9).[42] One recalls Jesus' irrefutable relativizing of earthly possessions when compared with spiritual ones in the Sermon on the Mount (Matt. 6:19–34 par.) or His forceful inquiry, "What good is it for you to gain the whole world, yet forfeit your soul?" (Mark 8:36 pars.). One observes the ways in which Luke praises Dorcas and Cornelius for their exemplary almsgiving (Acts 9:36; 10:2, 31).

Conversely, those who had the ability and opportunity to work and refused to do so, opting instead to "mooch" off the generosity of the church, were forbidden from eating at the daily communal meal among Christians in Thessalonica (2 Thess. 3:10).[43] And the famous but oft-abused passage in 1 Corinthians 11:29 about eating or drinking unworthily at Communion does not refer to people who either feel like or really are unworthy sinners, lest we all be excluded, but bans those who have behaved like some of the rich church members in Corinth did—overeating and overdrinking at the love feast (the original church "potluck"), so that there was very little or nothing left for the poorer members who could not bring as much in the first place.[44] What a revolution it would cause in our churches if pastors regularly explained that, among Christians, those and only those who should refrain from the Lord's Supper are people who are not adequately caring for the poor and needy in their midst!

A rich diversity of terms for the collection for the saints in Judea appears in 2 Corinthians 8–9, including such words as "fellowship" or "sharing," an "act of grace," "this grace of giving," an "offering," a "liberal gift," and a "service" or "liturgy." All this amply justifies Paul Barnett's conclusion that grace is the theme of this entire two-chapter section. "Christian giving represents a gift from the grace of God, which he enables Christians to exercise."[45] Contrary perhaps to our expectation, but consistent with numerous subsequent examples throughout church history, it was not the richer Christians in Corinth but the poorer ones farther north in the province of Macedonia who proved the most generous. Paul had not even wanted to trouble them in view of their economic plight, but they took the initiative to insist on contributing to the collection. As Ralph Martin puts it, "Normally we think of the fundraiser as 'begging' the would-be donors. Here it is the donors, who could least afford it, who entreated Paul for the favor of having a part in this enterprise" (2 Cor. 8:1–4).[46]

What is more, the Macedonian believers gave themselves "first of all to the Lord," and then also "by the will of God" to the apostles (2 Cor. 8:5). Their gift formed part of their larger and more fundamental consecration of themselves to God in Christ. The second half of this verse may suggest that they recognized Paul's apostolic authority over them. At any rate, this was no isolated or spontaneous response to some emotional appeal. It was a carefully thought-out request and an outgrowth of a broader understanding of what Christian discipleship demands. The ultimate theological rationale for such behavior appears four verses later: "For you know the grace of our Lord Jesus Christ, that though he was rich, yet for your sake he became poor, so that you through his poverty might become rich" (2 Cor. 8:9).[47] Indeed, we may bring all five of our New Testament themes on possessions together under the rubric of *whole-life transformation*. As we are indwelt by Christ and allow His Spirit to fill us, we will view wealth as a good to be shared to moderate social disparities, not something merely to be accumulated for ourselves. We will recognize that it is not a case of giving a certain amount to others and then doing anything we want with the rest. All of life will increasingly come under the lordship of Jesus Christ. Sanctification and stewardship go hand in hand.[48]

Conclusion

As I reflect on these themes and this rubric of whole-life transformation, there are many conclusions I could suggest. However, within the focus of this book let me suggest that generous giving is the natural outgrowth of a life devoted to Christ, and above all, any of us who ask for money for ourselves or for others must be good models, and be *known* to be good models, of the principles we seek to teach others—both in our overall stewardship and in our personal giving.

As models of Christ, then, fundraisers need to take a genuine interest in the entire lives of those they contact. Anything less than a concern for the entire spiritual and material well-being of supporters does a disservice to the gospel.[49] The gen-xers and millennials are even more sensitive than baby boomers to those who would exploit them just for their money, even as baby boomers are often catching on faster than the post-War "builders."[50] I get the impression that sincerity and genuine connectedness will be the highest priorities in looking for a fundraiser in the decades ahead.

If we know through a thorough study of Scripture and sense in the depths of our hearts that the causes for which we seek to raise funds please God, further His Kingdom, and meet crucial spiritual and material needs in our world today, and if we can say in all honesty that we treat every gift with utter integrity, then it just remains for us to share our passion and opportunity with others. One of the best gifts we can offer our supporters is an honest assessment of whether our ministry cause best fits their desires of whom to support, and then to assure them that their money will truly be used in that cause.

I suspect that most of us need to study the Bible in more detail, separate biblical from unbiblical practices, seek first God's transformation in our own lives so that prospective supporters can clearly see how our practices differ from secular ones, teach others how giving is essential for them if they are to grow in Christ, renounce every form of manipulation and deception when it comes to how we use their money, and make sure that we are working for organizations that are above any form of legitimate reproach. If we are concerned most about God's ultimate response to our lives on judgment day, then the details will fall into place and we can look forward to Him saying to us, "Well done, good and faithful servant" (Matt. 25:21, 23)!

CRAIG L. BLOMBERG (Ph.D., University of Aberdeen) is distinguished professor of New Testament at Denver Seminary. He is the author or editor of sixteen books, including *The Historical Reliability of the Gospels*; *Interpreting the Parables*; *Matthew* for the New American Commentary series; *1 Corinthians* for the NIV Application Commentary series; *Jesus and the Gospels: An Introduction and Survey*; *Neither Poverty nor Riches: A Biblical Theology of Possessions*; *Preaching the Parables*; *Contagious Holiness: Jesus' Meals with Sinners*; and *From Pentecost to Patmos: An Introduction to Acts through Revelation*. He can be reached at craig.blomberg@denverseminary.edu.

---

1. See esp. Craig L. Blomberg, *Neither Poverty nor Riches: A Biblical Theology of Possessions* (Leicester: IVP; Grand Rapids: Eerdmans, 1999; Downers Grove: IVP, 2001); *Heart, Soul and Money: A Christian View of Possessions* (Joplin, MO: College Press, 2000); "Is Affluence Good?" *Faith and Economics* 40 (2002), 11–14; "Mastering Mammon," in *Consumerism*, ed. Robert B. Kruschwitz (Waco: Baylor, 2003), 19–26.

2. See esp. William W. Klein, Craig L. Blomberg, and Robert L. Hubbard Jr., *Introduction to Biblical Interpretation*, rev. ed. (Nashville: Thomas Nelson, 2004).

3. Sondra E. Wheeler, *Wealth as Peril and Obligation: The New Testament on Possessions* (Grand Rapids: Eerdmans, 1995), 123–27.

4. On "The Old Testament and the Material World," see Hugh G. M. Williamson, *Evangelical Quarterly* 57 (1985), 5–22. For critique of the "prosperity gospel," cf. Bruce Barron, *The Health Wealth Gospel* (Downers Grove, IL: IVP, 1987); and Robert M. Bowman Jr., *The Word-Faith Controversy: Understanding the Health and Wealth Gospel* (Grand Rapids: Baker, 2001).

5. All biblical quotations are taken from the TNIV, unless otherwise indicated.

6. Cf. Jerome Murphy-O'Connor, *The Theology of the Second Letter to the Corinthians* (Cambridge: Cambridge University Press, 1991), 93.

7. Cf. further Craig L. Blomberg, "On Wealth and Worry: Matt. 6:19–34—Meaning and Significance," *Criswell Theological Review* 6 (1992), 73–89.

8. See esp. David M. May, "Leaving and Receiving: A Social-Scientific Exegesis of Mark 10:29–31," *Perspectives in Religious Studies* 17 (1990), 141–54.

9. Christopher J. H. Wright, *Walking in the Ways of the Lord: The Ethical Authority of the Old Testament* (Leicester: IVP, 1995), 181–87.

10. N. T. Wright, *The Resurrection of the Son of God* (London: SPCK; Minneapolis: Fortress, 2003), 31 and throughout.

11. See Justo L. González, *Faith and Wealth* (San Francisco and London: Harper & Row, 1990).

12. The pioneering work on the minority of well-to-do Christians in the first-century church was Edwin A. Judge, *The Social Pattern of Christian Groups in the First Century* (London: Tyndale, 1960). On the proliferation of these in Acts, see David W. J. Gill, "Acts and the Urban Élites," in *The Book of Acts in Its Graeco-Roman Setting*, ed. David W. J. Gill and Conrad Gempf, eds. (Carlisle: Paternoster; Grand Rapids: Eerdmans, 1994), 105–18.

13. On which, see esp. Ben Witherington III, "On the Road with Mary Magdalene, Joanna, Susanna, and Other Disciples—Luke 8,1–3," *Zeitschrift für die neutestamentliche Wissenschaft* 70 (1979), 243–48.

14. Cf. esp. his *The Scandal of the Evangelical Conscience: Why Are Christians Living Just Like the Rest of the World?* (Grand Rapids: Baker, 2005); *Just Generosity: A New Vision for Overcoming Poverty in America* (Grand Rapids: Baker, 1999); and *Completely Pro-Life: Building a Consistent Stance* (Downers Grove, IL: IVP, 1987).

15. Cf. esp. Jacques Ellul, *Money and Power* (Downers Grove, IL: IVP, 1984; Basingstoke: Marshall Pickering, 1986); Richard J. Foster, *The Challenge of the Disciplined Life: Money, Sex and Power* (San Francisco: Harper & Row, 1989).

16. See my *Interpreting the Parables* (Downers Grove, IL and Leicester: IVP, 1990); and *Preaching the Parables: From Responsible Interpretation to Powerful Proclamation* (Grand Rapids: Baker, 2004).

17. On the two James passages, cf. Craig L. Blomberg and Mariam J. Kamell, *James* (Grand Rapids: Zondervan, forthcoming).

18. Bruce W. Winter, *After Paul Left Corinth: The Influence of Secular Ethics and Social Change* (Grand Rapids and Cambridge: Eerdmans, 2001); and the literature cited therein.

19. Ronald F. Hock, *The Social Context of Paul's Ministry* (Philadelphia: Fortress, 1980), 59–62.

20. Dieter Georgi, *Remembering the Poor: The History of Paul's Collection for Jerusalem* (Nashville: Abingdon, 1992).

21. Gerald W. Peterman, "'Thankless Thanks': The Epistolary Social Convention in Philippians 4:10–20," *Tyndale Bulletin* 42 (1991), 261–70.

22. George W. Knight III, *The Pastoral Epistles* (Carlisle: Paternoster; Grand Rapids: Eerdmans, 1992), 169.

23. I. Howard Marshall, *The Acts of the Apostles: An Introduction and Commentary* (Leicester: IVP; Grand Rapids: Eerdmans, 1980), 336.

24. J. Nelson Kraybill, *Imperial Cult and Commerce in John's Apocalypse* (Sheffield: Sheffield Academic, 1996); Eugene H. Peterson, *Reversed Thunder: The Revelation of John and the Praying Imagination* (San Francisco: Harper & Row, 1988), 148.

25. Richard Bauckham, "The Economic Critique of Rome in Revelation 18," in *Images of Empire*, ed. Loveday Alexander, (Sheffield: JSOT, 1991), 47–90.

26. Craig S. Keener, *Revelation* (Grand Rapids: Zondervan, 2000), 442–43.

27. Matt. 23:23 par. refers to the Old Testament Law, still in force for Jewish leaders, prior to Jesus' death and resurrection.

28. Robert A. Oden, "Taxation in Biblical Israel," *Journal of Religious Ethics* 12 (1984), 162–81.

29. David Croteau, "A Biblical and Theological Analysis of Tithing within the Framework of the Law-Gospel Relationship" (Ph.D. Diss., Southeastern Baptist Theological Seminary, 2005).

30. Cf. David E. Garland, *2 Corinthians* (Nashville: Broadman & Holman, 1999), 381: "Some can give far more than the tithe and have more than enough to provide all the necessities of life. Others barely have two mites for their daily needs."

31. E.g., Ronald J. Sider, *Rich Christians in an Age of Hunger*, 3rd ed. (Dallas: Word, 1997), 193–96.

32. For a succinct overview, see Leslie J. Hoppe, *There Shall Be No Poor among You: Poverty in the Bible* (Nashville: Abingdon, 2004).

33. Cf. Michael O'Hurley-Pitts, *The Passionate Steward: Recovering Christian Stewardship from Secular Fundraising* (Toronto: St. Brigid, 2001), 77–79.

34. Walter E. Pilgrim, *Good News to the Poor: Wealth and Poverty in Luke-Acts* (Minneapolis: Augsburg, 1981), 133.

35. Gary Burge, *The Letters of John* (Grand Rapids: Zondervan, 1996), 169.

36. Cf. e.g., Bob Goudzwaard and Harry de Lange, *Beyond Poverty and Affluence: Toward an Economy of Care* (Grand Rapids: Eerdmans, 1995).

37. Linda L. Belleville, *2 Corinthians* (Downers Grove, IL and Leicester: IVP, 1996), 225.

38. Sze-Kar Wan, *Power in Weakness: The Second Letter of Paul to the Corinthians* (Harrisburg, PA: Trinity, 2000), 110.

39. Cf. John and Sylvia Ronsvalle, *The Poor Have Faces: Loving Your Neighbor in the 21st Century* (Grand Rapids: Baker, 1992).

40. Craig L. Blomberg, "'Your Faith Has Made You Whole': The Evangelical Liberation Theology of Jesus," in *Jesus of Nazareth: Lord and Christ*, eds. Joel B. Green and Max Turner (Carlisle, UK: Paternoster; Grand Rapids: Eerdmans, 1994), 75–93.

41. On these points, cf. esp. Marshall, *Acts*, 88.

42. Craig M. Gay, *Cash Values: Money and the Erosion of Meaning in Today's Society* (Vancouver: Regent; Grand Rapids and Cambridge: Eerdmans, 2003), 73–99.

43. For this interpretation, see Robert Jewett, *Paul: The Apostle to America* (Louisville: Westminster John Knox, 1994), 73–86.

44. Cf. Anthony C. Thiselton, *The First Epistle to the Corinthians* (Carlisle, UK: Paternoster; Grand Rapids: Eerdmans, 2000), 890.

45. Paul Barnett, *The Second Epistle to the Corinthians* (Grand Rapids and Cambridge: Eerdmans, 1997), 388–89.

46. Ralph P. Martin, *2 Corinthians* (Waco: Word, 1986), 256.

47. John P. Meier, *Jesus: A Marginal Jew*, vol. 1 (San Francisco: HarperSanFrancisco, 1991), 282.

48. Robert Wuthnow, ed., *Rethinking Materialism: Perspectives on the Spiritual Dimension of Economic Behavior* (Grand Rapids: Eerdmans, 1995). Cf. also William Schweiker and Charles Mathewes, eds., *Having Property and Possession in Religious and Social Life* (Grand Rapids and Cambridge: Eerdmans, 2004).

49. See esp. R. Scott Rodin, *Stewards in the Kingdom: A Theology of Life in All Its Fullness* (Downers Grove, IL: IVP, 2000); and Wesley K. Willmer with Martyn Smith, *God and Your Stuff: The Vital Link between Your Possessions and Your Soul* (Colorado Springs: NavPress, 2002). Cf. also Terry Axelrod, *Raising More Money: A Step-by-Step Guide to Building Lifelong Donors* (Seattle: Raising More Money Publications, 2003).

50. For much of what needs to be done, see Kay S. Grace and Alan L. Wendroff, *High Impact Philanthropy: How Donors, Boards and Nonprofit Organizations Can Transform Communities* (San Francisco: Jossey-Bass, 2000).

Chapter

GOD AND GIVING:
THE ROAD TO GENEROSITY

By WALTER B. RUSSELL, *Professor of New Testament*
at Talbot School of Theology, Biola University

T he road to generosity is a journey that few Christians successfully complete. Some never get started on the journey. Probably
most Christians start on the road, then quickly pull off at a rest
stop and just stay there, idling. A few take seriously their Christian faith and
choose to travel faithfully, like Bunyan's "Pilgrim,"[1] and complete the journey. They arrive as mature believers and generous stewards.

This book is about a revolution in generosity created by stewards transformed to be rich toward God. At the core of its thesis is the belief that generosity is the natural outcome of God working in individuals so that they are
conformed to the image of Christ and become generous, as Christ is generous. As a result of this journey, they will grow in the grace of giving and will
take hold of that which is life indeed (1 Tim. 6:19).

The purpose of this chapter is to break this journey down into under-
standable pieces, to explain the road to generosity as Christians become rich
toward God. Our journey on the road to generous giving (1) starts with faith

in Christ, (2) is motivated by gratitude toward Christ, (3) is directed by biblical examples, (4) picks up speed as faith matures, and (5) encounters distractions or roadblocks that must be overcome. This chapter will examine each aspect in turn.

GENEROSITY STARTS WITH FAITH

The road to generosity starts when we first become aware of Jesus Christ's generosity toward us and respond by placing our trust in Him. The apostle Paul says, "But now that you have been set free from sin and have become slaves of God, the fruit you get leads to sanctification and its end, eternal life. For the wages of sin is death, but the free gift of God is eternal life in Christ Jesus our Lord."[2] The journey of the Christian life is from death and sin's slavery to eternal life, made possible through the generous gift of Christ. Between the beginning of faith and our destination is the transforming process of sanctification, which includes imitating Christ's generosity (see especially Scott Rodin's chapter). Despite the fact that we have been freed from *slavery* to sin, we still struggle with sin and a propensity toward earthly things. Our sinful past and its habits make us selfish and miserly, desiring the goods of this world rather than service to Christ. Generosity, the outgrowth of faith, sets us free from the things of this world—material possessions and selfish desires—and assists us in being conformed to Christ's image. When we refocus our sights on the spiritual inheritance found in Christ, we generously give back to God as His stewards.

By accepting our God-given role as stewards rather than owners, we recognize that everything we claim to possess is not ours but God's, entrusted to us for a period of time to use as He directs.[3] Mark provides a stirring example of recognizing our role as stewards: "Calling his disciples to him, Jesus said, 'I tell you the truth, this poor widow has put more into the treasury than all the others. They all gave out of their wealth; but she, out of her poverty, put in everything—all she had to live on.'"[4] In a day when widows and orphans relied on benevolence from others, this woman demonstrated complete trust in God's ability to provide for her needs. Rather than hoarding what little she had, she freely gave everything to God. While many of us will not have the faith to go to such lengths, we should at least begin to develop the mentality that undergirds the widow's beliefs and practices: God owns everything; He'll care for my needs; therefore, I will embrace my role as His steward.

Our stewardship should be shaped by our calling to be rich toward God, heeding the warning Jesus gives in Luke 12:20–21 (ESV): "But God said to him, 'Fool! This night your soul is required of you, and the things you have prepared, whose will they be?' So is the one who lays up treasure for himself and is not rich toward God." This Scripture admonishes us to care more for the Kingdom of God than the riches of this world, and to manifest these priorities in the ways that we dispose of our resources. Our focus should be on God and His work, not wasted worrying about whether we have "enough." Too often we view giving as a chore, something that ought to be done, rather than an opportunity to be a steward who is rich toward God and a living image of His generosity.

God's love and generosity are manifested most vividly and powerfully in Christ's incarnation, death, and resurrection. Paul eloquently proclaims that Jesus

> did not count equality with God a thing to be grasped, but made himself nothing, taking the form of a servant, being born in the likeness of men. And being found in human form, he humbled himself by becoming obedient to the point of death, even death on a cross. Therefore God has highly exalted him and bestowed on him the name that is above every name, so that at the name of Jesus every knee should bow, in heaven and on earth and under the earth, and every tongue confess that Jesus Christ is Lord, to the glory of God the Father.[5]

The giving of all on earth, even His life, out of a place of supreme abundance in heaven is the ultimate act of generosity. This love and generosity of Christ are what empowers us to be generous.[6] As Dallas Willard observes, "Living under the governance of heaven frees and empowers us to love as God loves. But outside the safety and sufficiency of heaven's rule, we are too frightened and angry to really love others, or even ourselves."[7] As God's love flows through us, we become like Him. As His generous nature transforms our souls, we become more generous. It is not about giving from our own strength; rather, as Gordon MacDonald points out, "We are called to put on the essence of our heavenly Father. And how is this done? By living a life of love in the pattern of Christ's love . . . at the core of the generous person's heart is this penchant for Christ's love—the desire to receive it and to give it to everyone along the way who is in need."[8] Through God's power, we are able to embark upon the road of generosity set before us and become stewards who are increasingly rich toward God.

MOTIVATIONS FOR GENEROSITY

While the road to generosity starts with faith, the fuel or motivation for giving grows out of our gratitude toward Christ. Generosity comes from a blessed heart, as a response to God's generosity to us in sending His Son. Moreover, it frees us as His adult children from our attachment to earthly possessions. Karl Barth said it beautifully: "Grace and gratitude belong together like heaven and earth. Grace evokes gratitude like the voice an echo. Gratitude follows grace as thunder follows lightning."[9] The following observations explore this indispensable principle.

First, as just pointed out, generosity grows from a blessed heart—not out of manipulation or out of a resentful sense of obligation. When it comes to giving, it is the "cheerful giver," not the arm-twisted one, whom God loves (2 Cor. 9:7). Even within the old covenant's highly structured giving format, God gave His people opportunity to be cheerful in their giving. Perhaps this is best illustrated in the freewill offerings. Voluntary offerings supplied the materials for the building of the tabernacle (Ex. 35:20-29), the temple (1

Chron. 29:1–9), and the rebuilding of the temple six hundred years later (Ezra 1:4–11; 8:24–30). Note the cheerfulness enveloping the giving to the temple's construction: "Then the people rejoiced because they had given willingly, for with a whole heart they had offered freely to the Lord. David the king also rejoiced greatly" (1 Chron. 29:9 ESV).[10]

While the Old Testament is instructive about cheerfulness in freewill giving, it is also informative about the baseline for giving that God established for Israel. Should we be as generous under the new covenant as God encouraged His people to be under the old? Should we set 10 percent as a baseline for giving? Perhaps. But if the old covenant percentage was actually 19–22 percent, then such a baseline would need to be rethought.[11]

The bigger problem is that we are really comparing apples and oranges when we compare giving in the theocratic state of Israel with giving under the new covenant. If the tithe in Israel is viewed as a theocratic tax, then it corresponds to our modern pattern of paying taxes to state and federal governments. This means that the only correspondence left would be between the old covenant's freewill giving and the new covenant's grace giving. If this is the case, then we do not have any fixed percentages to go by. Rather, we must rely on the patterns and motivations of both the old and new covenants that encourage generous giving. With such adultlike freedom comes adultlike responsibility. This is why we must do a significantly better job of teaching our people in the area of giving. Biblical teaching and biblical motivations to give become immensely important with the new covenant freedom of grace-giving. Generous love breeds generous freedom. As God's love transforms our hearts, we are able to genuinely respond to the call of generosity. Though we have the freedom *not* to give, God motivates us *to choose* to give by appealing to our desire. The filter that separates good motives from bad in giving is that of *cheerfulness*. If a spirit of freedom and cheerfulness does not accompany our giving, then we need to check our motives. No freedom; no cheerfulness; keep your money! *Grudging compulsion* should give way pretty quickly to *cheer-*

ful choosing as a person is transformed.

Second, generosity flows as our response to Christ. Reflection on the life and work of Christ should inspire praise and gratitude. Thus giving can properly be thought of as an expression of gratitude toward Christ. C. S. Lewis notes:

> If you asked twenty good men to-day what they thought the highest of the virtues, nineteen of them would reply, *Unselfishness*. But if you asked almost any of the great Christians of old he would have replied, *Love*. . . .The negative ideal of *Unselfishness* carries with it the suggestion not primarily of securing good things for others, but of going without them ourselves, *as if our abstinence and not their happiness was the important point.*[12]

It seems that the substitution of the negative term *Unselfishness* has also triumphed quite grandly over the positive virtue of *Love* in many of our discussions of biblical giving. We fall into the narcissistic modern pattern of assuming that *our self-denial* is the primary point. The Bible's emphasis on giving is rooted in an appeal to our desires to love others in response to God's lavish love of us in Christ. To learn to give generously, therefore, is not to learn to vigorously deny self but to learn to love God and others generously, as we are loved. Giving generously is about loving generously. Randy Alcorn explains, "Giving is a response of the heart triggered by God's grace. We give because God first gave to us."[13] The Bible's emphasis on giving is rooted in our desire to love God in response to His love of us (1 John 4:19).

Third, generosity indicates mature faith. God commands and provides opportunities for generosity throughout salvation history, but the parameters become broader over time. Abram's tithing to Melchizedek in Genesis 14:20 establishes the historical foundation of tithing within the Mosaic covenant. The Mosaic Law simply develops in covenantal format the tithing principles established by Father Abram.

Paul considers the old covenant believing community as a child, a minor who is under the tutelage of the Mosaic Law (Gal. 3:23–26) until the time set by the Father. In Galatians 4:1–11, the apostle Paul's basic appeal is to persuade his readers to enjoy the freedom that comes from being adult children under the covenantal maturity of the messianic age, i.e., the new covenant. What is left behind is the developmental immaturity when God's children were minors under the Mosaic Law (Gal. 3:23–26). Their time of childhood was characterized by the tutelage of the Law covenant. Their time as adults is now to be characterized by the indwelling of the Holy Spirit (Gal. 4:6).

This developmental shift is of great significance to the change in God's emphasis on generous giving from the Old to the New Testament. What does *not* change is the importance of giving generously. What *does* change is the amount of structure and percentages surrounding the giving from the time when God viewed His children as minors. God's shifting of the age to adulthood brought the disappearance of many of the guidelines of childhood as well as the responsibility of giving generously according to the direction of the Holy Spirit.

Finally, generosity turns our focus and love away from our possessions and toward God's Kingdom. Jesus challenges us to keep a proper focus on our heavenly home. Linked to the seductive power and serving of riches (instead of God) is the corresponding focus on creating earthly wealth and security (rather than heavenly wealth). As both Jesus and Paul assert, such a focus is plagued with *uncertainty* due to the multiple threats to such wealth. God loves us too much to allow us to build our lives on flimsy stuff that will fail, that is a very little thing, that is not true riches, and that actually belongs to another (Luke 16:9–13; 1 Tim. 6:17–19). The only way to reach solid ground is to set our heart and focus firmly upon our heavenly home and heavenly treasure. This is the point of Jesus' words, "for where your treasure is, there will your heart be also" (Matt. 6:21 KJV). Choosing to give back to the Lord what He has given us will keep our hearts focused on that which really matters and that which is life indeed, increasing our longing for His Kingdom and weakening our attachment to this world.

BIBLICAL EXAMPLES OF GENEROSITY: TO WHOM SHOULD WE GIVE?

Mature giving comes from an overflowing response of gratitude for what God has done for us—moved by gratitude, we become stewards who are rich toward God. Scripture provides three broad categories for where our generosity should be directed: those who have blessed us spiritually, believers who are in material need, and those who have committed their lives to spreading the gospel beyond the local church.

Giving to those who gave us spiritual things springs from the old covenant practice of providing for the Levites, but is clearly reiterated in the New Testament: when others minister *spiritual things* to us, we are indebted to minister to them with *material things* (Rom. 15:27). The apostle Paul emphasizes this principle: "If we have sown *spiritual things* among you, is it too much if we reap *material things* from you?" (1 Cor. 9:11 ESV, emphasis mine). Note that the principle is one of "indebtedness" or very real obligation. Particularly, we see that while it is something that new covenant believers *ought to do*, it is nonetheless also a voluntary thing we should *choose to do*. At stake is the loving care of those who have given their lives and "careers" for the sake of the gospel. Of all people, these dear saints should be well cared for financially.

A second part of living under the spiritual adulthood of the new covenant is being aware of the needs of believers around us. Paul understands this mutual sharing of resources as so foundational to the life in Christ that he states it as part of *the purpose* for a Christian working: "Let the thief no longer steal, but rather let him labor, doing honest work with his own hands, *so that he may have something to share with anyone in need*" (Eph. 4:28 ESV, emphasis mine). Statements like this naturally raise questions about how far our duty extends, and what is the nature of our responsibility to fellow Christians who are in other geographical areas or other countries. As we are made aware of their needs, should we be sharing from our little pile of the world's goods to meet their deficiency?

The New Testament seems to focus on sharing resources with needy believers in other areas at the church-to-church level. This is a very neglected area of study when we discuss new covenant giving. The longest discussion of giving in the Bible, 2 Corinthians 8–9,[14] motivates a local church to follow through on its pledge to give to churches in another part of the world. Here Paul was exhorting the exuberant and immature Corinthian church to give to the collection for the poor saints in the Jerusalem and Judea area. Many churches in Macedonia, Asia, and Galatia had already given to this collection (e.g., 2 Cor. 8:1–4, 16–24; Acts 20:3–4 recounts their messengers carrying the collection). They were simply following the example of international generosity set nine years earlier by the new church in Antioch of Syria (Acts 11:27–30). The question that then emerges is how one cares for those in areas as yet unreached by the gospel, and so lacking a local church to facilitate church-to-church giving. This leads us to the third facet of giving: investment in the spreading of the gospel beyond one's local church.

Several years ago my fellow pastoral elders and I were confronted with the financial challenges of planting and growing a church. In light of the teaching of Philippians, one of our fundamental commitments was the priority of investing in the advance of the gospel beyond our own local church. Early in the life of the church, we committed to have *koinōnia* (New Testament Greek for "fellowship") with other ministries beyond our borders. We committed to invest 30 percent of every dollar that was given to us for the broader advance of the gospel. Every six months we wanted to increase this by 5 percent until we got to 50 percent.

Our idealism was soon tested when our church treasurer said that we could either pay the staff salaries in two weeks or pay our financial commitments to our missionaries and mission organizations. My wife and I had two young children and absolutely no financial buffer at the time. Missing a paycheck would be devastating to us as a family. However, as the other elders and I meditated on Paul's words about investing in the gospel cause in Philippians 4:10–20, we took heart. The Lord knew that local churches like us would regularly feel the conflict between investing in their local needs and investing in the broader gospel advance. This is why the Lord stirred Paul to include the promise to local churches in Philippians 4:19 (ESV): "And my God will supply every need of yours according to his riches in glory in Christ Jesus." As a group of elders, we claimed this promise and went ahead and made our missions investments. Sure enough, the Lord met our local needs and we were able to pay our staff salaries in the next two weeks.

By continuing to give priority to our investment in the broader advance of the gospel, we were always able to meet our local needs in the seven years I was at the church. God was astonishingly faithful to supply all our needs as He promised in His Word.

STAGES OF FAITH AND GENEROSITY[15]

Sinners do not become saints overnight—the Christian life is a journey toward maturity. When writing to the Philippians regarding their deliverance from "selfishness and empty conceit" and merely looking out "for your own personal interests" (Phil. 2:3–4), Paul exhorts them to "work out your own deliverance with fear and trembling, for it is God who works in you, both to will and to work for His good pleasure" (Phil. 2:12–13).[16] As Christians, we desire to be generous as Christ is generous, but this only comes as a part of the sanctifying process, through stages and growing our faith.[17] Contemplating stages people tend to pass through can help us as we walk along the road to generosity (see Todd Harper's chart in his chapter for greater detail).[18]

First, as children toddling on the road to mature stewardship, we give because we see those around us giving. This imitation is good in that it habituates our character in the ways of godly generosity; but the motivation quickly becomes inadequate, as the pressures of life force Christians to know *why* they give. Hopefully this pressure results in the understanding that it is good, in itself, to give. This "modeling stage" is characterized by people who give, often out of guilt or duty, knowing it is the "right thing" to do. Like the previous imitation stage, modeling is not founded on internal change, but external pressures. As we mature, however, the motivation deepens slightly to include concern for those in need, as well as a desire for personal recognition. Here, giving is possibly motivated by internal concerns, but it is a strictly horizontal activity and has little apparent relationship to the Christian's spiritual life.

The transition from external to internal motivation can act as a catalyst for transformation, where the Christian begins to understand that there is a strong connection between giving and his or her soul. Understanding this leads to a lifestyle where one is willing to become detached from one's possessions. This process results in a mature steward, a Christian who views generous giving as a vertical experience between oneself and God. This steward gives "not knowing where money will come from." Dallas Willard writes of this process: "His is a revolution of *character*, which proceeds by changing people from the inside through ongoing personal relationship to God in Christ and to one another. It is one that changes their ideas, beliefs, feelings and *habits of choice*, as well as their bodily tendencies and social relations."[19] Recognizing that generous giving is a process, and that maturity therefore accrues over time, is important in evaluating both our own and others' progression on the road to generosity.

ROADBLOCKS AND COMMON EXCUSES: REASONS WE PULL OFF THE ROAD

Unfortunately, it does not take much to distract us from God's faithfulness, and, like children, we would much rather run around at the rest stop than return to the road. Excuses for not giving abound, but some recur more frequently than others. These "common excuses" fall into four broad categories:

(1) I am not required to give, (2) I cannot give, (3) I have given enough already, and (4) I'm too disillusioned with the church or parachurch group to give.

The first category of excuses—that I am not required to give—includes statements like: "It's my money; I earned it," "God doesn't need my money," "The tithe does not apply to Christians today," and "The Bible says that each man should give what he has decided in his own heart to give. So I am free to give as much or as little as I choose, even not at all." This attitude ignores the fact that one aspect of God's generosity toward us consists in providing opportunities for us to be rich toward Him by distributing His money to those in need. It stems from a misunderstanding of stewardship and an improper posture toward our possessions.

The second category of excuses—that I cannot give—typically involves the following: "I am in the lower or middle income bracket, and giving is really the responsibility of wealthy people," "I am up to my ears in debt," or "I have spent a lifetime securing my financial independence. I can't throw it all away now." This set of excuses usually flows from a lack of trust in God as a provider, from the assumption that God helps those who help themselves and that He won't necessarily provide for us if we give sacrificially to further His work in the world.

Third, there are those who feel that they have already done their fair share—that they have given enough already: "I already tithe; that's all God requires of me"; "Stewardship is a lot more than money. I give my time and talents by teaching Sunday school and opening my home, and I consider that to be my giving"; "I've already maxed out my tax deductions for this year. My gifts won't count until next year, so I'll give then"; or "I have more than I need, but I am not prepared to live like a pauper." This set of excuses comes out of underestimating the importance of giving as a vital part of our whole spiritual transformation.

The fourth category is perhaps the fastest-growing complaint among the church's younger generations. It is the excuse of disillusionment with the local church or parachurch ministries. While there can be many legitimate reasons for being disillusioned with how God's people model His Kingdom, there is no legitimate reason for not giving back *to God* in spite of the imperfections of His people's institutions. We return again to the widow whose sacrificial giving at the temple elicited Jesus' robust praise in Mark 12:41–44. Jesus and the widow both looked past the corrupt temple system in her act of giving. While Jesus knew that He would later cleanse and judge this system, He also knew that the widow was ultimately giving *to the Lord* and not to the spiritually bankrupt temple structure. If Jesus found praiseworthy her act of giving to the Lord via an institution awaiting divine judgment, imagine how pleased He will be when we give *to the Lord* via His church, even with all her present spots and wrinkles.

There are many variations on these excuses, and it is important to be on the lookout for such attitudes. They tend to rear their heads when we least expect them and can generally be answered by reviewing the Bible's teaching on generosity. It is helpful to remind ourselves that everything we have belongs to God, and He commands us to steward His resources wisely to accomplish His priorities (not ours) in advancing His Kingdom (not ours).

May God help us respond to His overwhelming generosity with a generosity of our own, acting as grateful stewards who know the joy of service. A revolution in generosity will occur when believers move out of the rest stop and down the road of conforming to the character of Christ. While this is the less-traveled road, it is the assured route to a happy destination toward which the Bible urges us.

WALTER B. RUSSELL (Ph.D., Westminster Theological Seminary) is professor of New Testament at Talbot School of Theology (Biola University) in La Mirada, California. His areas of expertise are exegesis, hermeneutics, and New Testament theology, especially as they relate to world evangelism and the spiritual growth of the church. He authored *The Flesh/Spirit Conflict in Galatians* and *Playing with Fire: How the Bible Ignites Change in Your Soul*. He can be reached at Walt.Russell@biola.edu.

1. John Bunyan, *The Pilgrim's Progress from this world to that which is to come: delivered under the similitude of a dream, wherein is discovered the manner of his setting out, his dangerous journey and safe arrivals* (Urichsville, OH: Barbour, 1984).

2. Romans 6:22–23 ESV.

3. R. Scott Rodin, *Stewards in the Kingdom* (Downers Grove, IL: IVP, 2000), 56.

4. Mark 12:41–44 NIV.

5. Philippians 2:6–11 ESV.

6. Paul appeals to this concept in motivating the Corinthians to give in 2 Corinthians 8:9 (NIV): "For you know the grace of our Lord Jesus Christ, that though he was rich, yet for your sakes he became poor, so that you through his poverty might become rich."

7. Dallas Willard, *The Great Omission: Reclaiming Jesus's Essential Teachings on Discipleship* (San Francisco: HarperSanFrancisco, 2006), 25.

8. Gordon MacDonald, *Secrets of the Generous Life: Reflections to Awaken the Spirit and Enrich the Soul* (Wheaton: Tyndale House, 2002), 12.

9. Karl Barth, *Church Dogmatics* (Edinburgh: T & T Clark, 1957), IV-1, 41.

10. Randy Alcorn, *Money, Possessions and Eternity* (Wheaton: Tyndale House, 1989), 233.

11. The 19–22 percent figure comes from the probability that there were two or three tithes in Israel. The first tithe was 1/10 of all (Lev. 27:30–33; Num. 18:21–32), the second tithe was 1/10 of the remaining 9/10 (Deut. 12:5-19; 14:22–27), and the third tithe was 1/10 of the remaining 8/10 balance every third year (Deut. 14:28–29). Given the diversity of the three sets of instructions and their different emphases, it is hard to correlate them with only one tithe. Additionally, given the "theocratic tax" dimension of the tithes, it seems far more likely that 19–22 percent of each Israelite family's income would be needed to keep the theocratic infrastructure going rather than simply 10 percent.

12. "The Weight of Glory," in *The Weight of Glory and Other Addresses* (Eerdmans, 1949), 1; italics are mine.

13. Alcorn, *Money, Possessions and Eternity*, 207.

14. See 2 Corinthians 8-9 and Craig L. Blomberg, *Neither Poverty nor Riches: A Biblical Theology of Possessions* (Leicester: IVP; Grand Rapids: Eerdmans, 1999; Downers Grove, IL: IVP, 2001), 190–99.

15. Wesley K. Willmer, *God and Your Stuff: The Vital Link between Your Possessions and Your Soul* (Colorado Springs: NavPress, 2002), 43.

16. Translation is mine. Gerald F. Hawthorne, *Word Biblical Commentary: Philippians* (Waco: Word, 1983), 98, makes this observation about Paul's exhortation in 2:12-13: "Paul has just spoken sharply against Christians looking out for their own individual, personal interests (2:4). Hence, it is highly unlikely that he here now reverses himself by commanding them to focus on their own individual salvation." Hawthorne's and my understanding of the context of this passage is that Paul is speaking of the Philippians' (and our) "deliverance" from *the present threat* of selfishness and empty conceit, where we look out for our own personal interests rather than the interests of others (Phil. 2:3-4). Paul gives four examples in Philippians 2 of humble, selfless persons who showcase this deliverance from self-interest: Jesus Christ (2:5-11, the preeminent example), Paul himself (2:16-18), Timothy (2:19-24), and their own Epaphroditus (2:25-30). The "salvation" Paul exhorts us to work out *in this context* is a deliverance from our own selfishness, not a deliverance from eternal damnation. This interpretation would also fit the more common first-century usage of "deliverance" or "salvation" from an immediate threat, rather than from an eternal one.

17. For example, well-known theorist Lawrence Kohlberg identifies six stages of moral development in a person's life. See his book *Essays on Moral Development, Vol. I: The Philosophy of Moral Development* (San Francisco: Harper & Row, 1981). See also James W. Fowler, *Stages of Faith: The Psychology of Human Development and the Quest for Meaning* (San Francisco: HarperSanFrancisco, 1995). More recently, see Janet O. Hagberg and Robert A. Guelich, *The Critical Journey: Stages in the Life of Faith*, 2nd ed. (Salem, WI: Sheffield Publishing, 2005).

18. I have also found Hagberg and Guelich, *The Critical Journey*, to be immensely helpful. They summarize the six stages of the Journey of Faith as follows (p. 17):

        Stage 1 – Recognition of God

        Stage 2 – Life of Discipleship

        Stage 3 – Productive Life

        Stage 4 – Journey Inward

The "Wall"

Stage 5 – Journey Outward

Stage 6 – Life of Love

It is particularly in Stages 5 ("faith is surrendering to God") and 6 ("faith is reflecting God") that we become more like Christ in the many facets of His loving generosity.

19. Dallas Willard, *The Renovation of the Heart: Putting on the Character of Christ* (Colorado Springs: NavPress, 2002), 15; second italics is mine.

Chapter

GOD AND ASKING:

THE **CHOICE BETWEEN** TWO **ROADS**

BY RICHARD A. HAYNIE, *Director of*
Development for OC International

F undraising advice is easy to find and presents us with a myriad of options. Books on this topic fill store shelves, and seminars declare "how to do it" to get results. Countless voices loudly proclaim the ways we can go about asking for money—and each of these alternatives presents choices. We are faced with divergent paths and must decide which to follow. Though there seems to be a plethora of options, the choice is simple. As Jesus proclaims in Matthew 7:13–14, we must choose either God's way or humanity's way; God's narrow, less-traveled road or the wide, popular road. In recent decades the distinction between these two choices has become muddied because often the same terminology is used to signify diametrically opposed approaches. As a result, definition is crucial if we are to understand exactly what it means to raise resources God's way.

This book makes a distinction between choosing either the transactional or the heart-transformational road in fundraising. Popular and widely used transactional techniques get people to give by providing them something of earthly value in return, such as premiums, a naming opportunity, or membership in exclusive VIP clubs. The less-used approach is the belief that generous Christian giving is the result of the transformation of a person's character as he or she is conformed to the image of Christ, becoming generous as Christ is generous (see especially the chapters by Craig Blomberg and Walt Russell). Once you accept God's way for giving, you realize that asking for funds is a transformational process of growing givers' hearts to be rich toward God (Luke 12:21). These ideas represent what I see as the more perfect way that has been revealed to me after years of involvement in raising money. I believe that if Christian ministries adopted these principles, they would help create a revolution in generosity.

We will begin by looking at the principles and priorities, practices, and outcomes of the two roads. In this context, we will contrast a biblical model of development with the road of secular fundraising, specifically in regard to research, cultivation, asking, follow-up, and handling accountability. This comparison will leave us with a clear and practical understanding of the way of biblical development.

PRINCIPLES AND PRIORITIES

In fundraising, the underlying, foundational principles we set out determine the priorities that frame our strategies and the direction our road will take. Looking at the basic principles that undergird each of the two roads will start us on our way to understanding where and why the biblical road diverges from the popular road of fundraising. To set the stage for this section, understanding the answers to three foundational questions is essential: (1) who owns the money, (2) what motivates people to give money, and (3) the purpose behind the entire process of raising money.

Principle #1: God Owns It All

In today's culture the popular manner of looking at fundraising is pragmatic and horizontal: people own resources that must be accessed through a transactional process of getting people to give up some of what they own to the organization that needs the money.

Contrary to this belief structure is the principle underlying the other road—God owns it all. David expresses this in the fundraising context of 1 Chronicles 29: "Yours, O Lord, is . . . everything that is in the heavens and the earth . . . Both riches and honor come from You . . . and it lies in Your hand to make great and to strengthen everyone" (vv. 11–12). Further on he prays, "O Lord our God, all this abundance that we have provided to build You a house for Your holy name, it is from Your hand, and all is Yours" (v. 16). [1] As David understood, God is the source of all things.

If God owns it all, then spending money is spending *God's* money, and therefore spending is always a spiritual decision. [2] Each person is a manager of God's money, charged with stewarding it on His behalf; therefore, each one of us should be intensely interested in how God wants us to spend and give what He has entrusted to us. The principle holds true regardless of the amount of money involved. We must respond with submission to God; as R. Scott Rodin writes, "It was this total submission to God alone that Jesus was demanding from the rich young ruler of Matthew 19. For him, only the total abandonment of his earthly kingdom that demanded of him the worship of money could free him fully to embrace the living God." [3] We cannot choose both God's and humanity's way. Faithful stewardship or management of all God has entrusted to us is central to our obedience to Him, and thus the fundraising process should reinforce this God-honoring lifestyle.

If God has entrusted us with the management of His money, then our priority should be using it as He wants it used. [4] Since God owns it all (and He has no lack of resources), He implores us to handle our possessions in a way that edifies the body of Christ, reflects His glory by our trusting obedience to His plan, and gives credit to Him alone. We should dwell less on the amount He has entrusted to us, and be much more concerned about what God wants us to do with the resources He is providing and how He wants us to relate to the people through whom He is providing them. This attitude cannot follow from the principles on which humankind's road is based, but it is the natural result of embracing the biblical truth that God owns it all.

Principle #2: God Is the Fundraiser

The second principle of fundraising concerns how people are motivated to give. On the human road, where it is believed that money belongs to people, fundraisers shoulder the burden of persuading potential donors to give over some of their money to an organization. These fundraisers strive to make things happen through transactions; theirs is the road that guarantees programs (too frequently involving emotional manipulation, deception, and appeals to the donor's ego) and promises returns for efforts. The responsibility to get people to give rests entirely on the fundraiser, and it becomes too easy to do whatever works.

On God's road, where we recognize that God owns everything, we see that God moves people to distribute the resources He has entrusted to them. God cares for His stewards and He entrusts money to them so that, in giving it generously, they may be conformed to the image of His Son and participate in His work in the world. The Bible repeatedly demonstrates that generous giving comes from a transformation of people's hearts. First Chronicles 29:9 tells us, "The people rejoiced because they had offered so willingly, for they made their offering to the Lord with a whole heart." Exodus 35:21 records, "Everyone whose heart stirred him and everyone whose spirit moved him came and brought the Lord's contribution for the work." Second Corinthians 9:7 instructs, "Each one must do just as he has purposed in his heart, not grudgingly or under compulsion." In each instance, people became aware of a need, their hearts were stirred and their spirits moved, and they gave willingly. Giving, then, is a matter of a heart that is conformed to the image of Christ, and since God alone (through the work of the Holy Spirit) can change hearts, God is the One who motivates people to give. God is the fundraiser.

If God is the fundraiser, then what is the job of the person asking? To answer that question, we need to notice what preceded the above scriptural events of generous giving. In 1 Chronicles 29, David presented the need in obedience to God's issuing a vision, recounted in 1 Chronicles 28. In Exodus 35, Moses presented the need, or giving opportunity, based on God's command from Mount Sinai (cf. Ex. 34:32). In 2 Corinthians, Paul presented the need (chap. 8) and followed up (chap. 9) based on his calling as an apostle (Rom. 1:1 and elsewhere). Each of these biblical fundraisers told the people of a need that arose from a task God gave them to accomplish, and God moved the people's hearts to generosity.

The following story from my own experience illustrates the same biblical truth.

My supervisor and I had made arrangements to visit the home of a long-time friend and monthly supporter of our organization's missionaries. After we presented the vision of what we felt God wanted us to do to complete a multimillion-dollar project and shared how we thought that could successfully occur, the donor, with his spouse's enthusiastic approval, leapt up from the sofa and ran over to the bookcase. He quickly grabbed a book entitled *Lord, Help Me Give Away One Million Dollars* and said, "I've been waiting for someone to share God's plan with us . . . this title expresses my response!" God had been preparing this couple's heart to give generously and, when the organization presented an opportunity to give, God moved them to respond. God is the fundraiser—not us!

Scripture teaches that our job is to be ambassadors for Christ, to deliver the message of the King. As we sow the seed of the gospel, God reveals the truth of His Word and causes growth. As Oswald Chambers observed, "Our work begins where God's grace has laid the foundation; we are not to save souls, but to disciple them."[5] In fundraising, as in evangelism, we are called to present the opportunity and allow God to move givers' hearts to give whatever amount He reveals to them as their proper participation. We are dependent on the Holy Spirit's work in the hearts of our constituents.[6] When we understand our role as an ambassador—to advance and facilitate a believer's faith in and worship of God—we are liberated. God gives us a vision of work to do and leads us to tell people what we need in order to accomplish that work, and we communicate the vision and opportunity without having to worry about the financial results, since they do not depend on us. We can think of ourselves as matchmakers, pairing people whom God has moved to invest in a vision with ministries that God has created to carry out that vision. God has already appropriated the funding: He already owns it all. The job of the person asking is to simply share the giving opportunity as God directs in His work of growing givers' hearts and transforming people to generosity.

Principle #3: Fundraising Is about Transformation

The third foundational difference between the two roads is the *goal* of fundraising. On humanity's road, the completion of fundraising is a transaction. The goal is for a donor to transfer some amount of money from his or her pocket into an organization's bank account. The people involved become nothing more than a means to the all-important end of getting the money. Fundraisers have to interact with people in order to persuade them to part with their money. We want more and more people involved, because more people mean more money. We spend time with people with a view to increasing the size of their donation. Everything we do is for the sake of the transaction.

On God's road, the end purpose of raising funds is not a financial transaction but a whole-life transformation of growing givers' hearts to be generous and rich toward God. Those asking for funds on the biblical road see that their goal is to be instruments that God can use to transform Christians, from the heart, into godly, generous stewards of His resources and worshipers of Him. The purpose is to see Christians mature in their faith[7] (see Wes Willmer's chapter), that they may become cheerful, Spirit-led givers (see Todd Harper's chapter). Our purpose is to further an ongoing process that God is conducting in the hearts of believers. We recognize that people are God's priority—He is continually working by His Spirit to transform hearts to conform to the image of His Son.

Fundraisers are in a unique position of ministry to participate in God's work of transforming the hearts of His children, if they will take advantage of the biblical road stretched out before their feet. Fundraising can play an integral part in the fulfillment of the Great Commission (Matt. 28:18–20)—both indirectly, by gathering the funds necessary to send people to "all the nations" to make disciples; and directly, by helping facilitate the transformation of people into the image of Christ by "teaching them to observe all He commanded" about money and possessions. In both aspects of the fundraising effort, transforming people into closer followers of Christ is the goal.

If spiritual transformation is the goal of fundraising, then the fundraiser is called to be a minister. Jeavons and Basinger write, "Exemplary organizations are intentional about relating to donors and others in ways that allow space and time for God's work in individual hearts. In this way, they help donors find great joy and satisfaction in their giving."[8] As ministers, God can work through fundraisers to transform givers' hearts. We must evaluate all our priorities and strategies in light of this potential work. Do we consider it our purpose to be shepherds of stewards and agents of transformation in the hearts of potential givers? The answer to this question will define the road we take in fundraising. If we truly desire to see people's hearts and lives transformed to be like Christ, there is only one road that will take us toward that goal. This is the narrow road of God's way that will result in a revolution of giving.

How then do we put these principles to work?

PRIORITIES IN PRACTICE

The Bible underscores what we have observed of the two fundraising roads: God's ways are not humanity's ways (Isa. 55:8). Most people do not travel the road of asking for funds that is founded on biblical principles. But if we have become convinced of the truth of those biblical principles and desire to align our priorities with them, then how should we seek resources? We will look at research, cultivation, asking for gifts, follow-up, and accountability in order to understand how priorities derived from biblical principles should shape our practices.

Research

Research to identify who will be contacted to ask for support is an initial step in seeking funds. On humankind's road, research involves identifying the prospects with the financial ability to give to an organization's need. Most researchers focus their attention on a prospective giver's potential: What are the prospect's financial resources? What is the prospect's organizational position? Does he or she run the company, own it, hold stock in it? How much does the prospect have that we can use?

Unfortunately, when we emphasize this aspect of research, we neglect to consider the importance to the prospective giver of how his or her money would be used or directed. We must complement research into financial potential with research into the personal probability that the prospect might be led to give money to *this* ministry, with its particular vision and work. On God's road, then, research is about identifying those prospects who both have resources and have a God-given desire to become involved in the work God is doing through the ministry.

The "top prospect" in a biblical model of development is at the top not because of the amount of money he or she is giving but because of what is happening in the transformation of his or her heart toward God. For a biblical example, look at the widow's offering in Luke 21:1–4. As Jesus was watching the rich make their contributions in the temple, a woman gave two copper coins and received this response from Jesus: "this poor widow put in more than all of them." The rich people gave a large amount of money, but their large gifts represented a small sacrifice, for they still had plenty to spend as they pleased; the poor woman gave a tiny amount of money, but she sacrificed all she had to live on, out of her desire to serve God with everything He had entrusted to her. The person who gives the fewest dollars may be your "top" giver, if they are giving generously and sacrificially from a heart that is rich toward God. God's litmus test is not how much, but the state of the heart.

If the heart is the standard by which God evaluates the act of giving, then we should research prospective givers with God's values in mind. The prospect who is not wealthy is still worth your time. Your energy will be better invested in efforts to find people whose hearts are already becoming transformed and convicted to support the kind of work God is doing through your ministry, than in trying to "sell" your ministry and convince the wealthiest people you can find to donate toward what you are doing. Remember, we are matchmakers whose job is to present the vision and the need to people who have a passion for it, while God is the One who works in people's hearts, giving them that passion and transforming their hearts toward generosity.

Cultivation

Understanding the term *cultivation* correctly is critical to keeping us on the biblical road. For both roads, cultivation is a means to an end—but the ends are completely different. On the popular road, the process of cultivation involves whatever tactics will move the prospect to begin and continue donating money, the desired destination being a transaction. For those on the road less traveled, God's road, the final destination of fundraising is the transformation of givers into godly, generous stewards of all God has given them. Cultivation becomes synonymous with ministry, which must be administered lovingly and unconditionally—that is, not dependent on the quantity of money the prospect is likely to give to the organization, but rooted in the fact that the prospect is a believer whose spiritual growth is important to God.

During the process of cultivation, we should be continually pointing every prospect toward an understanding and acceptance of the biblical truths that

God owns it all and giving and asking are about heart transformation and growing givers' hearts to be rich toward God. Our goal is to motivate each prospect to seek God's direction for their financial participation in our ministry and for everything they do with the resources God has entrusted to them.

How do we best prepare ourselves for cultivating prospects? Before calling on any giver, adjust your attitude and motivation to Philippians 2:3-4. Do nothing and say nothing that would contribute to selfish ambition, pride, or ego in raising money. Be there for the sake of the other person—for his or her best interests—with the goal of helping him or her grow more like Christ. Sometimes God wants us to minister to someone from whom we have no prospect of receiving a gift, simply because it is good for that person.

Oftentimes it is hard to envision how money will be raised if we do not raise it. It is my testimony, after more than twenty years of following this biblical road of development, that the majority of finances received come in apart from any one person or department being responsible for raising a particular gift. Sales statistics—which predict that one in ten requests will yield a gift—will be turned upside down when you do research to find people whose hearts God has moved to care about what He is doing through your ministry and cultivate them unconditionally for their spiritual growth.

Asking for a Gift

God gives us the liberty and urges us to ask those who have been touched by our ministry (see the apostle Paul's example: 2 Cor. 10:13-16; Phil. 4:15-16). But only the Holy Spirit can recognize the proper timing to ask someone for a gift; our responsibility is to listen for His direction, and then obediently act as ambassadors for Christ. As ambassadors, we represent Christ and speak for His interests, not our own (this is why it is so important to know that the vision of our ministry actually seeks the interests of Christ).

We cannot step over the line between cultivation and asking without God's permission; but once the Lord has directed us to cross that line, our responsibility is straightforward. We should give the message or present the opportunity. Direct the prospective giver back to the three foundational principles—God owns it all, God is the fundraiser, and finances are a transformation issue. Exhort him or her to consider the truth of these principles and to ask God to make them a vital part of his or her lifestyle. Rodin writes, "We minister when we focus first on our donors' relationship with God and only secondarily on their relationship with us, for we know that faithfulness to one will result in necessary benefits to the other."[9]

In asking, we must therefore be motivated to minister to our fellow believers' spiritual condition, understanding that their financial participation is a decision strictly between them and God. Our part in asking is to help equip the body of Christ for the work of service (Eph. 4:12). We do this by offering ourselves to God to use as instruments of His transforming work in people's hearts; this means directing people to the Lord for their participation in our work for the Kingdom.

If heart transformation is our priority, then honesty and urging people to pray for God's guidance will characterize our practice. An important aspect of allowing God to move people's hearts is making sure that our techniques and programs do not interfere with His work of conforming believers to the image of Christ. Any strategy that involves deception is unacceptable; God is a God of truth, and our job is to give people a true picture of the vision and activities of our ministry. We should not create funding "crises" in order to play on people's fears and motivate them to donate money. Rather, we should teach potential givers what the Bible says about money, communicate truthfully the vision and giving opportunities of our ministry, and encourage people to seek and follow the leading of the Holy Spirit regarding their giving. Carl Henry contrasts this with the popular fundraiser who is "seldom . . . content to mention a need for which he is 'looking to the Lord in faith' without the further suggestion that the Lord in turn is looking to the [person solicited] to handle the matter in His absence."[10] The biblical road of fundraising is inherently revolutionary in its dependence on God's provision and the Holy Spirit's leading.

Fundraisers who believe that God is working in people's hearts should not even consider using emotional manipulation and guilt to motivate giving, for God is cultivating gratitude that will overflow in generosity. A subtler consideration is the use of premiums—if we offer material incentives as rewards for gifts, or recognition that appeals to givers' egos, we may distract them from seeking the leading of the Holy Spirit and erroneously correlate spirituality and material gain. We need to be careful to communicate, as Henry suggests, that godly stewardship and generosity is "first and foremost a spiritual exercise for the glory of God and the advancement of His goals," and that it "yields distinctive compensation of character"—though not necessarily of finances—to the steward.[11] We should always place the emphasis in asking on communicating the vision and opportunity, and encouraging givers to seek God's direction.

The popular road says that we must "close" the deal in order to receive. The Bible teaches us, on the other hand, that we must ask God what to do, obey, and trust Him to provide our needs. If the Holy Spirit leads us to ask, then our job is to deliver the vision, ensure that it has been communicated effectively, and urge the giver to seek God's will in regard to his or her response. In the meantime, we should pray for the giver's heart growth, allowing time for him or her to digest the vision and seek the Spirit's leading, and for God's provision for the work of our ministry.

One of the largest gifts I was privileged to be involved with was consummated without even a request, much less a close. The CEO and I called on a major giver to present our latest vision for the ministry. Within ten minutes, the giver had to excuse himself due to a company emergency. He apologized for having us travel so extensively to see him and then being unable to complete the call. Without any further presentation or discussion, we left to return home. Within a week of our "failed" visit, the giver, at the "behest of the Lord" (in his words), sent a larger gift to the ministry than we had even imagined in our planning (see Eph. 3:20). All we did was present the vision for the ministry; God moved the giver to participate financially, and he responded to God's leading with a generous gift.

Follow-Up

Follow-up is an activity that demands that we maintain a proper perspective and an unswerving dedication to service. We minister by making the spiritual welfare of others our first priority. We are not seeking benefits for ourselves or even for the success of our program. We are helping others grow conformed to Christ's image and lay up treasures in heaven (Matt. 6:19–20). Moreover, it is only as a giver obeys God in the stewardship of His money that the giver grows. If the transformation of others is our goal, then we will not urge anyone to give except as God has led him or her to give. Paul told Timothy to instruct the wealthy to be rich in good works (1 Tim. 6:18). Our ministry is spurring people on toward those good works that are ordered by God Himself (Heb. 10:24; Eph. 2:10) for the purpose of following Christ and storing up treasures (1 Tim. 6:19).

How can we rejoice in our follow-up just as much over a "No, I am not going to donate," as a "Yes"? Our rejoicing depends on our understanding of why we do what we are instructed to do on the biblical road of development. God alone is the provider for us and for the ministry. The purpose of our part is to help equip the body of Christ for the work of service (Eph. 4:12). We do this by offering ourselves to God to use us as instruments of His transforming work in people's hearts; in the instance of follow-up, this means directing people to the Lord for their participation in our work for the Kingdom. Whether God leads them to give or not give, if they follow His leading, then the Bible says that they have laid up treasures in heaven (1 Tim. 6:19–20). We all grow and receive rewards from God because of our wholehearted obedience *to* Him, not because of what we do *for* Him. The act of giving should be an expression of love from a human's heart toward God, so our follow-up should encourage that.

In light of these considerations, it is more important in God's evaluation that development professionals seek God's direction and obey than that they get the gift. In the same way, it should be more important in our evaluation that givers follow God's direction than that they give to our ministry.

Accountability to God

Accountability is best expressed in the words of the apostle Paul: "Not that I am looking for a gift, but I am looking for what may be credited to your account" (Phil. 4:17 NIV). We ask for a gift, but our purpose in asking is ultimately the transformation of the giver's heart and the growth of their account with God. It is not the *act* of giving that is important, but our obedience to God. Fundraisers are therefore accountable to understand this truth in order to appropriately minister to those whom they ask. If our aim is to help believers grow in conformity to Christ, then we should encourage them to imitate Christ in their generosity (John 5:30; Eph. 5:1–2; 1 John 3:16–18).

Accountability is misunderstood in our culture. The popular road of fundraising says that the donor and organization are accountable, in some sense, to each other. But what does Scripture have to say? A giver is a steward of God's resources, who seeks His directive as to whether to give, and is led by Him to do so. He or she is accountable to God. The organization that receives the gift is likewise accountable to God, to faithfully steward the resources for ministry. Part of the organization's stewardship is to keep the giver, who has invested money that God entrusted to him or her for God's work, informed about that work. Thus, biblical accountability requires that both parties are ultimately accountable to God.

Although financial reports are necessary and effective to communicate basic information, the most useful reports to a giver are "stewardship reports." Tell the giver what God has accomplished through the ministry by his or her participation. Report much more often on what God is doing than on what the ministry is doing. The giver is giving in order to participate in God's work, so he or she should be informed how God is working. (See Gary Hoag's chapter for communication suggestions.)

THE PREDICTABLE OUTCOMES

Where do the two roads lead? How do travelers look when they reach the end of each? On the culturally induced road, everything depends on the asker—success or failure is a function of the accountant's numbers at the end of the year, and depends solely on our expertise in persuading the right people to give money. Burnout is common.

Likewise, when Christians try to follow a human way of raising money, they often fall into what Carl Henry calls "heresies."[12] Henry outlines seven pitfalls that are common when a fundraising program is not firmly grounded in biblical principles:

Substituting slogans for Scripture: Reaffirm the Bible as the "all-sufficient guide to faith and practice and . . . honestly submit every campaign principle and slogan to biblical scrutiny."[13]

Substituting supposed proof texts for intrinsic principles: Be careful not to force isolated Scriptures to fit preconceived plans or desires. Unintentional misapplication of Scripture demonstrates sloppiness and a lack of study; deliberate misapplication demonstrates a lack of respect for God's revealed Word and of love for people.

Substituting a motivation of giving for a motivation of getting: When asking for funds be careful to communicate that the blessing of giving is promised to the giver's soul, not to his or her bank account. Scripture consistently reinforces that it is more blessed to give than to receive, thereby keeping motivations correctly prioritized.

Substituting secular sources for spiritual resources: Avoid reliance on non-Christian donors instead of generous Christians for support and on secular fundraising strategies instead of prayer and a ministry to grow givers' hearts.

Substituting material incentive for Spirit-led generosity: Avoid premiums and "hucksters of merchandise." "Fundraising premiums raise serious ethical problems,"[14] due to exaggerated values, assumed material blessings to the donor, and even spiritual attributes being attributed to trinkets and relics.

Substituting methodology for ministry: Urgent appeals, overstatements of the personal relationship between organizations and givers, telephone intrusions at unacceptable family hours, appeals to a person's ego, and publishing donor lists all place transactional methodologies above transformational goals of growing givers' hearts.

Substituting fear for faith as the motivation for giving: Fear-driven, artificial crises that play on emotions rob givers of the opportunity to respond to the quiet leading of the Holy Spirit to give for the expansion of the Kingdom of God.

These seven heresies can act as a diagnostic for Christians in resource development, providing us with practical guidelines for determining whether we are following humanity's road or God's road of fundraising.

In contrast to the popular road that leads us into unbiblical practices, on God's road, we recognize that God is the One who owns everything, who moves people's hearts to give, and who uses the work of askers in the process of conforming believers to the image of Jesus Christ in generosity. On this road, everything we do is motivated by prayerful trust in God and the desire to see givers transformed into generous stewards who are rich toward God. Since God is the One who changes hearts, it is not our responsibility to close a deal, but to consistently and earnestly seek God's direction and faithfully minister to potential givers. Success or failure is not determined by dollars but by givers' growth in faith and Christlike character, evidenced by their generosity. And since God owns it all, He is more than able to provide for the needs of every ministry that exists to accomplish His mission in the world.

The real question is why believers would ever choose the popular road once its underlying principles and motivations have been revealed. The answer can only expose our tendency to operate apart from faith, particularly in the area of finances. But if we truly believe that God owns all resources and has them properly placed for distribution, then God's road does not seem so lonely or forbidding. Here it is that we truly become God's ambassadors, His partners in transformation, His instruments in accomplishing His will on earth. It is as we travel down this road that God will create a revolution in giving to transform His children and fully fund His work.

HUMANITY'S ROAD	GOD'S ROAD
The road popularly traveled	*The road less traveled*
We decide what to do and ask God to bless it (maybe)	We ask God what to do and then do it
PRINCIPLES AND PRIORITIES	**PRINCIPLES AND PRIORITIES**
People own the resources	God owns it all; we are His stewards
We are the fundraisers	God is the fundraiser
Fundraising is about a financial transaction	Fundraising is about a spiritual transformation
PRIORITIES IN PRACTICE	**PRIORITIES IN PRACTICE**
Research—look for those with money to give	Research—look for those God is inclining to give to your ministry
Cultivation—build relationships so they will give	Cultivation—build relationships so you can help them grow
Asking—technique intensive; hype the need; close the deal	Asking—information/vision intensive; present the opportunity; direct to prayer
Follow-up—pressure and persuade to meet the goal	Follow-up—encourage obedience to help donor lay up treasure in heaven
Accountability—financial report to the giver; legal motivation	Accountability—to God alone; givers receive stewardship reports; spiritual growth motivation
PREDICTABLE OUTCOMES	**PREDICTABLE OUTCOMES**
Success/failure depends on us	Success/failure according to God's will
Burnout	God's glory through transformed lives and funded ministries

RICHARD A. HAYNIE is director of development for OC International, a fifty-five-year-old missionary organization. Rich's two decades of experience in fundraising development have taken him from the Air Force Academy to his work with ministries including The Navigators, International Bible Society, Fellowship of Christian Athletes, and Dawn Ministries in Colorado Springs, Colorado. Rich is an internationally known speaker and teacher. He can be reached at richhaynie@aol.com.

1. Unless otherwise noted, all Bible quotations are from the New American Standard Version.
2. R. Scott Rodin, *Stewards in the Kingdom: A Theology of Life in All Its Fullness* (Downers Grove, IL: IVP, 2000), 71.
3. Ibid., 205.
4. Ibid., 71.
5. Oswald Chambers, *My Utmost for His Highest* (Grand Rapids: Oswald Chambers Publications Assn., Ltd., 1963), entry for April 24.
6. Rodin, 209–10.
7. Wesley K. Willmer, *God & Your Stuff* (Colorado Springs: NavPress, 2002), 50.
8. Thomas Jeavons and Rebekah Basinger, *Growing Givers' Hearts* (San Francisco: Jossey-Bass Publishers, 2000), 117.
9. Rodin, 212.
10. Carl F. H. Henry, "Heresies in Evangelical Fund-Raising," in *Money for Ministries*, ed. Wesley Willmer (Wheaton: SP Publishers, 1989), 273.
11. Ibid., 274.
12. Ibid., 271.
13. Ibid., 272.
14. Ibid., 276.

Chapter 5

THE TRANSFORMATION
OF THE GODLY STEWARD:
PROMISE, PROBLEM,
AND PROCESS

BY R. SCOTT RODIN, *Former President,*
Christian Stewardship Association

O ver the past twenty-six years I have had the privilege of meeting many generous Christians. Looking back I recognize one consistent characteristic: they were engaged in the process of personal, spiritual transformation. A man I visited frequently while working for Eastern Seminary illustrated this. His giving record showed a modest but consistent pattern of giving, although he had the means to contribute considerably more. Our invitations to him to get more involved and increase his support were always met with a polite but clear decline.

One day an envelope from him arrived on my desk containing a letter and a very large check. The letter was his personal testimonial. In it he explained how he had been bargaining with God over the years about his giving. He confessed that he considered his money to be his own and he chose to give God what he felt was adequate, which meant just enough to assuage his guilt. Recently he had gone with his church to the Holy Land, and he came back a changed man. "As I stood where Jesus stood, walked the path to Calvary, and sat outside the empty tomb, I came to realize that Jesus wanted all of me. Not just Sunday but every day. Not just my leftovers but everything I had. So I am starting my new life by giving away what never belonged to me anyway, and I have never known so much joy."

The Christian life is a journey of spiritual heart transformation. On that journey we are shaped and formed into godly stewards who are generous. I believe this is the cornerstone for the entire enterprise of Christian fund-raising and development work, and therefore the focus and purpose of this chapter.

From conversion to final glory, Christians are called into a process of continual change, breaking from the bondage of our old sinful nature and embracing the freedom of God's transforming grace. It is not cheap grace, but grace that calls us to die to self and live for Christ. It requires us to lose a counterfeit life in order to find our true life. It is a shedding of our old nature that we might be conformed to the image of Christ. It is a quest that promises nothing less than our re-creation as a new, holy, and Christlike child of God. While we will never attain the full end of this quest on this side of heaven, we are compelled by the grace of God to enter unequivocally and sacrificially into the pursuit.

The transformation of the Christian as a whole person includes our vocation as godly stewards. The two are inseparable, for a Christian's stewardship is integrally tied to the process of transformation worked in us by the Holy Spirit.

When we use the term *steward* in this chapter, we mean one who is being transformed by God in response to the understanding that everything we have and everything we are has been redeemed and given back to us as a gift to be treasured and invested generously in the work of the Kingdom. "Stewardship" then is the daily practice of the steward who places into God's service the entirety of his or her life and resources with great joy.

We will look at three components of this journey that are specific to the

Spirit's work of transforming us into generous stewards in the Kingdom of the God of grace. Each has profound implications for Christian development professionals. We will look at the *promise* of this transformation, the *problem* of this transformation, and the *process* of this transformation.

THE PROMISE OF TRANSFORMATION

As Christian resource development professionals, we are participants in God's work of transforming God's people into Christlike stewards who are generous givers. I believe we must embrace this statement with all of our heart, understanding it as our purpose and core vocation in this ministry of Christian fundraising.

For Christians, godly stewardship is our destiny. It is the purpose for which we were called into being and redeemed by the blood of Christ. This destiny presupposes a true knowledge of God and His nature, as revealed to us in the life and work of Jesus Christ. Our purpose was founded in creation, lost in the fall, bought back for us on Calvary, and is given to us now as a precious gift through transformation. We will briefly examine the importance of the knowledge of God and then trace the history of God's transforming grace in order to understand the rich promise of change that we have in Christ.

Knowing the God Who Transforms

Transformation requires relationship. The God who created us is the God who calls us to be "transformed by the renewing of your mind" (Rom. 12:2).[1] This renewal is possible only in a relationship with our creator God. The spiritual theme of human history has been the quest to attain some reliable knowledge of God; however, outside of Christianity, that quest always leads down the futile path of seeking after God either somewhere inside ourselves or within the created world. For the Christian, genuine knowledge of God is found solely in the self-revelation of God Himself, in the person of Jesus Christ.

Our hope of transformation lies in the fact that the God who transforms is the God who has revealed Himself to us in a way sufficient to remove all doubt as to His intentions for our lives. In Christ we have the ability to know God with certainty. Karl Barth writes,

> Can God be known? Yes, God can be known, since it is actually true and real that He is knowable through Himself. When that happens, man becomes free, he becomes empowered, he becomes capable—a mystery to himself—of knowing God.[2]

Our transformation began in Bethlehem, was lived out in Galilee, was sealed on Golgotha, and was completed outside an empty tomb. In Christ our humanity has been transformed. Now we are called to make that transformation our own, and we can do so because we know, with certainty, the God who calls and invites us into that transforming relationship.

We also know that our self-revealed God is a triune God. We are transformed into the image of the Son by the power of the Spirit for the glory of the Father. The triune nature of our transformation—our worship, our mission, and our stewardship—bears witness to God's triune nature. The same is true for our knowledge of our own selves. We only know what it means to be God's child by looking at God's Son. From here we see who our God is, who we are, the One into whose image we are to be transformed, and what we are created to do. Our transformation by the power of the Spirit begins here and here only, for transformation is impossible without these certainties about God and His Son.

This is the viewpoint from which we are called to take on our work as Christian resource development professionals. We start with the knowledge of who God is in light of His self-revelation to us in Jesus Christ. We seek to carry out our work in ways that reflect the nature of this loving and gracious God. As we challenge our givers to embrace their true identity as God's beloved children, we pray they will better understand their calling, preparing them to be more faithful stewards. Our goal is that every gift given by a godly steward will be given out of a deep sense of gratitude, an obedient heart, and a joyful desire to glorify God through being conformed to the image of His Son and imitating His generosity. Our vocation is to allow God to use us and our resource development work as tools in this process of transformation, empowered by the knowledge that it is the will and work of our Creator.

The Story of God's Transforming Grace

Scripture tells us that we were created to bear the image of our triune God and therefore created for relational wholeness. There are four levels in this wholeness: our relationship with *God*, our relationship with *ourselves*, our relationship with *our neighbor*, and our relationship with *the created world*. We were created to bring glory to God at each level. This was, from the very beginning, a vocational calling, a calling to godly and faithful stewardship. We were called to be caretakers of our relationships at each of these levels by loving God with all our heart, strength, and mind; by loving our neighbors as ourselves; and by our charge to be caretakers of God's creation. This is the purpose of our creation and the source of our contentment and fulfillment in life.

In the devastation of humanity's fall into sin, our relationships were destroyed on all four levels. Everything that had been created for us and given to us in God's good creation was lost in the fall. From Genesis 3 to the end of Revelation, and throughout human history, we see the effects of sin writ large across the ages. Onto this ugly, devastating scene comes the hope of our transformation, for the gospel tells us that *all* that was lost in the fall was *fully* redeemed in Christ (1 Cor. 15:22; Rom. 5:9–17; 8:19–21). Our reconciliation with God through the work of Christ is the central conviction of our faith. However, we must not miss the miracle of the restoration of our other relationships in that same work. In Christ we have been reconciled to God, given new birth as God's children, empowered to live under a new commandment to love our neighbor, and restored in our call to rule over, subdue, and have dominion over God's good creation. These relationships were restored with the precious blood of Christ, and they have been given back to us as gifts to be stewarded. At each level we are challenged to give up our old, lost, and sinful ways and become Christlike in our nurture and care of these relationships. In this way we worship and glorify God through our stewardship, and in the process we are transformed.

As Christian fundraisers we miss the mark when we focus our work so singularly on the level of material possessions. When we are only concerned about money, we miss the opportunity to be the vessels through which God can work transformation on the other three levels. We must care about our givers' relationship to God, self, and neighbor as much as their relationship to their resources. What would our development strategies look like if we embraced a more holistic understanding of stewardship? How could we be used by God to help our givers become more godly stewards on all four levels?

The call to godly, holistic stewardship should be a foundational principle in the ministry goals of every church and parachurch organization. Too often, however, it is "tacked on" as a somewhat embarrassing necessity that is rolled out occasionally, only to be stuffed back into the ecclesiastical closet so the organization (and pastor) can get back to the "real ministry issues." However, when we understand biblical stewardship in the holistic sense described above, we will understand that Christian fundraisers are engaged in ministry that is as vital to the transformation of sinner to saint as any other ministry of the church. If our resource development work is truly transformational and not merely focused on a financial transaction, the results will be a revolution in generosity as we facilitate the growth of stewards that are transformed, rich toward God, and generous toward Christian ministries.

THE PROBLEM OF TRANSFORMATION

The transformation of sinful individuals into godly, Christlike stewards runs absolutely counter to the prevailing values and forces within North American culture. Tom Sine comments, "The call to follow Christ was an invitation to a whole-life faith that was profoundly countercultural both then and now."[3] At every turn we are being tempted, cajoled, urged, manipulated, and bullied into making decisions that directly conflict with the Spirit's transforming work within us.

This conflict is present at all four levels of our created being, but it confronts us most powerfully in our understanding of our relationship to the created world, including our possessions.

Our place and vocation as citizens of the one Kingdom of God are challenged by the myth of a second, earthly kingdom, a kingdom that promises the illusion that we can be the ruler in one sphere and servant in the other. Even more problematic is the reluctance of church and parachurch organizations to confront this distortion. We will look squarely at the problem and its paralyzing effects on how we view the world and the daily work of resource development.

The Lure of the Two-Kingdom Myth

Consider these two stories in Matthew:

> The kingdom of heaven is like treasure hidden in a field. When a man found it, he hid it again, and then in his joy went and sold all he had and bought that field. (Matt. 13:44)

> Jesus answered, "If you want to be perfect, go, sell your possessions and give to the poor, and you will have treasure in heaven. Then come, follow me." When the young man heard this, he went away sad, because he had great wealth. (Matt. 19:21–22)

In the first story Jesus tells a parable about the Kingdom of heaven, whose worth is so great that nothing is too much to pay to attain it. It is worth giving up everything in this life in order to secure a place within this Kingdom. This is a glimpse of God's purpose for us—to be children in this extravagant and audaciously expensive Kingdom that Christ came to establish on the earth. The only possible response we could render is to give over our entire life to God in childlike faith and absolute obedience.

In the second story Jesus encounters a rich young man who wants to maintain his place in two kingdoms. He has built an earthly kingdom made up of stuff, and now he inquires of Jesus as to how he might also gain access to this glorious new Kingdom of God. Jesus' answer is simple; you can't. You can't, that is, while still holding on to your earthly kingdom. Entrance into God's Kingdom requires an absolute abdication of the throne of your earthly kingdom. It is one or the other, never both. Unable to embrace a one-kingdom lifestyle, the wealthy young man goes away sad. His sadness is juxtaposed to the overwhelming joy of the man who has lost everything for the prize of the one Kingdom. What does this losing look like? Richard Foster offers this image: "Without question, money has taken on a sacred character in our world, and it would do us good to find ways to defame it, defile it and trample it under our feet. So step on it. Yell at it. Laugh at it." But even more powerful is our ability to, with joy, give it away. Foster concludes, "The powers that energize money cannot abide that most unnatural of acts, giving."[4]

While Scripture is clear about our call to be devoted solely to God's Kingdom, living this way is profoundly complex and difficult. Our sinful nature works in us a yearning to be sovereign over our own earthly kingdoms. Our culture tempts us to be earthly kingdom builders in our resource development activities.

Several years ago I worked with a wealthy giver on naming a gift for a school. His battle with a two-kingdom worldview became clear during our "negotiations" over the gift. He included so many stipulations and requirements of how the gift was to be used and how the name was to be displayed that it was clear he was using his gift to buy further prestige for himself. The board made the courageous decision to decline a major gift and, in doing so, made a statement to the giver about one-kingdom stewardship.

Like this man, we are continually tempted to measure our success according to the value of our earthly kingdoms, made up of reputation, fame, experiences, extravagances, and excesses. We live in a society obsessed with "extremes." What money cannot buy we seek in "edge-of-death" experiences as we push the envelope to try to inject some meaning into our satiated lives. Serving as sovereigns in our own kingdoms is an all-consuming task.

The Three Lies of the Two-Kingdom Myth

At the heart of this two-kingdom myth, we find three lies. The first is the *compatibility lie*. It whispers to us that there is no harm in living in two kingdoms. If God is Lord in our churchly kingdom, why can't we be the ruler of our own time and possessions? Give God His due and He will not care what we do with the rest. This can also be called the "selective steward" temptation. This subtle distortion promises us that godly stewardship offers us a cafeteria-like set of options. We simply choose which areas we believe we are called to practice stewardship and which we are not. It is "stewardship by convenience."

The second is the *compartmentalization lie*. It suggests that we live our lives in disconnected, isolated compartments. So our spirituality fits well in one box and our possessions, relationships, and time commitments in others. Each can operate independent of the others, and even in distinction and contradiction. It is perfectly normal for us to be consumers, exploiters, manipulators, and kingdom builders in our "secular" life, while maintaining godly stewardship practices in our "spiritual" arenas. If this sounds like dressed-up hypocrisy, it is. Craig Blomberg writes, "Different people will experience that transformation in different ways, and to different extents, but the person who never displays any concern for the Lord's work and for the poor and who never gives anything to help them *by definition* is not someone whom the power of the Spirit has touched."[5]

Third is the *transactional lie*. This fabrication is a logical extension of our capitalistic system, which reduces much of what we do to a transaction. Everything can be bought and sold, traded, and bargained for. We are tempted to view all of life as a series of transactions. And so it is with Christian resource development work. It is easy, and desperately wrong, to reduce giving to the transaction of exchanging money, time, and talents for goodwill and the contented feeling of having given generously. The focus of this lie is in the idea that we are able to make our giving another transaction where we "buy" the peace of mind and contentment we desire. We mix in with this the biblical commands on stewardship and create a distorted picture that confuses sacrificial giving out of love and gratitude with the purchase of peace of mind. We can believe the lie that we can buy God's favor, compensate God and the church for our lack of obedience and discipleship, and atone through occasional generosity for the greed and self-centeredness that permeates the rest of our lives. Against this background, the holistic transformation of the godly steward to true generosity stands in radical relief.

The Price of the Two-Kingdom Myth

Unfortunately, the church and parachurch's historic silence on the subject of stewardship has opened the door for these three lies to become firmly embedded in American Christian culture. In John Bright's book on the Kingdom of God, he laments,

> God help the church that so blends into society that there is no longer any difference! Such a church will produce no quality of behavior other than that which society in general produces. It will take on the prejudices of society, and even demand that its Gospel support those prejudices. It will make itself a tool of society whose main business is to protect and to dignify with divine support the best interests of its constituents. And this is a stark tragedy! . . . Such a church is not the

peculiar people of the kingdom of God.[6]

The price of the perpetuation of the two-kingdom myth has been enormous. We face a significant loss of kingdom effectiveness. God's blessings are lost, which He so dearly seeks to pour out on those who would deny themselves, take up their cross, and follow Him. Joyful giving vanishes—the devastating legacy of the total disregard of stewardship by the church. Vocation suffers, where the lure of self-actualization has unseated costly discipleship as the purpose in life for so many. Many of our resource development efforts have been pulled into the earthly kingdom patterns and as a result do not reap the bounty of generosity that could be available.[7] Two-kingdom people can never fully glorify God or fulfill His purpose in their lives, or in His church.

In the wake of this disastrous legacy, we are faced with the challenge of being used by God to facilitate the transformation of Christians into generous, godly stewards. Our call as Christian leaders is to attack this myth at its very core. It begins with clear, courageous biblical teaching and preaching in the church and parachurch at every level, from preschool through adult education. It receives support from Christian resource development work that educates and calls givers to a holistic understanding of biblical stewardship and the generosity that results. Consequently, Christian fundraisers must themselves be on a journey of heart transformation, and they must clearly understand their vocation as ministry in this holistic sense. Our work requires persistence, consistency, and passion. In attacking this myth we are striding headlong into the Enemy's camp and staking our claim to what is rightfully ours.

There can be no transformation without an unequivocal denial of the two-kingdom myth. We are called to be a one-kingdom people. Dallas Willard reminds of this joyful reality, "What is most valuable for any human being . . . is to be a part of this marvelous reality, God's kingdom now. Eternity is now ongoing. I am now leading a life that will last forever."[8] As we denounce all claims to the throne of a second, earthly, and counterfeit kingdom, we prepare ourselves to be transformed both in ourselves and in our work in this Kingdom that lasts forever.

THE PROCESS OF TRANSFORMATION

In speaking about the process of transformation, we must make a clear distinction at the outset between biblical transformation of the heart and the notion that we are in a continuing evolution toward a higher level of existence. The two could not be in greater contradiction. Secular humanism preaches an ever-evolving process in human development that will lead us toward a utopian future through the advancement of science and technology. The secular humanist's goal is a self-actualized world society in which human growth and the liberation of human intellect create a paradise on earth.

This striving for a better world based on human development and the continuation of an evolutionary process is not to be confused with the biblical command to *Spirit-empowered* transformation. In fact, they are antithetical. To distinguish biblical transformation from popular ideals of progress, we will look specifically at six areas that mark the forming of the godly steward. In each we will seek to understand the unique work of the Spirit and how this applies in our resource development work.

Holistic, Not Compartmental

Transformation is holistic, requiring our whole being: heart, soul, strength, and mind. If the Holy Spirit is the transforming agent, then every miniscule particle of our being will be affected by His work in us.

This transforming work overcomes our attempt to compartmentalize our lives. It calls us to die to the old nature, to the lies we have been told and believed about our vocation. Transformation involves nothing less than the complete abandonment of our thrones and the dismantling of our earthly kingdoms. It is a transformation from the struggle of two-kingdom living to the joy of one-kingdom service.

There is a real losing of our life and a real finding (Matt. 10:39). The life we find is the new life in Christ, the life of the generous steward in the one Kingdom of the triune God of grace. Stewards are transformed people, and stewardship is the life of the disciple of Christ who has been and continues to be transformed into the image of the Son of God.

Embraced, Not Imposed

We seek to be transformed because we are overtaken and overwhelmed by God's love and grace. In Paul's words, "Christ's love compels us" (2 Cor. 5:14). John Frank writes, "Just as Christ made the ultimate sacrifice for us, He desires that we learn to be givers in our everyday lives in response to His generosity."[9] Joy-filled obedience and servanthood, which frequently take the form of generous giving, are our individual and communal response to the unmerited grace of God. When you are freely given a treasure beyond all value, how can you receive it but with joy, thanksgiving, and praise? These are the transformational marks of the godly steward, and this is what resource development professionals are called to manifest in their own lives and work.

The Enemy, on the other hand, wants to turn this joyful response into dogmatic servitude. In Christian development work, this can take the form of manipulation through the use of guilt as a motivator for giving. When we succumb to the use of guilt, peer pressure, and the exaggeration of need, we will not further the work of the Kingdom of God. Our profession must continually be a call and opportunity for God's people to express their love of Christ and gratitude for His blessings through cheerful, generous giving in response to a real need that is presented honestly and passionately. This connection of the heart of the steward of God and the needs of the Kingdom produces the kind of development work that *is* ministry, and the kinds of generous gifts that bless the hearts of the asker, giver, and receiver.

God-centered, Not Human-centered

The work of transformation in the life of Christians is utterly selfless. The Spirit's work always has one primary goal: the glorification of Christ in every area of our lives. Our transformation is not a self-help process, but it does require our participation. As Jim and Molly Davis Scott remind us, "The point is that we participate in the decision to move away from self-centered to God-centered. It is arguably the most important decision we will ever make."[10]

This participation is not self-actualization or self-improvement. In a culture that values the improvement of the individual above all else in the quest for purpose in life, the Christian understanding of transformation is radical. The transforming work of the Holy Spirit in the life of the godly steward is all-encompassing, and it leads to a generosity that runs counter to the core of humanistic teachings and ethics.

In the end, godly stewardship is all about *lordship*. Before money, tithing, or time, it is about submission to the lordship of Christ. Our transformation has a direction and goal. That goal is Christlikeness. We are called to imitate Christ in His complete and absolute obedience and generosity toward God.

Our work in Christian resource development must be in sync with the ongoing transformational work of the Holy Spirit that engenders this radical submission to lordship in the life of the godly steward. Whether it is pastors preaching and teaching on generous stewardship or our fundraising practices themselves, we must be sure at every turn that our work has the marks of a transforming submission to Christ's lordship. (See especially Richard Haynie's chapter for a discussion of biblical fundraising practices.)

Process, Not Pronouncement

While Christ's work is once and for all, it is worked out in us throughout our lives. Transformation is, by definition, a process, a faith journey, a growing, reaching, and pressing on. Wes Willmer writes, "The Christian life begins at the moment of faith, but it does not end there. It involves a steady march of spiritual growth and change. A person's eternal destination is settled at the moment of faith, but building a life pleasing to God takes the rest of his or her life."[11]

Transformation requires a daily commitment to the continual life-changing work of the Holy Spirit. It does not happen automatically or instantaneously. It has to be entered into and pursued.

Stewardship and discipleship run parallel in the lives of believers. Disciples are generous stewards, and generous stewards are disciples. These words describe two foci of one transforming work of grace in us. When we hear Jesus' command to "take up [your] cross and follow me," do we not also hear His words to "sell your possessions and give to the poor, and you will have treasure in heaven. Then come, follow me" (Matt. 16:24; 19:21)? When Jesus calls us to "worship the Lord your God, and serve him only" is He not also telling us that we cannot "serve two masters . . . both God and Money" (Matt. 4:10; 6:24)?

Scripture calls us to faithful discipleship and holistic, generous stewardship as one calling, one vocation.

> Stewardship is no longer concerned with matters—including religious matters—on the periphery of existence; it belongs to the essence of things. For the call to responsible stewardship encounters us precisely at the heart of our present-day dilemma and impasse.[12]

This calling and work is never fully finished, but because it is motivated by grace, it is a calling of pure, joyous response. As such it will never devolve into mundane ritual, rigid legalism, or divisive ideology. As Foster reminds us, "Giving brings authenticity and vitality to our devotional experience."[13] David Young sees our decision as leaders to submit to the transforming work of God typified in Jesus' act of washing the disciples' feet: "Transformation originates from the One who transforms. As leaders, we never do the changing. We never have the total power of insight. We never carry the power on our own shoulders. We can merely enter the drama, the first part of which is allowing our feet to be washed."[14] When we humble ourselves and submit to God's transforming work, we are being prepared to lead others in the act of generosity and sacrificial giving. We "enter the drama" and allow God to work in us and through us as development professionals and ministry leaders.

It is through submission and sacrifice that you are shaped and formed into a steward leader. It is in the process of losing our life that we find true life, and that paradoxical process is our transformation.

Doxology, Not Dogmatism

As just noted, the process of transformation is a journey of joy because it is a journey with Christ. No greater freedom is available to humankind than that of a godly steward. For this reason our transformation can only result in doxology.

We might say that there is a "legalistic stewardship" and an "evangelical stewardship." By "legalistic stewardship," we mean that dogmatic, transactional command to give x percent of our excess to buy our peace of mind. It represents a two-kingdom worldview that yields guilt-inducing stewardship programs and high-pressure fundraising techniques. It is a money-focused, manipulation-based approach. It seeks a change of bank balance but not of heart, and it leaves stewardship solely associated with money. Tacked on to the work of the church like a necessary evil, pastors hate to preach on it and congregants hate to hear about it. It is done apologetically and seldom if ever results in a truly joyful act of giving. In so many ways "legalistic stewardship" has crippled the church and fostered the myriad of misconceptions about money, tithing, and transformation.

"Evangelical stewardship," on the other hand, is the generous, joyous response of grace. Its generosity is compelled by God's gracious and extravagant acts toward us and for us. It is the exuberant "amen" to God's love and mercy to us and, as such, every act of the godly steward is an act of worship. Commenting on the Great Collection in 2 Corinthians 9, Jouette Bassler concludes that for Paul, "Giving to others thus glorifies God (v. 13) and an act of charity is thereby transformed into an act of worship."[15] We must hold together the act of worship and the act of stewardship as one response to divine action.

If our stewardship is worship, does it not make sense that our work toward stewardship is ministry? Does it not follow that Christian fundraisers are involved in ministry as they promote godly stewardship and acts of generosity among God's people? Does it not make sense that stewardship should be part of every worship service, every Sunday? Would it not be true that raising up godly stewards is a core calling of church and parachurch organizations? And should we not be just as concerned about the stewardship faithfulness of our congregants and Christian neighbors and colleagues as their faithfulness in discipleship, personal devotion, and Christian service?

When we see stewardship as worship, empowered by our ongoing transformation to the image of Christ, we take a major step forward in putting the call of the godly steward back where it belongs—at the center of the Christian life. Randy Alcorn states it clearly: "Stewardship isn't a subcategory of the Christian life. Stewardship is the Christian life."[16]

Death, Not Denial

Finally, we achieve this attitude of the joyous, generous response of the godly steward only through death. Dietrich Bonhoeffer comments, "The cross is laid on every Christian. It begins with the call to abandon the attachments of this world. It is that dying of the old man which is the result of his encounter with Christ.... When Christ calls a man, He bids him come and die."[17]

Paul tells the church in Colossae, "You died, and your life is now hidden with Christ in God" (Col. 3:3). He reminds them that in following Christ they have "died with Christ to the basic principles of this world" (Col. 2:20). Paul exhorts the Christians in Rome that they have "died to sin" and that in being baptized into Christ Jesus they were "baptized into his death. . . . We were therefore buried with him through baptism into death" (Rom. 6:2-4). For Paul this death is critical: first because "anyone who has died has been freed from sin" and second, "if we died with Christ, we believe that we will also live with him" (Rom. 6:7-8). Paul tells the Galatians, "I have been crucified with Christ and I no longer live, but Christ lives in me" (Gal. 2:20).

This death is the single most critical step in our transformation into godly stewards because it is the abdication of the throne of our own kingdom. It is the first act of submission, obedience, and discipleship. It is selling all we have to purchase the treasure hidden in the field. It is a real death, death to a sinful nature that values things over people and places our pursuit of happiness ahead of our pursuit of holiness.

We begin our journey of transformation by dying this death, or we do not start it at all. There is no shortcut, no second way. In place of this death, the world wants us to embrace a denial of our real sinfulness. If we can somehow soften our sin, we can eliminate the need for this very real death, and so denial is the final lie of the Enemy in the guise of a human-centeredness that focuses us inward to save ourselves. Christ tells us that we are in need of holistic transformation that starts with the confession of our sinfulness and death to its bondage. We cannot set ourselves free, for true freedom is a gracious gift of God and not a result of our own works. And as we accept and embrace that gift, we experience death to our old nature and all the lies that it regurgitates to us daily.

Thus it is through death to sin and not a denial of our sinfulness that transformation begins. For that reason, the great stewardship question is not, "Are you living the Christian life?" but, "Have you died?" As we answer "Yes," we start on the journey of holistic, life-changing transformation to the image of Christ that daily remakes us into the generous stewards we were created to be. This book is a road map to that transformation, and it is my prayer that through the words of my colleagues you will be inspired and guided in the glorious calling of the steward in the Kingdom of the triune God of grace.

R. SCOTT RODIN (Ph.D., University of Aberdeen) has worked in Christian fundraising and not-for-profit leadership for eighteen years and served as the president of the Christian Stewardship Association. He has held posts and served as a fundraising consultant in the United States and Great Britain. He also served as president of Eastern Baptist Theological Seminary in Philadelphia. Dr. Rodin is a nationally sought speaker and preacher and has consulted with colleges, seminaries, churches, museums, parachurch ministries, and denominations. Recent books include *Stewards in the Kingdom* and *Seven Deadly Sins*. He can be reached at rodinconsulting@aol.com.

1. All Bible quotations are from the New International Version.
2. Karl Barth, *Dogmatics in Outline* (London: SCM, 1949), 24.
3. Tom Sine, *Living on Purpose* (Grand Rapids: Baker, 2002), 96.
4. Richard Foster, *Money, Sex and Power* (San Francisco: Harper & Row, 1985), 61.
5. Craig Blomberg, *Heart, Soul and Money* (Joplin, MO: College Press, 2000), 56.
6. John Bright, *The Kingdom of God* (Nashville: Abingdon, 1953), 263.
7. I have discussed the pitfalls of this situation in my book *The Seven Deadly Sins of Christian Fundraising* (Spokane: Kingdom Life, 2007).
8. Dallas Willard, *The Divine Conspiracy: Rediscovering Our Hidden Life in God* (San Francisco: HarperSanFrancisco, 1998), 208.
9. John Frank, *The Ministry of Development* (Woodinville, WA: Steward Publishing, 2005), 15.
10. Jim and Molly Davis Scott, *Kingdom People* (Woodinville, WA: Steward Publishing, 2004), 157–158.
11. Wes Willmer, *God & Your Stuff: The Vital Link between Your Possessions and Your Soul* (Colorado Springs: NavPress, 2002), 23.
12. Douglas John Hall, *The Steward* (Grand Rapids: Eerdmans, 1990), 95.
13. Foster, 43.
14. David Young, *Servant Leadership for Church Renewal* (Scottsdale, AZ: Herald, 1999), 137.
15. Jouette Bassler, *God and Mammon* (Nashville: Abingdon, 1991), 107–8.
16. Randy Alcorn, *Money, Possessions and Eternity* (Wheaton: Tyndale House, 2003), 140.
17. Dietrich Bonhoeffer, *The Cost of Discipleship* (New York: Macmillan, 1948), 73.

II.

The Church's Role in Transforming STEWARDS

*The church should be the center for developing Christians'
understanding of generosity and nurturing their heart
transformation. This section discusses how the church can
be an effective headquarters for biblical stewardship
education and formation.*

Chapter

THE CHURCH'S LEADERSHIP ROLE
IN **BRINGING STEWARDSHIP
FRONT** AND **CENTER**

BY RICHARD J. TOWNER, *Executive Director,*
Good $ense Stewardship, Willow Creek Association

CONTEXT FOR THE CHURCH

The church should be the central place for believers to come to understand biblical stewardship in a way that transforms their hearts, conforms their lives to the image of Christ, and results in overflowing generosity. Therefore it behooves us to look closely at the role of the church and church leadership in this process.

Every church has a stewardship culture, either by design or by happenstance—a set of beliefs and values regarding an individual's relationship to their money and possessions. A sub-biblical stewardship culture creates behavioral expectations for Christians that hinder a scriptural response to the culture's mores about wealth and property.

Much has already been said about the cultural context in which we live and minister—a culture of materialism in which possession has become an obsession. Given the cultural milieu, it could be said that for many Christians money is the chief rival god and materialism is the competing ideology in their lives.

This worship of material wealth in our culture takes on an insidious form that imitates Christianity. There is a gospel, the "good news," of materialism: "Things bring happiness." Materialism has a liturgy called consumerism, which is performed in temples of worship called shopping malls. The deity of materialism—called money—has been imbued with godlike characteristics. It is deemed omnipotent—"Give me enough of that stuff and I'll be powerful enough to make things happen!" It promises ultimate security—a promise that can only rightfully be made by God Himself. Yet materialism's news is not good, its liturgy is hollow, its god is false, and its promise of security is empty—but many, even in the church, have bought its lies.

The growing influence of materialism has far-reaching implications for the church and for our world as a whole. Arguably, the macroissues facing the world today—the destruction of the environment, the plight of the poor, war and conflict, and the decline in the value of human life—are, at their core, stewardship issues. On these issues, the church "may be the last place left in our culture that can engage the public conversation with non-market values."[1]

The key question is, how can the church engage the public conversation in a cogent, grace-filled, and convincing way to effectively counter the pervasive and persuasive messages of materialism? This chapter will examine the roles of the pastor, the nonpastoral staff, and the corporate church. But first it is critical to understand why it is important to discuss possession issues in the church.

Why Is Stewardship Important to the Church?

There are those who feel the church shouldn't talk about money. Why should it? First of all, financial issues are a large part of the day-to-day lives of everyone, including believers. Many of us spend the majority of our waking hours making money, spending money, worrying about money, fighting over money, and/or trying to protect money. Failure to address such a major issue in people's lives may be one of the greatest acts of self-marginalization in the history of the church. It also ensures that giving to God's work in the world through the local church suffers. Those who succumb to the materialistic pull of the culture have little motivation and few resources to offer, and God's vision for the local church goes unfulfilled for lack of financial support. Scarcity of resources creates other negative effects within the church:

- Unhealthy competition for limited resources arises between ministries.
- Those skilled in financial matters have undue influence in church affairs.
- The budget drives ministry rather than ministry driving the budget.
- Morale of staff and congregation suffers as the pressing issue becomes how the budgetary needs can be met.

The fact that finances are such a major issue in our people's lives and in the life of the church could be reason enough for every church to address the topic of biblical stewardship. But an even more important reason is that a person's relationship to their money is a significant spiritual issue, a central matter of discipleship, and a transformational issue of the heart, as highlighted throughout this book. Pastor and author Ben Patterson observes, "There is no such thing as being right with God and wrong with your money."[2] At first glance, that statement may seem a bit strong. But a cursory review of just four of the hundreds of references in Scripture concerning our relationship to money would suggest that Patterson's statement is right on target. For example:

- Matthew 6:21—"For where your treasure is, there your heart will be also."[3] In this context the heart refers to the essence of who we are. The New Living Translation says "the desires of your heart" will be where your treasure is.
- Matthew 6:24—"You cannot serve both God and Money." "Cannot" is in the indicative tense in Greek, suggesting it is *impossible* to serve both

God and money.

- Matthew 13—In the parable of the sower, Jesus explains that the thorns that grew up and choked out the good growth (the Word of God) and made it unfruitful were concern over things of the world and the deceitfulness of riches.
- 1 Timothy 6:10—Paul warns Timothy, "For the love of money is a root of all kinds of evil."

What these four verses say is that an improper relationship to our money and our stuff can steal our hearts from God, keep us from serving God, make God's Word unfruitful in our life, and lead us to all kinds of evil. Pretty serious stuff!

The bottom line is that if we care about our congregation's day-to-day lives, if we are concerned about their spiritual well-being, if we profess to teach the whole Word of God, then leadership *must* address the vital topic of financial stewardship. We are in a battle of competing ideologies, perhaps the major spiritual battle of our day—and we are losing badly!

The reality is that most churches do *not* deal with the topic. Money tends to be the great "silent subject"[4] in both seminary and church. When money *is* talked about, it usually is in the context of "stewardship Sunday," what United Methodist Church (UMC) Foundation president Michael Reeves refers to as "the annual lamentation of desperation for the church budget."[5] If a church is to successfully address the area of financial stewardship, it must have a holistic, year-round, churchwide financial stewardship ministry that teaches, trains, and supports and encourages individuals in implementing biblical stewardship principles into their daily financial lives.

The Specific Role of Church Leadership—Clergy and Laity

Given the importance of biblical stewardship in the lives of their congregants, a key responsibility of leadership—pastoral, staff, and lay—is to ensure that the church consistently and effectively models and teaches biblical steward-ship and provides training opportunities for personal implementation. In short, a church must intentionally craft a stewardship atmosphere or culture. We are called to reshape the values of our people, who live in the flawed econ-omy of a kingdom other than the Kingdom of God. As a stewardship culture is created within the church, our people receive a great gift. Their hearts are transformed, they are more fully conformed to the image of Christ, and they experience the benefits of the economy of the Kingdom of God. Those bene-fits include:

- The unique joy and freedom that comes with generous giving compared to the fear and anxiety that accompanies a hoarding mentality.
- The certainty of God's promises and faithfulness compared to a sys-tem based upon uncontrollable and unpredictable human and natural events.
- The opportunity to experience God's provision in uncertain circum-stances and a sense of peace and contentment that transcends those circumstances.

Pastoral Leadership Challenges

In spite of the overwhelming benefits, pastoral leadership often face signifi-cant challenges in effectively bringing to light the countercultural truths of God's economy. Many pastors feel unprepared—and are, in fact, ill equipped—to teach and train others in biblical stewardship. They have a knowledge gap. Few seminaries offer a course on stewardship, and only a small percentage of those that do make it a requirement. In addition, most pastors do not make financial expertise or monetary accumulation a central focus. Combine lack of preparation and lack of expertise and interest with the typically modest income of most pastors and it is easy to understand why many feel intimi-dated and ill equipped to lead in this arena.

In addition, pastors are as susceptible as any of us to the seductive materialism of our culture, as well as to general financial difficulty. The expense of seminary and educational loans paired with the modest starting salary of the typical pastor may complicate their finances.

Yet another challenge can be the perception that messages about stewardship are self-serving (after all, the pastor's salary is part, often a significant part, of the church budget). There are also those who feel the church simply should not talk about money—that it is a "personal" matter. Their voices can be loud and intimidating.

However, the preaching pastor is the most important individual in ensuring that biblical stewardship is taught and permeates the church's culture. He or she cannot avoid being, in the words of Richard Borg, the "chief steward."[6] Bill Hybels of Willow Creek indicates that one of the biggest surprises of his early ministry was becoming aware that he, as senior pastor, had the ultimate (earthly) responsibility to see that there was money to pay the church's bills and salaries.[7]

The pastor has a multidimensional stewardship role—as leader, educator, and communicator—so let's look at some constructive responses to the challenges the pastor faces. Howard Dayton's chapter provides specific content ideas for preaching.

Closing the Knowledge Gap

Self-study can offset the lack of seminary training on the topic of stewardship. Obviously study of Scripture is foundational, and the good news is that there is no lack of texts to be studied. Imagine what could be accomplished in just thirty minutes a day, five days a week, 130 hours a year of New Testament study on money and possessions, in equipping you to preach and teach more powerfully and confidently in this area.

A growing number of websites can be helpful sources of messages and information on stewardship. Notable among them is Generousgiving.org. A growing number of excellent books that deal with both the practical and the theological aspects of church financial stewardship include the following.

Money, Possessions and Eternity, by Randy Alcorn, challenges the leader at both a personal and organizational level and provides numerous practical suggestions. One need not agree with all the author's conclusions to benefit greatly from the book.

God and Your Stuff, by Wesley Willmer. Note particularly the chapter entitled "What You Should Expect from Your Church." Willmer points out that James W. Fowler's six stages of faith as outlined in his book by the same title can be a useful framework for viewing the development of a steward.

Wealth as Peril and Obligation, by Sondra Ely Wheeler, professor of Christian Ethics at Wesley Theological Seminary, delves deeply into the question, "How can the New Testament canon form and inform the contemporary moral discernment of the church regarding the holding and use of possessions?"

Dealing with personal finances

While self-study may be the answer to lack of biblical knowledge, reaching out to someone with expertise and experience beyond our own is often the solution for getting our personal financial lives in order. Admittedly this can be a humbling experience, and clearly the person should be chosen carefully. But one can be certain that in every congregation there are those who are able and willing to help in this area.

While the encouragement and accountability of a trusted individual is always helpful, an additional option is to participate in a teaching/training experience such as the Good Sense biblical principles and money management course (aka "Budget Course").

For those of us who have not had good financial role models or do not have an affinity for managing our financial resources, the effort to get our financial lives in order may appear overwhelming. It need not be so. Discipline is required, but the principles of sound financial management are not rocket science and are spelled out in Scripture. Trusted counsel and a basic understanding of key financial principles can transform our financial lives. This transformation is crucial, especially since the personal practices of pastoral leadership have a direct impact on their effectiveness from the pulpit. Teaching and preaching can only have transformational power if they flow out of a life consistent with what is being taught. Since our relationship to our money is a key indicator of our spiritual maturity, and since giving is a reflection of where our heart is (Matt. 6:21), the tithe as a minimal level of giving seems a reasonable requirement for church staff and leaders. But keep in mind that the point is not a particular amount that one gives, but the transformation of the heart that conforms it to the image of Christ—becoming generous as He is generous.

Dealing with misperceptions and opposition

Opposition to the church speaking about money usually arises from one of two sources: lack of information or spiritual resistance. Some in the church may simply be uninformed about what and how much Scripture has to say about money. For cultural reasons or because the church has not done so in the past, they feel we should not talk about such a personal subject in church.

Most often, taking time with these individuals to ask why they have this feeling, and pointing out how often Jesus talked about money and our relationship to it, can win them over. It might also be worth exploring the origin of their belief that personal matters should not be discussed in church. It certainly did not originate in Scripture!

Spiritual resistance can be a more difficult issue. Some individuals may, consciously or unconsciously, not wish for this topic to be discussed because they are not honoring God with their finances and do not want to be convicted in this area of their lives. Clearly, they should not be allowed to set the agenda on this topic. And should their opposition to biblical teaching on money lead to them leaving the church, it is well to remember, as pastor Richard Borg said, "Church health and growth does not depend upon the people who leave for the wrong reasons, but those who stay for the right ones."[8]

In preparing for potential resistance, any transition in a stewardship culture should be initiated by a unified church leadership. Study and discuss together why it is important for the church to move in this direction. Once key leadership is on board, they should be highly visible in their support of the pastor bringing this topic "front and center." The most effective person(s) to talk to the church about giving may, in fact, be lay leadership. But the task—the privilege—to *preach* a biblical perspective on money and possessions remains with the pastor.

College Hill Presbyterian Church in Cincinnati provides an example of one way to respond to misconceptions about money in the corporate church. The leadership at this church took an extra step to ensure they heard and included the whole congregation in a building campaign.[9] The congregational vote was over 80 percent in favor of a building program that leadership was convinced was a God-led project and for which they had solicited extensive input. But the fact that almost 20 percent of the congregation had voted against the project was a surprising and unacceptable outcome.

The leadership's response was, "We thought we had heard God regarding this project, but obviously there is something additional He wants to tell us through the dissenting 20 percent." They held meetings to determine what the problem was and, interestingly, everyone agreed the building program was needed and the plan was an excellent one. The issue for those who voted against the proposal was not lack of understanding or spiritual opposition, but that they had a heart for missions and could not bring themselves to approve spending that much money on bricks and mortar alone.

The solution was to have a dual campaign. The church developed a two-part pledge card. One part was for "Up-building the Body" (for the new facilities). The other part was for "Up-building Others" (for missions/outreach ministries). Members were invited to pledge to either one or both as God led them.

The result of combining the two needs into one campaign resulted in 100 percent approval of the project, and the campaign resulted in complete funding for the building project and a significant amount of money raised for missions and outreach.

One further thought on dealing with misconceptions: preaching a biblical perspective on our relationship to money need not always be labeled a "stewardship" message. Simply preaching the whole Word of God will broach the topic regularly! By all means, aspects of financial stewardship other than giving should be addressed. The perception in the pew that stewardship is strictly about giving money to the church is far too common and exists because that is often the only context in which it has been presented. While giving is perhaps the most tangible and easily measured indicator of a transformed heart, the totality of financial stewardship is far deeper and broader.

Overcoming hesitation to approach those with significant resources

A lack of knowledge about financial affairs and modest income compared to marketplace peers can lead pastors to feel intimidated around people with significant resources. Truth be known, the intimidation is most often self-imposed and pastors do, in fact, have a great deal to offer wealthy individuals.

It should be noted that the ability to make money does not automatically carry with it the ability or the wisdom to manage it well even in a worldly manner, much less a Kingdom one. Many wealthy individuals have had their lives literally turned around and incredibly enriched when they were introduced to a God-honoring perspective on the handling of their wealth.

Still further, persons who have acquired considerable wealth often feel isolated and are cautious regarding those who reach out to them in "friendship," because many have ulterior motives. Scripture also makes it clear that their resources put them in a place of spiritual vulnerability (Matt. 19:23). Many face life issues brought about by heavy stress in their work environments and workaholic tendencies that often accompany wealth acquisition. In short, they have tremendous pastoral needs!

A pastoral relationship that cares about their soul and not just their money, that enables the individual to embrace their true identity as a beloved son or daughter of God, not just a "successful" businessperson, and that provides them with the spiritual counsel of 1 Timothy 6:17–18 ("so that they may take hold of that which is life indeed") is one of the greatest gifts they could receive.

A pastor can be the one to introduce a wealthy person to the unique joy and satisfaction that comes from being conformed to the image of Christ and giving generously. It is an incredible loss not only for the Kingdom but also for the wealthy individual when they do not generously share.

A pastor may hesitate to reach out to the wealthy due to a misunderstanding of the admonition in James 2:1–7 to not show favoritism to the wealthy over the poor. The aforementioned reasons for pastoring the wealthy do not fall into the category of favoritism but simply recognize that neglecting the rich would be just as bad as neglecting the widows and orphans. As Gary Moore said:

> Ironically, despite their material poverty, the poor are precisely those who Jesus saw as blessed. It was those of us with excess wealth that he saw as challenged. Yet many pastors still ask me how to approach the wealthy. Some even believe I'm wrong to associate with the rich. Neither group has been taught why Jesus lovingly asked Zacchaeus to come down to earth and chat over dinner.[10]

John Paul II summarized the attitude behind that simple act with these words: "Love for the poor must be preferential but not exclusive."[11] The leading sectors of society have been neglected, and many people have thus been estranged from the church. If evangelism of society's leaders is neglected, it shall come as no surprise that many who are a part of it will be guided by criteria alien to the gospel and at times openly hostile to it.

Nonpastoral Staff Responsibilities

In addition to having their personal financial lives in order and generously supporting the work of God in the world, staff—other than the pastor—must also be equipped to teach and discuss stewardship with their constituencies. Stewardship is a discipleship issue that is involved in all areas of ministry, and all staff must be prepared to support and from time to time actively participate in stewardship-related activities.

Worship staff needs to understand that the offering is an act of worship. Therefore, the worship leaders are instrumental in preparing the hearts of the congregation to give. These moments leading to and following the offering present an opportunity to provide a brief but compelling counterpoint to the messages of the culture that have bombarded the worshiper all week.

In similar fashion, financial stewardship has nearly universal ministry application. Whether it is the benevolence ministry, premarital counseling, children's ministry, or new member orientation, there is opportunity to teach godly financial principles—introducing the congregation to what the Bible has to say about earning, giving, saving, debt, and spending. Richard Edic's and Howard Dayton's chapters provide some specific guidelines and materials for integrating biblical teaching on financial stewardship into the church's various ministries.

Another way in which all staff can be involved in creating a stewardship culture is by consistently holding one another accountable for God-honoring handling of the funds entrusted to their areas of ministry. In turn, as staff members work with teams of volunteers, they can incorporate "stewardship moments" as they make ministry decisions that involve expenditure of funds. Staff can lead by taking time with their volunteer team to thank God for the availability of the funds and for the people who gave a portion of the resources entrusted to them to the church, and petitioning God for wisdom in spending those resources.

Last but not least, there is the stewardship ministry core team of individuals who understand the life-transforming potential of the ministry and are committed to it. I am convinced that within every congregation there is a person or persons who are qualified and have the passion to provide leadership for this ministry. In many cases, because of the church's historic avoidance of the topic, they have never dreamed there was a place for them to serve in such a capacity.

The stewardship ministry team should have overall staff support and access to the church's top leadership body. Because stewardship ministry is not about raising funds but about raising stewards, it should organizationally be located within the church's ministry area, not under the finance department. Useful models for leadership teams can be found in Richard Edic's chapter.

A word to staff members who do not have the support of the senior pastor for their stewardship ministry efforts: I know of no substitute for open, honest, nonjudgmental dialogue. Hopefully the prior discussion regarding the spiritual significance of stewardship ministry and the degree to which finances are a major issue in the life of our people and the church will be useful in ultimately gaining support. It may be very helpful to present the pastor with the testimonies of people who have benefited from whatever fledgling ministry efforts exist or by the testimonies of those from other churches where effective ministries are in place. Once understood, the spiritual significance of one's relationship to his or her money should be a compelling rationale for any pastor to lay aside personal hesitancy in approaching this area. Listening carefully to the pastor's reasons for hesitation, attempting to discern what may be deeper reasons behind the proffered ones, and eventually addressing the issues that surface will be important.

THE ROLE OF TRUST

Trust is a prerequisite to change. It is a central factor in the effective functioning of any organization and is of particular importance within the body of Christ. In few areas can the seeds of distrust be more easily sown than in the area of finance. No one wants to be the person fooled into giving to something ineffective or harmful.[12]

Many factors contribute to the building of trust. Checks and balances, policies and procedures, and adherence to Generally Accepted Accounting Practices (GAAP) are all precautions that church leadership can take so that their actions are not discredited in the administration of the funds entrusted to them and are, in the words of Paul, honorable "not only in the eyes of the Lord but also in the eyes of men" (2 Cor. 8:21).

These standards of fiscal responsibility and accountability must be in place from the moment money is collected in the offering receptacle until it is wisely, efficiently, and effectively expended for ministry purposes. One pastor's criterion for expenditures is the question, "If a reporter with an agenda found out about this expenditure, would they have any grounds for a negative story?" The leadership's handling of money should be above reproach.

An additional aspect of financial accountability and building trust is open access to financial records. An audit should be performed annually, whether this is in-house for smaller churches or a full independent audit for larger churches. Making copies of the audit available and providing the opportunity to ask questions of the appropriate staff can establish a strong foundation of trust for the congregation. Very often, the more open the financial records are, the fewer people will even be interested in looking at them—trust has been established.

I served for five years as director of finance for Willow Creek Community Church. During that time it was my privilege once each quarter to stand before the congregation in the worship service and give them a brief financial report. The report had only a little to do with numbers and a whole lot to do with building and maintaining trust. Reports contained:

- A bit of information—"Here's a brief overview of last quarter's income and expenses," and, "Here's a follow-up on the mention I made last quarter that the board of directors was going to decide what to do with a large undesignated gift we had received."
- A story about a ministry their giving had allowed to take place—"Let me tell you about the family who came to our food pantry and how they wound up being touched by six different ministries."
- Examples of how we were being good stewards of the resources they made available to us—"Thought you'd be interested in how ministry X maximized their funding this year," or, "I'd like to share a new procedure we've implemented to ensure the security of our funds."
- A "thank-you" for their generosity, which made all we were doing possible.

A good starting point for trust building (and for assuring that good financial practices are being followed) is for churches to become a member of the Evangelical Council for Financial Accountability (ECFA). The prerequisites for membership are benchmarks that all churches should be able to clear. Doing so is valuable, as strengthening trust in leadership's handling of resources lays the foundation for the congregation to direct their generosity to the church.

THE CORPORATE CHURCH

How the church budgets and spends funds, how it approaches the issue of debt, and how it allocates funds to ministry outside the church body are corporate parallels to individual stewardship. Does the church practice what it preaches?

I am sure there are many examples of churches that corporately model good stewardship and a generous spirit, but two of which I am aware are the Vineyard Church and Crossroads Community Church, both in Cincinnati. Years ago the Vineyard Church had outgrown its location and had purchased ground for a new facility.[13] They owed several hundred thousand dollars on their existing property, which could have been sold for what was owed and more. However, leadership felt led to give the property to another church, mortgage free. So the church had a capital campaign to do just that. The deed to their church property was turned over, debt free, on Easter Sunday, 1999. *Then* they began their campaign to build their new facility.

Crossroads Community Church is a vibrant, creative church that feels part of its call is to freely share whatever they learn or develop with the body of Christ at large.[14] All its CDs, DVDs, publications, and ministry resources are given away for free to anyone who attends or asks. Their resources are marked "Please reproduce and distribute." These two churches are great examples of corporately exhibiting the generous spirit that every church should seek to embody.

CONCLUSION

For the sake of their spiritual well-being, Christians must be taught "why" and "how" to incorporate biblical stewardship principles into their daily lives. They often must be supported and encouraged in the transformation from a secular to a God-honoring lifestyle and the practice of generosity that comes with being conformed to the image of Christ.

Not only the congregation but also those who are charged to lead in the church must perform the difficult task of aligning our finances with biblical principles. Avoiding the challenge is not an option for leaders if they are to effectively shepherd the sheep and preach the whole Word of God.

It is important to keep in mind the goal, which is a transformed heart. Be assured: the rewards are worth the effort! In closing, let me share a vision for your church.

Imagine that it is a number of years from now and you and your team have successfully created a stewardship environment in your church—you've taught and trained, supported and encouraged your people in biblical financial stewardship. People are implementing biblical financial principles in their lives; they are growing in generosity, saving regularly for the unexpected, and freeing themselves from the bondage of consumer debt. Their lifestyles are marked by moderation, discipline, and contentment. Money has been eliminated as the rival god, and they are growing in their relationship with the true God.

On Sunday morning they arrive for services and in their countenance is joy radiating from their generous hearts. In their demeanor is a sense of peace—a lack of anxiety over financial matters, a pervading sense of contentment and gratefulness. Marital conflict over money has been largely eliminated. They enter worship with a sense of anticipation and expectation of God's presence and work among them. Imagine this visible transformation flowing from the hearts of those in your church.

Continue to imagine: the church is debt free. The church's ministries are fully funded. The church has a strong outreach to the local community and beyond in both evangelism and compassion ministries. Resources have made quality, well-maintained church facilities available for use in ministry. The question before leadership is, "What is God calling us to do with the abundant resources with which He has entrusted us?"

That can be your church—a united body of men and women whose hearts have been transformed and whose lives have been conformed to Christ! Out of that conformity to a generous Savior who gave *everything* on our behalf will flow a generosity that enables the fulfillment of God's vision for your church.

RICHARD J. TOWNER is the Willow Creek Association's (WCA) executive director for the Good Sense Stewardship Movement. He is also the primary author of the WCA's Good Sense curriculum. Prior to arriving at Willow

Creek Community Church in 1992, Dick served thirteen years as the minister of administration at a church in Cincinnati. He also spent fourteen years in university administration. Dick serves on the board of the Christian Stewardship Association and on the president's council of the Christian Management Association. He can be reached at dtowner@willowcreek.org.

1. Cornel West, quoted in Ched Myers, *The Biblical Vision of Sabbath Economics* (Washington, DC: Church of the Saviour, 2002), 7.

2. Ben Patterson, quoted in Dick Towner, "Ministry Connections: Stewardship," *WCA News* (2007).

3. Unless otherwise noted, all Bible quotations are from the New International Version.

4. Brian Kluth, "Biblical Stewardship: Christianity's Silent Subject," Maximum Generosity, http://www.kluth.org/church/SilentSubject1.htm.

5. Michael D. Reeves and Jennifer Tyler, *Faith and Money: Understanding Annual Giving in Church* (Discipleship Resources, 2004).

6. Richard Borg, "The Chief Steward: Leading Your Church to Excellence in Financial Stewardship" (working paper, 2007).

7. Bill Hybels, Keynote Address (speech presented at the WCA Resource Challenge Conference, Chicago, Illinois, May 13, 2003).

8. Borg, "The Chief Steward."

9. College Hill Presbyterian Church, Cincinnati, Ohio, spring, 1980.

10. Gary Moore, "Feed My Sheep, Corral My Bulls" (lecture, Nashville, Tennessee, May 24, 2002).

11. Pope John Paul II, "Ecclesia in America" (Post-Synodal Apostolic Exhortation, Mexico City, Mexico, January 22, 1999).

12. See Paul Nelson's chapter for a fuller exposition of these issues.

13. Vineyard Church, Cincinnati, Ohio, 1999.

14. Crossroads Community Church, Cincinnati, Ohio, 2006.

Chapter

7

Organizing and Implementing a
Church Stewardship
Ministry

By Richard E. Edic, *Founder and President*
of Vision Resourcing

H aving worked with hundreds of churches, it is my observation that
most churches have no plan or program to teach biblical stewardship. Friends of mine who have also worked with churches in the
area of stewardship education have confirmed my observation of this unfortunate reality. Often these churches' only concept of stewardship revolves
around their annual budget and the yearly struggle to meet it. Meanwhile
their members are being pulled by the secular culture toward materialism and
consumer debt. As a result, according to surveys, including some by Barna
Research Online, giving among Christians averages 3 percent of their annual
income.[1] Although churches may conduct various fundraising campaigns over
the years, they are not necessarily getting at their people's core need to become
mature disciples and stewards of what God has given them. Their need is to
enter into the intimate and joyful experience of being godly stewards and generous givers.

Since pastors and church leaders are responsible for leading their congregations in resourcing the church's vision and ministries, they also need to understand and implement the financial principles addressed in the previous chapters of this book. They need to see themselves as facilitators of heart transformation. This is part of their calling to help disciple their congregations to be conformed to the image of Christ.

Often, the first need of a church is to teach financial management truths even before giving truths. Without the church's effort in teaching these truths to their people, generous giving is not likely to occur. Growing stewards to be rich toward God takes time, but it should happen in the church. Churches need to provide a comprehensive stewardship education ministry through all their ministries and to all age groups. You want to get stewardship into the church's ministry "water system," so that whichever ministry "faucet" a member drinks from, they will occasionally receive some aspect of stewardship teaching. This chapter seeks to provide a practical structure for a church to apply in organizing and implementing a stewardship ministry. This is only an overview of what it takes to lead a stewardship ministry, and the end results will vary with individual churches, so the reader is encouraged to seek more detailed information and help at www.visionresourcing.com and www.crown.org, along with the other resources listed in this book.

ORGANIZING YOUR STEWARDSHIP MINISTRY LEADERSHIP TEAM

Once the pastor, staff, and church lay leadership commit to the process of implementing or expanding a stewardship ministry, they can form and train a lay Stewardship Ministry Leadership Team. This vital team will carry out the daily details of managing a stewardship ministry. It is best to take your time in recruiting the right people to serve on this team. The size and structure of the Leadership Team will vary according to the size and needs of each church. Here are some suggested positions on the team:

- **Team Leader**–Provides overall leadership to the ministry. He/she will manage, support, and coordinate the efforts of each team member. He or she will work with the pastor, staff, and board. He or she, along with the pastor, will cast the vision for the stewardship ministry with the congregation.

- **Communication**–Creates and coordinates all communications and promotions relevant to stewardship activities, programs, and general education. This will involve the use of strategies such as video, printed material, email, website, and vocal communication.

- **Christian Education Teaching**–Plans, schedules, and coordinates the teaching of stewardship in all adult and youth classes, working closely with assigned pastors or lay leaders.

- **Small Group Ministry**–Promotes, schedules, recruits, and coordinates any small groups involved in teaching some aspect of stewardship, such as a Crown Financial Ministry small group. This person will probably want to form their own leadership team within the main Stewardship Ministry Team in order to be able to accomplish this responsibility.

- **Special Events and Campaigns**–Coordinates all the details of running a special event or campaign to raise funds for selected projects. This job can include scheduling, promoting, and coordinating stewardship seminars, whether live or video.

- **Estate and Gift Planning**–Ensures that church attendees and members are motivated and instructed in the "why" and "how" of estate and planned giving.

- **Counseling or Coaching Team**–Develops a trained team of counselors, or coaches, who can be available to personally counsel and mentor individuals and couples seeking help with their money management and debt reduction. Two excellent resources for training these counselors, or coaches, are Crown Financial Ministries and Willow Creek's Good $ense Ministry.

For smaller churches, the key positions to fill are Team Leader, Communication, and Christian Education Teaching. Rather than attempting a full-scale, comprehensive stewardship ministry, a small church might opt for scheduling specific events or activities, such as one of Crown Financial Ministry's "Church Solutions" or the "Budget Course" by the Good $ense Stewardship Ministry.

Once the Stewardship Ministry Leadership Team is formed and trained, they should plan and activate their agenda. It is important to remember that this is a long-term teaching effort to raise up stewards to be rich in generosity toward God. It is not just an occasional campaign, although a campaign can be part of the stewardship ministry. (See Brian Kluth's chapter for insights on conducting resource development campaigns in the church.)

A church's comprehensive training involves learning how to organize the Stewardship Ministry Leadership Team; formulate individual job descriptions; and decide what subjects to teach, what activities and events to schedule, and where to find helpful resource materials. Three suggested sources of assistance are Crown Financial Ministries, Vision Resourcing, and Good $ense Ministry.

PREPARING FOR YOUR AGENDA AND ACTIVITIES

Once you have formed and trained your Stewardship Ministry Leadership Team, it is time to start the process of introducing stewardship into your church's ministry "water system."

Start by bathing the whole effort in prayer. Have your prayer groups and church leadership spend several weeks praying over your anticipated ministry effort. Remember to pray for: (1) wisdom in deciding which activities you should do and when, (2) strong support from your church staff and lay leadership, and (3) the congregation's hearts to be receptive to future efforts and teaching on stewardship principles.

The questions on your mind at this time might be, "What are the activities we should include in our stewardship ministry? Where do we start? Which ones are priority?" This chapter lists many activities that your church may engage in over time. Do not try to do them all at once. Pick the ones that seem most important to your people and that you have the capability to implement. It will take time to train your team members and church staff who will teach as well as coordinate a particular activity. Obviously, some stewardship activities are easier to implement than others, and you must decide which ones come first for your church.

Three tools that may help you decide your agenda are the Congregational Stewardship Questionnaire, Church Stewardship Survey, and Your Church's Giving Potential Worksheet. Samples are included at the end of this chapter.

A good first step is to survey your church congregation in order to determine their stewardship maturity and climate. Use the Congregational Stewardship Questionnaire to gather information about your people. This is an *anonymous* questionnaire that your congregation takes home, completes, and drops in a box at the door of your worship center. Your Team members then can complete the Church Stewardship Survey by entering the tabulated information gleaned from the Congregational Stewardship Questionnaires and by surveying church staff and officers. Modify the questions to fit your particular church situation.

Because you may encounter some resistance to very personal questions, here are some ideas to share with your congregation to motivate them to complete the Congregational Stewardship Questionnaire:

- The church leadership is committed to educating you in the whole counsel of God's Word. Stewardship is a vital part of this process.
- Evidence indicates that there is a strong felt need for help in becoming better managers of our money and time.
- The Bible and Jesus have a lot to say about finances.
- The church wants to know the spiritual and stewardship health of its congregation.

- Your help will guide us in designing a stewardship educational ministry that will help you grow in your walk with God.
- We want your *candid* and *anonymous* response. Do not write your name on the questionnaire!

If you have the technical capability to put the Questionnaire on your website, you could have your people complete them electronically over the Internet. A good sample of completed Congregational Stewardship Questionnaires will supply you with much of the information you will need in order to complete your Church Stewardship Survey. The evaluation of the results of this second tool will help you design your agenda.

The third tool is Your Church's Giving Potential Worksheet. The results from this worksheet will give you an idea of your people's giving potential toward your church ministry vision. You can compare this to what they are currently giving. Another source for calculating this information is the "Giving Potential Calculator" on Vision Resourcing's website, www.visionresourcing.com/potential.htm.

The evaluation of all this information will guide you as you design and schedule your agenda. What is the strongest need your people feel, by age group? Where are they the weakest? Your team, along with counsel from your pastoral staff, will need to decide which activities are the most important at the start. Commit to what your current leadership resources can handle, start slowly, and gradually add activities over time. Remember, it will take time to bring your people to their full stewardship maturity. To successfully penetrate the hearts of your people, you must continually teach stewardship themes from every ministry platform, or "faucet," that you can.

MINISTRY "FAUCETS"

Below are suggested venues for teaching. These are the various ministry "faucets," each providing a unique aspect of stewardship education.

Preaching: Preaching must be a consistent part of your stewardship education process. Four or five sermons on the subject can provide good motivation and basic education in stewardship principles. Preaching, by itself, does not always cut deeply, but it gets the message out to almost everybody. And it is important because it shows the people where your pastor stands on the subject and demonstrates his faithfulness to teach the whole counsel of God's Word. Coordinate other avenues of teaching, such as personal devotionals or small group study outlines, with sermon topics to complement and reinforce the stewardship message. Also, remember that stewardship sermons should not only be on giving but also on debt reduction, budgeting, saving, and other stewardship topics. Specific content ideas for this can be found in Howard Dayton's chapter.

Worship: The offering time during worship services provides another important opportunity to teach stewardship. Instead of just asking the ushers to come forward and then praying, take a minute or two to try one of the following:

- Have a brief testimony from someone in your church who has been transformed into a godly steward in areas such as giving generously or getting out of credit card debt. Be sure to check the testimony for brevity and preparation! It might be best to put their testimony on video, if your congregation is very time sensitive.
- Have someone from your worship team or Stewardship Leadership Team read a verse or quotation relating to stewardship. An extensive list of verses, quotations, and factoids is available in Vision Resourcing's Resource Guide, pages 60 to 70 (available at www.visionresourcing.com). Another great source of verses on finances is Larry Burkett's book *The Word on Finances.*
- Include drama, music, and other forms of art in teaching stewardship.
- Include ministry reports of what God is doing through the church's

ministries or missions, indicating that the congregation's giving helped make it possible.

Keep these moments positive, to complement the other activities of stewardship education.

All-Church Tithing Sunday: Challenge the entire congregation to bring a full 10 percent of their monthly income as an offering on a designated Sunday. A second option is to have people write on a card (without indicating their name) how much their tithe would be if they gave 10 percent of their annual household income to the church. Tally this information, and report the totals back to the congregation. People will be amazed to discover that if they faithfully gave 10 percent of their income to the Lord's work through their local church, they could expand the church budget two to four times for missions, staff, new ministries, and regular operations.

Christian Education: You can create your own class lesson outlines or draw from the resources listed in this book. For your youth and children's classes, you can either modify these adult outlines or utilize the resources for different ages available through ministries like Crown Financial.

Small Groups: One of the greatest benefits of a small group approach is the opportunity to build close personal relationships. You can modify lesson outlines from larger classes for use in a small group setting, where participants can be most effectively motivated to apply what they learn about stewardship.

One on One: As part of your stewardship ministry, you may form a small group of trained financial counselors, or coaches, who can be available to help people individually with budgeting and debt reduction. Most churches have people in their congregation who are struggling with money management, keeping a budget, and debt—particularly credit card debt. Those people seeking individual counsel should be encouraged to also enroll in a small group financial Bible study. Most congregations also have members with the expertise and willingness to help. Interested counselor or coaching candidates need to be reminded of the intensive time commitment this entails before they sign up. Also, do not advertise this resource until you actually have a committed and trained group of counselors or coaches. You may receive more requests for help than you can handle!

Written Materials: Knowing that people in churches today experience information overload via TV, radio, twenty-four-hour instant news, email, Internet, cell phones, etc., we need to infuse clear communication about stewardship into the mix. Here are some suggestions for using written materials:

- *Church Newsletter*-Include a section in your church newsletter on the subject of stewardship. This section could include people's testimonies about their stewardship pilgrimage. A possible title for this column is "T3," which stands for "time, talent, and treasure." The intro to your "T3" column could look like this:

   Where is your heart? If you are not sure, look for your "treasure." Jesus said in Matthew 6:21, "For where your treasure is, there your heart will be also."[2] If you want to have a heart for His Kingdom, give generously of yourself to it, and your heart will follow. This is the introduction to our new "T3" column in (name your newsletter here). In determining where your heart is, ask yourself how you are doing with your three "Ts." In this column we will be sharing encouragement and ideas to help all of us become better stewards of our time, talent, and treasure.

- *Church Library*-There are many excellent books, booklets, videotapes, CDs, and DVDs on the subject of stewardship to include in your church library. Obviously, you will want to publicize their availability to your congregation.

- *Worship Folder*-Along with any announcements on stewardship activities, this is a good place to include quotes, verses, and mini-articles on aspects of stewardship.

- *Articles*–You may want to occasionally distribute to your people copies of good articles on some aspect of stewardship.
- *Bulletin Boards*–Develop displays and provide a "people friendly" bulletin board located strategically in the church facility. Provide informational handouts. Change the material frequently.
- *Thank-you Letters*–Send these to individuals who have been faithful in their giving. Also, mail and/or email general letters to your congregation, thanking them for their support and reminding them of how their giving has produced indicated ministry results.

New Member Classes: Your New Member Class is the opportunity to share the vision and mission of your church, and a wonderful opportunity to share your heart for stewardship. Use this class to "start them right" toward both understanding the basics of stewardship and recognizing their responsibility and privilege of supporting the mission of the church.

Premarital Counseling: Encourage couples to take a small group Bible study class on biblical finances. Have them attend one of your Sunday school stewardship classes or the Good $ense Budget Course. This can save them a lot of grief later on, since a major cause of marital stress is financial mismanagement.

Retreats and Seminars: *Repetition* is important for learning. Both retreats and seminars are good exposure for stewardship principles. You will want one of your Team members to lead in coordinating, promoting, and conducting the seminars. The actual teaching may be a video or live presentation by trained professionals.

Miscellaneous:
- **Say Thanks!** Print thank-you comments on giving reports, ministry updates, and vision-casting materials. Make personal thank-you phone calls to your *consistent* givers, not just your "big ones." Divide these calls among staff and key leaders.

- **Collect and Share Ministry Stories.** Collect stories from your church ministry leaders, and from missionaries and organizations your church supports, about the difference that the giving in your congregation is making, both within the church and beyond. Print these stories in your church newsletter, or use videos to share them at worship services or other church functions. They put a "face" on the facts and figures, so we know what God is doing through the generosity of the congregation.

- **Hold a Ministry or Mission Fair.** Annually have every ministry represented with displays in a single place to share their focus, service, and stories. This will excite members who do not realize the full scope of the ministries their church supports about their opportunity to give generously to the church.

- **Fund Your Stewardship Ministry.** It costs money to implement a stewardship ministry, year after year. Be sure to include a line item on your church budget to cover this expense.

- **Consider Establishing an Endowment Fund.** A good one to start with is a "Missions Endowment Fund" where you invite people to make major gifts, both current and deferred, into the fund that disperses the annual earnings to designated missions or ministries. Consult a professional who can assist you with the legal aspects of setting up the fund. Many givers want to give to an endowment fund where their money can "work" annually for their ministry of interest.

- **Offering Envelopes.** Provide offering envelopes to members and friends to encourage regular giving and serve as a reminder to give when members are away on a given Sunday.

- **Electronic Transfers.** More and more people today are comfortable using electronic transfers for regular payments, and some would like the convenience of giving this way to their church. This also helps in keeping them consistent in their giving. Consider setting up your receipting system and web page to accommodate this way of giving.

- **Home Visits.** Organize visits or focus groups in the homes of church members, not to secure commitments but to get better acquainted. You will want to find out how they are doing, what their ministry passion is, and if they have any suggestions for church leaders regarding the operation of the church and its ministries. Ask about their needs and prayer requests, and thank them personally for their commitment and financial support.

- **Conduct a Time and Talent Survey.** Annually promote and carry out a broad-based survey that allows members and friends to indicate ways in which they want to invest their time, talent, and energy in the coming months. Give them a list of ministry needs in the church. This will remind them of the responsibility and blessing of getting involved and giving of themselves.

- **Have a Brokerage Account.** It is relatively easy for a church to open an account with a stockbroker for the purpose of receiving gifts of stock. Gifts of appreciated stock are valuable to the church and also have significant tax advantages for the contributor. Clear policy guidelines should be in place regarding the processing, holding, or sale of such stock. Professional counsel regarding these transfers is essential.

- **Include Your Youth and Children in Your Stewardship Ministry.** Challenge them to give. Provide offering envelopes. Place your mature youth on some of your committees in order to gain from their perspective, to encourage them to have a sense of participation in what God is doing through their church, and to train them to lead their generation in coming years.

PROMOTING THE CHURCH'S STEWARDSHIP MINISTRY

To maintain momentum of your stewardship emphasis within the church, an ongoing communication strategy is important. This can be done regularly as you activate the different parts of the ministry. How promotion happens will depend on the communication resources of your church, but the goal is to keep the stewardship "message" in front of your people year after year. Look for creative ways to repeatedly remind your people of the importance of generosity in their Christian discipleship.

Occasionally tie your stewardship promotion and ministry needs directly to your church vision and mission. You should balance among general stewardship education, vision casting, and the promotion of a specific ministry need, such as a project that needs to be funded. All three are necessary. When your people understand who they are as a church and where they are going and why, they will begin to join you in owning it and supporting it.

Activating Your Agenda

So, how do you weave all of this together? Where do you start? Much of *what you do* and *when you do it* will depend on the size and culture of your church. It will depend on how ready your leadership is to commit to a stewardship ministry. To help you determine this, take the free Church Stewardship Health Survey on the Vision Resourcing website (www.visionresourcing.com/index.htm).

Wherever you start, your congregation needs to perceive that you are inviting them to become a part of the church mission through their stewardship and, most importantly, helping them be transformed into the image of Christ—and reflecting His generosity. Your goal is not just to get them to support the church budget, so avoid giving that impression. Make it a priority of the Stewardship Team to emphasize the connection between generous stewardship and Christian discipleship.

Finally, as you approach the one-or two-year mark in your agenda, it is time to evaluate how you are doing. One option is to go through the Stewardship Ministry Evaluation Checklist at the end of this chapter to evaluate your progress.

ESTATE AND GIFT PLANNING

In 2 Kings 20:1, the prophet Isaiah came to King Hezekiah, saying, "Put your house in order, because you are going to die; you will not recover." Basically, God told Hezekiah to complete his estate planning so that when he died his wishes could be carried out by those who survived him. Proverbs 13:22 says, "A good man leaves an inheritance for his children's children." Estate planning is the process of arranging your resources in such a way that, after you die, it properly affects the people in your life, transfers your property efficiently while minimizing probate and tax expense, and guides those who will assist you in achieving your goals. Included in this process is the opportunity to leave a charitable gift. It allows you to direct the material blessings with which God has endowed you away from government control and into the hands of people who will use it for God's work. We need to inform our church members of this opportunity and show them how to take advantage of it.

Planned giving, which is a part of estate planning, is an area of stewardship ministry that most churches neglect. Planned giving refers primarily to "deferred gifts" after members die and go to be with the Lord, although it can refer to current gifts that require special legal and tax assistance. Consider these two questions in this regard:

- How many funerals of church members and attendees did your church hold the past five years?
- How much money was given to your church through those decedents' estate plans?

Chances are, the amount was minimal. Statistics reveal that about 60 to 70 percent of Americans do *not* have a will or trust. Unfortunately, this is also representative of Christians. The real tragedy is that of those 30 to 40 percent who *do* have a will or trust, approximately 5 percent have remembered the Lord (including their church) in their estate plan.

The tiny minority of Christians who include God's work in their estate plans often leave it to a ministry other than their local church. Your people are being asked by other ministries and institutions to leave a portion of their estate to them when they die. This is wonderful, as it contributes to funding God's Kingdom. Many of these people would give to their church as well, if their church had a program to secure these planned gifts and bequests.

Experts estimate that between $10 and $45 *trillion* will be subject to estate transfer during the next fifteen to twenty years, the largest transfer of wealth in the history of the world. The April 1998 issue of "Give & Take" newsletter states, "90 percent or more of charitable bequests and a large percentage of bequest dollars are realized from the estates of lower and middle income persons who are seeking to make their 'gift of a lifetime.'"[3] Therefore, you do not have to have a large number of wealthy people in your congregation to benefit from deferred giving, since most charitable gifts come from individuals with average-sized estates.

A planned giving program in your stewardship ministry helps your people become better stewards of the estate that God has given them to manage. It not only saves potential probate expense and estate taxes, but it gives them peace and joy in knowing that their estate will help advance God's Kingdom. It is a win-win situation.

How do you provide basic estate and gift planning education for your congregation? The most productive way is to conduct estate-planning seminars once or twice a year. Invite qualified financial planners and estate-planning attorneys from your community to conduct seminars for your people. A good source of referrals for these is www.kingdomadvisors.org. Also, provide literature on aspects of estate and gift planning. Such literature can be obtained from denominational offices and companies that serve this area of financial planning.

CONCLUSION

Keep in mind that, as your stewardship ministry gradually helps your people grow and be conformed to the image of Christ, they will grow in stewardship maturity, and their increasing generosity in giving will provide the resources you need to fulfill your God-given vision. You will discover that you will need to rely less on campaigns and fundraisers to resource your vision. Your "asking" will be reporting what God is doing through your church ministry and inviting your people to participate in the blessing of giving. It will be an opportunity for them to worship and experience a deeper intimacy with God. This is transformational stewardship; this is the generosity that results from being conformed to the image of Christ.

RICHARD E. EDIC is founder and president of Vision Resourcing, a ministry that trains church leaders how to implement a successful stewardship ministry utilizing his training kit, "Resourcing Your Vision–A Church Stewardship Ministry Guide." For more than ten years he was the assistant to the president, Ministry Partner Services, of the Baptist General Conference, serving churches in the southwest region of the United States. He is a member of College Avenue Baptist Church in San Diego, California, and formerly led their stewardship ministry. Dick is also an Advanced Certified Stewardship Executive (A.C.S.E.) with the Christian Stewardship Association, and serves on the Crown Financial Ministries leadership team for San Diego County. He can be reached at dedic@visionresourcing.com.

1. Barna Research Group, "Americans Donate Billions to Charity, but Giving to Churches Has Declined," http://www.barna.org/FlexPage.aspx?Page=BarnaUpdate&BarnaUpdateID=187.
2. All Scripture quotations are taken from the New International Version.
3. "Give & Take" is a charitable giving publication of the Sharpe Group. Current issue and archives are available at http://www.sharpenet.com/gt/.

(SAMPLE)

Stewardship Ministry Evaluation Checklist

• How many people have received stewardship instruction in our adult Christian education classes, and what instructions were given? _____
_____
_____

• How many have been through a small group financial Bible study, and how many groups have been held? _____

• How well is our pastor providing effective leadership for stewardship ministry through
  • Preaching on stewardship? _____
  • Setting an example in stewardship? _____
  • Telling how God is using church member gifts? _____

• Do our members see our budget as a "mission statement" made tangible? Explain.
_____
_____

• Are we including a stewardship education column in our church newsletter? _____

• How are we involving our new people in our stewardship ministry? ·
_____
_____

• How many stewardship seminars have we held? _____
Which ones? _____
_____

• Are we holding stewardship "moments" just before taking the offering during our worship services? Explain. _____
_____

• How has our stewardship emphasis changed in the last year and a half? _____
_____

• How have we informed our people about estate and gift-planning options and given them an opportunity to exercise those options? _____
_____

• Knowing that most members will not grow in giving unless asked, how effectively have we challenged them to grow in their stewardship of:
   • Time? _____
   • Talents? _____
   • Treasure? _____

• How much has annual income increased to the church? $_____% _____

• How are we doing with teaching our youth and children in the area of stewardship?
_____

• What other observations can we make about our stewardship ministry?
_____

(SAMPLE)

Congregational Stewardship Questionnaire

We would appreciate your **candid** and **anonymous** response. In order to serve you better in the area of stewardship education and carry out our church's vision and global mission, we need your input and information. **DO NOT WRITE YOUR NAME** on the questionnaire. **It is anonymous**. Give totals as a family unit, not individual family members. Your candid answers will help us in designing an effective stewardship teaching agenda. Thank you so much! Your Stewardship Ministry Leadership Team.

1. How long has your family been attending _____(your church)_____?
1-5 yrs_____ 6-10 yrs_____ Over 10 yrs _____

2. How many total years have your family members known the Lord Jesus Christ as their personal Savior? _____ Describe the quality of their walk with the Lord. _____
_____
_____

3. Do your family members know their spiritual gift(s)? Yes _____ No _____

4. Is your family currently giving of their time and talent in a church ministry? Yes__ No__

5. What is your average gross family annual income? $25,000 to $49,999 _____
$50,000 to $74,999 _____ $75,000 to $99,999 _____ More than $100,000 _____

6. Do you have a current written budget that you follow daily? Yes _____ No _____

7. On average, are you spending more than your income each month? Yes _____ No _____

8. What is the current balance of your credit card debt? Zero __ $1000 to $5000 __ More__

9. What percentage of your gross family annual income do you currently give to the church?
1-3% ___ 3-4% ___ 4-5% ___ 5-6% ___ 6-7% ___ 7-8% ___ 8-9% ___ More %___

10. What percentage of your gross family annual income do you currently give to other ministries? _____What is the total percentage given to ministry? _____

11. Do you have a current written will or living trust? Yes _____ No _____

12. If you have a current written will or living trust, does it include a charitable bequest for the Lord's work? Yes _____ No _____ Is our church included? Yes _____ No _____

13. Would you be interested in receiving training in biblical money management, stewardship principles, and estate planning? Yes _____ No _____

14. What specific subjects or themes do you want to learn about? _____
_____
_____
_____

15. Any special needs, observations, or comments? _____
_____
_____
_____

(SAMPLE)

Church Stewardship Survey

CHURCH _____

PHONE _____

ADDRESS _____

CITY _____ ST _____ ZIP _____

PASTOR _____ AVERAGE ATTENDANCE_____

1. Describe the demographics of your church, i.e., age and ethnic mix, professional, "blue collar," single versus married, etc. _____

_____

2. Describe your *perception* of the spiritual condition of your members and attendees.

_____

_____

3. Does your church teach spiritual gifts? _____

4. How well do your people offer their time and talent to the ministry of the church? _____

_____

_____

5. Is your church receiving adequate finances? Are you meeting your budget requirements? __

_____

_____

6. What was your church's *average* income per year the past three years? _____

7. What is your Sunday morning attendance percentage growth per year compared to giving income percentage growth, if any, for the past five years?_____

8. What money did your church receive the past five years from bequests? _____

_____

9. How do you "raise money" for your church? Events? Preaching? Other?_____

_____

10. If the church had sufficient finances, what would be its priority goals for ministry? _____

_____

_____

11. What percentage of the church budget is allocated for missions? _____

12. How are missions funds raised? It is part of our church budget ___ Faith promises, over and above regular giving ___ Specific designation ___ Other _____

13. The individual average annual *gross income* of our people is _____

14. What is the average percent of gross family income that your people *say* they are giving to the church? _____ To other ministries? _____ Total? _____

15. What percent of their annual *gross income*, on average, are they actually giving to the church? _____

16. What is the *potential* giving of your congregation if they were to tithe the *full 10 percent* of their gross income to the church? _____ (To calculate, multiply the number of households, or giving "units," by their *average* gross family income by 10 percent. You determine the *average* household, or gross family income, from the replies you receive from the questionnaires you distributed.)

17. What percentage of your people have a written will or living trust? _____

18. What percentage of those who *have a will or trust* have included a charitable bequest for the Lord's work, including your church? _____ What percent would like to? _____

19. What percentage of your people have a written budget that they are following daily? _____

20. What percentage of your people are spending, on average, *more* than they make each month? _____

21. What is the average amount of credit debt (other than house mortgage) that your people are carrying each month? _____

22. What stewardship education has been provided by the church for your people?
_____
_____

23. What specific training in stewardship have your people requested?
_____
_____

24. How well do you think your people are managing their personal finances?
_____

25. Do you think they would benefit from some practical and biblical training in the area of financial management and estate planning? Yes ___ No ___ Explain _____
_____
_____

26. In what priority areas of stewardship education and development do you as a church most feel the need for help and training?
_____
_____

27. Any other observations or comments? _____
_____
_____
_____

Your Church's Giving Potential Worksheet

(by Pastor Jay Pankratz, Rialto Baptist Church, California)

Your Church	Example	Calculations
1. Number of households in the congregation is:	125	_____
2. The average household income (estimate) is:	$26,122	_____
3. Total estimated income of congregation is: (#1 x #2)	$3,265,250	_____
4. Last year's total giving:	$75,133	_____
5. Average dollar giving per household was (#4 divided by #1)	$601	_____
6. Average percentage giving per household of total income was: (# 4 ÷ # 3)	2.3%	_____
7. If each home increased giving by 1% of income, the church would receive: (add 1% to #6 x #3)	$107,753	_____ (or 3.3%)
8. Dollar and percentage increase next year: (dollar = #7–#4; percent = #7–#4 divided by #7)	$32,620	_____ (or 30.3%)
9. If every family tithed to the church, it would receive: (multiply #3 x 10%)	$326,525	_____

TEACHING
FINANCIAL PRINCIPLES
IN THE CHURCH

BY HOWARD L. DAYTON,
Co-founder of Crown Financial Ministries

L ook at my new car, my beautiful home in the suburbs, my pool and deck, my golf club membership, and my latest, greatest everything!" After proudly strutting his stuff, the guy in the commercial admits, "I'm in debt up to my eyeballs." Then, with a plastered-on smile that attempts to hide his desperation, he pleads, "Somebody help me!"

He is one of hundreds of thousands sitting in our churches: looking good, trying hard to get it right, and extremely confused. Although it is unfair to blame the church for all of the confusion and financial stress of its members, we must admit that it has not adequately prepared them for the onslaught of our unrelenting consumer culture.

Many Christians in church pews today resemble the rest of the culture when it comes to money. Many of them: (1) give little, (2) save little, (3) spend more than they earn, (4) are slaves to debt, and (5) have a mixed commitment to honesty in their financial struggle. Identifying these symptoms is certainly a beginning, but it does not provide a strategy for treatment. Simply saying "give more," "save more," "be honest," etc., doesn't get to the heart of the matter.

These symptoms of financial illness require more than a simple Band-Aid. They are broken bones that need to be reset in order to heal properly. As seen throughout this book, a faulty worldview (particularly one neglecting truth about God's nature and plan for us to become conformed to the image of Christ) underlies the problem. Generally, it is when believers improve their understanding of who God is that they can move into a closer relationship with Him and then experience positive change in their lives.

Many believers are shocked to learn that God has provided over 2,350 verses dealing with money and possessions *for their benefit*. Unfortunately, teaching within the church has largely neglected these truths, leaving God's people to conclude that His interest is limited to 10 percent of their income—as though He cares only about what they give. Struggling to manage the other 90 percent from the perspective of popular culture, they conclude that they cannot afford to honor God with even the 10 percent they think He cares about.

While Christians frequently declare a faith that sets them apart from the culture, they are often indistinguishable from it in the ways they handle their resources.[1] They do not realize God cares enough about their daily lives to help them earn, save, and spend wisely, give generously, maintain integrity, get out of debt, experience contentment, develop an eternal perspective, and teach their children to do the same.

The good news is that the current dilemma offers an unprecedented opportunity to teach and show God's love and wisdom through church and parachurch programs. Effective demonstrations of love and wisdom create a receptive environment for churchwide stewardship and its resulting global outreach. In previous chapters, Richard Towner described the church's role in this endeavor, and Richard Edic provided examples of how to structure the church's stewardship education program. Now it is time to suggest specific stewardship teaching content for educating church members. This content can be used in sermons, seminars, Sunday school classes, small groups, and similar settings. A more comprehensive listing of resources is available at the end of the chapter. The information that follows will provide church members with a solid biblical foundation of key financial principles. These principles form the core of a Christian worldview of possessions and are the basis for growth toward mature Christian stewardship.

CONTENT THEMES

In considering what to teach, it is important to remember that the Bible is teeming with passages on money—not because of what God wants *from* believers but because of what He wants *for* believers (see, e.g., Job 7:17–18). God sent His only Son to redeem the world (John 3:16). He has given believers His truth to set them free (John 8:31–32). He does not want them to return to bondage of any kind (John 8:34–36), including financial (Prov. 22:7).

It is in this context that we emphasize God's heart and base our teaching on the authority of His Word (2 Tim. 3:16; Titus 1:7–9) rather than the needs of a church budget. Even when talking about giving, the motivation should not be about getting something *from* believers; rather, it is what God wants to do *for* them. It is about growing givers' hearts to be rich toward God. God wants to show His power on their behalf. He wants them to be generous because they are conformed to His Son's image. He wants them to be free to serve Him. Therefore, when teaching about God's financial principles, the focus should be on transforming the heart so believers are conformed to the image of Christ and become generous, just as He is.

Effective teaching utilizes both principles and stories to facilitate heart transformation. Principles are taught well through asking good questions and the ensuing process of discovering the answers. Here is a model for a logical flow of good questions on the topic of biblical financial principles:

1. Is there an authority on the issue in question?

2. Is the authority credible?

3. Does the authority speak clearly to the issue?

4. What does the authority say?

5. How does it apply to our situation?

6. Do we need to change our thinking?

7. Do we need to change our actions?

These questions, although not usually acknowledged explicitly in the lesson itself, lead the thinking process that satisfies our need for logical explanations.

With the underlying assumption that the Bible is an authority on this topic, I offer the following questions to assist in the preparation of your own teaching. They logically cluster around four themes: (1) God's power, (2) God's care, (3) God's character, and (4) God's design. All four themes reveal ways in which we have marginalized God and not allowed Him to transform our hearts to be rich toward Him. The first three themes create a solid, thoughtful foundation that helps us establish trust in God, encompassing what we often refer to as "God's Part" in our finances. Until believers have a solid sense of God's trustworthiness, any tactical instruction falls on less than fertile ground. But once they see God more accurately and their trust begins to grow, they are ready for the fourth theme: God's design. This we refer to as "Our Part" in our finances, and it answers the question, "What does He want *me* to do?"

This list of questions and references will springboard you to many others. Although the answers to some of these questions may be a simple yes or no, they have far-reaching implications. Do not pass too quickly over them. Dare to be dramatic. As you unpack these questions, take your congregation with you on a journey of exploration. Through freshly awakened minds, changing perspectives, and the power of God, your church will be transformed.

GOD'S PART

Teaching first about God's role as owner and provider gives the necessary context for us to understand our role as stewards.

God's Power

We have marginalized God by underestimating His power.

- Did God create everything? *(Gen. 1:1)*
- Does He own it all? *(Pss. 24:1; 50:10–12)*
- Does He control events despite our perception that our free will is the ultimate determiner of outcomes? *(1 Chron. 29:11; 1 Sam. 2:3–10; Ps. 135:6; Prov. 20:24; Dan. 4:34–35; Isa. 45:6–7; Rom. 8:28)*
- Is it reasonable to think, when we disagree with God, that we are right? *(Job 40:1–5; Isa. 55:8–9)*
- How should we approach our inevitable disagreements? Shouldn't we assume He is right and that we need to adjust by increasing our understanding of Him and His ways? *(Job 42:1–6; Isa. 55:7)*
- Can (and does) God thwart our efforts to "get ahead" when we fail to put Him first? *(Deut. 28:15–68; 2 Chron. 24:20; 26:5; Jer. 10:21; 48:7; Prov. 10:22; 11:28; Hos. 2; Hag. 1:4–11)*
- Do we understand that "getting ahead" means more than mere accumulation—that accumulation without contentment is misery? *(Ps. 106:14–15; Num. 11:4, 33–34; Eccl. 5:10–13, 18–20; 1 Tim. 6:6–10, 17)*
- Does it make sense to stay on the wrong side of God on any issue? Do we want to hang on to a strategy that is guaranteed to lose?
- Is there any priority in life that should come ahead of moving in God's direction?

When we acknowledge God's ownership, every spending decision becomes a spiritual decision. No longer do we ask, "Lord, what do You want me to do with *my* money?" The question is restated, "Lord, what do You want me to do with *Your* money?"

We should manage God's possessions to the best of our ability, but we need not fear their loss to circumstances beyond our control. We can say with Job, "The Lord gave and the Lord has taken away. Blessed be the name of the Lord" (Job 1:21).[2]

God's Care

We have marginalized God by thinking He is uninterested in our welfare, including how we handle our finances.

- Does the Bible demonstrate God's unwillingness to give up on us despite our chronic refusal to obey His better way? *(Matt. 23:33–39)*
- Of all of the blessings God has promised in the covenants He has made with us, which ones failed because of His unfaithfulness rather than ours?
- What basis do we have for believing that God will provide for and reward those who put Him first? *(Lev. 25:20–22; Deut. 7:12–15; 8:15–18; 15:4–6; 28:1–14; 29:9; 30:9–10, 15–16; Josh. 1:8; 1 Sam. 18:14–15; 1 Kings 2:3; 2 Chron. 25:6–9; Pss. 33:18–19; 34:9–10; 37:4; 81:13–16; 128:1–2; Prov. 10:3; 22:4; 28:25; Jer. 27:5; Matt. 6:33; Luke 12:30–31; Phil. 4:19)*
- Why are we tempted to think God is holding out on us—that His will for us is less beneficial than what we want for ourselves? Why have we not learned the most basic lesson of Satan's temptation of Adam and Eve?

God's Character

We have marginalized God by thinking His attributes do not apply to the fallen world in which we live.

- **Eternal**
  - What implications does God's eternality have for cultivating a long-term perspective rather than our natural short-term perspective; for cultivating eternal values that satisfy deeply rather than immediate gratification that quickly turns to emptiness and regret?
  - How do we retrain our minds to live for the line (eternity) rather than the dot (this brief life on earth)? *(Ps. 90:10, 12; Matt. 6:19–21; Rom. 14:10–12; Col. 3:1–6; 1 Tim. 6:7; Heb. 11:24–26; 2 Peter 3:10–11)*
- **Righteous**
  - What integrity compromises do we make because we don't trust

God to "keep the books"? Do we realize He judges and vindicates? *(1 Sam. 24:12–20; Pss. 35:24–28; 43:1–5; 54:1–7; 135:5–18; Jer. 51:5–10; Rom. 12:17–21; 1 Cor. 6:7–11; Matt. 6:1–6)*

- How can we, in light of God's power and goodness, ever rationalize personal dishonesty?

- How do we conclude that God is either unable or unwilling to hold us accountable for our dishonesty? *(Ps. 101:6–7; Prov. 13:11; Heb. 12:4–11)*

- Do we not understand—regardless of momentary appearances—that the eternal playing field favors righteousness? *(Rom. 8:18–39; Eph. 3:14–20; 2 Peter 1:3–4; Jude 1:24–25)*

- How do we conform to God's requirement for justice and absolute honesty? *(Lev. 6:4–5, 19:11; Prov. 4:24–26; Luke 19:8; John 14:15; Rom. 13:9–10; Gal. 5:16–17; 1 John 1:9)*

• **Loving**

- Do we judge God's love by His willingness to "fix" things for us?

- Do we understand that "fixing" things would mean annihilating us? We *are* the problem when we demand freedom to act and simultaneous freedom from consequences.

- Do we see God's love in the fact that He chooses to weep for us and with us rather than eliminate us from His presence? *(Matt. 23:37; Rom. 5:8–11; Col. 1:21–22)*

- How can we grasp the mercy of God's patience with our rebellion? *(Rom. 9:22–26; 11:32; Eph. 2:1–10; Titus 3:3–7; 2 Peter 3:9)*

- How do we reflect His love (generosity, mercy, patience, etc.) to those around us?

The Lord is the One who provides our needs. In Genesis 22:14 God is spoken of as Jehovah-jireh, which means "the Lord will provide." The same Lord who fed manna to the children of Israel during their forty years of wandering in the wilderness, and who fed five thousand with only five loaves and two fish, has promised to provide for our needs.

OUR PART
God's Design
We marginalize God when we think He has not given us practical, effective instructions for managing what He has entrusted to us.

- **Earning**
  - Has God given us work as a blessing or a curse? *(Gen. 2:15)*
  - From where do we get our aptitudes, interests, and abilities? *(Ex. 36:1; 1 Cor. 12)*
  - What is God's role in our level of promotion? What is ours? *(Ps. 75:6–7; Eph. 6:5–8)*
  - What instructions does He give us as employees? As employers? *(Eccl. 9:10; Prov. 12:27; Col. 3:23–24) (Deut. 24:14–15; Job 31:13–15; Mal. 3:5; Col. 4:1; Eph. 6:9)*

- **Giving**
  - How can we understand that God wants the best *for* us, not *from* us? *(Luke 6:38; Acts 20:35)* Our possessions are meaningless to the One who created and owns everything. But our hearts are His treasure *(Mark 12:30; Heb. 8:10)*, and He knows our hearts follow our possessions. *(Matt. 6:21)*
  - Can we understand that developing the habit of giving *first* (before saving, paying bills, etc.) both develops and proves our faith? *(Prov. 3:5–10)* We *cannot* please God without faith. *(Heb. 11:6)*
  - Do we see the discrepancy of being Christ-followers—mortal images of God to a dying world—and being unlike Him in generosity? *(Deut. 15:10–11; Prov. 14:31; Jer. 22:16; Ezek. 16:49; Matt. 25:31–45; John 3:16; Heb. 13:16)*

- Do we understand that God desires to bless our giving so that we can continue it and even grow in it? *(Mal. 3:10; 2 Cor. 9:6–11)*
- Can we cultivate an eagerness to give as an opportunity to demonstrate our gratitude and loyalty to the One who has given us everything? *(Ex. 35:21–29; 2 Cor. 8:1–4; 1 Tim. 6:17–19)*
- Can we learn to give gladly and generously to the poor—not because it will fix everything for them but because it is in keeping with God's character and command—and trust Him with the practical results? *(Deut. 15:11; Prov. 14:21; 2 Cor. 9:12; Heb. 13:16)*
- What does it say about our values if we will plan and sacrifice for a bigger house or newer car but not for the opportunity to give more?

• **Saving**

- Do we understand that God expects us to live prudently—with wisdom—and gives us instructions on how to do it? *(Gen. 41:34–36; Isa. 48:17–18)*
- Do we see that the perspective and discipline required to develop the habit of saving will help us acquire a long-term (mature) mind-set? *(Prov. 21:5, 20; 28:20, 22)*
- Do we recognize the temptation to allow our savings and investments to become our security, competing with God's unique role as Provider in our life? The early leaders of our nation had the wisdom to stamp on our currency "In God We Trust." In other words, "Here is my money, and it is important, but my trust remains in God." *(Luke 12:16–21; Phil. 4:19; 1 Tim. 6:17)*
- Do we understand that God wants us to be conduits—even in our saving—through which His blessings can flow for the benefit of others? *(Lev. 19:9–10; Deut. 15:7–10; Ps. 112; Prov. 11:24–25; Isa. 58:6–11; Ezek. 16:49; Luke 6:38; 2 Cor. 8:13–15; Gal. 6:10)*

• **Spending/Avoiding Debt**

- Do we understand that debt is a form of slavery, making us a servant of our debtors? *(Prov. 22:7)*

– Do we understand that consumer debt (not a home mortgage or business loan) is the result of spending more than we earn? Why do we think it will not catch up with us? *(Prov. 21:20; James 4:13–15)*

– Do we know where our money is going? Exactly? How can we find our way out of a mess without knowing where we are? Do we think ignorance can be a part of spiritual maturity? *(Prov. 27:23)*

– Do we understand that how we handle money and possessions is a test designed by God? *(Matt. 25:21; Luke 12:14–21, 32–34; 16:10–12)*

- **Contentment**

  – Do we understand the difference between needs and wants? *(1 Tim. 6:8)*

  – Do we realize there is no end to uncontrolled appetites? *(Phil. 3:18–19; 1 Tim. 6:9–10)*

  – Do we recognize the connection between discontentment and covetousness? *(Ex. 20:17)*

  – Have we learned the secret of contentment and the power and peace it brings? *(Phil. 4:11–13; 1 Thess. 4:11–12)*

  – Do we recognize the promise of God's presence as the source of contentment? *(Heb. 13:5)*

  – Do we understand the meaninglessness of "success" apart from serving Christ? *(Luke 12:20–21; Mark 8:36; Phil. 3:7–14)*

These questions and the study of the corresponding Scripture references should supply enough content for the congregation to begin implementing the principles that are important for heart transformation, conforming to Christ, and becoming generous, godly stewards.

Once both God's role and our role are identified in a broad sense, the audience often is ready for practical application. This should focus on four core areas of our financial lives: earning, honesty, debt, and saving. Earning refers to one's attitude toward work and diligence in completing it. Work is designed for more than utilitarian benefit; it is also a vocation or calling, a way to glorify God on this earth.[3] If the Christian's work is intended to glorify God, then that work and all resulting financial responsibility should be conducted with honesty. Honesty is crucial because it reflects the truthfulness of the Creator, strengthens our faith, and establishes credibility so that evangelism can be effective.[4] In being responsible stewards, we also need to strive to stay debt free. Although Scripture never calls debt a sin, it discourages it, considering it a form of slavery.[5] The final component of practical application is saving. Saving is a form of godly stewardship because in intentionally setting aside money, generosity toward God's Kingdom can grow.

Teaching to the Heart

Our hearts are God's treasure. Imagine standing face-to-face with Him and asking the question, "What do You want from me?" His answer might vary depending on what *you* value, but from His perspective the meaning is always the same: "Give Me your heart."

This book is about creating a revolution in generosity. For some who have lived long without practicing biblical generosity, it may take a few steps to reach the point where giving for the church's expenses is a fulfilling experience. One of the early steps in that transformation is teaching generosity for the sake of the poor. Participating in a campaign focused on a specific need of our hurting world helps many people learn the joy of generosity.

All of our church teaching should have the same ultimate goal: helping people surrender their heart to be conformed to Christ and become part of His great reconciliation plan. When we talk about money, it is not because God needs money; it is because money is a heart issue. Remember at all times the end goal: transformation of the heart. The following is a letter that exemplifies how money issues can be the catalyst to heart transformation.

My life was in good shape. I was a civil engineer with a master's degree before I married Maria. We figured we were entitled to the life-style our parents had. In fact, we thought we should have more—and have it right away. Almost overnight, we had a mortgage, family loans, and an additional $55,000 in debt.

We were carrying about twelve credit cards at the time, shifting the balances among them to stay ahead—not a good situation.

When my reserve platoon went on a two-week training exercise, I spent a lot of time in the command center. Wouldn't you know it? I heard fourteen straight days of Crown broadcasts. And I accepted Christ as Savior.

A short time later, the Lord allowed me to suffer a fever during which I dreamed that I died and left my wife with huge financial problems. It was time for a change.

When I got back home, Maria and I began attending church, tithing, and growing in our faith. And with all the input I was getting from Crown, we started paying off our debt. There's no way we should have been able to pay off $55,000 in four years, but God blessed us in unexpected ways. Crown's small group study and Money Map Coach training have prepared us to help ourselves and others.

Business by the Book, the "Dividends" newsletter, and Crown's Career Direct assessment have all been instrumental in the success of my business partnership, which is now debt free and tithing.

I guess we've become fanatics.

—*Ken and Maria Atkins*

In conclusion, remember that the essence of the content we teach concerning financial principles is heart transformation. Jesus, understanding that money is the key to most hearts, highlighted it in His teaching. I pray that the Lord will bless your efforts to equip the people of your church to handle money God's way. It is one of the most helpful things you can do for your congregation and the financial health of your church.

LINKS AND OTHER RESOURCES
Resources for Pastors

- Generous Giving: **http://www.generousgiving.org**
  - Including an index of Scripture passages related to stewardship: http://www.generousgiving.org/page.asp?sec=9&page=618
- Maximum Generosity: **http://www.kluth.org**
  - Ten things pastors should know: http://www.kluth.org/church/10Th ingsPastorsNeedToKnow.htm
  - Helpful quotations for sermons: http://www.kluth.org/1quotes.htm
  - Audio and downloadable resources that include outlines and handouts, which can be used as seminar resources as well: http://www. kluth.org/1audio.htm
- Leadership Skills Inc.: **http://www.leaderskillsinc.com**
  - This website, the online home of Rod Rogers, has multiple resources including articles and kits: http://www.leaderskillsinc.com/christian-pastors-resources.htm
- Rick Warren's Pastors Network: **http://www.pastors.com**
  - Free sermons include a few on stewardship: http://www.pastors.com/en-US/FreeSermons/RicksFreeSermons.htm

Seminars

- Crown Financial Ministries: **http://www.crown.org**
  - Partner with Crown to host a seminar at your church: http://www.crown.org/Seminars
- Good $ense: **http://www.goodsenseministry.com**
  - This ministry through the Willow Creek Association offers seminars for church leaders to attend.

Sunday School, Small Groups, and Personal Study

Numerous books could be helpful, but the ideal solution is a study course designed specifically for small groups, such as Crown's ten-week Biblical Financial Study, which presents a comprehensive approach that incorporates all of the necessary practical application tools and forms along with video support and a strong accountability component.

Study Courses:

- Maximum Generosity: Available from **www.kluth.org**
  - Kluth's "40 Day Spiritual Journey to a More Generous Life": This booklet is good for the whole church or small groups.
- Crown Financial Ministries: Available from: http://www.crown.org/store
  - *Road to Financial Freedom:* four-week introductory, churchwide curriculum that teaches an entire church how to handle money God's way
  - *Discovering God's Way of Handling Money:* Video-driven study
  - *The Treasure Principle Workshop* By Randy Alcorn and Howard Dayton
  - *Business by the Book Workshop* By Larry Burkett, Howard Dayton, and Dave Rae
  - *Biblical Financial Study*, Crown's flagship study for life groups

Books by Howard Dayton (www.crown.org/store):

- *Your Money Counts: The Biblical Guide to Earning, Spending, Saving, Investing, Giving, and Getting Out of Debt*
- *Free and Clear: God's Roadmap to Debt-Free Living*
- *Your Money Map: A Proven 7-Step Guide to True Financial Freedom*

God and Your Stuff: The Vital Link between Your Possessions and Your Soul by Wes Willmer and Martyn Smith, NavPress. This ten-chapter book has group study questions in the back.

Children

Crown Financial Ministries: Available from: http://www.crown.org/store

- *The ABC's of Handling Money God's Way:* For ages 5–7
- *The Secret of Handling Money God's Way:* For ages 8–12
- *Family Times Stewardship Virtue Pack:* For K–5th grades. Made in partnership with Crown Financial Ministries and the reThink Group.
- *Discovering God's Way of Handling Money Teen Study:* For ages 13–17

HOWARD L. DAYTON is the co-founder of Crown Financial Ministries, which he started with the late Larry Burkett. Crown is an interdenominational ministry with the global mission of equipping people to learn, apply, and teach God's financial principles. Howard is heard nationwide on his syndicated radio broadcast, "Money Matters." He is the author of several books, including *Your Money Counts, Free and Clear,* and *Your Money Map.* After graduating from Cornell University, Howard served as a naval officer and developed successful businesses before founding Crown. Howard can be contacted at Howard.Dayton@crown.org.

1. Jeffery Sheler, Caroline Hsu, and Angie C. Marek, "Nearer My God to Thee," *US News & World Report* 136, no. 15 (2004), 59.
2. Unless otherwise noted, Scripture quotations are taken from the New American Standard Bible.
3. Dorothy Sayers, *Letters to a Diminished Church* (Nashville: Thomas Nelson, 2004), chapter 11.
4. Philippians 2:15 ESV.
5. Dèuteronomy 28:12 ESV.

Chapter

CONDUCTING GENEROSITY
INITIATIVES AND CAPITAL
CAMPAIGNS IN CHURCHES

BY BRIAN P. KLUTH, *Senior Pastor of the First Evangelical*
Free Church in Colorado Springs, CO

INTRODUCTION

One of the most vital and life-changing topics a church can address in spiritual transformation is moving people from being self-centered misers toward being Christ-centered, generous stewards. Planning a holistic stewardship ministry is vital to the lives of the people in your church and the health of its ministry.

This chapter will focus on practical ways to conduct *generosity initiatives*, both *campaigns for ongoing generosity* and special *capital projects* in your church. First we will look at the purpose of such inititiatives, and then at their application—with essential ingredients to help your onetime and ongoing financial support programs to succeed.

A generosity initiative is a churchwide focus on the biblical calling for people to be faithful and generous givers to God's work. This initiative should include a specific timeline, a plan, and resources that encourage giving to God as a vital aspect of people's spiritual lives and growth. When a congregation's pastor and leaders begin a generosity initiative, they will find themselves on common ground with spiritual leaders from the pages of Scripture. The Bible reveals numerous leaders who were used by God to encourage support for regular ministry funding, including Moses, Nehemiah, Solomon, Hezekiah, and Malachi. The Gospels recount Jesus Christ's challenges to move to greater levels of generosity. Scripture recounts six building and renovation project initiatives and additional generosity efforts for itinerant ministry, benevolence ministries, relief work, and missionary efforts.[1]

The Lord delights in leaders who direct His people away from the quicksand of materialism, consumerism, greed, and idolatry to the solid ground of being conformed to the image of Christ and living with a generous heart for the glory of God. When you have a vision for teaching God's Word on finances and generosity, transformation will follow, and it will be exciting to see how lives are changed in the area of giving for the glory of God and the benefit of others.

Living unselfishly and giving generously to God's work are common themes throughout Scripture. Generosity initiatives in the Bible are divided into two fundamental groups: teaching initiatives that generated faithful support for the Lord's work on an *ongoing basis*, and campaigns for *special projects*, usually related to building expansion and renovations, or missions and relief ministry. Both will be discussed later in the chapter.

Campaigns to Encourage Faithful Giving

Teaching on finances and generosity is a "silent subject" in many churches. I often tell church leaders, "No church has a money problem; they have a faithfulness problem." While God has generously given financial blessings, resources, and provisions to many of His people, they need solid teaching, encouragement, and opportunities to faithfully share the best of what God has given them for the Lord's work at their church and beyond.

When you intentionally instruct for and facilitate people's transformation to be rich toward God by giving generously to the Lord's work at your church, you are helping them become conformed to the image of Christ. Matthew 6:21 says, "Where your treasure is, there your heart will be also."[2] Sadly, in many churches, 25 to 40 percent (and sometimes even 50 percent) of those attending most weeks have giving records of zero dollars. When someone attends church weekly but does not learn to give faithfully and generously, then his or her heart is not with the work of the church. But when you help people grow in the knowledge and grace of giving, you are helping them attach their hearts, with their money, to the Kingdom of God, where Christ's heart is.

KEY INGREDIENTS FOR CULTIVATING ONGOING GENEROSITY

Ingredient 1: Sermon message or series by the pastor or guest speaker. As a rudder steers a sailing ship, the pulpit steers the congregation. A pastor can find great freedom and boldness to preach a generosity message when it is based on the authority of God's Word, not only the needs of the church budget (see Howard Dayton's chapter). Of course, preaching on generosity with passion and conviction can only follow the pastor's own commitment to living and giving generously. Learning to give faithfully, even on a meager salary, will embolden a pastor's faith in God to enable him or her to teach authentically. Additionally, a guest speaker can effectively deliver a generosity message that deeply penetrates lives and transforms giving attitudes and habits, in ways that its own pastor cannot.

Ingredient 2: Written communications and/or devotional reading materials mailed to homes. While preaching can steer the ship, study of Bible devotional readings at home is the engine that will propel people's stewardship to new destinations. Devotional reading on this topic should be clear, biblical teaching and easy to read. The material should help people assess their giving to the Lord's work in light of their income sources, lifestyle choices, and financial assets. It is more effective to mail materials, as opposed to just placing them on a back table to pick up. When you mail your generosity materials to every household, people have the quietness of their own home to read, reflect on, and discuss the topic. You can use these materials to highlight the key goals the church has already met and potential subsequent plans, through examples of how giving has helped in the past and will be useful in the future.[3]

Ingredient 3: Sharing testimonies on giving. Personal testimonies have the power to inspire. You can incorporate into the service two- to four-minute testimonies (live or on video) of how individuals learned spiritual lessons about giving, or include quotes and stories in materials you mail out. I remember a single mother who once stood in front of the congregation and told how she was raising three young boys on a $24,000 per year income while she was also $24,000 in debt. Despite her situation, she was led to begin faithfully giving at least 10 percent of her income to the Lord's work even though it seemed highly impractical. God faithfully provided in creative ways, and eventually she was completely out of debt. She spoke with such joy and passion that it moved everyone listening to think about his or her own need to trust God in regard to money.

Ingredient 4: Family, class, or small group discussions. In order to help people process what they are reading, hearing, and learning, it is helpful to provide opportunities and questions for discussion. Thought-provoking, memory-jogging, soul-stirring questions can help transform people from miserly, tightfisted takers to joyful, generous stewards who are rich toward God. In these smaller settings, people often feel more willing to share and a generous spirit can be not only *taught* but *caught* from others in the group.[4]

Ingredient 5: Commitment/Consecration Sunday(s) with response cards. If you are going to take people on a stewardship journey, make sure you help them recognize where they should arrive—whether that is a new mindset about giving, a new desire, or a new plan to be more faithful and generous to the Lord's work—and help them take steps in that direction. Choose a specific Sunday or Sundays when people turn in a response card indicating their intended financial giving or ways they can provide their time and talent to specific ministries in the coming year. When John Maxwell was a pastor, for instance, he conducted a four-week preaching series every January on finances and generosity that culminated in people turning in cards that indicated: (1) I will start tithing this year, (2) I will continue to tithe this year, or (3) I will increase my tithes and offerings to the church this year.[5]

A list of places to find more resources for generosity initiatives is provided at the end of this chapter.

SPECIAL CAPITAL PROJECTS

Any congregation that is around long enough will find that eventually facilities need to be expanded, renovated, or maintained, requiring funds beyond the normal operating budget of the church. Occasionally, a church may need to relocate because of space problems or drastic changes in the neighborhood or congregation. There are also times when previous projects were accomplished with the use of borrowed funds, causing monthly payments that hamper ongoing ministry costs. Special multiyear capital campaigns can be used to accomplish church expansion, renovations, relocation, or debt retirement and move the church forward.

A *one-year capital campaign drive* can be used to raise dollars for projects requiring 15 to 40 percent of the church's annual budget. *Multiyear pledge drives* should be used to secure financial commitments to accomplish expansion, renovations, relocation, or debt-retirement projects that will require gifts equal to 50 percent to 300 percent of a church's annual budget. Below are some key reasons to conduct a capital campaign, followed by practical steps for success.

Reason 1: Move forward in your ministry. If you attempt to do everything needed for your church with funds from your annual operating budget, you may quickly discover you are restrained from taking any great strides forward. Building projects, renovations, and major maintenance projects require a significant influx of cash that cannot be generated without the clarion call of "It's time to build," expand, fix, relocate, etc. The focus, energy, and passion of a capital campaign will marshal energy, leadership, and resources to take your church to a new level.

Reason 2: Facilities facilitate ministry. I'm not a big believer in "if you build it, they will come," but I do believe that "if they're coming, you need to build it or expand it." Ultimately, church is not about building buildings but building lives. But facilities that meet the needs of the ministries that use them enhance discipleship opportunities. Youth groups need space to operate, nurseries need room for babies, sanctuaries allow God's people to worship together, and fellowship halls allow people to gather.

If your church uses an older facility, it is important to properly care for what God has entrusted to you. It should not look sloppy (e.g., peeling paint, torn/dirtied carpets, broken light fixtures, and cracked windows). A capital campaign can be conducted to bring in financial resources that people do not give for the regular budget but would use to improve, renovate, or expand facilities. In the Scriptures there are a number of places where God raised up leaders to mobilize the people to give generously and to fix facilities that had fallen into disrepair (e.g., Haggai, Joash, Nehemiah). A friend and former staff member of mine took the pastorate at a small struggling church in Nebraska with only twenty-five people in attendance. For years the steeple was broken, the shingles were coming off the roof, and the boiler was not working properly. He mobilized this small congregation to fix up God's house as an act of worship. Not only did the building get fixed up, but the momentum generated also led to a men's early morning discipleship group with eighteen men in attendance, an AWANA Bible Club program for children that grew to ninety in attendance, and a cooperative youth group with a number of the other churches in the area.

Reason 3: Big gifts flow to big vision. The Bible says, "Where there is no vision, the people perish."[6] A wise pastor once quipped, "Without vision, the people go to another parish."[7] And a fundraising consultant would say, "Without money, the vision perishes."

A man once approached his pastor and said, "Pastor, if you could have any amount of money to help this church, how much would you need and what would you do with it?" The pastor thought for a while and said, "If I could just receive an extra $500, I would fix up the ladies' restroom." Unbeknownst to the pastor, the man had come in with $100,000 to give to the Lord's work. If the pastor had had a $100,000 vision (or greater), the man would have given the entire amount to the church. Instead, he said, "Pastor, that's great. Here's $500 to get the job done." The pastor was happy, but the man was saddened and went out and found a ministry with a vision big enough to strategically and effectively use his remaining $99,500.

When you have a God-given vision for the future and action plans to get there, you may experience some of the biggest gifts your ministry will ever receive. Do not be afraid to dream big about ways God can use your church. Then, when He gives you a vision for what He wants you to do and how to accomplish that vision, go ahead with planning to allocate the necessary resources, and watch God provide in surprising ways.

Reason 4: God has blessed people with resources that need to be released into God's work. God is often at work behind the scenes, preparing people to give by pouring significant financial resources into their lives. The Lord wants to use those resources for His glory, and at just the right time they will be released—sometimes in unexpected ways. On their way out of town, the Israelite slaves plundered the Egyptians of gold, silver, and fine clothing. God orchestrated this in advance so the former slaves would have sufficient resources to build the tabernacle in the wilderness. God allowed David to accumulate vast wealth from his military campaigns because He wanted to use those resources for the building of the temple. It is during times like a church's capital fund drive that God causes people to look at what He has given them so they can lavishly, generously, and sacrificially give to a special undertaking.

There may also be some people in your congregation who only give a few thousand dollars a year, but during a capital campaign would commit to giving a five-, six-, or seven-figure gift. During a recent project in our church, a retired couple that I barely know (they only come to our church a few months a year) committed to giving $100,000! You do not always know the ways in which God has blessed people. See your church's project as an opportunity for heart transformation for those clinging too fast to those blessings; allow the church's need to encourage Christians to be generous as Christ is generous.

TEN INGREDIENTS FOR A SUCCESSFUL CAPITAL CAMPAIGN

Years ago I studied eighteen churches that conducted capital fundraising campaigns. Regardless of the amount a church was seeking to raise—from a few hundred thousand dollars to millions of dollars—the churches that were successful used the ten following ingredients in their recipe for success. The churches that left these out were often frustrated and disappointed with their results. These ten essential ingredients fall into four categories:

- Identifying and igniting a vision
- Instructing and inspiring
- Leading and informing
- Inviting and involving

Phase 1: Identifying and Igniting a Vision

Ingredient 1: Receive God-given vision. Make sure your vision for future growth is from God and not just a dream to promote your own self-interest or agenda. Consider how biblical leaders in the past looked for clarity. Moses spent forty days on a mountaintop with God, David met quietly with the Lord and wrote down what he heard, and Nehemiah fasted, prayed, and planned. If we walk humbly with the Lord, and open ourselves and our churches to His ways and timing, He may choose to do mighty things in our generation for His glory.

Ingredient 2: Write the vision. A vision must be clear and compelling for people to get excited and support it from their hearts with their financial resources. If a vision cannot be clearly articulated, it may not be from God. Exodus 24–34 shows how Moses received and listed in detail a clear vision of God's desire for the future. Habakkuk 2:2–3 reads, "Write down the revelation and make it plain on tablets so that a herald may run with it. For the revelation awaits an appointed time; it speaks of the end and will not prove false." Invest in writing the vision you receive so that it clearly communicates what you believe God wants for your church.

Ingredient 3: Gain leadership support. For a capital campaign to succeed, you need a cohesive, united team effort from your most dedicated top leadership. This team should give sacrificial gifts that meet 40 to 60 percent of your total campaign goal. In 1 Chronicles 28 and 29, David gathered, inspired, and challenged his leadership, and the result was the modern equivalent of $35 billion dollars in resources for a building project. In Exodus 35 and 36, Moses inspired those around him to give and they had to restrain the people from bringing in more. Your project will not surge forward if you are primarily counting on the average non-leader in your church to carry the campaign; your top leadership needs to lead the way.

Phase 2: Instructing and Inspiring

Ingredient 4: Provide biblical teaching. During your capital campaign, build momentum and inspire people with biblical stories of building expansion, renovation, and major maintenance projects. Use written materials to take your congregation deeper into the Scriptures. For example, I wrote a Bible devotional booklet for a church campaign called "A 40-Day Spiritual Journey to a More Generous Life." It takes a congregation through over five hundred Scripture verses in a forty-day period. With weekly projects and discussion questions, readers can assess their giving in light of their income sources, assets, lifestyle choices, and giving priorities. One church that used the forty-day devotional booklet in their campaign raised 50 percent more than their consultant had predicted they could raise[8] (see also Howard Dayton's chapter for content ideas for teaching and writing).

Ingredient 5: Include personal testimonies. Sharing real-life stories of sacrificial giving with your congregation inspires everyone to greater levels of generosity. Use them in sermons, live testimonies, video testimonies, or pamphlets and written materials. One story I share is that of a church where we distributed $5,000 in $20 bills to the congregation and challenged people to use the money and multiply it for our building project. People got enthused and creative. One twelve-year-old boy used his seed money to purchase dog shampoo and washed people's dogs in his neighborhood for donations. The original $20 entrusted to him ultimately returned $187 in donations for the building project. Remember that the most inspiring stories often come from the least expected or neediest people.

Ingredient 6: Aim to make the fund drive a rich, spiritual experience. A fund drive is about more that just brick and mortar; it is bigger than a building effort. Help people to see that it is about God and His vision and believers and their transformation. The aim is to learn deep lessons in faith, generosity, obedience, and sacrifice. Here is a growing opportunity for the church to work as a family, pulling together to reach the lost and do more in the future for God's work and His Kingdom. Many churches testify that a capital campaign not only increases giving in the church but also increases the spiritual maturity of its members.

Phase 3: Leading and Informing

Ingredient 7: Get experienced counsel. How safe would you feel in a building erected by inexperienced people who thought they could save you money with a do-it-yourself construction project? When it comes to hiring fundraising consultants, people in your congregation may say, "We can save money by doing the campaign drive ourselves!" What follows is usually neither safe nor successful. One church I observed felt this way and ran a campaign on its own. They raised hundreds of thousands of dollars *less* than what was needed, borrowed the rest of the money, and spent hundreds of thousands of dollars in interest payments. All of this happened because an individual or individuals strongly voiced opposition to paying for professional counsel and guidance.

What does a fundraising consultant do? He or she will not personally go out door-to-door and raise the money for you. On the contrary, this professional will provide customized and proven fundraising plans and help you stay motivated and on track. A consultant can also effectively mediate and settle differences of opinion between leaders that would otherwise lead the church toward disastrous results.

The general rule of thumb about companies that provide capital campaign consulting services to churches is that a church will normally raise two to three times their annual operating income over a three-pledge period. Many variables affect the final amount of cash and pledges, but about 80 percent of the time this is a reasonable expectation for a church retaining the services of an experienced consultant or church fundraising firm. It is wise to request at least three consultants or consulting groups to make a no-charge presentation to your leadership before making a final selection about who will partner with you.

Ingredient 8: Form a strong leadership team and comprehensive plan.
Many details need to come together in a timely and coordinated manner for a campaign to gain and maintain momentum to achieve your desired goals. As you move forward with your capital campaign, it is important to follow a plan (approved by leadership) that outlines specifically the tasks (what), timeline (when), and people assigned to each task (who). The steps below are essential to the plan's success.

a) *Consulting selection phase:* If you use an experienced consultant or consulting firm for your capital campaign, you will need to do the following:

- Talk with other church leaders in your community or denomination (or any personal connections) for recommendations and to hear their experiences in working with specific consultants or firms.
- Review the consultant's/firm's websites and references. Make sure the consultant is knowledgeable and experienced in conducting campaigns for your size, style, and type of church.
- Schedule a no-cost interview meeting with potential consultants/firms. Make sure the consultant who would be assigned to your campaign is present at the meeting. It is important that your leadership feels the consultant is a good fit for your leadership and congregation.
- Obtain upfront and as clearly as possible all costs that are associated with retaining a particular firm/consultant, including consulting fees, feasibility study (if applicable), travel, office, equipment, mailings, multimedia, and promotional materials.

b) *Leadership selection phase:* To move the initiative forward effectively, you will need key leaders on your team: the Campaign Consultant, Campaign Chairman, Senior Pastor, Administrative Support, Communications Director, Prayer Coordinator, Home Groups or Home Visits Coordinator, Major Events Coordinator, Lead or Leadership Gifts Coordinator, and others. If your church already has an ongoing stewardship ministry (as detailed in Richard Edic's chapter), its leadership team can fill many of these positions and help recruit any additional people needed to run a special campaign. An excellent resource to read *before* putting together your team and plan is Michael Reeves's *Extraordinary Money: Understanding the Church Capital Campaign.*[9] The book gives a comprehensive overview of specific job descriptions for leadership positions and provides step-by-step guidance on conducting a successful capital campaign.

c) *Planning phase:* Hold a comprehensive planning session and develop your vision materials (sometimes called a "case statement" or a "case for support"), which will picture the future and what it will take to get there. You should develop an informational piece with answers to commonly asked questions and craft a master calendar. Develop a detailed, multitiered giving chart or pyramid (i.e., how many gifts/pledges at different amounts will be needed to meet your goal), so people can clearly see what is needed and where they can fit into the big picture.

d) *Leadership commitment phase:* Leaders need to lead in their giving. During this time, prior to the whole congregation being invited to pledge a gift, your top leadership groups (elders, board members, church council, committee members, and staff) will be asked to turn in their financial commitments. Key biblical passages that support this step are 1 Chronicles 29:6–9; Ezra 2:68–69; and Nehemiah 7:70–71. This phase is frequently the most important part of the whole campaign. Depending on the church, you may find that anywhere from 60 to 90 percent of the total financial resources come from your lead giver(s) and leadership group.

e) *Quiet or advance funding phase:* This phase includes personal visits with key people and receiving advance lead and/or leadership gift commitments. It is often called the quiet phase since it comprises work done before the campaign moves into a larger, more public phase. It is wise to identify major lead gifts that will spark the campaign's movement. In 1 Chronicles 29:2–5, King David announced his personal lead gift and challenged others to give. Nehemiah and Ezra also received generous "lead gifts" in the form of government grants before they began their building renovation projects.

Phase 4: Inviting and Involving

Ingredient 9: Provide informative and inspiring materials and meetings. You will need to invest time, effort, and money in providing quality communication materials that share the vision for the future, the campaign plan, and the timeline, along with biblically based devotional materials that provide people with the information and inspiration to give sacrificially and generously. Ultimately, you must answer the key underlying questions: "Why is this important?" and "Why should I get involved in giving to this project?" Communication methods can include: PowerPoint presentations, literature, DVDs, Bible devotionals on generosity, skits, video clips, pamphlets, drawings, models, website information, email updates, and much more.

Holding personal meetings, home group meetings, dessert meetings, or informational meetings at the church allows the pastor and/or key leaders to share the vision and answer questions in a warm and open environment. This is also the time to use multimedia, literature, drawings, models, mailings, testimonies, and preaching messages.

Ingredient 10: Set specific times of commitment and utilize follow-up communications in the campaign. Once people have been informed and inspired, they need clear instructions on *when* and *how* to give for maximum participation and return. Without intentional, clear communication and systems for receiving pledges and gifts, all of the information and inspiration generated may be wasted.

It is important to offer a variety of options for people to fulfill their pledges: Do they want to donate stock? Do they need estate-planning assistance? Are they donating land or a gift-in-kind asset? Do they want to fulfill their pledge electronically?

Depending upon your consultant's experience and your church's desires, your campaign can culminate in a major banquet, a celebration event, and/or a dedicated worship service where everyone who has not already done so is asked to turn in their specific cash gifts and financial pledges/commitments. David and his leaders modeled this approach in 1 Chronicles 29 when he had a great celebration and the leaders turned in their commitments for the temple building project.

Finally, follow-up is very important for the long-term success of the campaign. Be intentional about providing written information and pledge updates to your congregation throughout the entire pledge period. People need to see information, in writing, concerning what is happening and how things are progressing in fulfilling their pledges.

As you teach your congregation about generosity, I trust that you and those you influence will be forever transformed by God's amazing grace, as you excel in a revolution toward godly generosity.

HELPFUL CHURCH RESOURCES FOR GREATER GENEROSITY MINISTRY IN YOUR CONGREGATION

- **www.MAXIMUMgenerosity.org**—Articles, pamphlets, flyers, and preaching helps for money and generosity topics, PowerPoint slides, articles, a free monthly generosity newsletter, and more.
- **www.GenerousLife.info**—Website for "A 40-Day Spiritual Journey to a More Generous Life," a Bible devotional booklet to accompany all church generosity initiatives.

- **www.generousgiving.org**—A wide variety of generosity resources, with links to many additional resources.
- **www.Crown.org**—Resources to help train people to manage their finances and giving according to sound biblical principles.
- **www.visionresourcing.com**—A resource manual and leadership training materials for stewardship in the local church.
- **Denominational Resources**—Some denominations provide stewardship pamphlets, curriculum, and campaign materials.
- **www.Stewardshipdirect.com**—The Southern Baptist church's stewardship materials for use in local churches.
- **www.DynamicGiving.com**—Written materials and training and consulting resources.
- **www.stewardshipresources.org**—The Ecumenical Center for Stewardship Studies in Indianapolis, Indiana, offers materials that can be used in annual stewardship drives.
- **Abingdon Press**—*Consecration Sunday Stewardship Program.*
- **KLW Enterprises**—Effective Stewardship program.

HELPFUL RESOURCES FOR SPECIAL GENEROSITY EVENTS AND INITIATIVES

- **Run-your-own-campaign resources**—Saddleback Church's "It's Time to Build Campaign Kit" and Brian Kluth's online resources at www.MAXIMUMgenerosity.org.
- **National firms**—INJOY Stewardship Services, RSI, Generis, The Gage Group, Cargill Associates, and The Rogers Company.
- **Regional firms**—These consulting groups tend to be made up of the owner of the firm or a network of two to ten associated consultants that serve a three to fifteen state area.
- **Denominational consulting services**

BRIAN P. KLUTH is senior pastor of the First Evangelical Free Church in Colorado Springs. He is the founder of www.MAXIMUMgenerosity.org and www. GenerousLife.info. His websites receive top search engine rankings on "biblical generosity" and "church giving" and provide a wealth of generosity materials and resources for pastors, church committees, and congregations. Kluth also offers a generosity e-newsletter that is sent free to thousands of pastors, church leaders, and denominations. He is the author of a Bible devotional booklet, "A 40-Day Spiritual Journey to a More Generous Life," used by numerous churches and denominations. Brian can be contacted at bk@kluth.org.

1. See Brian Kluth, www.MAXIMUMgenerosity.org.
2. Unless otherwise noted, Scripture quotations are taken from the New International Version of the Bible.
3. Woodmen Valley Chapel of Colorado Springs, annual report.
4. Brian Kluth, *Count Your Blessings*, http://kluth.org/tracts.htm.
5. Lawrence W. O'nan, "Lifestyle Stewardship," in *Money for Ministries*, ed. Wesley K. Willmer (Wheaton: Scripture Press, 1989).
6. Proverbs 29:18 KJV.
7. Olan Hendrix, president, Leadership Resources Group.
8. Related by Jon Peach, http://www.kluth.org/40Day/40DayBookletInfo.htm.
9. Michael D. Reeves, *Extraordinary Money: Understanding the Church Capital Campaign* (Discipleship Resources, 2002).

III.

The Asker's Role as a Facilitator of Heart
TRANSFORMATION

*The frontline workers in the revolution in generosity
are those who facilitate God's work through the process of
asking for funds. This section explains in practical terms
the process of heart transformation that grows generous
stewards who are rich toward God and applies biblical
principles to Christian asking practices.*

Chapter
10

MAXIMIZING GENEROSITY BY
ALIGNING GOD'S CALLINGS

BY LAUREN D. LIBBY,

COO, Vice President of the Navigators

ne morning twenty-five years ago, while I was presenting a strategic ministry opportunity to a couple, the husband looked me square in the face and said, "This is a great project. It has a huge potential for impact, and it's in line with where the Lord has called us." The Holy Spirit moved that morning, and the couple responded with a generous gift. As I reflected on this interaction while flying home, I realized that the key to this gift was the alignment of this giving opportunity with the calling this couple sensed upon their lives and that calling is an important aspect of working for God's eternal Kingdom.

From God's perspective, giving is a spiritual act. Giving is our reflection of Christ's generosity, a means of participating in the work of God. Rodin writes, "As we work in the power of the Spirit, we seek to be stewards and to train up stewards in gracious response to the love of God in Christ Jesus. Our work is our participation in the faithfulness of the Son to the will of the Father."[1] As a result, the alignment of the following three callings within the giving and asking process will maximize participation and generosity:

1) the call of the asker to the ministry of asking for funds,

2) the call of the organization to the mission and purpose they are fulfilling, and

3) the call of ministry partners (givers) to distribute God's resources to facilitate the ministry's mission.

In the ideal world of God's economy, when these three callings are aligned, God is glorified and generosity is maximized. The goal of those who ask is first to be sensitive and discern these callings, and second to match the callings of the organization and giver, effectively drawing together what (and whom) God has provided.

This chapter will examine (1) the spiritual dynamics of calling, and apply this to three different parties: (2) the asker, (3) the organization, and (4) the giver. The fundamental premise is that those who are called to ask will seek the guidance of the Holy Spirit in finding givers who are called to support their particular ministry purpose (see Craig Blomberg's and Richard Haynie's chapters), aligning these three callings of God to maximize generosity.

THE SPIRITUAL DYNAMICS OF CALLING

God is a God who communicates with His people. God calls individuals and groups of individuals to particular tasks. God called Nehemiah to rebuild the walls of Jerusalem. God told Ananias that Paul was "a chosen instrument of mine to carry my name before the Gentiles and kings and children of Israel" (Acts 9:15).[2] Paul was chosen for a specific purpose; by following this calling he was transformed by the power of God to be rich in good works. God works both supernaturally and naturally through His people, using their particular gifts and activities to further the work of His Kingdom. It is important to understand the dynamics of this call before applying the idea to resource development.

God Calls Us to Work

"Kingdom activity. . . takes place only through the operation of the Spirit through, although at times in spite of, God's people."[3] We see throughout Scripture that the Holy Spirit works in and through people to accomplish God's purposes in the world. Horace Bushnell writes: "We are all called by God to share in His life and His kingdom. Each one of us is called to a special place in the kingdom."[4] God calls people to places and purposes. For some, God's call is very specific; for others it is a more general path. Either way, God's call directs His people toward what He wants them to do.

God Calls Us through Our Gifts, Talents, and Life Circumstances

Thomas Merton writes that "in choosing what will please God [we] take account of all the slightest indications of His will."[5] God guides us through every circumstance of our lives, sometimes dramatically, sometimes quietly. In his book *The Call*, Os Guinness says, "Giftedness does not stand alone in helping us discern our callings. It lines up in response to God's call alongside other factors, such as family heritage, our own life opportunities, God's guidance, and our unquestioning readiness to do what He shows."[6] Similarly, John Henry Newman writes that God "works through our natural faculties and circumstances of life."[7] God creatively weaves our lives in such a way as to guide us toward His plan for our life. God reveals more and more of His calling as people's lives go on, and provides the material resources for them to invest in this calling.

God Expects Us to Obey His Call

God's call isn't always manifested in the same manner, but when we receive it our best option is to follow it. Robert Hudnut notes, "To hear in Hebrew means to obey. A call heard is a call obeyed."[8] There is not space in God's economy for ignoring His call. A quick read through the story of Jonah emphasizes the value God places on listening for and obeying His direction.

Martin Luther wrote, "God does not guide me, he pushes me forward, he carries me away. I am not master of myself."[9] When, as transformed stewards, we submit our lives and resources to God's control, we open ourselves to the dynamic call of God on our lives. We are ready to respond with generosity to the burdens, desires, and interests He places on our hearts.

This generosity, as depicted in Figure 10-1, is maximized when we align God's separate callings of individuals, uniting them around a common goal. This alignment is the correct positioning of the various components (i.e., asker, organization, and giver) relative to one another, so that they all are within God's calling.

- God calls believers into the ministry of resource development, to provide people with the opportunity to support God's work. The **asker** communicates

- an **organization's** calling to fulfill a specific ministry purpose

- and the potential **giver** is called by God to be generous to the specific ministry purpose of the organization.

As seen in Figure 10-1,[10] when these three separate callings align, the asker presents the ministry opportunities of the organization to a potential giver whom God has called to support that particular ministry. As the givers' heart is transformed to be rich toward God, and they become sensitive to the work of the Holy Spirit in their lives, their alignment results in maximized generosity to God's work.

THE ASKER: CALLED TO ASK

The primary role of a Christian fundraiser is to advance and facilitate a believer's faith in and worship of God, which results in generosity (see Joyce Brooks's chapter). When fundraising is understood this way, as the ministry of raising up stewards to be rich toward God, it is no longer merely a job or a duty, but an extension of God's eternal Kingdom work and a ministry to which God calls those who ask. This can come as a supernatural calling, a biblical realization, a recognition of giftedness, a need expressed in the Kingdom of God, or even a movement from within the church that God initiates. However the asker receives the call, what he or she is called to is the vital role of explaining an organization's purpose and ministry opportunities, as well as often being the instrument through whom God calls givers. Nehemiah exemplifies this calling. God laid a vision—the rebuilt walls of Jerusalem—on his heart, calling Nehemiah to ask all those around him for support. Based on this foundation, Nehemiah rallied everyone from kings to stone layers to bring this vision to fruition. Nehemiah could not build the walls of Jerusalem single-handedly; he was called to ask

Figure 10-1:
The Alignment of Three Callings

the people to support God's vision. In essence, askers are shepherds of God's stewards.

After receiving this call to ask, the asker is responsible to communicate the God-given vision to God's people and invite them to be involved. Often askers rely on their ability to persuade or even manipulate givers into supporting a vision. But when askers instead rely on God to call givers, the results are enduring. Instead of persuasion, their job becomes one of recognizing the alignment between God's calling of an organization to an eternal kingdom purpose, and God's similar calling of a giver to support that purpose. The asker relies upon the Holy Spirit's work, rather than his or her own charisma, charm, and shiny brochures. The asker communicates the vision and purpose, and the Holy Spirit transforms people's hearts to grow rich toward God, guiding them to invest generously in alignment with God's calling.

Askers who have received a calling from God are uniquely equipped to gather resources from the people God touches to respond to their appeal. For example, God's calling is evident throughout the passionate ministry of Wes Stafford, the president of Compassion International. When Wes speaks about investing in the lives of needy, hungry children, people's hearts resonate with the message and vision. His childhood, spent in Africa, is a circumstance that God used in calling Wes and that gives a sense of authenticity to his calling to raising funds.

Several years ago I was consulting with a broadcasting ministry in the area of major gift recruitment. After several days of developing an intricate strategy, the leader of the ministry said he would not be talking to any potential supporters because that was the job of the staff. I persuaded the leader to accompany me as I called on a potential giver; after praying in the car before entering the office, the president confided that he was fearful enough that he might become physically sick. We engaged the potential giver, and he ended up writing a large check on the spot to help fund the project we were presenting; in fact, it was for half of the total need. As we were leaving his office, the man turned to the leader of the ministry and said, "If you had not been here, I would not have given. But because you believe in the project so much you would take the time to see me personally, I really want to have a part. I sense that God's hand is on you and the project." Needless to say, the president's mind-set toward his role in fundraising changed dramatically in about an hour.

I would be so bold as to say that the raising of resources—namely, personal and financial resources—is an integral part of the job of any nonprofit leader. There are parts of the role that can be delegated, but the overall responsibility of supplying the organization rests with its top leaders. This fits the biblical pattern of God calling a leader to the role of asking and energizing the movement of resources from His people as their hearts align with the particular opportunities presented. The leader is best suited for communicating the calling of the organization and presenting it to individuals with the same calling.

God's call to the asker is to present potential givers with the opportunity to align their giving with the work God is doing through an organization.

THE ORGANIZATION:
CALLED TO A SPECIFIC MINISTRY PURPOSE

God calls Christian organizations to fulfill specific ministry needs in the world. Often this calling is expressed in the organization's mission, vision, and values statements. Not every Christian organization is called to minister to the same group of people. Paul describes this in Galatians 2:7: "I had been entrusted with the gospel to the uncircumcised, just as Peter had been entrusted with the gospel to the circumcised." The book *The Prospering Parachurch* contains a taxonomy showing the wide range of ministries that come alongside the church.[11] This variety of callings results in a plethora of opportunities for God's people to be involved in His work.

When organizations follow God's call, they are able to fill a unique role in God's Kingdom. I vividly remember Campus Crusade for Christ founder Bill Bright speaking to a group of potential givers about the vision God had called him to initiate. As Bill spoke, one could sense that he was called by God for a mission; that here was someone whom God had personally touched to accomplish His purposes. Bill spoke of investing his own retirement account in a strategic project in Russia. After the presentation one couple told me, "We gave generously because we sensed an affinity with what Bill was talking about." This is an example of how God matches organizational callings with individual givers' callings through leaders communicating visions that cause people's hearts to respond with an investment of their resources. Dr. Bright's calling to communicate a particular vision from God gave him the ability to align callings, facilitate growing givers' hearts to be rich toward God, and release generosity that supported the purpose to which God called the organization.

It is important to remember that God does not make value judgments based on the different callings of organizations. Jeavons and Basinger write that "God has no favorite causes…Fundraisers who truly believe that God is enough and that no one ministry is inherently more valuable than another are free to encourage right motives for giving and let donors follow their hearts and feed their souls."[12] When the focus of fundraising efforts is on raising up stewards who are rich toward God and called to a particular ministry, then there is no fear of competition in aligning stewards with ministries other than your own (see Shelley Cochrane's chapter). What is important is discerning God's call, and then following Him. Aligning givers with ministry opportunities to which they are called becomes the primary goal, rather than merely gaining donors for your own organization. As noted in Paul Nelson's chapter, it is often when organizations try to raise funds for purposes outside their ministries' mission that they get into ethical and legal problems.

THE GIVER: CALLED TO GIVE TO SPECIFIC MINISTRIES

Through His personal relationship with them, God places burdens on givers' hearts, sparks their interest in a vision, and gives them the opportunity to invest strategically in His Kingdom. Os Guinness defines *calling* as something that God initiates "so that everything we are—everything we do—everything we have is invested in response to His summons and service."[13]

Paul Johnson, a businessman from Detroit, was once sitting with a man in front of a campfire at a Christian camp. The man had invested huge sums of money from his once thriving business in the youth camp. His fortunes had turned from having a substantial trucking company down to one truck he and his wife operated to provide for their family. This man told Paul that the only thing from his business that really would last was the investment he had made in the lives of the next generation of young believers. Because he invested resources in God's work rather than merely his own, the man experienced the fulfillment that comes from obeying God's call.

Returning to the couple I mentioned at the beginning of this chapter, when God touched their hearts to respond to Jesus Christ, they answered with an enormously generous spirit toward investing in the work of God. They embodied what Mark Powell describes when he says, "We give out of glad and generous hearts as an expression of love and devotion to the God who is so good to us. When we do this, we discover the very essence of Christianity: a heartfelt relationship with God in which joy and thanksgiving replace self-interest or guilt."[14] When I visited them in their small, three-bedroom home on several acres of property, the only way you could even guess they had substantial resources was that they drove a ten-year-old Mercedes. Yet as a part of their calling, God used this couple to provide millions of dollars for Kingdom work. They understood that they were simply stewards of material resources with a calling to give those resources that was recognized by askers who exposed them to organizational callings that matched their sense of calling as a couple.

This couple is a living example of aligning individual callings with organizational callings to provide abundantly for the work of God. When God uses an asker to unite a giver and an organization under a common Divine calling, there is a revolution in generosity.

CONCLUSION

In writing to the Philippians regarding their gift to him, Paul says, "Not that I seek the gift, but I seek the fruit that increases to your credit" (Phil. 4:17). Paul is not worried about a monetary transaction for his support; he has "learned the secret of facing plenty and hunger, abundance and need" (Phil. 4:12). Rather, he is concerned with the good of the Philippians; he desires blessing for those who have given to him. Paul understands that when we give out of gratitude and obedience to God, when we are rich toward God, we "lay up for ourselves treasures in heaven" (Matt. 6:20). It is these eternal rewards that he desires for the Philippians. This is the attitude of a person God has called to ask.

The investments we make in light of our gifting and calling will continue right into eternity, into life beyond our existence on earth. This gives a feeling of destiny to both the person asking and the person giving toward an organization's ministry. The reality of God's calling answers the ultimate question of *why*? For those asking, calling plugs them into the eternal purposes of God. For those giving, calling gives a sense of investment in God's Kingdom. They do not give of their own independent volition but in response to the call of God—and in this act of obedience, we can hear the voice of the Master saying, "Well done, good and faithful servant" (Matt. 25:23).

When givers, askers, and organizations submit to God's call, generosity is maximized and great things are accomplished individually and corporately in the present world that result in eternal rewards. The alignment of an asker with a giver, who are both passionate for the same mission, is the synergy that revolutionizes the work of stewardship professionals.

LAUREN D. LIBBY is senior vice president and chief operating officer of the Navigators and has been active in recruiting resources for Christian causes since the 1970s. He became involved in fundraising "accidentally" when a financial crisis arose in his organization. This started a biblical study of the process of how God provides for His work. Libby earned an MBA from Regis University in Denver. He served on numerous boards, including: Northwestern College (Minnesota), Educational Communications of Colorado Springs, Chairman of the ECFA Standards Committee, and the Christian Stewardship Association. Lauren can be reached at lauren.libby@navigators.org.

1. R. Scott Rodin, *Stewards in the Kingdom: A Theology of Life in All Its Fullness* (Downers Grove, IL.: IVP, 2000), 71.

2. Scripture quotations are from the Holy Bible, *English Standard Version*.

3. Eddie Gibbs and Ryan K. Bolger, *Emerging Churches: Creating Christian Community in Postmodern Cultures* (Grand Rapids: Baker Academic, 2005), 140.

4. Howard Bushnell, "Every Man's Life Is a Plan of God," *Callings: 20 Centuries of Christian Wisdom on Vocation*, ed. William C. Placher (Cambridge: Eerdmans, 2005), 421.

5. Thomas Merton, "No Man Is an Island," *Callings: 20 Centuries of Christian Wisdom on Vocation*, 422.

6. Os Guinness, *The Call: Finding and Fulfilling the Central Purpose in Your Life* (Nashville: W Publishing Group, 1998), 4.

7. John Henry Newman, "Divine Calls," *Callings: 20 Centuries of Christian Wisdom on Vocation*, 437.

8. Robert Hudnut, *Call Waiting: How to Hear God Speak* (Downers Grove, IL: IVP, 1999), 18.

9. Martin Luther as quoted in Hudnut, *Call Waiting*, 32.

10. *God, Money, Giving and Asking*, Presentation by Wesley Willmer to the Christian Stewardship Association in Denver, CO, on January 21, 2006.

11. Wesley K. Willmer and J. David Schmidt with Martyn Smith, *The Prospering Parachurch* (San Francisco: Jossey-Bass, 1998), 201-14.

12. Thomas Jeavons and Rebekah Basinger, *Growing Givers' Hearts: Treating Fundraising as Ministry* (San Francisco: Jossey-Bass, 200), 98.

13. Guinness, *The Call*, 29.

14. Mark Allan Powell, *Giving to God: The Bible's Good News about Living a Generous Life* (Cambridge: Eerdmans, 2006), 5.

Chapter

PRACTICING GOD'S PRESENCE:

AN **ESSENTIAL TOOL**
FOR RAISING **FUNDS**

BY **MARK L. VINCENT,** *Lead Partner,*

Design For Ministry

I n order to grow givers' hearts and help believers become rich toward God through their giving, those seeking funds should be individuals of spiritual depth. This chapter focuses on how to achieve that maturity and depth of theological reflection by practicing God's presence. It will examine the need for a devotional life, contemporary biblical principles, and examples of practicing God's presence.

Practicing God's presence means being aware that God is with you in the small and large moments of life—in your conversations, decisions, and responses. It is praying with your eyes open as you move throughout the day, communing with God on the spot instead of waiting for the next scheduled appointment with the Divine Creator.

Those who raise ministry support professionally spend many hours on the road, sleep in many strange places, and, ironically, spend many hours alone while working with large numbers of people. Everyone finds him or herself tempted. Another donor dinner or another night in a look-alike hotel room can move individuals outside the peace of Christ, leaving them vulnerable to attack—especially when they have not cultivated the understanding that God's presence is with them wherever they go.

Those who seek support also face ethical pressures as they work. They must juggle their call to ministry with the demands of their organization's mission and a giver's intent for a gift. On some occasions they discover that their organization's mission is inadequate for the situation or the giver's desire is unsuitable for the ministry need. It is even possible that the grandness of the vision leads to significant donor response that can lead the development professional to trust in the money more than the God who supplied it. Dallas Willard points out that "when our own kingdom has a good year, we quit longing for the kingdom of God."[2] Those who invite gift giving see all of money's beauty and all of its ugliness—sometimes simultaneously. The peaceful and Christ-centered condition of one's soul is in regular jeopardy.

If faith is only an appendage to one's ministry, what will be the response in pressure-packed moments? The temptation will be to focus on acquiring money to meet an annual goal, instead of helping supporters grow more deeply in Christian generosity as a response to God's mercy. If she or he is not spiritually well and attending to God's work in the giver, the Christian who invites giving will offer no qualitative difference from a secular fundraising effort. Faith will only be window dressing, a thin veneer that covers mere fundraising technique.

WHY A DEVOTIONAL LIFE?

So much of this has to do with the spiritual and personal transformation of turning from sin and becoming a follower of Jesus Christ. As Scott Rodin writes, "Transformation involves nothing less than the complete abandonment of our thrones and the dismantling of our earthly kingdoms. It is a transformation from the struggle of two-kingdom living to the joy of one-kingdom service."[3]

A Christian transformation reorients a person away from self, family, or corporate satisfaction and toward the mission of bringing the good news that God wants to forgive sin—indeed, has forgiven sin in the person and work of Jesus Christ. It is tragic for the asker, the organization, and the supporters, when self-serving activity replaces servanthood, and such activity is justified as "necessary for organizational survival." The gospel becomes a mere add-on—if it remains at all. "Christian" fundraising becomes a description of the cultural environment in which fundraising is done, rather than a distinctive style of fundraising centered in a Great Commission to make disciples everywhere (Matt. 28:19–20).

The devotional life of a person in ministry is central to cultivating spiritual well-being and maintaining this important transformed perspective. In using the term *devotional*, I do not mean merely setting time aside each day for Scripture reading, prayer, and journaling, although doing so is a most useful exercise. Instead, I am writing about practicing God's presence.[4]

Practicing God's presence goes beyond learning more about the Scriptures and reaches into moment-by-moment application of what one finds there. Jesus invites us to this when He calls us to care for the least of these (Matt. 25: 31–46). The apostle James reminds us when he points out that true religion cares for orphans and widows in their distress (James 1:27). Paul reminds us when he tells us not to let the sun set on our anger (Eph. 4:26). The person who requests financial support from others cannot merely affirm that these are Christian actions but must also lead an exemplary financial life—living well within their means so they are generous to God with their firstfruits giving and use the remainder to develop an expansive, hospitable, and neighborly life.[5]

Remaining aware of God's presence in a support-raising vocation is not easy—especially given the many and varied interactions with colleagues and constituencies. Doing so, however, makes for a rewarding discipline that drives one's spiritual transformation forward. Even though inviting others to support ministry is a special and satisfying profession, it offers unique pressures, as noted earlier. God is present and active in those pressure-filled moments, and we are able to respond well not because we had devotions earlier that morning, but because we live a devoted life with a heightened awareness of God's ongoing presence. Thus, a devotional life is not only bracketed as an appointment with God; it is constantly integrated into the work of inviting support for ministry. Here are some examples for your consideration.

REFLECTING ON REAL-LIFE CASES

Work through the following cases and reflect on how someone who practices God's presence might respond. You may wish to use these cases in conversation with your colleagues, having first revisited R. Scott Rodin's chapter on transformation. Identifying details have been changed, but the scenarios are real.

Case #1: Jacqui Parker raises support for an orphanage and school near Phoenix. Many of the students are Native American. On her way to see a grant-making agency, she hears a breaking news radio report that two former houseparents have been arrested for molestation. The incidents are connected to the agency where they work now, but the radio report mentioned they once worked for the orphanage. Jacqui knows this will mean an investigation into their tenure at the orphanage and fears something might be uncovered. The agency seemed poised to make the grant. She wonders if she should say anything, but worries it would damage the possibility of the grant.

Case #2: Gospel Purveyors is a Bible society in the middle of a capital campaign. A major donor promised a $300,000 U.S. matching gift for the first $300,000 raised, and a $1,000,000 U.S. gift when the campaign reached $1,000,000. The first $300,000 was raised, and the donor gave the gift. A lot of celebration and publicity followed. A year later, the campaign pledges totaled $1,000,000. Packy Stark, the vice president for development, had informed the matching donor as each $100,000 plateau was reached. The donor did not respond, but Packy was not worried, as the donor was very private and had requested to be informed of the campaign developments so they could have the gift ready when it was time. Packy called the donor at home to deliver the good news and discovered the phone was disconnected. He then drove out to the donor's home and found it empty. Neighbors told Packy they heard something about a repossession and bankruptcy.

Without cultivating an ongoing devotion to God, it is difficult to maintain the perspective that raising support is ministry in cases like those above. Panic sets in, and desperate actions follow. The way to prevent acting rashly is to maintain a transformed and eternal perspective. Fundraising techniques do not provide this perspective—neither do college degrees nor professional associations nor credentials. To see these situations as opportunities, a person must cultivate a deep and attentive spirit toward God's intention to show mercy, to forgive sin, and to call people to return to their Creator. They need to develop their time management, their devotional life, and their understanding of biblical stewardship in order to be ministers in such a situation.

If we are not spiritually well, we will analyze management issues associated with raising support according to data alone, forgetting spiritual discernment, prayer, and theological reflection. This is not to point to a shallow spirituality that offers perfunctory prayers or says "Praise the Lord" as a substitute for proper preparation. Neither is it to point away from administrative rigor or learning about the development profession. Rather, it is bringing heart, soul, mind, and strength to one's work—connecting the knowledge one has gained about inviting financial support with attention to God's work in the world. Study and meditation on God's Word can help us gain this eternal perspective, as the transformational examples that follow illustrate.

THE DEVOTIONAL LIFE OF THOSE WAITING FOR MESSIAH

There are strong biblical examples of people who, through their lives of devotion, embraced their transformation and its implications for ministry. Luke begins both his gospel and the Acts of the Apostles with portraits of communities with active devotional lives.[6] In his gospel, people like Zechariah, Elizabeth, Mary, Simeon, Anna, John the Baptist, and Jesus of Nazareth were part of a community that believed God was doing something in the world that would make a special difference for those who were oppressed, marginalized, or lost. They prepared themselves to be ready to respond and to point to God's advent. Their life of prayer, waiting, reflecting, gaining familiarity with the Scriptures, and remaining in fellowship with people of like faith prepared them to point to the Messiah and celebrate His life and ministry.

Luke emphasizes that the Holy Spirit moved in these people, leading them to do what they might not have done if left to themselves. Miraculous events accompanied their devotional faith. Those who witnessed these events were in awe and spread the word about what they had seen (Luke 1:65). God's work was done because of them.

THE DEVOTIONAL LIFE OF THE FIRST CHURCH

Luke opens the book of Acts with Jesus promising His disciples that the same power that accompanied His ministry would rest on them. The Holy Spirit that previously filled Zechariah, Elizabeth, Mary, and Simeon would fill His disciples as they completed their transformation for ministry. The power behind His ministry as teacher, miracle worker, and Savior would now expand into their varied lives and send them to all the peoples of this world with His message.

The disciples returned to Jerusalem and began to wait for the promised Holy Spirit. They spent this waiting period building up their unity and remaining in constant prayer (Acts 1:14), strengthening themselves devotionally to be poised for action when God's work broke out.

Luke writes that the Holy Spirit did come and propel the early believers into the marketplace, where people from all over the world had gathered for a festival. By the time the marvel of that Pentecost celebration passed, and Peter preached his first marketplace sermon, thousands of global believers had emerged. As they went home from the festival, they took the transforming power of the gospel with them. It was as if a giant stone had been thrown into the population pond, causing ripples that affect the world even today (Acts 2). We bear its momentum. When we invite others to support our ministry, we are in essence inviting them to join the movement that began at Pentecost.

Believers all over the world share in the belief that God has given the Holy Spirit to the church—empowering, comforting, gifting, guiding, aiding, and prompting. With this knowledge, a person who invites support for ministry is reminded that she or he is now God's instrument, working on behalf of a ministry organization that also attests to being an instrument of God.

A person in a support-raising role can be confident the Holy Spirit will send them to places and into the lives of people where they would not otherwise have gone. If a person inviting support allows the Holy Spirit to be an abiding presence in their lives, they will be given ability to love the donor as God loves them, and to speak to them within their life experience and language. The Holy Spirit makes it possible for a person who invites giving to be an extension of God's priesthood, connecting people more deeply to God's good news. Their internal state of practicing God's presence begins to affect their external actions of raising support for ministry (see Todd Harper's chapter). Fundraising letters, thank-you notes, public speaking situations, and private conversations take on a tone of growing the giver's heart rather than merely raising support.

WHAT SHOULD WE DO?

If the Holy Spirit's presence completes the spiritual transformation of someone's life and makes them an emissary of God's Kingdom in the life of all those they meet, then it is right and good to ask, just as those who witnessed the power of God in the lives of the early believers: "What should we do?" And like those early believers, a ministering person should be eager to answer their question.

Luke provides a specific list of devotional habits the early church practiced. Those who invite giving are wise to appropriate them (Acts 2:42-47). Why not use it as a checklist to see where you might shore up your devotional well-being? I added the application each one has for those of us who request support for ministry.

- They daily shared meals with other Christians in a fellowship environment. (We benefit from purposefully developing authentic Christian friendships among colleagues and supporters.)
- They devoted themselves to prayer. (The implication is exactly as written: devotion to God involves devotion to prayer. Pray for the ministry organization that you represent. Pray for the donors. Pray for integrity. Pray for God's work to be done.)
- They continued to point to signs and wonders God performed through the apostles. (We should make the case again and again that we are doing God's work. This benefits far beyond the asking activity of the organization; it also plays a significant role in preventing an organization's mission from drifting.)
- They did not claim private ownership of their possessions but made them available for the work of the church. (We who invite others to give ought to be exemplary givers—giving the firstfruits of income to God in worship and using the rest in generous ways that honor God.)[7]
- They spent daily time in the temple. (We need to participate in regular and consistent worship and reflection on the Scriptures. Notice this encompasses far more than attending a weekly worship service.)
- They had the goodwill of the people. (We benefit from cultivating meaningful relationships with internal and external constituencies.)

216

- The Lord added to their number daily. (Such a life results in people invited to commit or recommit to follow Jesus.)

It is no stretch to make this list of devotional acts the outline for an annual report from the fundraising office. Looking over the list, one might wonder when asking would actually get done. The response to this observation is that these activities contribute to the credibility of the ministry professionals' efforts to invite people to respond to the grace of God, and to be generous toward God's continued work through the organization they represent.

Without a highly developed devotional life, those who invite giving will not be highly developed Christians. Without the necessary spiritual maturity on the ministry professional's part, the most godly and generous of Christians will kindly refuse to contribute or give far less than they might, continuing to look for ministries that enjoin them to God's work. Fundraising tools can only carry us so far. The best tools we have are ourselves and God's Spirit resident within us. When we let God's Spirit have its way, the possibilities increase for unplanned, lavish, and incredible gifts from God's people. Why? Because givers and potential donors witness God at work through the person inviting the support, and through the organization they represent.

A biblical example of this is Barnabas in Acts 4. He sold his property and placed the proceeds at the apostles' feet because he witnessed God's work through the apostles and was moved to respond. There simply is no better means of raising support than the display of earnest faith and ministry results among God's servants. Earnest faith becomes marketplace cultivation when accompanied by a regimen of fellowship, prayer, devotion to the teaching of Jesus, worship, and the practice of generosity. The rigor of such a fully integrated and devoted life is, in and of itself, a tool for raising ministry support.

The Bible is also quite serious in reminding us that we cannot fake our way to this earnest and rigorous faith. Acts 5 tells us of Ananias and Sapphira, who tried to look as if their gift were motivated by the same source as

Barnabas's. They wanted to be honored for their gift, while only pretending a commensurate level of sacrifice. Their tragic end reminds us that engaging in ministry and gathering support is holy activity and requires purity of intent—in both the giver and the asker.

Scripture provides other examples and concepts that are important to remember for a successful career in growing givers' hearts. You might consider Paul's fundraising appeal for suffering believers in Jerusalem (2 Cor. 8– 9) as a starting point for your study.

MAKING THE DEVOTIONAL LIFE SIMPLER

We can also learn from advice and examples of people in the field. Earnest faith and devotional rigor make possible a long and wonderful career, and possibly a lengthy tenure with a single ministry organization. If the job is solely about achieving fundraising benchmarks, then the temptation is far stronger to relocate frequently to take on the next fundraising challenge at the next organization. I am reminded of what I was told when I began in ministry—advice I think also applies to the vocation of asking people to give: *It is better to have forty years of ministry than to have four years of ministry ten times.*

This winsome phrase has remained with me and challenged me to think about ministry as a body of work, rather than the position one holds or the merit pay one achieves. It also speaks of durability and developing a long-term perspective. Without a long-term perspective, the person who raises financial support for ministry will live from fiscal year to fiscal year. Their barometer will be the current operational picture, without reference to the organization's mission or long-term goals. Their sense of well-being will fluctuate with the comparison of weekly receipts to the previous year.

Living a life of devotion to God, and doing so for the long-term as a member of God's transformed priesthood, not only raises money for the organization but also develops a larger population of generous people. These newly transformed generous people will bless God through their congregations and ministry organizations, both during the current fiscal year and for many years to come.

So, how does one build this devoted life and function for the long-term? Consider the following tools:

- **Realistic Time Management**—Knowing the boundaries of one's time allotment helps focus our work and maximize productivity within these limits. Individuals called to raise support for ministry need to be their own best friend in these matters, as there are no assurances that anyone else will care to define the limits of a support-raising position. It can be helpful to use the expertise of consultants or coaches to establish realistic and increasingly productive workloads.

- **Self-care**—The world is awash with messages that we should sleep adequately; eat a balanced diet; take time off for rest, reflection and play; and get moderate exercise several times a week. But, just like being devoted to God is of limited benefit without integration into one's daily activities, self-care is useful only when it is practiced. Self-care involves investing in one's home life just as much as one's work life. Without the anchor of family, friends, and congregation, it is difficult to maintain perspective on what truly matters in life.

- **Lifelong Learning**—Raising resources for ministry for a long time means one must cultivate a knowledge base and then convert it to wisdom that can be passed to others. This does not happen by having a reading pile that is never touched, foregoing professional development workshops, or delaying the development of a network of professional colleagues at other ministry organizations. It is important to challenge ourselves. Becoming well-rounded and acquiring new skills prevents a ministering person from becoming a grouchy dinosaur whose favorite subject is "how we once did it."

These three habits help to create the reflective space where one's life with God and God's work in the world intersect with the varied constituency relationships of the ministry organization. At the end of the chapter I have included some Scriptures for your reflection, along with reflection questions you might ask. I would especially encourage you to look at the heroes of the earliest chapters in Luke and Acts. They are among the best examples we have of people who lived this life of devotion that cultivates support for ministry.

IN SUMMARY

Hopefully, as you read this chapter you recognized how multiple pressures can lead a person away from practicing the presence of God. Ironically, raising support for ministry provides many opportunities to become disconnected from the faith and inhibits the potential for the transformation God can work in both the asker and, *consequentially,* the giver. Whether the problem is rooted in one's personality or brought on by a supporter or the ministry organization for which one works, the devotional life of the asker is open to spiritual attack.

The example of those waiting for the Messiah and those waiting for and responding to the Holy Spirit show us the habits involved in living a life of devotion to God. They also show how those habits become an invitation for others to support ministry. We can follow these biblical examples as we take care of our own life of devotion and as we wait for and respond to the Holy Spirit. We can invite others to devote themselves through giving ongoing material support for continued ministry in God's name.

TEN SCRIPTURES UPON WHICH TO MEDITATE

1. Genesis 8:20-9:17—Noah leaves the ark and offers a thanksgiving sacrifice to God. God is prompted to promise not to destroy the earth by a flood again.
2. Exodus 12:33-36—The Hebrew people are asked to leave Egypt, and as they

do they ask for gifts. They are given the plunder of a war that was never fought by soldiers or military weapons.

3. 1 Kings 17:8-16—In the midst of famine and death, a widow shares the last of her food with a stranger from another land. God blesses her for her gift.

4. 2 Chronicles 3—A storehouse is prepared for the contributions of God's people in support of the priesthood. This stands in contrast to number 7 below.

5. Psalm 96—Worship includes bringing gifts to God's house. Giving in response to God's gifts is a central act of corporate worship.

6. Malachi 3:6-12—Often used to remind people to give what is often overlooked is that this is a statement first and foremost to ministry leaders. This text contains more promise than it does judgment.

7. Luke 12:13-21—A rich man prepares a storehouse for his own benefit and takes personal credit for it. God is not pleased.

8. 1 Corinthians 2:1-5—Paul relied on the gospel and demonstration of the Holy Spirit's power as he engaged in ministry.

9. James 1:14-17—The devotional life integrates faith with action.

10. Revelation 5—The Christian mission fulfilled. This is the reason the Christian fundraiser does their work.

A POSSIBLE DEVOTIONAL EXERCISE

A. Read one of the above passages three times.

    1. After the first time, ask: "What do I notice or observe?"

    2. After the second time, ask: "What is God saying or doing in this text?"

    3. After the third time, ask: "What is God saying to me through this text?"

B. Pray, asking for grace to put what you observe into practice.

C. When next you meditate on one of these passages, return to your notes from the previous session and evaluate how well you are putting your observations into practice. Repeat A and B above.

MARK L. VINCENT (Ph.D., Capella University School of Business) leads Design For Ministry™—a network of experts who assist congregations, ministry organizations, and service-minded businesses. Mark has pioneered work in neighborhood ministry to children, congregational leadership development, decision making, The Giving Project, MMA's Stewardship University, firstfruits funding systems for denominations, strategic interim ministry, and the ENQUIRE™ system for capital campaigns. He is the principal writer for *Depth Perception*, and his books include *Speaking about Money*, *A Christian View of Money*, and *The Offering as Worship*. Mark edits *GIVING*, the annual periodical of the Ecumenical Stewardship Center. He can be reached at marklv@ DesignForMinistry.com.

1. Thomas H. Jeavons and Rebekah Basinger, *Growing Givers' Hearts: Treating Fundraising as Ministry* (San Francisco: Jossey-Bass, 2000).

2. Cornelius Plantinga Jr., "Dr. Willard's Diagnosis," *Christianity Today*, September 2006, 50.

3. See Scott Rodin's chapter in this book.

4. David Winter, *Closer than a Brother* (Wheaton: Harold Shaw, 1971).

5. Mark L. Vincent, *A Christian View of Money: Celebrating God's Generosity*, 3rd ed. (Eugene, OR: Wipf & Stock, 2007).

6. Luke and Acts are, in effect, one body of literature. The volume of words written in Luke and Acts exceeds that of all of Paul's epistles combined.

7. Vincent, *A Christian View of Money*.

Chapter

12

DISCIPLESHIP AS A TOOL
TO TRANSFORM HEARTS
TOWARD GENEROSITY

BY TODD W. HARPER, *Executive Vice President*
of Generous Giving

M y focus in childhood and young adulthood was to become rich. From as early as I can remember, I was consumed with money and the things money could buy. Everyone in my family knew it and would make reference to this fact in a variety of ways. For example, I grew up in a middle-class family of five children. For Christmas each year, my grandmother and aunt would give each of us $50. Each of my siblings would receive a single $50 bill, but not me. I would receive fifty $1 bills because they knew I liked to count money. In high school I had a lawn business, which generated an income of $1,000 per week during the summer months. At eighteen years old, I received my license to sell securities and worked for a small brokerage firm. I oriented my life and my focus on becoming "successful" and wealthy.

During my freshman year at college, the Lord convicted me of my misplaced priorities. He made it clear that, although I had grown up in a strong Christian family, I was conflicted about what was most important in my life. Matthew 6:24 accurately describes what I was unsuccessfully trying to do:

"No one can serve two masters. Either he will hate the one and love the other, or he will be devoted to one and despise the other. You cannot serve both God and Money."[1] At that time, I made a decision to turn my life and will over to God and trust Him for my future.

I have observed that many others among God's children are struggling in different ways to serve two masters. Some wrestle with money in subtle ways and others in more obvious ways. My motivation for writing this chapter may be surprising. I am primarily motivated to liberate people to be spiritually rich toward God and then, as a secondary result, to liberate resources to God's work. As explained in chapter one, this liberating comes as a person is conformed to the image of Christ and becomes generous as He is generous.

Unfortunately, many people are missing out on the blessings God has for them because they are focused on creating and accumulating wealth for themselves rather than stewarding it for God and experiencing the joy of giving to Him. Those involved in asking others for funds have the opportunity to facilitate the steady transformation of people to follow God wholeheartedly, releasing financial resources for Kingdom work and experiencing the blessings of the abundant life: freedom, joy, peace, contentment, meaning, and purpose. This chapter will address the opportunity to transform people's hearts so they are conformed to the image of Christ through a process of discipleship.

Since leaving fundraising several years ago, I have worked with Generous Giving, an organization that seeks to motivate followers of Jesus Christ toward greater biblical generosity. My role at Generous Giving is to encourage individual believers to experience the joy of giving and embrace a lifestyle of generosity, according to God's Word and Christ's example.

This chapter will outline some principles and methods for ministering to God's people that God can use to transform their hearts to be rich toward Him and generous with their resources. Four sections in this chapter will provide a road map of the process of discipleship toward the goal of heart transformation: (1) the importance of the asker's heart, (2) the process of discipleship in raising resources, (3) transformational tools, and (4) special considerations for discipling the wealthy. My experience validates this four-pronged approach to raising resources that can grow the giver spiritually, bless the asker relationally, bless the ministry financially, and expand God's Kingdom exponentially.

THE IMPORTANCE OF THE ASKER'S HEART

The first critical question those involved in raising resources must ask themselves is this: "Do I see my role as a job or a calling?" People who see fundraising as simply a job or a business may not find this chapter to be very helpful. However, for those who recognize their calling from God to this role and seek to advance God's agenda in the hearts of givers, this chapter can provide inspiration and practical assistance. (For more on this calling, see Lauren Libby's chapter.)

God wants to transform each of us to be conformed to the image of Christ. The Holy Spirit transforms believers over time by means of God's Word, relationships, and experiences. The role of the asker is to actively facilitate and participate in this transformation in the lives of givers. A critical question to answer is, "What is my primary motivation in what I do?" Is it to raise money, or is it to spiritually grow believers, specifically in the area of handling money in a way that honors God and advances His agenda? Andy Stanley, pastor of North Point Church near Atlanta, Georgia, puts it this way when talking about the members of his church: "My people need to know what I want *for* them before I tell them what I want *from* them."[2]

While understanding the audience is critical for effective ministry, it is not sufficient for facilitating transformation. In this job, transformation begins with the one who disciples. A leader cannot take people where they have not been themselves. Paul exhorts in 1 Corinthians 11:1, "Follow my example, as I follow the example of Christ." In order to lead people into generosity effectively, one must possess three qualities: contentment, humility, and generosity.

Contentment

In Philippians 4:11–12, Paul writes,

> *I am not saying this because I am in need, for I have learned to be content whatever the circumstances. I know what it is to be in need, and I know what it is to have plenty. I have learned the secret of being content in any and every situation, whether well fed or hungry, whether living in plenty or in want.*

This passage describes Paul's personal journey toward contentment. Even the apostle Paul had to *learn* the secret of being content, which shows that this quality does not come naturally; rather, it is a quality God cultivates over time through sanctification. Contentment can be challenging, especially during times of working among the wealthy. Being around the trappings of wealth can be attractive and rouse covetousness in the hearts of even strong believers. For this reason, God must transform His people so that, like Paul, they can testify to being content in any and every situation. Because of God's work, believers can be confident of God's unique provision, for He knows what is best for His people.

It is especially important for askers to seek contentment. Askers cannot be effective in facilitating spiritual growth in others if they find themselves wishing they could trade places with the giver. People do not like being around those who, however subtly, covet their position, possessions, or prestige. On the other hand, the asker's freedom from the desire for wealth creates freedom and authority to help givers develop their perspectives, grow spiritually, and experience joy in giving generously.

The askers' authority rests in a genuine expression of spiritual qualities in their own lives. Because Paul was content, as described in Philippians 4:11–12, he could ask with authority and integrity in verse 17: "Not that I am looking for a gift, but I am looking for what may be credited to your account." The readers of this letter recognized that due to Paul's contentment, he was not seeking money for his own benefit but rather was teaching the biblical principle of generosity, "It is more blessed to give than to receive" (Acts 20:35).

Humility

Humility is one of the qualities I have consistently observed in my interactions with generous people. They know it is not about them, and they are focused on using God's resources for others. This is part of what makes generous people so attractive. Philippians 2:2–3 teaches,

> *Do nothing out of selfish ambition or vain conceit, but in humility consider others better than yourselves. Each of you should look not only to your own interests, but also to the interests of others.*

In fundraising, there is great temptation to focus solely on the needs of the organization. In order to move beyond fundraising to transformational disciple making, the focus must shift to the needs and interests of others. People are drawn toward those who are free from the need to look out for their own interests and can instead focus on the needs of others. As this quality becomes more evident in askers' lives, their effectiveness in discipling others greatly increases.

Humility cannot be feigned; the Lord must develop it in the lives of believers. Humility frees the asker to focus on the needs of givers and to exhort givers to focus on the needs of others in their giving.

Generosity

In 2 Corinthians 8:7, Paul writes,

> *But just as you excel in everything—in faith, in speech, in knowledge, in complete earnestness and in your love for us—see that you also excel in this grace of giving.*

Askers cannot take people where they have not been themselves or impart what they have not internalized personally. People who do not allow God to cultivate a spirit of generosity in their own lives will be handicapped when they try to exhort others to move into greater generosity. While this point seems obvious, it cannot be overlooked.

The experience of a dear friend in development, who was convicted of his lack of generosity, illustrates this fact. He realized that he was a faithful tither but not a generous giver. The Lord had enabled him to get out of significant debt, and he had been debt free for more than two years. He and his wife were living frugally, well within their means, and he began to question why he was so frugal. He concluded that the reason for his frugality was not a drive to increase his generosity; rather, it was because he was afraid. In order to be free from fear and to excel in the grace of giving, he and his wife decided to double their giving to over 20 percent. Needless to say, his effectiveness in encouraging others to give generously has increased dramatically through his stepping out in faith to give generously, and the new joy he has experienced is a result.

No one will embody these qualities perfectly; the process of being conformed to Christ is ongoing. However, askers who allow God to mold in them the fundamental qualities of contentment, humility, and generosity will be increasingly effective in discipling givers toward greater generosity.

THE PROCESS OF DISCIPLESHIP IN RAISING FUNDS

As we explore the topic of discipleship, it is important to distinguish between fundraising and discipleship. Fundraising means gathering financial resources to accomplish a cause, most often with a marketing and transactional focus. On the other hand, discipleship means teaching, modeling, and living with people so that they become devoted followers of Christ who, in being conformed to the image of Christ, are enabled to be increasingly rich toward God.

While fundraising can be effective in accumulating resources for a given mission, those involved in seeking resources miss an incredible opportunity to liberate people and resources when their sole focus is the transaction of gaining funds (the giver's wallet). Discipleship opens up the possibility of spiritual transformation and true generosity (the giver's heart).

During my time on staff with Campus Crusade for Christ, a mutual friend referred me to a successful businessman, "John." I called to ask for a lunch appointment. Being a busy man, John asked me what I wanted. For some reason I was emboldened to answer in an atypical manner: "John, I want you to give away far more money than you ever dreamed possible. But I don't care if you ever give $1 to Campus Crusade." John agreed to meet me the following day on my trip through his town. That meeting began a relationship that has continued to this day. On my second visit with him, he earnestly told me he was convinced that God brought me into his life to help him give his money away.

In the world of Christian fundraising, which often follows a secular model, those seeking resources tend toward one of two extremes: the relational fundraiser or the transactional fundraiser. While relational fundraisers are primarily concerned with being friends and "buddies" with givers, transactional fundraisers focus solely on the "gifts" and moving on to their next "prospect." Both extremes have downsides: The relational approach generally avoids the financial aspect of givers' lives, while the transactional approach tends to miss a relational connection. Both approaches limit the opportunity to transform the hearts of givers. I want to advocate an alternative to these extremes: financial discipleship. If askers take the discipleship of givers seriously, they will intentionally build relationships to address specific, spiritually significant financial issues in givers' lives.

The apostle Paul presents a blueprint for financial discipleship in 1 Timothy 6:17–19:

Command those who are rich in this present world not to be arrogant nor to put their hope in wealth, which is so uncertain, but to put their hope in God, who richly provides us with everything for our enjoyment. Command them to

do good, to be rich in good deeds, and to be generous and willing to share. In this
way they will lay up treasure for themselves as a firm foundation for the coming
age, so that they may take hold of the life that is truly life.

Paul presents two prohibitions and four exhortations in this passage. His first prohibition is not to be arrogant. This is a particularly relevant point for those living in the developed world. People tend to become arrogant when they believe they are in control of their future. Money creates the illusion of control, and the Bible teaches that the greatest danger of wealth is self-dependence rather than God-dependence. When people are assured that the money they possess will meet their future financial needs, they can become arrogant by believing they are in control.

A caveat is in order here: According to Paul, anyone living in the developed world would qualify as rich. From a global perspective nearly everyone living in the United States is overwhelmingly wealthy. For example, someone making more than $30,000 per year is in the top 5 percent of the world's population in terms of income.[3] Thus, this passage in 1 Timothy applies to nearly everyone in the United States.

Paul's second prohibition is not to place one's hope in wealth. Interestingly, he does not say that doing so is wrong but that wealth itself is uncertain. In other words, it is not wrong to trust in wealth, but it is stupid. However, it is ever so tempting to place one's hope in the security that one believes wealth brings. In my own life I continue to struggle not to place my hope in my retirement account, children's college funds, home equity, or general savings. These resources give a sense of security that Paul teaches is illusory. The more resources people have under their stewardship, the more tempting it is to believe that resources, rather than God, provide security.

After telling readers what not to do, Paul gives positive exhortations. His first is for believers to place their hope in God. Believers can be confident in God because He is trustworthy and good. He richly provides His children with everything for their enjoyment. This is an important point for askers' work with givers: that God is good. He gives good gifts to His children. Those raising resources are not the lifestyle police; it is not their job to define what is appropriate or not in terms of comforts and luxuries. That is not to say there is no place for discussion about these issues with people being discipled, but it is important not to become judgmental about people's lifestyles. Disciplers should lead with grace and let the Holy Spirit convict people of changes in lifestyle.

Paul's second, third, and fourth exhortations are to do good, be rich in good deeds, and be generous and willing to share. They are three different ways of saying the same thing, that we have been "blessed to be a blessing" (Gen. 12:3). He is reminding the readers of the reason they have been entrusted with more than they need. Why? Not for their own benefit exclusively, as the culture seems to proclaim, but for the benefit of others. In 2 Corinthians 8:13–15, Paul explains his reasoning further:

> Our desire is not that others might be relieved while you are hard pressed, but that there might be equality. At the present time your plenty will supply what they need, so that in turn their plenty will supply what you need. Then there will be equality, as it is written: "He who gathered much did not have too much and he who gathered little did not have too little."

Author and former pastor Randy Alcorn puts it this way: "God prospers me not to raise my standard of living, but to raise my standard of giving."[4]

The best part of this entire passage comes when Paul explains why he is instructing people to live in this manner: "so that they may take hold of the life that is truly life." Askers could approach their task with the goal of freeing people from the love of money so that they may "take hold of the life that is truly life." In this way, they can boldly step into people's lives, for they are not concerned with what they want *from* givers but rather what they want *for* them. This passage informs the process of everything they do. Those who are most generous are those who are experiencing the abundant life of which Jesus spoke in John 10:10, "I have come that they may have life, and have it to the full." This is the "life that is truly life" that Paul is describing to Timothy, his young protégé.

One example of the life of generosity is "Peter," a businessman in his late forties from the Midwest. He and his wife underwent a conversion related to their giving. In 2001 they attended a conference on giving, where they were challenged to give more generously. They responded by doubling their giving to the causes about which they were passionate. The following year, they paid for six couples to join them at the same conference, wishing for their friends to be blessed by the same experience and similarly increase their giving. Peter assumed that he was returning to this conference simply to encourage his friends, not to be personally challenged again in his own giving. God had a different idea, and before Peter left the conference, God had impressed him and his wife to increase their giving another two-and-a-half times. He said they spent less than $150,000 on personal expenses that year and gave away over $3 million.

That's the quantitative side of their story. The qualitative side is equally compelling. The joy, freedom, and contentment this couple experiences is uncommon and attractive. Additionally, their sense of purpose and calling is clear. God has given them the spiritual gift of giving, and they are exercising this gift with excellence. As they live in their calling, there is a profound sense of fulfillment in doing what God has designed them to do. Proverbs 11:24–25 applies for this couple and many others who are living out the principles of 1 Timothy 6:17–19: *One man gives freely, yet gains even more; another withholds unduly, but comes to poverty. A generous man will prosper; he who refreshes others will himself be refreshed.* When those called to ask approach their mission with a transformational, discipleship perspective, they can be God's instruments for freeing people to experience the joy, freedom, and purpose that come from living out one's calling.

USEFUL TOOLS FOR AIDING TRANSFORMATION

People do not change in an instant by their individual efforts. Rather, transformation into the image of Christ is the work of the Holy Spirit through genuine relationships over time. (For more on the process of transformation, see R. Scott Rodin's chapter.) For this reason, the presence of askers in meaningful relationship with the people they serve can be life changing. So what are some tools to aid in this endeavor?

Included in this chapter is a chart representing four stages of a giver's journey toward greater generosity. The chart is designed to be a useful tool for discipling a giver. It can be used by the discipler to intentionally move a giver along the journey toward greater maturity by employing the suggested tools in each stage. Alternatively, it can be given to givers to allow them to self-assess their own journey and serve as a road map for ongoing interactions with those God has called them to serve. This chart can also be used to discern the giver's current place in their journey so that the discipler can be better equipped to continue the discipling process. This chart of the giver's journey can be used in conjunction with the chart of spiritual maturity found in chapter 1.

There are four elements that contribute to transformation in a giver's life: teaching, relationships, experiences, and questions. The following are some of the useful tools within each category.

TEACHING is a primary component of transformation into the image of Christ. First and most important, God's Word changes people who take it to heart. Additionally, writers and speakers who communicate the life-changing message of God's Word in a compelling manner are meaningful resources to pass along to givers. Here are a few suggestions:

1. *The Treasure Principle*, by Randy Alcorn,[5] is a quick and easy read with a powerful paradigm-shifting message on the joy of investing in eternity, and it is based on Alcorn's excellent and exhaustive book *Money, Possessions*

and Eternity.[6]

2. Andy Stanley's book *Fields of Gold* is another short but powerful book that deals with the fear that keeps people from giving generously.[7]

3. John Piper's book *Desiring God* contains a chapter entitled "Money: The Currency of Christian Hedonism," which presents important biblical arguments for the faith and joy that accrue to the giver who lives a generous, God-oriented life.[8]

4. Richard Foster's book *Celebration of Discipline* has a chapter called "The Discipline of Simplicity."[9] Foster later expanded his writing on simplicity into an excellent book entitled *The Freedom of Simplicity.*[10]

5. Generous Giving's website (www.GenerousGiving.org) has an extensive library of talks delivered by renowned speakers such as Rick Warren, Randy Alcorn, Henry Blackaby, Joseph Stowell, Ravi Zacharias, and Bob Coy.

RELATIONSHIPS are a second component God uses to transform people. The purpose of this chapter is to encourage you toward a transformational relationship with many of the givers you serve. God can use you to help givers store up treasures in heaven. I often have described myself as an eternal investment advisor. There are millions of financial advisors in this country who help people with their temporal investments, but people also need guidance for their eternal investments.

One of the most effective discipleship services an asker can provide to givers is to introduce them to other givers who are generous. Whether or not these generous people ever give money to your ministry, exposing those with whom you work to people who are further along in their journey of generosity allows the givers to see how generosity positively impacts life. Proverbs 27:17 teaches, "As iron sharpens iron, so one man sharpens another."

Another way to positively influence givers is to introduce them to stories of other givers. For instance, Generous Giving's website provides a platform where people can learn one another's stories about giving and celebrate God's work through people's generosity. There is something very powerful about hearing the story of someone with whom you can relate.

Several years ago, a man was given a set of testimony CDs from a Generous Giving conference. He was known as one of the most generous men in his community, yet upon listening to the stories of other givers, he was deeply convicted. He shared with me later he had always thought of himself as generous, but listening to others' stories had convicted him that he had a long way to go. He and his wife immediately made significant changes to their estate plan and quadrupled their annual giving.

EXPERIENCES are a third element God uses in transforming His children. While teaching engages the mind, experience engages the person through all five senses. Talking with anyone who has traveled internationally for ministry will reveal how transformational this can be.

One of the most generous businessmen I know tells the story of a trip to Haiti to show an evangelistic film of the life of Christ. He was out in the villages for a week, but his group never arrived at half of the film showings they scheduled because the dilapidated truck they were driving broke down. Immediately upon his return home, he sent money for a new truck so that more people could hear the gospel in Haiti. His experience in Haiti had changed his perspective in a way that prompted him to give.

Another friend described his experience at an event Generous Giving hosted for givers. He explained how the event had changed his life because it was the first time he had been in a place surrounded by successful businessmen who were joyful about their giving. This experience made him wonder what he was missing out on by not giving more. It is one thing to talk about the joy of giving as an abstract concept, but it is another to see and feel the enthusiasm of one's peers as they describe the joy they find in giving. This friend has increased his giving more than ten times annually since this experience.

Meaningful local ministry involvement can be another transformational experience. A ministry leader I know works with a local prison ministry, seeking funds. He has had an incredible impact on local business leaders, getting them into the jail to minister and experience something most of them have only seen on TV. This experience changes people's perspective of the world from self-centered to God-centered. Facilitating experiences, even if they are not with one's own ministry, can be a powerful tool in facilitating transformation in givers.

The fourth tool in discipling givers is double-edged: **APPROPRIATELY ASKED QUESTIONS** and **ATTENTIVE LISTENING**. Often what you say is less insightful than the questions you ask, and listening allows one to discern where the giver is on his or her journey. If you are to be used of God to significantly influence givers, you should learn to ask powerful, appropriate questions in the context of a relationship. There is an art to asking good questions. As noted earlier in the chapter, one must be humble—that is, looking to the interests of others, not simply one's own interests. There is also an art to listening well. Rather than feeling the need to jump in with your own answers, listen closely to the giver's feelings and attitudes. After all, one asks the question in order to know and help the giver as effectively as possible. Asking good questions and listening closely to the answers demonstrate the discipler's priorities—the purpose of the questioning is to disciple, encourage, and help the giver mature spiritually. One can aid him or her in going from an "Emerging Giver" to a "Giving Champion." If a giver believes probing questions are for his or her benefit and that his or her answers actually are given attention, he or she will be more likely to engage in the discussion and invite challenging questions.

Second, one must know when to ask appropriate questions. Typically, as trust deepens in the relationship, one is able to ask more probing questions. Question asking is more art than science. If one is uncertain about the bounds of appropriate questions, one can always ask permission to ask a personal question. If permission is granted, be willing to ask intentional questions with grace and truth.

A few sample questions to ask givers include:

- Why do you give?
- Who is the owner of all you possess?
- How much (money) is enough?
- What is an appropriate lifestyle?
- Where do you experience the most joy in giving?
- Who is the next steward of your resources, and is that person prepared?
- Have you considered establishing annual and lifetime giving goals?

Asked at the right time and in the context of a relationship, these questions can be transformational in people's lives. Often, these questions suggest ideas people have never considered. Certainly the typical lawyer, accountant, or financial advisor is not asking these questions; givers' pastors probably are not asking them. God can use fundraisers to encourage many to become increasingly rich toward Himself—to disciple many to be conformed to Christ's image.

SPECIAL CONSIDERATIONS FOR DISCIPLING THE WEALTHY

Since effectiveness in ministry increases with an understanding of the audience one is seeking to serve, I would like to provide some insight into the heart of the wealthy. They spend their lives trying to discern people's agendas for having a relationship with them. They seem to have a sixth sense about people's motives. This is not the typical life experience of a development officer. It can be difficult to put oneself in another's shoes when their experience is dramatically different from one's own. However, the more attuned one becomes to the experience of those he or she is serving, the more effective that development officer will be.

So, how can those seeking resources live out their calling and at the same time mitigate the targeted feeling of many givers? The key is to first bring the message of biblical generosity for the Kingdom, and only secondarily bring specific opportunities to participate in the ministry or cause one represents. In this way, one can help persuade givers to believe and experience the truth of Jesus' words, "It is more blessed to give than to receive" (Acts 20:35). The biblical message of generosity is one of opportunity, not obligation; joy, not duty; grace, not law. How an asker invites people into the opportunity, joy, and grace of giving will be determined by his or her own commitment to seeking first God's Kingdom and believing that all these things will be added unto him or her (Matt. 6:33).

Ministering to the wealthy is a cross-cultural experience for many financial disciplers. It is helpful to recognize this and not presume that one knows what a wealthy person is thinking or how he or she is feeling. Generally the most significant thing a development officer can do is to pray for and seek out cultural insiders who can teach him the culture and life of the wealthy. Doing so will allow the asker to understand their culture and the lives they lead, helping him or her to become increasingly able to live and serve cross-culturally in the world of the affluent.

PAYOFF OF TRANSFORMATIONAL DISCIPLESHIP

With this financial discipleship approach to raising resources, everyone involved gains much for eternity. Askers/disciplers are not called simply to facilitate financial transactions between givers and worthy causes. They have the privilege of facilitating transformation in the lives of their brothers and sisters in Christ. As people are liberated from the love of money and the cultural pull of materialism, they are released into the joy of generosity, and they become increasingly rich toward God. They gain as they are freed to experience giving not under compulsion but "giving as much as they are able and even beyond their ability," as the Macedonians did for the believers in Jerusalem (2 Cor. 8:3). Those seeking resources also gain as they experience deeper relationships with their constituents. They understand that as disciplers of givers, they do not simply transact business but rather follow God's ways and do business very differently from most fundraisers. Most important, God's Kingdom is made more manifest on earth as people are transformed to become more like Christ and resources are released exponentially for His work. I know this approach is counter to most fundraising techniques; however, I also know that as we move in this direction, we will be used by God to create a revolution in giving and God's Kingdom will flourish.

TODD W. HARPER is executive vice president of Generous Giving, managing its interactions with givers. He holds a bachelor's degree in economics and entrepreneurship from Baylor University and comes out of an eleven-year career with Campus Crusade for Christ International, where he served in Russia, Yugoslavia, and the United States. Prior to joining Generous Giving, Harper was a partner with an investment firm, advising high net-worth clients on growing and using wealth wisely. Harper's passion is to disciple others; he has extensive experience in ministry leadership, major donor development, and philanthropic advising. He lives with his wife, Collynn, and five children in Orlando, Florida.

1. Scripture quotationa are from the Holy Bible, New International Version.
2. Andy Stanley, "Creating a Stewardship Culture: Three Critical Components," speech delivered at the Exponential '04 Conference for Pastors, Generous Giving's joint conference with Crown Financial Ministries, Alpharetta, GA, September 21, 2004.
3. Global Rich List, www.globalrichlist.com.
4. Randy Alcorn, *The Treasure Principle: Unlocking the Secret of Joyful Giving* (Sisters, OR: Multnomah, 2001), 75.
5. Ibid.,
6. Randy Alcorn, *Money, Possessions and Eternity* (Wheaton: Tyndale House, 2003).
7. Andy Stanley, *Fields of Gold: A Place beyond Your Deepest Fears, a Prize beyond Your Wildest Imagination*, Generous Giving Series (Wheaton: Tyndale House, 2004).
8. John Piper, *Desiring God* (Sisters, OR: Multnomah, 2003).
9. Richard J. Foster, *Celebration of Discipline: The Path to Spiritual Growth*, 20th anniversary ed. (San Francisco: HarperCollins, 1998).
10. Richard J. Foster, *The Freedom of Simplicity* (New York: HarperCollins, 1981).

Figure 12-1

THIS IS A JOURNEY

EMERGING GIVER	MATURING GIVER

Reasons for Giving (Why)

- I give primarily because of relationships, tax savings, public recognition, or a feeling of obligation.
- My primary desire is to pass on assets to children and family.
- I follow the advice of trusted advisors—not necessarily spiritual advisors.
- I may give in response to something that has personally impacted me.
- I may still seek greatness in the eyes of man.
- I am not sure I understand biblical stewardship.

Practice of Giving (How)

- I have more of a "here and now" mentality in my giving.
- I may provide a scheduled gift to church or charity.
- I may give 10 percent of my income.

Direction of Giving (Where)

- My giving is not based on planning or intentional strategies.
- I tend to give to those who ask.

Things to Possibly Read or Do:

Randy Alcorn *The Treasure Principle*
Andy Stanley *Fields of Gold*
Leo Tolstoy "How Much Land Does a Man Need?"
Listen to personal testimonies of generous givers
Attend a Generous Giving conference

Questions for Reflection:

1. Who has had a spiritual impact in my life?
2. What cause/event has been meaningful in my life?
3. What giving opportunity has brought me the most joy?
4. What, if any, is my annual giving goal?
5. Why have I been given more than I need?

Reasons for Giving (Why)

- I have a growing desire to give as I further understand God's plan.
- I wrestle with a desire to pass on wealth to children or give to the Kingdom.
- I am open to listening to trusted advisors based on spiritual truth.
- I understand that everything belongs to God and I am simply a steward of His assets.
- I am beginning to view giving as an investment in others.

Practice of Giving (How)

- Developing short-term giving strategies and goals is becoming more important.
- I have a deepening understanding of stewardship and ownership.
- I give a minimum of 10 percent and desire to give progressively more.

Direction of Giving (Where)

- I am discovering more causes where I find joy in giving.

Things to Possibly Read or Do:

Wes Willmer *God and Your Stuff*
John Piper *Desiring God* (chap. 7)
Richard Foster *Celebration of Discipline* (chap. 6)
Ralph Doudera *Wealth Conundrum*
Go on a mission trip
Listen to personal testimonies of generous givers
Attend a Generous Giving conference
Participate in a Crown Special Edition study

Questions for Reflection:

1. What is an appropriate lifestyle?
2. How much is enough?
3. What, if any, is my lifetime giving goal?
4. If time and money were no object, what would I do with my life?
5. Who is the next steward and are they prepared?

GENEROUS GIVER

GIVING CHAMPION

Reasons for Giving (Why)

- My giving is an outward material expression of my spiritual commitment, as God continues to mold my heart to willing obedience.
- I see assets as a sacred trust. I see that family estate decisions are to be based on an intentional transfer of spiritual, character, and financial capital.
- I actively seek spiritual guidance for all giving matters.
- I experience the blessing of generosity and of being a "cheerful giver."
- I am willing to give to people and/or organizations independent of tax benefits.
- I sometimes give anonymously.

Practice of Giving (How)

- I use systematic planning to accomplish the responsibilities of stewardship.
- I give generously (beyond conventional norms) out of both income and assets to multiple ministries/people.
- I may give sacrificially.

Direction of Giving (Where)

- I give intentionally and aggressively to causes God has given me a passion for.

Things to Possibly Read or Do:

Ron Blue *Splitting Heirs*
John Piper *Don't Waste Your Life*
Richard Foster *The Freedom of Simplicity*
Attend The Gathering conference
Attend a Generous Giving conference
Attend a Generous Giving boutique event
Teach children or grandchildren Crown for Teens
Go on a family mission trip

Questions for Reflection:

1. How do I steward all that God has entrusted to me?
2. What are the dangers and opportunities of wealth from a spiritual perspective?
3. How could my family be more involved in giving?
4. What does my eternal investment portfolio look like?
5. What are the benefits of simplicity?

- I attempt to pursue God's plan in every aspect of my finances.
- I encourage others to begin the journey of generosity.
- I give to facilitate generosity in others.
- I am motivated by transformation in others.
- I am a careful steward of all God has entrusted to me: time, talent, treasure, truth, and relationships.
- I intentionally seek to influence family, friends, church, and community with living ever more generously.
- I am comfortable around those with wealth.
- I can challenge without being judgmental.
- I find joy in seeing life change in others.
- I consider how I can utilize my influence and affluence for God's Kingdom.
- I seek the approval of God, not man (Gal. 1:10).

Things to Possibly Do:

Attend The Gathering Conference
Bring others to a Generous Giving conference
Host a Generous Giving boutique event
Go on a family mission trip
Spend time investing in others—mentoring
Lead a Crown Special Edition Study
Serve on the board of a local Christian foundation

Questions for Reflection:

1. Who would benefit from these experiences?
2. Who am I intentionally mentoring?
3. How do I discern my calling?
4. What might my church look like if it were generous?
5. Am I equipped to share my giving story?

Organizing Fundraising to
TRANSFORM STEWARDS
TO BE RICH TOWARD GOD

BY **ADAM J. MORRIS**, *Senior Director of Stewardship
and Resource Development at Biola University*

I 'll never forget that November day when I sat with an elderly widow in Long Beach, California. Her name was Lucille, and she and I had a strong friendship that centered on her love for God and her heart for ministry. We had wonderful talks about life, family, and the Lord. She lived a simple life. She grew up during the Great Depression and never seemed to find the material things of the world all that interesting. Her gifts to my organization were modest, yet consistent over the years.

I had asked her to prayerfully consider a generous gift to our capital campaign and was returning to her home to see where she was with this request. As we sipped tea at the kitchen table, Lucille began to cry. She was bursting with joy and couldn't wait to tell me that God had spoken to her the night before. She located several stock certificates and slid them across the table. She told me that this was her contribution to our project and that she couldn't believe that it took her eighty years to experience the true joy of giving. Lucille's gift was the largest contribution she had ever made. We rejoiced together and had a wonderful time of prayer. It was an incredible moment.

Right before my eyes, the Lord provided a vivid example of how engaged He is in raising resources. Through the work of the Holy Spirit, I saw in Lucille something that no development professional could have ever accomplished on his or her own. What I saw was a transformed heart, conformed to the image of Christ, and now desiring to be generous, as Christ is generous. Because Lucille's heart was focused on God's eternal values, she was rich toward God.

My time with Lucille ignited in me a desire to find a new approach to raising funds. No longer was I comfortable using many of the "techniques" I had learned at secular professional conferences. I began to understand that generous gifts happen when God does a transforming work in the heart of a believer who is then conformed to the image of Christ. They become generous as Christ is generous. I soon realized that it had less to do with my dark suit and starched shirt, my four-color brochure, my compelling case for support, or my persuasive nature. I was beginning to grasp the fact that my primary job as a stewardship officer was to help believers experience that same joyous heart transformation that so filled Lucille.

As I reflected on my time with Lucille and tried to reorient my understanding of fundraising to be God-centered, I began looking for resources to help me build an effective, God-honoring fundraising program. Unfortunately, I couldn't find many to help me discern how to apply the truth of God's Word to the practice of raising money. The purpose of this chapter is to be such a resource by outlining a philosophy and practice of raising funds that is centered on advancing and facilitating the transformation of stewards to be rich toward God, using the following eight components:

1. Establish a biblical philosophy of raising funds.
2. Encourage an organizational ethos that supports this philosophy.
3. Hire staff who share and articulate stewardship values.

4. Depend on the Holy Spirit as the "heart motivator."

5. Focus on facilitating a believer's faith in and worship of God.

6. Avoid practices that manipulate or encourage the wrong motive for giving.

7. Develop a sacred trust between the organization and its ministry partners.

8. Celebrate God's provision when financial goals are met.

1. Establish a Biblical Philosophy of Fundraising

John Frank defines Christian fundraising as "creating opportunities to involve God's people in God's work."[1] He believes this fundraising is the link that connects God's people with God's Kingdom work by placing greater emphasis on involving believers in ministry (engaging their hearts) than on meeting financial goals. From this perspective, the fundraiser recognizes that God is the creator and owner of everything, and it is as people are conformed to the image of Christ that they give generously. The fundraiser, then, becomes a facilitator who links the giver with the ministries that are building God's Kingdom. Therefore, a good fundraising office is one that helps believers realize that they are caretakers, or stewards, of their time, talents, and treasures.[2] Fundraising becomes more than simply recruiting volunteers, developing a case statement, asking for the gift, and publicly recognizing ministry partners. It involves a long-term commitment to growing givers' hearts, so that they are conformed to the image of Christ and are generous because Christ is generous.

Building a God-centered, heart-focused fundraising program begins with a well-defined philosophy of fundraising. One resource is the *Biblical Principles for Stewardship and Fundraising* (see Joyce Brooks's chapter). In wrestling with the biblical texts, you begin to formulate an understanding of why people give and acknowledge God's ultimate ownership of all things. An important step in developing your philosophy of fundraising is to write out a purpose statement for your organization's fundraising program. While it is not perfect, consider the following philosophy and purpose statement at Biola University. These principles not only guide its practice but are shared with ministry partners early in the relationship building process.

GOD, GIVING, AND ASKING AT BIOLA UNIVERSITY

One of the primary objectives of Biola University is to help Christians think Christianly from a biblical worldview perspective. This includes how we ask ministry partners to help equip men and women in mind and character to impact the world for the Lord Jesus Christ. When it comes to your giving and our asking, here are some thoughts on a biblical perspective that we try to follow.

1. GOD OWNS IT ALL (1 Chron. 29:14)

God has provided us with all of our time, wealth, possessions, and resources. God owns everything. These resources are His gifts to us, which God will use to accomplish wonderful things for His Kingdom.

2. WE ARE TO MANAGE GOD'S RESOURCES (1 Peter 4:10)

Since God owns everything, Christians are called to be managers or stewards of all that God entrusts to them, to honor and glorify Him.

3. OUR GIVING IS TO GOD (Rom. 12:1; Phil. 4:17)

Giving, then, is a worshipful, obedient act of returning to God from what He has provided. Your giving should be directed to God and His work, not to an organization. Therefore, giving is a spiritual decision.

4. GOD IS WATCHING OUR GIVING (Rom. 14:12; 2 Cor. 5:10; Luke 16)

From God's Kingdom view, our giving becomes a tool to further God's work on earth, a test to see how much responsibility we will be given in heaven, and our giving serves as a trademark of our lives as Christians.

5. GOD IS THE FUNDRAISER (1 Chron. 29:9; 2 Cor. 9:7)

When needs are shared, the response is from the heart. God is the only One who stirs hearts and moves spirits.

6. WHAT IS BIOLA'S ROLE? (1 Chron. 29:9; Ex. 35:21; 2 Cor. 8-9)

Examples from David, Moses, and Paul suggest that Biola University's responsibility is to share the need, provide opportunities for stewards to respond, and allow God the opportunity to stir hearts and move spirits.

BIOLA'S PURPOSE IN FUNDRAISING

From a biblical perspective, then, when Biola asks you to give, our greater purpose is for your accountability to God. Our primary concern is to provide opportunities for you to lay up (send ahead) treasures in heaven (Matt. 6:19–21), and a secondary motive is to have you further God's work by giving to Biola.

As a result of honoring God with a biblical approach to our giving and asking practices, we believe that in God's time, He will supply all our needs (Phil. 4:19). In addition, we believe that as we honor God in doing things His way and relying on God changing hearts, the resulting joy-filled generosity will fully fund God's work (Ex. 36:3–7).

We would encourage you to consider how your generous giving to Biola can become a joy for you as you honor God.

WHY WE SHOULD GIVE
Psalm 24:1

The earth is the Lord's, and all it contains, the world, and those who dwell in it.

Most people think they should give to simply do good for mankind. This is a popular, cultural idea used to raise money throughout the world and even among some Christian organizations. Biblical stewardship stems from the understanding that God is the owner of all that we have, and we are managers of God's resources. He has chosen to give us things to use for His glory. While "doing good for mankind" focuses on the individual who is giving, biblical stewardship focuses on the ownership of God.

Clearly establishing such guiding principles is important to anchoring the rest of your organization's fundraising program and practices.

2. Encourage an Organizational Ethos That Supports This Philosophy

Following a biblical philosophy of fundraising may be a radical shift away from your current fundraising practices. Adopting such principles may seem daunting if it means doing business differently. Or, a set of guiding principles may help bring into focus what the organization has believed all along. For those of you who are in organizations with sophisticated fundraising programs that are steeped in secular tradition, the shift to a biblical model may be quite difficult. A holistic approach to biblical fundraising requires that all fundraising functions be evaluated through the same biblical filter.

It is important to recognize up front that the leader of your organization will play a pivotal role in establishing a culture of biblical stewardship (see David Black's chapter). Schmidt believes that a distinctively biblical fundraising program is evident through the heart condition of its leaders.[3] If the ministry leader's heart is focused on God, it will bring forth right motivations that will ultimately produce right methods. Randy Alcorn says that fundraising will never rise above the spiritual quality and perspective of those leading the ministry.[4] Jerry White encourages boards (see Rebekah Basinger's chapter) to help evaluate the ethics behind their fundraising philosophy for biblical acceptability and the Holy Spirit's guidance.[5] Jeavons and Basinger claim that "only theologically reflective and spiritually mature leadership can move a development program toward the place where a concern about the spiritual condition of ministry partners is held in creative tension with concern about the financial condition of the organization."[6]

Let me be clear in saying that some organizational leaders will think you are crazy for adopting a biblical model of fundraising. While they will likely agree that they want their fundraising to be God-honoring, they may interpret your suggestions as softening their approach to raising funds and thus proving to be too great a risk to the bottom line. Developing and implementing a biblical model of fundraising takes time. Be patient . . . and be diligent to bring about the change that will honor God and result in a revolution of giving. Pray that God will change hearts. Find colleagues within your organization and at others that share your values, and start by taking baby steps.

3. Hire Staff Who Share and Articulate Stewardship Values

An important next step is to build a team of stewardship professionals who embrace these values and apply them to their work. However, finding good people can be very difficult. In a survey of 521 parachurch CEOs, I found that few leaders felt spiritual maturity was a top qualification/requirement when hiring fundraising personnel.[7] The primary requirement, according to these CEOs, was hiring people with a proven track record of fundraising success and the ability to close a deal.

When my organization hires major gift officers, they often follow a general outline to assess skills, gifts, technical proficiencies, and spiritual development. Interviews tend to be comprehensive. In addition to ascertaining that they are attentive listeners, have a track record of responding in a timely fashion, and embrace the organization's values and technical competence, staff should have the biblical competencies required to minister to the heart of your constituents. To assess this in the interview process, one might consider asking the applicant the following questions:

- Can you explain how God views money and possessions?
- What has God taught you personally about His view of money and possessions?
- How do you handle your own giving?
- What are some guiding stewardship principles you might share with a prospective ministry partner?

- If a ministry partner asked you to show him or her some key steward-ship passages in Scripture, where would you have him or her turn?
- What process would you want to take a person through to help disciple them in the area of faith and finances?

4. Depend on the Holy Spirit as the "Heart Motivator"

When an organization has built a God-honoring fundraising program that has established trusted relationships with ministry partners, the Holy Spirit can be clearly seen moving in the hearts of people—motivating them to give. Moving beyond the surface motivations (such as tax benefits, recognition, duty, etc.) is not an easy task—in fact, there is no prescriptive formula to help "facilitate" the Holy Spirit. It is beyond our human capability. Yet there are some biblical guidelines that might help put motivation in perspective. If you are a stewardship officer charged with raising funds, consider the following as a means to disciple a believer into a posture of godly motivation (see also Todd Harper's chapter).

1. **Understand the heart**. The heart is the place where decisions are made; obedience or disobedience is directly connected to the condition of the heart (Mark 7:21; Prov. 22:15; Jer. 17:9). Generous giving results from a heart that is conformed to the image of Christ and is generous because Christ is generous.

2. **Promote godly obedience**. Mankind has the ability to choose to obey or disobey God (Gen. 3:5, 22; Deut. 6:13–19). This type of obedience can only be fostered through a deep, meaningful relationship with Him. As Rodin states, "You cannot be 'sort of' or 'occasionally' a Citizen of the Kingdom. It's an all or nothing proposition—a state that permeates every area of life."[8] Motivation should be rooted in a deep relationship with God, prompted by a desire to be obedient to Him.

3. **Encourage holiness**. In Leviticus 19:2 we are told to "Be holy because

I, the Lord your God, am holy." It is clear that those who follow God are called to be holy—to think and act differently than those who are not following Christ (Deut. 7:6; Lev. 11:44; Eph. 4:17).

4. **Lean on the Holy Spirit**. *Parakletos*, the Greek word for Holy Spirit found in the gospel of John, gives a clear depiction of God's provision of a helper, comforter, and counselor. In John 14:13–16 (NKJV), Jesus promises to leave His disciples with "another helper" to "abide with" them forever. For the ministry partner, there is the promise that this God-given Paraclete is available to help guide financial decisions. The choice of whether to give does not have to be made alone. For those willing to engage the Holy Spirit in the process, God Himself promises to direct and grow the heart. Likewise, the Holy Spirit works through the stewardship professional as a helper, comforter, and counselor.

It may feel like a risky thing to back off on the secular techniques of motivation and shift one's trust to God as the ultimate motivator. A few years back I was forced to put this belief to the test. Consider the following.

WHEN THE HOLY SPIRIT MOVES

For eighteen months I had the privilege of working with the widow of a prominent, world-renowned businessman. I met her and was quickly accepted as her trusted financial advisor. Her stated desire was quite simple—to get her financial affairs in order and make a large contribution to my organization. After months and months of planning (and countless hours of attorney fees), we finally had a plan that we all agreed to. Built into the plan was a $2.2 million dollar gift.

The day before the gift was made, she called me and said that she thought it would be good for our ministry to have her name on the building. She recounted the numerous other prominent organizations whose buildings bore her name. I took her request to my administration for their consideration. As that day unfolded and I had other conversations with the donor, we began questioning her motives. We began wondering if this gift was being given out of a heart conformed to Christ, or for personal recognition here on earth. It was my responsibility to communicate to her that we weren't willing to put her name on the building. In a fit of rage she hung up, saying, "You can kiss this gift good-bye."

Eighteen months of work and a $2.2 million dollar gift seemed gone. I was devastated. A few of us gathered that evening for prayer and simply put the situation in the Lord's hands. The next morning she called me. She asked if she could read me a short devotional that she had picked up the night before. "Coincidentally" the topic was pride, and she shared with me that throughout the night she felt convicted that her motives for making the gift weren't pure. She apologized profusely and asked if I could come to her home to complete the gift. She said that God told her to make the gift with no strings attached, and her relationship with our ministry was forever changed. She became one of our most loyal, generous supporters, making numerous gifts throughout her remaining years. How thankful we were that the Holy Spirit moved in such a profound way.

5. Focus on Facilitating a Believer's Faith in and Worship of God

As stated earlier in this book, generosity results as the believer is conformed to the image of Christ and becomes generous, as Christ is generous. The role of fundraising, then, is to advance and facilitate a believer's faith in and worship of God through a Christ-centered understanding of biblical stewardship. As a result, generosity will follow. It is easy to think about the *gift* as the "end product." But the gift is only a by-product. The end product, according to Smith, is the ministry partner—a friend who is growing in Christ, thriving spiritually, and joyfully being used by God in the mission of the organization.[9] Smith claims that believers need relationship and ministry far more than organizations need their money. Every fundraising activity needs to value and consider ministry partners, for it is the transformation of their hearts to be rich toward God that is the goal. As Rodin writes:

> Imagine designing a program that took God's promises of rewards seriously and saw the gift of giving as the greatest blessing in the [charitable] transaction. Imagine acknowledging the primary role of the Holy Spirit as the motivator of all our gifts and the peace and courage we would receive in our planning and asking. Imagine a program whose objectives were built around the desire to encourage and challenge donors to a greater and deeper walk with Jesus Christ.[10]

To accomplish this you first achieve the previous points in this chapter of having a biblical philosophy of fundraising, gaining organizational support, hiring like-minded staff, and learning to depend on the Holy Spirit.

Listed below are some guiding principles for facilitating a believer's faith that will result in generosity:

1. Realize that generosity is the result of a transformed heart that is conformed to the image of Christ and becomes generous as Christ is generous (see Walt Russell's chapter).

2. Focus first on the potential supporter's relationship with God and secondarily on your organization.

3. Acknowledge that God, not slick techniques, is the motivator (2 Cor. 9:7) who stirs hearts and moves spirits to give to a ministry opportunity.

4. The facilitator's role is to provide giving opportunities within the purpose of the organization so the giver can lay up treasures in heaven (Matt. 6:19–21).

5. The facilitator becomes a spiritual discipler who helps people become generous by growing in their understanding of godly giving (see Todd

Harper's chapter).

6. The facilitator becomes a shepherd of the stewards of God's possessions and aligns their giving interests with the right organizations.

7. The facilitator's practices are designed to grow constituents spiritually from believers to disciples. As they mature spiritually, they will become more generous.

8. The facilitator's program would provide a comprehensive communication plan, through publication, events, and direct mail (see Gary Hoag's chapter) to all constituents that would reinforce and educate toward this godly way of thinking and raising support. The language used (stewards, ministry partners, etc.) will reinforce this view.

9. Realizing that we are not in competition with one another, Christian organizations should therefore gladly support and encourage other ministries (see Shelley Cochrane's chapter).

10. Amend our practices so they avoid manipulation to give out of obligation rather than from a blessed heart.

The task of thinking and acting Christianly is not easy to accomplish and particularly so in raising money, because of the well-entrenched culturally accepted methods. If you develop your program around these principles and avoid those in the next section, you should be well along the way to creating a revolution in generosity.

6. Avoid Practices That Manipulate or Encourage the Wrong Motives for Giving

As you seek to apply the truth of God's Word to the practice of raising funds, sometimes it is easier to define what not to do than what *to do* in building a program that is truly God-focused. Making both a philosophical and practical shift in how your organization raises money will be difficult. To maintain a strong philosophy of fundraising, work with great diligence to avoid the following practices[11] that are often used to manipulate a person to give or encourage a motive for giving other than the Holy Spirit's working in the person's life.

- *Offering premiums that promise a return for a certain sized gift.* This is most common when a potential giver is offered a book, CD, DVD, etc., only if they are willing to give a specific sized gift. The problem is that this approach encourages and manipulates the ministry partner to give for what they get in return, rather than giving because they believe in the mission of your organization.
- *Writing appeals that are detached from the spiritual basis of the organization.* When presenting giving opportunities, they must be within the core purpose of your organization. Just because a topic is hot in the culture does not mean you should be raising money for that cause.
- *Raising funds in a way that is unconcerned with the giver's heart as a partner in ministry.* Giving opportunities should be God-glorifying, be connected to eternal perspectives, and result in joy for the giver.
- *Practicing fundraising in a way that robs the giver of the joy of giving.* Do not let your agenda, your programs, or your priorities distract the ministry partner from giving joyfully—out of obedience to God.
- *Making the giver feel like a "means to an end."* Avoid making givers feel like they were a pawn you used to accomplish your organization's goal outside of God's eternal purposes.
- *Not respecting the giver's privacy.* Do not push on a ministry partner for an appointment, for confidential information, or for a specific gift if God's Spirit does not allow this to freely happen.
- *Using impersonal fundraising language.* Direct mail appeals and campaign proposals tend to be rich in content yet very impersonal. Remember that those you are appealing to are partnering with you in ministry. Use language that demonstrates that you value this two-way relationship and are concerned about their spiritual well-being.

- *Making class distinctions by the amount given.* This is most common among organizations with multitiered giving clubs. Make certain that the giver is not motivated to give at higher and higher levels simply to receive "perks" (or earthly rewards) that come with moving up the ladder.

- *Hosting money-raising events that are not ministry-focused.* Fundraising auctions and golf tournaments tend to be focused on what a ministry partner gets for their gift. Be sure the focus of all events is rooted in the mission and vision of the organization and promotes eternal Kingdom values.

- *Utilizing deceptive or emotional asking practices, based on producing guilt.* Crisis fundraising appeals, dramatic pictures of underprivileged people, and exaggerated facts can play too heavily on the emotions of a potential giver. Be careful to choose your words and images very carefully and with integrity; be sure to not manipulate donors to give against their will.

- *Communicating in a way that does not support a stewardship approach to giving.* Remember that the words you use in print or speech can promote obedience or disobedience in how ministry partners steward their resources.

- *Providing naming as a carrot.* While it is appropriate to honor people for what they've done, it is not appropriate to offer naming opportunities as the motive for someone's giving.

Remember, the highest priority in building (or rebuilding) a fundraising program is to see the hearts and lives of ministry partners transformed according to the likeness of God. Your words, actions, and fundraising techniques play a vital role in helping people become effective stewards for the kingdom.

7. Develop a Sacred Trust between the Organization and Its Ministry Partners

J. Bassler, in her book *God and Mammon,* said that a biblically based approach to fundraising begins when the organization fosters with their ministry partners a spirit of trust, shared faith, and common goals. When this takes place, said Bassler, the act of giving becomes a joyous celebration of faith whereby the giver benefits more than the receiver, and everyone sees the requests for money as a "link in the operation of God's grace."[12] Most would agree that trusted relationships are a rare blessing these days, yet they are essential to raising money by growing givers' hearts.

It is clear that ministry partners need to feel extremely comfortable with the organization *and* the representative they are working with for the relationship to grow. Fostering trust within a stewardship office starts with the leader. She or he must be a leader of utmost integrity—leading by example and well respected by both the internal and external audiences. Following the example of this leader should be a team of stewardship officers that models this same level of trust within the team, with the organization, and ultimately with its ministry partners.

When trust has been built with a ministry partner, private and confidential information tends to flow freely. It is as if the person has been waiting for years to share this information with another party but has never found someone "safe" enough. Common statements are, "I can't tell my attorney these things . . . it would take too long and he'd bill me for the time," or "I can't talk to my kids about this . . . they'll think I'm giving away their inheritance." A telltale sign that deep trust has been formed is when a ministry partner is willing to talk to a stewardship officer about the distribution of their assets. When a staff member is viewed as an unbiased, trusted friend, the ministry partner trusts that the stewardship officer will put his or her spiritual growth before the financial needs of the ministry.

To set the context for building trusting relationships with ministry partners, my organization has created a small booklet to help ministry partners understand our biblical posture with respect to raising funds. At the end of the piece is a section written directly to the ministry partner. It states that we promise to rely on the Holy Spirit and the Scriptures, to always focus on the hearts of givers rather than a financial bottom line, and to follow biblical principles of stewardship.

When an organization communicates commitments like these to ministry partners, it almost instantly dispels the fear that all the ministry wants is money. Ministry partners often tell us how much they appreciate knowing our philosophy of fundraising, as it helps define the relationship between them and the stewardship officer. Ministry partners know that we are working on behalf of the ministry to encourage financial support, yet they believe we are attempting to do so in a way that honors God.

In *Money, Possessions, and Eternity,* Randy Alcorn writes about abuses in the world of religious fundraising and says that if a charity is always begging for money, the logical conclusion is that they are either not doing God's work, or they are not doing it God's way.[13] When an organization fails to raise money in a way that honors and pleases God, the sacred trust between the ministry and giver is at risk. Once that trust is broken, any hope of a relationship leading to a donation is likely dead.

Trust can be broken in numerous ways—perhaps the most heinous is when a stewardship officer shares with a ministry partner their own personal financial needs. I know of numerous situations where stewardship officers have talked with ministry partners about how hard things are for them financially, how a family member has lost a job, how expensive it is to put kids through college, even how costly it is to buy a new pair of shoes. When this happens, the stewardship officer has obviously violated a sacred trust with both the ministry partner and the organization.

To avoid breaking the sacred trust with ministry partners, consider creating a list of organizational fundraising "commandments" that all stewardship officers agree to and sign. Should one of these commandments be broken, it must be clear to staff that it is grounds for immediate action on the part of the ministry. Consider the following "trust commandments" (and feel free to add to the list):

1. I will not share any personal financial needs with ministry partners.

2. I will discourage personal gifts of all kinds that a ministry partner may want to give to my family or me.

3. I will not involve myself in any gift transaction where I receive personal financial compensation.

8. Celebrate God's Provision When Financial Goals Are Met

We know from Scripture that fundraising campaigns and celebrations go hand in hand. Perhaps the quintessential "party" that was thrown in celebration of what God had done was the dedication of the wall in Nehemiah 12:27–47. We can learn a lot from this one event. The Levites who had settled in neighboring towns around Jerusalem joined together with others in the Holy City to dedicate the rebuilt wall. The event was to be a time of singing songs of thanksgiving to God and praising Him with musical instruments (1 Chron. 25:1).

Two great choirs assembled at the wall—bringing with them two full processionals of important dignitaries. At one stage of the event, members of the processional were singing praise to God from atop the wall (12:31, 38) to visually demonstrate that the walls were stronger—a rejoinder to Tobiah's earlier mocking (4:3). Perhaps Nehemiah wanted Tobiah to see that with God's help the project was completed despite the opposition. In 12:40–43, we read that the event moved into the temple and music leader Jezrahiah led the two large choirs. Scripture says that they could be heard in neighboring villages.

In my many years of fundraising experience, I have been to very few Nehemiah-like celebrations. I am convinced that most Christian fundraising offices fall woefully short in this important area. I recently spoke to an organization that avoids such celebrations in order to keep the pressure on the fundraising staff. "After all," they said, "we wouldn't want them to slack off."

There is no prescribed way to appropriately celebrate fundraising success. It will vary from ministry to ministry and will look different from project to project. Consider the following ideas:

How Should We Celebrate?

- Hold a big event (i.e., dedication ceremony, ministry partner dinner, etc.)
- Host intimate luncheons/dinners with ministry partners and key staff/administrators
- Host regular events with fundraising staff to celebrate mini-milestones
- Hold a prayer/thanksgiving meeting with key stakeholders to praise God for His faithfulness
- Share the good news with others (through ministry publications, email, etc.)

What Should Anchor Our Celebration?

- *It should be worshipful.* When believers give as an act of obedient worship, the ministry should worship God with them for His faithful provision.
- *It should be joyous.* When reading Nehemiah 12, one can sense the pure joy at the party.
- *It must be God-centered.* While God likely worked though certain members of the fundraising team to help channel the funds to the ministry, the team itself is not to be the center of attention. We are celebrating God at work in the hearts of the believers.
- *It should reflect hearts of thanksgiving.* Celebrations must acknowledge God's goodness and reflect a heart of thanksgiving for all He has provided.

What Does Celebration Do for a Ministry?

- It unites the ministry.
- It motivates staff.
- It serves as a reminder of God's faithfulness.

Certainly there are many ways to celebrate with others when there is success in fundraising. Whether it is a big event or a small gathering with staff, celebration plays an important part in developing a healthy fundraising environment. J. Bassler, commenting on 2 Corinthians 9:13, says that giving glorifies God, and the act of charity is thereby transformed into an act of worship.[14] Just as giving is an act of obedient worship to God, so is the purposeful act of celebrating His faithfulness.

CONCLUSION

As you seek to apply the truth of God's Word to the practice of raising funds, you will be tempted to fall back on traditional fundraising methodology. The adage "old habits die hard" will likely apply to your organization as you work to sever ties with the world's way of raising money and seek to build a program that is truly God-focused. Be careful not to give yourself credit for God's work; recognize that it is the Spirit of God who motivates people to give. Practically show this dependence on the Spirit by praying for your ministry partners, organization, and God's abundant blessing. Focus on God's priority of raising up stewards to be rich toward Him and make the heart condition of the giver your number one priority.

Remember, the highest priority in building (or rebuilding) a fundraising program is to see the hearts and lives of ministry partners transformed according to the likeness of God. Your words, actions, and fundraising techniques play a vital role in helping people become effective stewards for the kingdom.

One might ask why fundraisers should concern themselves with biblical stewardship and the heart of the giver. After all, isn't that really the job of the church? A thorough review of the writing and research on this topic uncovers the grim reality that churches are failing at teaching biblical stewardship, parachurch organizations are failing to practice biblical fundraising, and religious fundraisers do not view themselves as stewardship educators.[15]

This reminder provides today's stewardship professional with an unprecedented opportunity to make a lasting impact in the world of Christian fundraising. I challenge you to be part of the solution. Be a pioneer in your sphere of influence and build a development program centered on God's Word—focused on the transformation givers' hearts.

I firmly believe that any organization that pursues the God-honoring way of centering your fundraising efforts on transforming stewards to be rich toward God will be richly blessed. While the eight principles outlined in this chapters are far removed from the secular techniques of fundraising, I believe wholeheartedly that by building a fundraising program around them, you will be positioning your organization to receive God's richest, most abundant blessing.

ADAM J. MORRIS (Ph.D., Biola University), the senior director of stewardship and resource development at Biola University, has devoted his career to working in Christian college advancement and has received widespread recognition for his involvement in the nonprofit sector. In 1989, Morris received the Southern California Carnation Award for outstanding leadership in fundraising and volunteerism. Morris also received recognition from former President George H. Bush and was granted a national "Point of Light" award for his significant service to the community. Adam has been a contributing author to several publications, including the chapter "Survey Trends: What They Say about Advancement Today," which appeared in *Advancing Small Colleges*. He can be contacted at Adam.Morris@biola.edu.

1. John Frank, *The Ministry of Development* (Dallas: EDM, 1996), 13.
2. C. Zech, D. Hoge, and P. McNamara, *Plain Talk about Churches and Money* (Bethesda, MD: Alban Institute, 1997).
3. Wesley K. Willmer and J. David Schmidt, *The Prospering Parachurch: Enlarging the Boundaries of God's Kingdom* (San Francisco: Jossey-Bass, 1998)
4. Randy Alcorn, *Money, Possessions, and Eternity* (Wheaton: Tyndale House, 1989).
5. Jerry E. White, "Integrating Faith into an Organization's Fund-Raising Practices," *Money for Ministries*, ed. Wesley K. Willmer (Wheaton: Victor Books, 1989).
6. Rebekah Basinger and Thomas Jeavons, *Growing Givers' Hearts* (San Francisco: Jossey-Bass, 2000), 161.
7. Adam J. Morris, "The Fund-raising Techniques of Evangelical Parachurch Organizations and God's View of Money and Possessions" (unpublished dissertation Biola University, 2002).
8. R. Scott Rodin, *Stewards in the Kingdom* (Downers Grove, IL: IVP, 2000).
9. T. Smith, *Donors Are People Too* (Akron, OH: Berkey Brendel Sheline, 2003).
10. Rodin, *Stewards in the Kingdom*, 214.

11. Wesley K. Willmer, *God & Your Stuff* (Colorado Springs: NavPress, 2002), 109. Thanks also to Rebekah Birch Basinger and Thomas H. Jeavons for many of these ideas.

12. Jouette M. Bassler, *God and Mammon: Asking for Money in the New Testament* (Nashville: Abingdon, 1991), 135.

13. Alcorn, *Money, Possessions, and Eternity.*

14. Bassler, *God and Mammon: Asking for Money in the New Testament.*

15. Morris, "Fund-raising Techniques."

Chapter

A COMMUNICATIONS PLAN FOR
RAISING UP STEWARDS
TO BE **RICH** TOWARD **GOD**

BY **GARY G. HOAG**, *Vice President of*
Advancement at Denver Seminary

T o create a revolution in generosity, you must have a plan. To send a penetrating message to the hearts and minds of your constituents, your methods should be both spiritual and strategic. To move beyond asking people to make gifts to encouraging them to become givers, you have to shift the focus of your communication beyond transactions to transformation. And, as you may have already discovered in this book, you need to be willing to adopt an approach that goes against the norm in our culture. Rather than merely advancing the cause of your charity or organization, your ultimate goal must be to challenge people to conform to the image of Christ, who is generous.

R. Scott Rodin writes, "While we have produced resources for understanding what stewardship looks like, we have failed to raise up stewards. The result is the continual need to develop new fundraising strategies and innovative approaches and clever campaigns to balance the budget and further the work of the church."[1] If you are tired of fundraising gimmicks and want to help people actually grow in the grace of giving, then you must take intentional steps to communicate the message and reach the goal of heart transformation.

The purpose of this chapter is to help you develop a spiritual and strategic communications plan for your ministry, which, when implemented, will change the way your constituents live as well as the way they give. As a framework for your plan, this chapter will cover six basic components of communication: (1) *who*, (2) *what*, (3) *where*, (4) *why*, (5) *when*, and (6) *how*. Each of these six areas will challenge you to rethink how you can enact your program to target transformation. This study can serve as a practical manual for setting up a program that communicates stewardship principles and starts a revolution in generosity.

1. WHO—THE COMMUNICATOR OF THE MESSAGE

Change within an organization starts with you. When you grasp head knowledge about stewardship and apply biblical principles in your life, your personal character grows. The Holy Spirit works in your life to conform you to the image of Christ and transform you to become more generous. As a leader, you serve as a model for others and a voice for spreading Kingdom values related to stewardship.[2] As others join you, a movement begins at your ministry. When movements sparked by a host of ministry leaders come together to confront the competing theology of secular philanthropy, we can create a revolution in biblical generosity.

Alcorn writes: "Only 15 percent of pastors say they have been equipped by their denomination or seminary to teach biblical financial principles"[3] —and it is no better in parachurch organizations. With little or no stewardship training, incarnating transformational biblical stewardship principles can be a daunting task. Henri J. M. Nouwen suggests a proper starting point: "Those of us who ask for money need to look carefully at ourselves. The question is not how to get money. Rather, the question is about our relationship with money. We will never be able to ask for money if we do not know how we ourselves relate to money."[4] What is your relationship with money?

It is necessary, if you are to be the communicator of a transformational message, to study biblical stewardship principles, seeking to apply what God has to say about money and submitting to the work of the Holy Spirit in your life. One resource option is the *40 Day Spiritual Journey to a More Generous Life*.[5] This booklet immerses the reader in the Scriptures and suggests exercises for assessing areas for growth. Tools like this one spiritually prepare you and your team for creating a God-honoring communication plan that will start a revolution in generosity.

Your actions and words send a message about stewardship. Does your example reflect that of a "giving champion"[6] or "mature steward" who "develops a firm conviction that God truly owns everything…who gives not knowing where money will come from and gives more so that others can experience spiritual and material benefits?"[7] As you become a mature giver, the transformation will spread through your board, administration, and organization with the potential to impact your entire constituency. Again, the movement at your ministry starts with you. What message do your personal giving practices communicate in relationship to biblical stewardship? If you are to be the *who* in your communication plan, your financial life must reflect biblical principles and generosity.[8]

2. WHAT—THE CONTENT OF THE MESSAGE

The topic of possessions and the Christian's role as steward of them is a central theme in Scripture. As noted in the book *God & Your Stuff*, "Our stuff and the spiritual development of our soul are very important topics to God—so important that 17 of the 38 parables of Christ are about possessions. Possessions are mentioned 2,172 times in Scripture—three times more than love, seven times more than prayer, and eight times more than belief."[9] God has much to say regarding our stuff. Because of this, we have plenty of material from which to craft our biblical stewardship message. The language in our personal communications, the copy for our direct mail, and the talking points at our events should all be drawn from the Scriptures.

While a more intensive discussion of biblical stewardship principles can be found in chapters two through five of this book, let us briefly consider seven themes from the Scriptures that summarize the stewardship message.[10] By right of creation, **(1) God is the ultimate owner and sustainer of everything** (Gen. 1; Col. 1:16–17). This is the starting place for any biblical model of stewardship. It is under the authority of God, and in obedience to Him that **(2) Christians are stewards or managers of God's resources** (1 Cor. 4:1–4). The role of each Christian is to serve as a steward or manager as opposed to being an owner, and **(3) resources are to be returned to God, shared with others, and enjoyed by all** (1 Chron. 29:10–14; 1 Tim. 6:17–19). We recognize that this "returning" cannot be forced (2 Cor. 8–9); but rather **(4) the Holy Spirit prompts Christians to give** (John 15:4–5; 2 Cor. 9:5–7). Like all activities in the Christian life, **(5) practicing stewardship is a vital part of our spiritual growth** (2 Cor. 8:7; Phil. 4:17). Following the work of the Holy Spirit and the recognition of the vital nature of stewardship, **(6) generosity flows from transformed hearts that are conformed to Christ** (Mark 12:41–44; Luke 7:36–50). Finally, based on all these principles, we conclude that **(7) resource development professionals should place growing givers' hearts toward God above ministry agendas** (2 Tim. 3:16; James 3:1).[11]

Whether you use this list or come up with a summary of your own, an essential starting point is to determine *what* you believe about biblical stewardship before you engage in resource development. Your message impacts the response you get; it takes a message that targets growing the hearts of your audience to see heart-transformational outcomes.

Revolutions generate slogans and catchy phrases. They are crafted in an effort to quickly and concisely pass along the important themes of a movement. The words and sayings through which the content of the biblical stewardship message is communicated must be clear and consistent for heart transformation to take place. Examine your language. Are you using the best terms and phrases to communicate transformational biblical stewardship?

It is easy to slip into the trap of using culturally accepted words or phrases in a merely transactional way when referring to money, resources, and the act of fundraising. Below is a list of statements that capture the essence of the transformational message; make an effort to be intentional and consistent in your communication so that your every word may further the revolution. Do these kinds of statements appear in your direct mail? Are these phrases spoken in your *ask* at events?

(1) God is the ultimate owner and sustainer of everything

"Everything we have belongs to God."

"The Lord provides for the needs of this ministry."

"If the Lord has blessed your family with financial abundance..."

"Our trust is in God to provide, as this is His ministry, not ours."

(2) Christians are stewards or managers of God's resources

"How are you using your spiritual gifts and financial resources to further God's Kingdom?"

"It is required of stewards to be found faithful."

"Seek the Lord as to how you should allocate the resources He has placed in your stewardship."

(3) Resources are to be returned to God, shared with others, and enjoyed by all

"Giving to the church and parachurch ministries is returning resources to God."

"Enjoy the fruit of God's blessings and share with brothers and sisters who are in need."

(4) The Holy Spirit prompts Christians to give

"Following the leading of the Holy Spirit, please give generously..."

"Pray about how God would have you participate with us in this ministry."

"Would you consider prayerfully how God would have you respond to this need?"

(5) Practicing stewardship is a vital part of our spiritual growth

"Giving is storing up treasures in heaven."

"How are you growing in the grace of giving?"

"Giving is an act of obedience and worship that produces joy and glorifies God."

(6) Generosity flows from transformed hearts that are conformed to Christ

"After praying about it, they determined to give far more than they had planned."

"We invite you to be strategic about making a Kingdom impact with the money you have."

"If God has richly blessed you, consider what it means for you to be rich back to God."

(7) Resource development professionals should place growing givers' hearts toward God above ministry agendas

"What priority do money and giving take in your life?"

"We care more about your relationship with God than whether or not you make a gift."

"Our ministry generally does not ask people for a specific amount, unless we feel led to do so."

"Give as God leads you."

"I want to challenge you to give to a portfolio of ministries, starting with your church."

In our verbal communication to groups as well as in our mail, should we refer to financial partners as *donors* or *givers*? Should we talk about the act of giving as *making donations* or *practicing generosity*? Do we *schmooze certain people and show favoritism* or is our goal *to invite everyone to participate*, realizing that sacrificial giving often comes from sources we least expect? Should our ministry professionals be called *development professionals* or *stewardship officers*? The point here is to analyze the words you are using and choose those that best communicate what you believe.

These phrases and terms are only a sampling of a vocabulary that is consistent with biblical stewardship. They make up the *what*, or the content of the message. Effectively communicating this message via various channels of communication will be discussed further in the *how* section. Before we can apply these communication themes, we must identify our target audiences to determine *where* we hope to create a revolution in generosity.

3. WHERE—THE TARGET AUDIENCES OF THE MESSAGE

The third aspect of an effective plan is to map out your publics. You must understand your audiences in order to deliver appropriate messages. Each ministry should prioritize its communication to three main sets of constituents: internal publics, religiously oriented publics, and external publics.

Internal publics are people often considered as "family" and include subgroups like employees, alumni, givers, board members, etc. You must target messages to this group with rifle-like accuracy, as your internal family members often serve as your ambassadors to the other two sets of publics. *Religiously oriented publics* would include other Christian organizations within the reach of the mission and vision of your ministry, such as churches, denominations, parachurch ministries, etc. If these groups perceive that you have a Kingdom focus related to stewardship, they will probably be eager to encourage people to partner with you. *External publics* have some knowledge of your organization but would not necessarily consider themselves among your constituency. This group includes the general public and mass media. By taking a shotgun approach in inviting this broad audience to join you in your endeavors, your ministry may move from making a local difference to having a regional, national, or even global impact. Habitat for Humanity, for example, has rallied millions of people to assist them in providing families with a decent place to live through strategic messages to all three kinds of publics.

If your ministry is like most, you have a limited budget and so you must choose carefully what communication channels you will use to send your stewardship message most efficiently and effectively. Regardless of the size of your organization, determine your target audiences so that you can craft your stewardship messages to them accordingly.

4. WHY—FOUR OBJECTIVES

After the *who*, *what*, and *where* areas are addressed, the next step is to ask the question: *Why?* Why send the transformational stewardship message? Is it just a gimmick for securing gifts? Is it just about the money? If you believe that a faithful steward is one who prays, serves, grows in their understanding of stewardship, *and* gives generously, then you must focus on four objectives, not just one! To facilitate the growth of generous givers is to exhort constituents to be conformed to the image of Christ and thereby participate with God in His work, employing the gifts and goods He has entrusted to them. For this reason, your spiritual and strategic communication should seek to accomplish these four objectives: intercession, involvement, instruction, and investment.[12]

Intercession

Prayer is often overlooked because efforts in this area may not show outwardly a return on investment. Whether you are running a campaign or raising annual support for your ministry, it is easy to fall into the trap of thinking that *people* fund *your* work. However, the reality is that *God* funds *His* work, and He does it through people and organizations. Just as you can be an agent of transformation by communicating the message of transformational stewardship, your constituents can serve as agents of provision through their faithful prayers.

God's Word says, "The effective prayer of a righteous man can accomplish much" (James 5:16 NASB). As a leader, do you demonstrate that you personally believe this—do you intentionally seek prayer support?

Asking people to seek the Lord on your behalf is only the beginning of intercession. Trusting God to transform people's hearts and lives and move them to respond with generosity is a privilege that stretches the faith of those praying as well. Ultimately, by raising up an army of intercessors, you are teaching your constituents holistic stewardship and inviting them to be a part of what God is doing at your ministry through prayer.

Involvement

A second objective in your communication must be involvement. Involvement with a ministry covers a broad spectrum of participation, from serving as a board member to helping out as a volunteer. From top to bottom, each role is important and requires commitment and sacrifice. Sacrificial service helps ministries and transforms those who get involved. Often generous giving flows from the life of a person who had the privilege of participating with the mission of an organization through volunteering.

When ministries start viewing stewardship holistically, they get people involved using their spiritual gifts and skills, and in so doing, both the involved stewards and the ministries experience transformation.[13] Web-based tools like *The Call* can make this process of matching stewards with ministries easier.[14] Whatever the method, rallying involvement takes careful communication. When we do not invite people to be involved, we send the message that they do not have anything to contribute to the mission. On the contrary, when we do send out the call for assistance and staff members are joined by wise advisors and willing servants eager to help, everyone is encouraged and blessed, while overall productivity increases.

Instruction

The third communication objective is instruction. "All [ministries] teach stewardship. Most do it poorly," George Barna proclaims. "As I [George Barna] studied the best fund-raising [ministries] in the nation, it was obvious that the practical, no-holds barred preaching and teaching of the biblical principles of stewardship, and relentless holding the Body of believers accountable to those truths in appropriate ways, were cherished distinctives of these families of Christians devoted to growing even in difficult, sacrificial aspects of the faith."[15] Good stewardship does not just happen; leaders must take steps to challenge people to grow in their understanding and practice of biblical stewardship.

When Christian organizations provide biblical instruction in this area, people grow spiritually. Anyone who hears and puts these principles into practice will experience a change of heart in relation to possessions, as these teachings are contrary to prevailing cultural values. To create a revolution in generosity, you must target people's hearts by instructing them in biblical stewardship. What better way to accomplish this than through a carefully crafted message sent through all communication channels?

Investment

The fourth stewardship objective is investment, and it must not be limited to gifts to *your* ministry. The paradox of the purpose-driven program (the purpose being to raise up stewards to be rich toward God) is that you want to encourage each of your constituents to generously give to God's work locally, regionally, and globally, regardless of whether or not they give to your ministry. Jeavons and Basinger punctuate this point, proclaiming: "God has no favorite causes. . . . Fundraisers who truly believe that God is enough and that no one ministry is inherently more valuable than another are free to encourage right motives for giving and let donors follow their hearts and feed their souls."[16] Each development professional must care more about growing givers' hearts than getting gifts. Any other approach results in manipulating people to make gifts, rather than inviting people to become generous givers.

The culture of secular philanthropy measures fundraising success by monetary results. This trains staff members to ignore the heart transformational outcomes and to measure their success only in dollars. What if your communication objectives were designed to grow givers' hearts and focus on involvement, instruction, intercession, and investment, with measurable outcomes in all those areas? Many ministry leaders argue that they cannot afford the staff time and energy to raise up stewards to be rich toward God. They say the *ask* must be focused on getting money for *their* ministry. Considering the eternal implications tied to giving, I answer that you cannot afford *not* to do it! Furthermore, I believe that generous giving at significant levels only flows from transformed hearts; thus our efforts should target transformation.

5. WHEN—CONSISTENTLY COMMUNICATING THE MESSAGE

The next step is to be consistent in communicating this message. Put simply, the *when* is all about branding! One of the *22 Immutable Laws of Branding* is the Law of the Name: "In the long run a brand is nothing more than a name."[17] Xerox and Kleenex are two of the most famous brands in the corporate world. When you see or hear the names, you know what they mean. When someone gets mail from your organization, your message forms the meaning of your name in the person's mind. Do people think that all you want is money from them? Do they think of how they have grown spiritually through your communication? Are they thankful for the privilege of partnering with you in ministry? What do you want them to think?

In order for your constituents to be transformed by the biblical stewardship message, your organization should consistently and regularly share spiritual principles that instruct them to be conformed to the image of Christ. This means that at every level—from staff titles to what you ask for in your mailings, and from personal conversations to remarks at events—biblical principles of stewardship need to be integrated and communicated. There is no area too small to be revolutionized by this transformation. Consistency results in a strong brand and leads directly to an examination of the various channels through which your organization communicates.[18]

6. HOW—THE CHANNELS OF COMMUNICATION

The purpose of this final section is to provide specific suggestions of *how* to communicate the biblical stewardship message through different communication channels. The many church and parachurch organizations joining the revolution in generosity can serve as good examples for other ministries to follow.

When forming fundraising plans, often ministry leaders opt for the *easy* routes and go with strategies that *work*, with little or no concern that the strategies may be inconsistent with biblical principles. Listed below are a few ministries, small and large, that have implemented practical strategies that both *work* and are consistent with the biblical principles discussed in this chapter. The illustrations are divided into four general areas: electronic media, printed materials, direct mail, and verbal communication to groups.

Electronic Media: E-Communications and Websites

Send emails to share specific opportunities for participation through prayer, service, and giving. This conveys a holistic stewardship message in a cost-efficient manner. Attract people to your website through your emails, making it convenient for them to discern how they can help. Don't just use emails to ask for money, and avoid overusing *need* language. The most common use of e-communication for ministries is to send news updates, urgent prayer requests, and praises to your people. Be sure to use special mass emailing software, as you do not want your ministry labeled as a spammer. Luther Seminary does an outstanding job using e-communication to provide biblical instruction for their constituents. If you visit their website, you can opt in to receive "God

Pause,"[19] a daily devotional that can be read in a minute and make a difference for eternity. "God Pause" has also helped build community within the seminary's constituency, as the devotionals are written by alumni. How are you e-communicating?

Use your website to invite people to join you in accomplishing the mission of your ministry. Many websites are like bulletin boards; they have all the information you need, but you have to go looking for it. Other websites are like billboards; they draw you in by piquing your interest and inviting you to respond accordingly. (Suggesting great websites can be dangerous because they can become dated in the length of time it takes for this book to be published.) One noteworthy example is Camp Id-Ra-Ha-Je, (which is short for *I'd Rather Have Jesus*).[20] It is a Christian camp in Colorado with a great website that clearly and concisely communicates the need for prayer support, volunteer involvement and gifts of different sizes to fund specific projects. Does your website function like a chaotic bulletin board or like an attractive billboard?

Encourage online giving in a manner consistent with your stewardship principles. Look at the language suggestions in the *what* section of this chapter as you carefully convey your dependence on the Holy Spirit rather than on the generosity of men and women. China Partner, a small parachurch ministry making a big impact, communicates this foundational belief by including the following philosophy of giving posted on its website: "Pray before giving. Ask the Holy Spirit to provide you wisdom in your giving decisions. Ask God what type of financial goals He wants you to set for you and your family. If China Partner resonates with you and you feel CP's vision and mission deserves your financial support, we welcome your involvement."[21] If a potential giver were surfing your site, would he or she find your philosophy of biblical stewardship?

Printed Materials: Articles and Magazines

Include articles on biblical stewardship in publications of your organization, whether magazines, newsletters, or books. This placement of the message reminds your constituents that stewardship is a ministry itself, not merely a means to ministry. Also, it assists in training their hearts and minds in biblical principles. Gordon-Conwell Theological Seminary's quarterly publication, *Contact*, includes a column "On Giving" by chief development officer Howard Freeman. In it he writes: "Is God calling you to exercise this spiritual gift of giving?"[22] "Get involved beyond giving. For while we are grateful for your treasures, we also want your hearts."[23] "The giving was not about her but about Him."[24] Columns in magazines can be utilized to effectively communicate specific biblical stewardship messages to constituents.

Emphasize great stories of transformed givers, not just stories about great big gifts. These testimonies are not only encouraging to constituents but can be used by God to transform their hearts. Biola University's magazine, *Connections*, featured an article in which they shared about a giver who "understood that God is the ultimate owner of all things, and they want to make sure that the things they hold dear are being leveraged for the Kingdom."[25] The article went on to detail the stages of growth in becoming rich toward God, presenting a solid path to follow for readers interested in growing in the grace of giving. What stories could you print? Do you realize that what you celebrate declares what you value? It takes work to present these stories, but the return is well worth the effort.

Produce annual reports to communicate dependence on God and the centrality of heart transformation. An annual report may give space to highlight God's provision, demonstrate fiscal integrity and accountability, and illustrate the impact of generous giving in the lives of constituents. These reports can serve as platforms for teaching stewardship principles through their presentation and focuses. SEND International's annual report is an example of a careful and strategic use of this tool.[26] Does your ministry do an annual report?

Direct Mail: Communication and Premiums

Demonstrate dependence on God and encourage biblical generosity through communi-

cation without manipulation. In your direct mail, avoid sending frequent urgent appeals, using language that motivates with guilt, and employing techniques that appear to be creating crisis situations calling for support. Such tactics can be accused of being inappropriate and unethical and may offend your constituents. "Much has been written about the abuse and overuse of direct mail. But studies and focus groups still show that many people want to be kept aware of ministry needs through regular appropriate letters."[27] Christian leaders should regularly assess their direct mail program through surveys and other feedback tools to ensure that their efforts are, in fact, ministering to people by sharing the progress of the mission, providing them with information they want, and nurturing transformational biblical stewardship. Should any of your terms or tactics change?

Evaluate your existing strategies and be sure they are consistent with your goal to raise up stewards and create a revolution in generosity. Philip Yancey tells the story of how a few years back, for one month, he saved every fundraising appeal he received and then analyzed the sixty-two items he had collected. He writes, "What struck me first is how closely [the appeals from the Christian organizations] resembled the appeals from everybody else: the same fake 'Express-Grams' with the red URGENT! headlines, the same P.S.'s underlined in blue ink, the same 'challenge grants' that require me to act within ten days if I want my donation to double in value." Yancey continues, "I was impressed mainly by all the gimmicks employed. A group soliciting money for Bibles for Russia had a catchy red 'Approved: Government of Russia' stamp on the envelope. One Christian television station promised me a miracle if I would give a multiple of seven: $7.77, $77.77, or $777.77; the largest amount also earns me a framed original page from a 1564 Bible."[28] He went on to say that none of the appeals expressed concern that he honor and obey God with his giving. This is the sad present state of Christian fundraising. Unfortunately the focus is on the desire for quick monetary transactions. What would people say about your direct mail communication strategies? Are you substituting slogans for Scriptures? Are your letters perceived as trying to make people to give gifts, or does your communication intentionally seek to help them grow in their understanding and practice of holistic biblical stewardship?

Exercise care in using premiums. Rather than encouraging people to give to receive premiums in return, consider sending unsolicited "front-end" gifts to constituents, such as *Secrets of the Generous Life* by Gordon MacDonald or *The Treasure Principle* by Randy Alcorn to encourage your people spiritually and communicate your desire to grow their hearts. Numerous churches, large and small, have taken this approach. As giving often comes from where you least expect it, be careful not to show favoritism by giving only to a select group but share freely with your constituents. Are you motivating people to give merely based on what they will get in return? Are you encouraging material reward and incentive for the giver or genuine Spirit-led generosity?

Verbal Communication: Meetings, Events, and Programs

In conversations with prospective givers, *emphasize their submission to the Holy Spirit and the vital nature of the transformation of their hearts to be like Christ.* This changes the focus of interactions from closing transactions to furthering transformation. Remind givers that they have been entrusted with God's resources and are thus responsible to steward those resources. Using tools like the *Stewardship Portfolio*[29] can help prospective givers become more strategic and intentional in their giving.

Host events that invite partnership in ministry, rather than VIP programs organized by the amount of money donated.[30] Encourage all your constituents to become ministry partners who may be transformed by giving of their lives, not merely their financial resources. Campus Crusade for Christ exemplifies this by asking people to give their LIFE (*labor, influence, finances,* and *expertise*) to God's work.[31]

Support wise stewardship by *giving clear and direct presentations of giving opportunities, and organizational commitments to biblical stewardship.* Be honest to givers regarding where the money goes, and how you as a leader and organization are modeling biblical stewardship. Become an ECFA member.[32]

Provide biblical stewardship instruction for your constituents. Encourage givers as well as pastors and ministry leaders to make use of resources offered by organizations such as Willow Creek and Generous Giving, which seek to further the growth of givers' hearts. Consider setting up a weekend training seminar for your staff and your constituents as well as local churches.[33] Denver Seminary, for example, hosts free *stewardship seminars* each semester.

Christian leaders and organizations must exercise wisdom and discernment in *how* they communicate, always targeting transformation and trusting God to provide. This takes faith and consistency, and can help raise up stewards and start a movement that could result in a revolution in generosity.

CONCLUSION

As you develop a communications plan for your ministry, start by ensuring that all **who** will communicate the message of transformational biblical stewardship understand **what** they are communicating. Transformation starts with the leader and must be articulated clearly. From there, determine **where** the message will be communicated and **why**. Map your target audiences and outline your communication objectives. Ministries that raise up stewards to be rich toward God strategically invite participation through intercession, involvement, instruction, and investment. **When** you communicate consistently, transformation will result. This also builds trust in the hearts of your constituents who realize you care more about their relationship with God than their participation with your ministry. And finally, **how** you utilize the various communication channels will ultimately determine the extent to which you will be successful in raising up givers. Shifting from focusing on transactions to targeting transformation is an adventure that must be lived out in dependence on and trust in the power of God to transform people to Christlike generosity. Godspeed as you lead!

GARY G. HOAG (M.Div., Talbot School of Theology, Biola University) is vice president of advancement at Denver Seminary and was ordained as a minister with the Evangelical Free Church in 1994. He has held development positions at Biola University and Colorado Christian University and teaches a class called Stewardship and Resource Development. Hoag passionately practices, preaches, and teaches that Christian fundraising is a calling to Raise Up Stewards to Be Rich toward God! He can be reached at gary.hoag@denverseminary.edu.

1. R. Scott Rodin, *Stewards in the Kingdom: A Theology of Life in All Its Fullness* (Downers Grove, IL: IVP, 2000), 17.
2. See Richard Haynie's chapter "The Road Less Traveled" for more insights on the transformation of the leader.
3. Randy Alcorn, *Money, Possessions and Eternity*, Rev. ed. (Wheaton: Tyndale House, 2003), xii.
4. *The Spirituality of Fundraising* (Richmond Hill, Ontario: Henri Nouwen Society, 2004), 11. Visit www.henrinouwen.org to request a free copy of this outstanding booklet.
5. Brian Kluth, *40 Day Spiritual Journey to a More Generous Life* (available online at www.kluth.org).
6. See Todd Harper's chapter "Discipling as a Tool to Transform Hearts toward Generous Giving" for an explanation of the "giving champion."
7. Wesley K. Willmer, *God & Your Stuff: The Vital Link between Your Possessions and Your Soul* (Colorado Springs: NavPress, 2000), 50–51.
8. See David Black's chapter "The President's Role as Transformational Leader" to dig deeper in this area.
9. Willmer, *God & Your Stuff*, 9.
10. For further study, see the appendix, "Understanding and Applying Biblical Principles for Stewardship and Fundraising."
11. These principles are drawn heavily from the Biblical Principles for Stewardship and Fundraising as well as the appendix.
12. Visit www.denverseminary.edu/giving/staff to see "the Four I's" in action in the purpose statement that guides the work at Denver Seminary.
13. For further study on the gifts of the Spirit as listed in Romans 12; 1 Corinthians 12; Ephesians 4; and 1 Peter 4, see: Leslie B. Flynn, *19 Gifts of the Spirit: Which do you have? Are you using them?* (Colorado Springs: Cook, 2004).
14. *The Call* (www.thecallonline.com) measures the gifts of giving, administration, teaching, serving, mercy, prophecy, and encouragement as outlined in Romans 12:4–8, and has been adopted by a number of ministries as the resource for helping their staff and volunteers assess job fit and giftedness.
15. George Barna, *How to Increase Giving in Your Church* (Ventura, CA: Regal, 1997), 91.
16. Thomas Jeavons and Rebekah Basinger, *Growing Givers' Hearts* (San Francisco: Jossey-Bass, 2000), 98.
17. Al and Laura Ries, *The 22 Immutable Laws of Branding* (New York: Harper Collins, 2002), 44.
18. One practical idea here is to hire a communications consulting firm like Keung & Associates. The communications audit they performed for Denver Seminary proved to be very insightful.
19. Visit www.luthersem.edu/godpause to check this out.
20. Visit www.idrahaje.org.
21. Visit www.chinapartner.org.
22. Howard Freeman, "On Giving," *Contact* (Gordon-Conwell Theological Seminary, summer 2005).
23. Howard Freeman, "Development Update," *Contact* (winter 2006–07).
24. Ibid.
25. Adam Morris, "Releasing Your Grip," *Connections* (Biola University, fall 2006), 26.
26. For a copy of SEND's annual report, contact personnel@send.org.
27. John R. Frank, *The Ministry of Development: An Introduction to the Strategies for Success in Christian Ministries* (Dallas: Press, 1996), 58–59.
28. Philip Yancey, *Finding God in Unexpected Places* (Colorado Springs: WaterBrook, 2005), 264–67.
29. Gary Hoag, *Denver Seminary Magazine* (Denver Seminary: summer 2006): 17.

30. The concept of point-of-entry events developed by Terry Axelrod in her book, *Raising More Money*, has proven to be a useful strategy for hosting events that seek to invite people to partner with the mission of your ministry.

31. See www.ccci.org/staff_volunteer_opportunities.html for examples of how Campus Crusade points people to specific service opportunities.

32. Visit www.ecfa.org to learn more about financial accountability guidelines.

33. Willow Creek (http://www.willowcreek.com/resources/ministry.asp) and Generous Giving (http://www.generousgiving.org) offer resources for ministries and church to train people in biblical stewardship.

IV.

The Leader's/Advisor's Role in Raising Up
STEWARDS

*Board members, CEOs, and advisors play an
essential role in facilitating an understanding of biblical
stewardship that will transform the hearts of Christians and
spark a revolution in generosity. This section calls the
Christian leader/advisor to personal transformation,
organizational renewal, and the growth of givers' hearts.*

Chapter

WHEN FAITH AND GOVERNANCE MEET:

THE BOARD'S ROLE IN GROWING GIVERS' HEARTS

BY REBEKAH B. BASINGER,

Basinger Consulting

O ver the past twenty years or so, a single theme—the conviction that fundraising, when done in the name of Christ, is the ministry of growing givers' hearts—has dominated my writing, speaking, and professional life.[1] In fact, there are those who say I've become a "one-note Nelly" in my work, and that's okay. I'm proud to wear that label if it gives me the opportunity to open more eyes to the amazing potential present within the fundraising process for transforming hearts and minds to be rich toward God. When my audience includes members of the boards of Christian organizations, I'm even happier.

It has been my experience that boards play a critical role in moving a Christian organization away from the single-minded, culturally driven, time-bound obsession with this year's bottom line, to a holistic, eternal view that builds its fundraising programs around God's work in growing givers' hearts. Don't get me wrong. I'm not suggesting that wise financial management and looking out for the organization's well-being aren't important. The Christian world is littered with the remains of ministries failing due to poor fiscal management and inattentive boards. However, if every boardroom conversation begins and ends with reports only about progress toward this year's bottom-line fundraising goals, the possibility and opportunity for growing givers' hearts may be lost.

From my experience, organizations that limp along from one financial crisis to the next are usually the victims of boards whose members have a fear of fundraising and an inadequate understanding of the holistic role of faith and heart transformation as the path to generosity. Financial issues are not the end-all and be-all of the board's work, but money does matter, and the board has a central role to play in helping secure, in a God-honoring manner, the funds necessary to support the organizational mission.

That said, as this book is suggesting, the definition of what constitutes a God-honoring fundraising program should be centered around encouraging supporters in their walk with God as a means to meeting the funding goals of the organization, because "it is only in this understanding of the relationship between spiritual growth and faithful stewardship that we can fully embrace Christian fundraising as ministry."[2] Ideally, the boardroom should be the place where the philosophical underpinnings of a ministry-centered approach to fundraising that focuses on growing givers' hearts are hammered out, endorsed, and embodied. In contrast to secular boards, the Christian board should be identified by their (1) common Christian faith, (2) holistic Christian worldview, (3) doctrinal and behavioral standards based in the Scriptures, and (4) accountability to God.[3] While members of the boards of ministry organizations have a similar outline of obligations to their governance peers in other organizations, they should accomplish them through God's grid of growing givers' hearts.

So it is not enough for board members to show up for meetings, listen politely to staff reports, vote on a few items, pat the CEO on the back, and head for the door. Board members have a double dose of responsibility in the area of resource generation. When it comes to fundraising, trustees are encouraged—indeed, expected—to wear both the policy hat as a member of the group and wear the separate hat of an individual active in fundraising. They contribute through their careful and wise work when meeting in quorum and also through their individual relationship building activities on behalf of the organization.

With this understanding of board work in mind, the material that follows is divided into three parts. First, I look at the role of individual board members in advancing the ministries they have been called to serve. Next, I explore the board's responsibilities as a corporate body for a ministry's success. Finally, I provide pointers for the persons responsible for recruiting and nurturing the board in its ongoing development. All three spheres of activity are mission-critical, and all are rightfully integrated with the board's responsibility in facilitating godly generosity of its constituents from a transformation process where a person becomes conformed to the image of Christ and as a result becomes generous, as Christ is generous.

IF IT'S TO BE, IT MUST BEGIN WITH ME:
THE ROLE OF THE INDIVIDUAL BOARD MEMBER

From this eternal perspective of focusing on God's work of growing givers' hearts, when you accept the invitation to serve on the board of a ministry organization, you have taken on the joyful God-given responsibilities of giving generously from your heart, asking others to act similarly, and lending a hand willingly in recruiting new friends to the cause. From your first day on the board and right through to your farewell meeting, the question uppermost on your heart should be, "What can I do today to advance the mission of this ministry by facilitating the growth of givers' hearts?"

You don't have to be the wealthiest person on the board to contribute in a big way to the fundraising success of the organization. It begins with the head knowledge of God's way of growing givers' hearts, and through commitment becomes a heartfelt conviction as you are conformed to the image of Christ. As you mature in your relationship to Christ, you are generous and model generosity to others, as Christ does. Generosity becomes a natural outgrowth of who you are (see Richard Haynie's and Wesley Willmer's chapters for more explanation). You become "a mature steward [who] gives not knowing where money will come from and gives more so that others can experience spiritual and material benefits."[4] As you pursue the following three requisites of board service, God will bless and multiply many times over the gifts you bring to the organization, be those large or small.

Grab Hold of the Transforming Power of Prayer

When approached about serving on the board of a Christian organization, prospective members are usually asked to commit the invitation to prayer. As seasoned board members can attest, the life cycle of every ministry includes times when prayer is all on which board members and other organizational leaders have to depend. Human wisdom and organizational finances ebb and peak, but God never fails. This is the root of the board member's confidence.

A good starting point is to pray that God will conform you to His image and show you how to disciple others to this end (see Todd Harper's chapter). As a result of prayer, you should be prepared to have your own heart grow bigger and more generous toward the work of the organization. In fact, encouragement to pray should probably carry a warning label or, more accurately stated, a promise label that reads: "Regular, sincere prayer causes extraordinary generosity." I have heard board members, half jokingly, say to a CEO, "Enough prayer requests, already. I can't afford to pray much more this month." When we lay our whole selves open to God in prayer, the Holy Spirit will nudge us into action, transforming our hearts toward generosity.

As you pray for the ministry, you are likely to notice some unanticipated other outcomes in your own life. For one, you're almost certain to find yourself growing smarter. After all, it is difficult to pray with enthusiasm without seeking more information about the organization. If you want to be specific in the matters you bring before God, you will need to educate yourself about the programs, people, and priorities of the ministry: "fulfillment of this responsibility requires the board member to spend personal time in reading, thought, contemplation and prayer on behalf of. . . the organization."[5] In short, as you pray, you should become more knowledgeable about the organization to which you are committing your work, wealth, and wisdom. Thinking about the various boards on which I have been privileged to serve, I praise God for what I've learned along the way.

Practice Joyful Generosity

Board members who are unwilling to give generously in support of the plans and programs they have had a hand in shaping constantly perplex me. It makes me cringe when a ministry head or development officer refers to giving as a "requirement" of board service. Giving is a privilege, and as a board member, you are triply blessed to be able to contribute time, talent, and money. Jesus was intentional in the word order when He instructed that "where your treasure is, there will your heart be also" (Matt. 6:21; Luke 12:34). Your support for the organization speaks volumes about the affections of your heart. The ways in which we allocate our money are an outward sign of our inward state.

Board members' generosity from a blessed (not obligated) heart also models the behavior the organization is seeking from others. During your time on the board, you should plan to sacrificially support the annual operations of the organization. Similarly, when a campaign rolls around, you and other members of the board should be the first in line. You may also want to consider including the ministry in your estate plans. In short, during your term(s) of service as a board member, and very likely beyond, the ministry will be among your top two or three giving priorities, second only to your financial commitment to your local congregation. This is not because it has to be, but rather, because board service is always more rewarding when coupled with joyful generosity as an outgrowth of your conforming to the image of Christ.

Over the coming years, you will have countless opportunities to be generous. Don't hide from what God will ask of you. Rather, open your heart to giving and step into His joy. As a board member said to me recently, "The most fun in my life comes from looking for the next place to give. Every day is a surprise from God."

Invite Others to Join You

Although organizational leaders are often quick in pushing board members to "get out there and ask," I am inclined to move more slowly. In fact, it's my view that board members must grow their way toward the privilege of inviting others to give, showing themselves faithful first with their prayer and financial support of the organization as they are conformed to the image of Christ. "It is important that board members are servant-leaders...that they have a passion for the mission and be there because of what they can contribute."[6] Prayer encourages an open heart, leading to an open wallet, and from there, to an open mouth. A significant step in getting to this point is to understand that it is the work of the Holy Spirit that changes hearts and you are a conduit/facilitator (see Richard Haynie's and Todd Harper's chapters). This is the holistic eternal view that you are not a manipulator but rather an agent of God's work to grow givers' hearts to be rich toward God. When you realize this, the pressure to perform is relieved, and instead helping others grow in their giving becomes a natural outgrowth of who you are in Christ.

Even with that said, asking for a gift doesn't come easily for most people. Our ingrained, culturally induced reluctance to talk about money gets in the way of our passions. But with each subsequent heart-directed gift that you make to the ministry, it will become easier for you to encourage others to support similarly. "Generous giving according to ability to give is a major spur to effective asking. Conversely, failure to give will and does inhibit many trustees."[7]

Men and women who never thought they could ask for money are surprised at how easily an invitation to give slips from their mouths in the wake of their own generous gifts given from a blessed heart. To paraphrase the Prairie Home Companion advertisement for powder milk biscuits, personal generosity gives shy board members the courage to get up and do what they need to do. I've experienced this reality in my own board work, and I've seen it in the lives of countless other board members.

ALTHOUGH IT BEGINS WITH ME, THERE IS ALSO WE: THE BOARD AS A CORPORATE BODY

Questions about the board's role in fundraising are almost always met with a cryptic response—give, get, or get off. Unfortunately, this oft-repeated mantra confuses the responsibility of individual board members with the work of the board as a corporate entity. As was noted earlier in this chapter, board work is not solely an *individual* activity. It is, in fact, first and foremost about teamwork. It's about a group of dedicated, enthusiastic "me's" coming together as a cohesive, committed "we." And although the majority of issues with which boards regularly deal are not about money *per se*, virtually everything a board does in its "we" mode has an impact on a ministry's ability to raise money.

That's why, when asked to speak to a board about its role in fundraising, I always begin with a description of good governance. As figure 15–1 illustrates, governance is at the center of organizational activity, and the quality of the board's work within the governance realm has a profound effect on the organization's overall effectiveness, including on the fundraising program. "Specifically, trustees must address two key issues: readiness of the board to provide the kind of leadership a first-rate [organization] deserves and worthiness of the [organization] to receive the goodwill and gifts it desires."[8]

At the end of the day (or the fiscal year), nothing builds givers' confidence in an organization like the actions taken by its governing board. Transparency is the watchword of our time, and within not-for-profits, the "buck" stops

WHEN FAITH AND GOVERNANCE MEET:
Mapping the Board's Role in Growing Givers' Hearts

Figure 15–1: The Board's Process in Growing Givers' Hearts

with the board for safeguarding organizational integrity. When it comes to revisioning the fundraising process to focus on growing givers' hearts, the board's role begins with a commitment to providing the best possible governance and then continues outward from the center like ripples in a pond. The board's influence starts in the boardroom and extends across the whole of the constituency in ever-widening circles. "It is important that board members are servant-leaders . . . that they have a passion for the mission and be there because of what they can contribute."[9] To paraphrase the apostle Paul, some among us are called to be board members, set apart for the glory of God, and ready "to serve Him in a unique fashion, exploiting the gifts, talents, abilities, experiences, passions, and opportunities He has provided."[10]

Setting the Context for Fundraising as Ministry

Within the space of a single week, I heard two board leaders speak about fundraising in starkly different terms. The first comment came during the inauguration of a new president. The board chair referred to the search committee's quest for someone who "wasn't afraid to beg for money" and then described the new president as "such a beggar." The second was part of a devotional at the beginning of a board retreat. With tears in his eyes, the speaker thanked the president for introducing him to the freedom that comes with sacrificial giving from a transformed, blessed heart. "You've changed the way I think about my money and what God expects of me," he said. I didn't need to talk with givers to determine which of the programs was perceived as ministry-centered.

The idea of giving and asking as a faith-building activity doesn't make sense unless the men and women on the board have experienced their own hearts growing conformed to Christ as a result of joyful giving. Sadly, too few board members report this kind of "heart growth," and in fact, a good many board members arrive at the organizational doorstep with basically secular attitudes about fundraising. Some have been admonished in a past setting to "get out there and twist a few arms," and they are still feeling bad about the experience. Others have been pressured or guilted into supporting initiatives that really didn't connect with their hearts.

Because the board is a policy-setting group, one way they can solidify and encourage this approach to growing givers' hearts is to approve the Evangelical Council for Financial Accountability endorsed Principles of Biblical Stewardship and Fundraising (see Joyce Brooks's chapter). These guidelines provide the biblical and philosophical directions the board should take and gives the organization policy to follow throughout the enterprise. It's no surprise if trustees look on fundraising as an unpleasant but necessary part of doing business and have trouble revisioning the development program as an extension of the organization's mission and ministry. Remedial education is almost always in order, and the boardroom is the place to start.

A well-rounded board education effort within the context of a Christian ministry organization must include a review of biblical and theological teachings about money and faith. The Biblical Principles of Stewardship and Fundraising mentioned above are a good starting resource. There should also be opportunities for board members to share personal stories of what giving has meant to their walk with God. It's crucial to allow ample time for the board to pray and worship together during every meeting. Although some board members may initially be uncomfortable with the money talk or question whether worship is the best use of the board's time, when continued over several meetings, these practices can transform a board's heart and thinking about its participation in the money-raising program. As a student of the management of Christian organizations has observed, "One of the most impressive aspects of the most effective organizations was the way they recalled the need to seek divine guidance in all their activities; planning and prayer were often integrated, frequently part of the same meetings or conversations."[11]

Ideally, the boardroom should be a place where the members encourage one another to be conformed to the image of Christ and where individual generosity is seen as contributing to the corporate whole. When a board is operating in top form (providing good governance), its members feel freer and more confident about branching out from the culturally influenced models of secular fundraising to focus on God's work in growing givers' hearts toward generosity.

In addition to formal times for reflection by the board, it is helpful for the board to keep track of comments and questions about the fundraising program that come up during meetings. "Imagine acknowledging the primary role of the Holy Spirit as the motivator of all our gifts, and the peace and courage we would received in our planning and asking. Imagine a program whose objectives were built around the desire to encourage and challenge donors to a greater and deeper walk with Jesus Christ."[12] Setting policies and goals in this way maintains concentration on transformation, on growing givers' hearts, rather than just transactions and the financial bottom line. In time, board queries should grow to include attention to givers' hearts as well as the organization's bottom line. When that happens, trustees will know that their commitment to board education has been worth the effort.

A sure evidence that a board has "gotten it" when it comes to a God-centered/growing-givers'-hearts way of thinking about fundraising are the goals that board members approve for the resource development program. Faith-encouraging goals reflect an understanding of the difference between targets that challenge supporters to stretch themselves on behalf of the organization's mission, and goals that are simply beyond the ability of a constituency to achieve. It is good to aim high, but too great expectations almost always lead to frustration, dashed hopes, and failed programs. Effective boards recognize that pushing the constituency beyond what they are able is not the way to encourage God's work in growing givers' hearts.

Addressing Organizational Climate

The next circle on the diagram for heart transformation focuses on interactions between the board and the organization's staff. After working through their own priorities about what the organization can—and should—accomplish through its growing givers' hearts fundraising efforts, board members are ready to hear through the CEO what the rest of the community has to say about the growing givers' hearts emphasis. Every organization has its "money myths," and it is crucial that the board be aware of the assumptions—both right and wrong—that inform internal thinking about giving and asking.

With the appropriate growing givers' hearts policies in place, the board must stand with the chief executive in helping the organization's workforce to appreciate the importance of resource development activities that grow givers' hearts. This is especially important when it comes to setting the budget for raising money. Program staff can be resentful or question the wisdom of directing precious ministry dollars toward resource development. But the simple truth of the matter is that it takes money to raise money, and especially so if fundraising is to be carried out as ministry.

297

Staff members whose duties don't include attention to an organization's budget can be ignorant to the realities of what it takes to fund the ministry. Further, because so much of what the resource development team does is external to the organization, their work is often a mystery to other staff. Without proper education, organizational insiders can make unkind comments about givers and the methods used by the fundraising staff.

If the CEO and the board define the success of a fundraising program solely by the financial bottom line, it is not likely that the development team will feel safe in giving attention to God at work in growing givers' hearts. Rather, fundraisers will assume that their performance will be judged solely on dollars raised, with little interest in how their work contributes to growing the generous spirit of God's people. Trustees can model a different way of talking about the fundraising program by proclaiming the potential that it is possible by giving attention to givers' hearts as a means to grow the bottom line.

A Word about Right Hiring

The board's greatest influence on organizational culture comes through the selection of the CEO. No other activity is of greater consequence to the long-term health of an organization or a greater litmus test of a board's performance than the selection of the ministry's chief executive officer. When the goal is to find an individual who can lead the way toward a transformational understanding of fundraising as growing givers' hearts, the stakes are even higher. It's no surprise that board members list CEO selection as their toughest assignment, and especially in today's competitive job market. Jockeying for quality leaders is almost as keen as for gifts themselves, and as a result, search committees aren't always as careful as they should be when hiring a new CEO. A good starting point is to have the criteria or opportunity profile/job description outline that a person must have head knowledge and personal understanding of, as well as model generous giving from, a heart conformed to the image of Christ. Only if this is the case will they be able to lead the organization with growing givers' hearts values.[13]

Often feeling pressured to fill the spot at the top as quickly as possible, boards are tempted to gloss over the importance of discussing with the would-be leader his or her attitudes about money, faith, and approaches to raising money. If, however, boards and search committees are purposeful in seeking out CEOs who have the heart and skills to imagine and help facilitate a godly vision for the development program, ministry organizations can lead the way in growing givers' hearts. The board dare not—must not—settle for less in the hiring process.

Checking In with Givers

With their own house in order, the right leader in place, and assured that the board and other personnel are all "singing from the same page" of a growing-givers'-hearts-centered fundraising program, the board is ready to check in (through the CEO) with the organization's support base. If the ultimate aim is to help create channels through which God's love and joy can flow, then the board can do no less than pay attention to what is happening in givers' hearts as a result of the way in which the organization goes about raising money.

Board members should seek opportunities through the CEO to hear for themselves what donors have to say about the messages and methods used by the organization in seeking funds by growing givers' hearts. They need to make sure there is a regular review of the resource-raising program that includes a plan for gaining candid feedback from givers and other important constituents.

Board members should also encourage (through the CEO) regular evaluation and timely reporting on the organization's progress in delivering on its claims. There should be clear and publicly available documentation that the organization is achieving what its mission declares. "The bottom line is that increasing numbers of major [givers] are looking for more satisfaction than just helping nonprofits reach their financial goals. They are looking for tangible evidence that their gifts are making a difference, and they want to know from the outset what the potential impact is."[14]

ENCOURAGING THE BEST IN "ME" AND "WE": RECRUITING AND NURTURING A TRANSFORMATIONAL BOARD

The likely question at this point in the chapter is: How can I fill up my board with people who individually give generously from a transformed heart, confidently ask others to do the same, thank willingly, and wisely guide the organization forward? The answer is simple: recruit board members with these purposes in mind.

Every member of the board should be busy doing God's work on behalf of the ministry organization to which they've committed themselves. A board that is contributing to God's transforming work in givers' lives relies upon a diversity of work and wisdom, along with the hope for wealth. Effective organizations benefit from a variety of gifts and giftedness within the board. In fact, "one of the most important attributes of effective leadership teams is that the leaders have a combination of gifts and skills that complement one another."[15] As board member Sharon Bell suggests, "Organizations need hard-nosed business people to keep the focus on the bottom line issues. We also need visionaries who say, 'Why can't we do A?' And we need people with critical thinking and a diversity of vision and expertise."[16] Ideally all your board members have a desire for growing generous givers' hearts as they maximize the gifts that each one brings to the mix, working as agents of heart transformation through the following activities.

» Orientation and Ongoing Board Education

If you want the great people whom you've wooed and won to your board to fulfill the expectations you have for them, you must make board orientation a priority. When done well, orientation programs set high standards for the work of the board, clarify expectations (including a "heads-up" regarding trustee giving), provide board members with a beginning knowledge base, and serve to welcome new members into a community of service, emphasizing their role of growing givers' hearts. A quality orientation program is also a powerful statement of respect and appreciation for each board member.

In order to give special attention to the education of board members in growing givers' hearts, a retreat using an outside facilitator may work well. Attending a Generous Giving conference and assigning reading that encourages growing givers' hearts are other excellent ways to educate board members to be generous and comfortable with their growing givers' hearts role. Also, encouraging the CEO to report stories of hearts transformed to be rich toward God can be a way to continue the education of the board.

I know of ministry leaders who devote as much as 50 percent of their time to educating and nurturing the board. Passionate, involved, and informed trustees are a powerful force in the fundraising efforts of ministry organizations. As a longtime board member of several Christian ministries was heard to exclaim following a board education session, "This was my first introduction to the idea of our fundraising program as an extension of the ministry of the organization. I had no idea there was so much involved and so much potential for God to work in givers' hearts."

» Maximizing the Board's Potential through Meaningful and Manageable Tasks

It's up to the CEO/president and the fundraising staff to make it as easy as possible for trustees to advocate for the ministry, introduce givers to the organization, or contact a denominational leader on behalf of the work. Avenues for involving board members in the development program are as varied as the many ministry organizations out there today. Trustee assignments can include:

- Writing thank-you notes or making follow-up telephone calls to givers
- Hosting fundraising events in their homes or at their churches

- Suggesting names of potential givers
- Participating in visits with the CEO or development officer
- Assisting in crafting a campaign case statement

The list goes on; the only limit is the imagination of the leadership team.

Ministry organizations with successful advancement programs are those where board members are well informed about the organization and are full partners in reaching out to the broader world. The "more board members exercise their roles as asker-advocates, the more committed they become to the mission. . . . They become effective agents in transformational giving as the stewards of relationships."[17] In essence they become the shepherds of the stewards. This is good news for ministry organizations, because we know that when someone trustworthy shows them a giving opportunity that speaks to their heart conformed to Christ, people will give.

» Caring Enough to Assess

Regular assessment helps assure board members that their work, both individually and as a group, is adding value to the institution. Self-assessment also sends a clear message to the wider community that board members are serious about their responsibilities. At its best, the assessment process should encourage board members to reflect upon and testify to the ways in which the organization's mission and faith commitments of growing givers' hearts are reflected in boardroom decisions.

A CONCLUDING THOUGHT

The pursuit of money is a constant and pressing aspect of ministry leadership. It is also a joyful responsibility when the ultimate aim is helping to grow givers' hearts. As board members are involved in asking donors to give as agents of God's grace, and when givers respond with faithful, generous hearts, they will help create a revolution in giving and ministries will have all that is needed. Money is necessary to support mission, and the giving record of board members does set the pace for other givers to follow. But when the development goals are bigger and bolder than organizational needs—when the goal for the fundraising program encompasses God at work in givers' hearts, the board's role can't be described in financial terms alone.

The board's God-given role in fundraising is to give voice and witness to the organization's commitment to growing givers' hearts as the best way to grow the ministry. As board members grab hold of the amazing potential present in the fundraising program committed to growing givers' hearts, they—both individually and as a group—will be better equipped to exercise faithful leadership on behalf of the organizations they've been called to serve.

For **REBEKAH BURCH BASINGER** (Ed.D., Temple University), helping to encourage strong boards and generous giving are longtime passions. In her half-time position as program director with In Trust, Rebekah's niche is fundraising, strategic planning, and presidential selection and evaluation. And as the director of congregational relations for the Brethren in Christ Church, the other half of her work life, she assists pastors and other congregational leaders with their stewardship programs. She has authored numerous articles on fundraising and various aspects of seminary governance. Rebekah was the lead author for "The President's Role in Institutional Advancement" in the Association of Theological School's *Handbook for New Presidents* (Eeerdmans, 2006). She is also the coauthor with Thomas Jeavons of *Growing Givers' Hearts: Treating Fundraising as Ministry* (Jossey-Bass, 2000). Rebekah serves on the boards of MAP International, Pacific Lifeline Ministries, and MOPS International, and recently completed two terms of board service with the Evangelical Council for Financial Accountability (ECFA).

1. Thomas Jeavons and Rebekah Basinger, *Growing Givers' Hearts* (San Francisco: Jossey-Bass, 2000).

2. R. Scott Rodin, *Stewards in the Kingdom: A Theology of Life in All Its Fullness* (Downers Grove. Il.: InterVarsity, 2000), 212.

3. Wesley K. Willmer and J. David Schmidt, *The Prospering Parachurch* (San Francisco: Jossey-Bass, 1998), 74–77.

4. Wesley K. Willmer, *God & Your Stuff* (Colorado Springs: NavPress, 2002), 50.

5. Willmer and Schmidt, *The Prospering Parachurch*, 81.

6. "Strengthen the Board," *Boardwise* November/December 2001, 4.

7. Henry Rosso, *Achieving Excellence in Fundraising* (San Francisco: Jossey-Bass Publishers, 2003), 138.

8. Rebekah Burch Basinger, "The Trustees' Role in Advancement: Beyond the Bottom Line," in *Advancing Small Colleges*, ed. Wesley Willmer (Washington, DC: CASE Books, 2001), 41.

9. "Strengthen the Board," 4.

10. George Barna, *The Power of Team Leadership: Finding Strength in Shared Responsibility* (Colorado Springs: Waterbrook, 2001), 84.

11. Thomas H. Jeavons, *When the Bottom Line Is Faithfulness: Management of Christian Service Organizations* (Bloomington, IN: Indiana University Press, 1994), 205.

12. Rodin, *Stewards in the Kingdom*, 214.

13. Jeavons and Basinger, *Growing Givers' Hearts*, 145–47.

14. Kay Sprinkel Grace and Alan L. Wendroff, *High Impact Philanthropy: How Donors, Boards, and Nonprofit Organizations Can Transform Communities* (New York: Wiley, 2001), 13.

15. Barna, *The Power of Team Leadership*, 25.

16. "A Macro View of the Issues," *Boardwise*, July August 2001, 4.

17. Grace and Wendroff, *High Impact Philanthropy*, 19.

Chapter

THE CEO'S ROLE IN
LEADING a MINISTRY COMMITTED to GROWING GIVERS' HEARTS

By David R. Black,
President of Eastern University

T he goal of this book is to radically change the vital activity of raising resources for Christian organizations. The previous chapters have explained how this revolution in generosity will result from a process of individuals conforming to the image of Christ, embracing the idea that Christ is generous and therefore as believers we should reflect Christ and be generous.

This approach is distinct from the outset, for the vast majority of Christian organizations have adopted the world's way (see Richard Haynie's chapter) of doing whatever works to get the largest financial bottom line. Most often these techniques focus on marketing/transactions that encourage people to give in order to get a premium, membership, or their name listed in return. The authors in this book build a case from a biblical worldview that the process of raising resources is not merely for the sake of a financial transaction but a whole-life transformation. Fundraisers on this biblical path see themselves as facilitators used by God to transform Christians into godly, generous stewards of His resources who then support Christian organizations.

The purpose of this chapter is to outline the role and responsibility of the CEO/president or senior pastor leading a Christian ministry with the goal of creating a revolution in biblical generosity by transforming hearts to be generous and rich toward God (Luke 12:21). My desire is to assist the CEO in changing his or her organization's fundraising program from one focused solely on financial results, using transactional methods, to one with a priority of spiritually transforming givers' hearts and minds to conform to Christ's. While this may seem nonsensical to those who are hearing it for the first time, the organization that focuses on encouraging its constituents in the process of being conformed to Christ in all aspects of life, including generosity, will see its financial needs more than met as a result.

To understand the CEO's responsibility in this process, we will begin with (1) the Christian CEO's distinctive purpose. We will then examine (2) how a Christian CEO needs to start with the transformation of his- or herself, and (3) how the leader can change his or her understanding of fundraising. Next, we will address (4) the CEO's role in the transformation of the organization he or she leads. We will close by discussing (5) how the transformed organization can educate its constituency in biblical stewardship.

1. THE DISTINCTIVE PURPOSE OF A CHRISTIAN CEO

The starting point is to acknowledge that the purpose of a Christian CEO is, first and foremost, to further God's eternal Kingdom, and only secondarily to build an organization. You serve the Lord first, not the board! The organization, like its CEO, exists for the purpose of being used by God. The CEO's role is to facilitate his or her organization to think and act Christianly toward their internal and external constituents. Being a servant leader, modeling the holistic transformation that we wish to see others embrace and facilitating their journey to generosity is part of this call. Genuine generosity from constituents flows out of a heart conformed to the image of Christ, not solely marketing transactions.

As Christians, we are new creatures in Christ. As a result, there should be a fundamental difference between the way a Christian approaches work as a CEO and the rest of the world's approach. This difference exists because the Christian's model for his or her new life is Christ and his or her aim is to be conformed to His image—to be like Him and, as a result, behave like Him. The Christian CEO learns from the Bible, for example, that God in the person of Jesus Christ was profoundly generous, and he or she therefore seeks to allow the Holy Spirit to develop generosity in his or her own heart. The Christian CEO observes Christ's concern for all His followers' attitude toward and use of money, and becomes likewise interested in the spiritual well-being of those who give financially to his or her organization.

Without a Christian worldview, the CEO focuses on maximizing the organization's bottom-line dollars, earning a lot of money, and attaining earthly success. This is in complete contrast to a Christian worldview, where the CEO gives priority to the spiritual maturity of the organization and its financial supporters, growing givers' hearts, raising up stewards to be rich toward God, discipling believers in Christlikeness, releasing resources to God's work, and fulfilling the Great Commission. What a difference!

2. LAYING THE FOUNDATION TO LEAD: START WITH YOURSELF

Transformation begins with you. You cannot ask others to go where you have not gone yourself, in both internal values and external actions. At the outset, the leader needs to understand and internalize these biblical stewardship values before he or she can make changes within the organization. The process of laying a foundation for an organization to seek resources in a way that furthers givers' growth in conformity to Christ begins in the hearts of its leaders. Unfortunately, most CEOs do not have a good understanding of a theology of money for their own life, let alone the organization they lead. The problem is systemic, because few of today's Christian servants have studied the life-changing topic of biblical stewardship. "Only 15 percent of pastors say they have been equipped by their denomination or seminary to teach biblical financial principles. Only 2–4 percent of seminaries offer courses, seminars, or Bible studies to teach stewardship principles, and only 1–2 percent of Christian colleges offer any training."[1]

If the CEO is to lead his or her organization in being transformed into the image of Christ, that process of transformation has to first begin in the CEO's own heart. The CEO would be wise to study and meditate on the Word of God to learn Christ's teachings and heart about money, as he or she seeks to be conformed to the image of Christ. As Christians grow to have the heart of Christ, they become concerned for the whole life and soul of the people they interact with, rather than only the financial aspects that affect their giving capacity. They learn that the Holy Spirit has power to change people's hearts, far beyond the ability of any person's persuasion. The Christian CEO becomes convinced from Scripture that generosity comes from the transformation of the heart to be rich toward God by being conformed to Christ's image, which results in the believer's desire to build God's Kingdom, as opposed to the prevailing cultural persuasion that giving is a transaction by which people gain tax benefits and personal recognition.

This learning needs to become deeply rooted in the heart of the CEO so that knowledge of the truth grows into acting according to it, so that the CEO not only understands what Scripture says about money, but actually believes that God owns all things and, trusting God to provide his or her needs, habitually and generously gives to others for the sake of the kingdom. Until the CEO models generous giving in his or her own life, he or she will not be able to lead their organization effectively down this road.

As posited earlier in this book, generosity is rooted in a heart conformed to the image of Christ. The practice of selected spiritual disciplines is a critical aspect of a CEO (or any person) conforming to the image of Christ and developing a generous spirit. The disciplines of confession, submission, study, meditation, prayer and guidance, fasting, service, and simplicity/frugality are particularly formative for Christian leaders (consult the Renovare Study Bible for insightful definitions of these eight disciplines).

Stephen, the New Testament church leader, exemplifies this transformation into Christlikeness, based on the enabling grace of God. The description of Stephen in Acts 6–7 brings to light seven particular qualities a Christian leader should possess. First, Stephen exhibited godly *integrity* such that the people he led respected him and trusted his intentions and words and thus risked changing from their ways to his. Second, Stephen was *full of the Holy Spirit*, who gives leaders the tools necessary for effective ministry and makes Christ's ways deeply our own. Third, Stephen was filled with *wisdom*: beginning with reverential awe for God and His holiness, Stephen demonstrated insight, sound judgment, and knowledge both about business and about the teachings of Jesus. Fourth, Stephen's fullness of *faith* resulted in a deep belief in the divinely ordained mission of the ministry as an extension of Christ's work and witness. His *grace*, fifthly, reflected God's purity, love, and faithfulness in a way that restored broken relationships and witnessed to Christ's transforming power. To confirm that witness, God imbued him with *power* to perform great wonders and signs among the people. Finally, Stephen demonstrated *generosity* when he gave his life for the sake of the Lord.

When biblical stewardship truths penetrate the CEO's heart, they should result in generosity consistent with financial ability. King David led by example, saying, "Now with all my ability I have provided for the house of my God" (1 Chron. 29:2 NASB), and the people of Israel followed. Consistent leaders practice and model the generosity they ask of others. Giving is part of "[making] sure your character is free from the love of money."[2] If your being is yet to be transformed when it comes to generosity, it is doubtful that you will be able to lead your organization in this area. It must start with you.

3. TRANSFORMING THE LEADER'S UNDERSTANDING OF FUNDRAISING

Many leaders view fundraising as a regrettable but unavoidable means to an end. The majority of CEOs are uncomfortable with the topic and would prefer not to deal with asking for funds, as Adam Morris discovered in his study.[3] I believe this discomfort would disappear if the CEO understood the biblical ways of God, money, giving, and asking. This book makes the case that raising support is an integral part of a Christian organization's core purpose in the kingdom of God, and that the call to raise money is a call to be a minister of the gospel. Leaders need to believe that claim with internal conviction if they are to take a serious interest in the resource collection practices of their organizations. Leaders should have a correct understanding that fundraising is about growing givers' hearts so that they are rich toward God. As such, asking activities should focus not on a certain institution or need, or even on what the giver wants to support, but rather on what God is calling them to support as they are conformed to the image of Christ. Wesley Willmer notes that the God-honoring way of development focuses first on our supporters' relationship with God, and our primary job is to help people trust in God[4] and become rich toward Him through their giving. Christian resource development should be concerned first and foremost with raising people to be rich toward God, and as a result generous giving will pour forth from a blessed heart.

As Walt Russell's chapter outlines, generosity flows from a heart conformed to the image of Christ. The leader's role is to proclaim the Word of God to people and then trust God to cause growth. "And God is able to make all grace abound to you, so that always having all sufficiency in everything, you may have an abundance for every good deed" (2 Cor. 9:8 NASB).[5] In the tabernacle campaign, God, without mincing words, told Moses to ask people to give. "Tell the Israelites to bring me an offering. You are to receive the offering for me from each man whose heart prompts him to give" (Ex. 25:2 NIV).[6]

Paul gives insight as to how to ask when he reminds the Corinthian church that they should give "not grudgingly or under compulsion, for God loves a cheerful giver" (2 Cor. 9:7 NASB). Henri J. M. Nouwen captures the leader's asking role well in his booklet the *Spirituality of Fundraising* when he says: "We are inviting those with money to a new relationship with their wealth. . . . If our security is totally in God, then we are free to ask for money. . . . Asking people for money is giving them the opportunity to put their resources at the disposal of the Kingdom."[7]

So how do leaders transform their understanding of asking for funds into the view this book presents? Nouwen recommends that leaders begin by acknowledging the spiritual nature of giving: "When those with money and those who need money share a mission, we see a central sign of new life in the Spirit of Christ. . . Those who need and those who give meet on the common ground of God's love."[8] He suggests further that, from the perspective of the gospel, fundraising is a ministry that includes *proclamation, invitation*, and *conversion*. Through it, leaders announce a divine vision and invite people into a sacred mission. Through it, they extend the Lord's call into a spiritual relationship that includes people conforming to the image of Christ and becoming generous, as Christ is generous. Asking a person for money not only provides them with the opportunity to invest resources in the Kingdom, it also invites them into a new spiritual communion with God and with a ministry's constituents. This spiritual communion reveals itself in a new fruitfulness, "thirtyfold and sixtyfold and a hundredfold" (Mark 4:20 ESV). In this way, generosity leads to communion, to fruitfulness, to gratitude, and ultimately to a constant awareness of God's goodness. A humble confidence in the vision and mission grows as leaders grasp the faithfulness of the one who said, "Ask and it will be given to you; seek and you will find; knock and the door will be opened to you" (Matt. 7:7 NIV).

Giving is not only the way we invest in the Kingdom of God, but is also a means to spiritual communion with God and neighbor. Done sacrificially and generously, it transforms hearts. Once the CEO has been personally transformed and understands the role of fundraising from God's perspective, he or she can then influence his or her organization.

4. TRANSFORM YOUR ORGANIZATION

While organizations are often known for their buildings or geographical locations, the values of the employees are what really sustain and maintain an organization's mission, vision, and long-term viability. As the CEO's heart becomes aligned with the biblical stewardship message, the leader can begin to direct his or her attention to influencing the employees' values, so the organization can begin to facilitate their constituents' growth in generosity toward the work of God in the world.

There are six key areas in which a Christian CEO can influence the organization he or she leads to embrace the biblical stewardship ideas espoused in this book: (1) seek agreement with the leadership, (2) set the vision, (3) provide the policies, (4) direct the hiring, (5) educate the employees, and (6) guide the board. Let's take a look at each of these areas in regard to the emphasis of growing givers' hearts to be rich toward God.

Seek Agreement within Leadership

As a first step, the CEO might bring together board members and/or key staff to agree on what their organization believes regarding stewardship issues, before developing strategies and programs. Many will not have thought through these ideas, so the leader starts as an educator. From their study of a variety of ministries, Thomas H. Jeavons and Rebekah Burch Basinger conclude, "An organization and its fundraising program must be clear about the essential theological tenets of its own tradition and how that tradition should shape the work of raising money."[9] Their findings illustrate that, "though Christian organizations seem to agree on putting confidence in God's abundance, assumptions about human responsibility for organizing the work of bringing in those resources, however, differ greatly."[10] Coming to consensus will be hard work, but the result is essential for each leader and for the organization. (See Rebekah Basinger's chapter for more about the board's role.)

The document Biblical Principles for Stewardship and Fundraising (see Joyce Brooks's chapter) is a resource that can provide a starting place for ministry leaders to discuss these issues with one another and the board of their organization.[11] Walking through this template in a staff meeting or on a board retreat can surface potential differences and help build consensus through the formation of new opinions and perspectives. Whether leadership adopts this document as is or forms their own set of biblical principles for your unique ministry context, the result serves as the foundation for the organization's resource allocation efforts. When the Scriptures serve as the anvil for hammering out foundational principles, everyone experiences transformation.

Many, if not most, Christian organizations have based their fundraising policies and procedures on the study of best practices in the secular marketplace. Those practices are based on assumptions about human nature and motivation that often do not align with the spiritual elements of stewardship discussed in this book, including our central premise that fundraising is a ministry of the gospel and that its ultimate goal is transforming self-centered hearts to God-centered hearts. Morris's research confirms the tendency of parachurch organizations to employ secular practices, yet finds that such organizations' fundraising methodologies are also influenced heavily by the heart and agenda of their president/CEO.[12] The reality is that fundraisers will generally wind up applying secular practices to presidential agendas, and CEOs often just turn their heads away as long as it is working. This chapter and book suggest you take a much different approach, by getting involved yourself.

This revolution in fundraising is dependent on a president leading a transformation of the organization's fundraising program into one that focuses more on a giver's relationship to God than on his or her relationship to the organization. Romans 12 describes a Christian organization that has been transformed in its totality, including activities related to leadership, asking for gifts, and serving. Paul's theology of the whole Christian organization begins with spiritually disciplined people whose hearts and minds have been transformed; that is, turned away from things deemed desirable by a fallen world and toward holy lives that discern and fulfill the will of God. Rodin writes:

> The new creation in Christ is not just a detached, spiritual creation but a holistic transformation of everything we are and everything we have. If the kingdom of God is occupied by the people of God who are this new creation, then there is simply nothing left with which we can build a second, earthly kingdom.[13]

This personal transformation equips us to join with others in the formation of a body of believers empowered by the Holy Spirit to carry out the will of God. In other words, we become a Christlike organization. Our organizational culture (the prevailing set of standards and values that influence our attitudes, habits, and beliefs) is now distinguished by its fealty to the Lord whose name we take.[14]

Set the Vision

The next step is to set the vision for biblical stewardship within your organization. One possible vision proclamation would be:

Our vision is to create a revolution in giving among our organizations, employees, and constituents by focusing on the transformation of their hearts, so they conform to the image of Christ and are generous.

Let your employees and constituents know this bold target at which you are aiming. The organizational model presented in Romans 12 begins with a prophetic message expressed as vision and mission by a person whom the Holy Spirit has gifted specifically to enunciate that message. A ministry without such a message is incomplete. The CEO called to declare this message must be faithful in doing so if the organization's fundraising program is to become truly transformed. By proclaiming this vision, he is serving the organization. Visions that inspire changes of heart through fundraising relationships have two specific qualities. First, they picture for others a redemptive ministry that has discerned "the good and acceptable and perfect will of God" (Rom. 12:2 NIV). Next, the vision captivates employees' and constituents' hearts and draws them toward that same will of God.

Provide Policies

Once the vision is proclaimed, the CEO has a responsibility to ensure that their organization is going to operate on these biblical stewardship values and to put policies in place that support this vision. Every Christian organization should have a written statement that lays out its core beliefs, vision, and mission. This statement should inform the organization's planning, strategies, and day-to-day operations. It should declare for all of its publics why the organization exists, whom it serves, the expected consequences of that service, the beliefs underlying the service, and the values (including biblical stewardship) that frame the organization's work. Unfortunately, most organizations have failed to incorporate biblical stewardship values into their policies. A recent review of fifty statements of mission and values among members of an association of Christian educational institutions found common references to teaching, student formation, Scripture, and Christian witness. However, only two of the fifty made any reference to the stewardship of resources. It is not enough for us to assume that an obligation to stewardship is central to our ministry; we should declare it in writing both missionally and publicly. It is essential, if we are serious about these stewardship values, to set down in our organizations' written purpose statements our commitment to grow givers' hearts.

An inquiry into how the stewardship references made their way into one of those two organizational foundational statements revealed that they grew out of a planning retreat. Two board members questioned the absence of any stated commitments to biblical stewardship. A president led a strategic planning team, which added the statements presented above. Now all strategies and operational guidelines are framed in part by those references to biblical stewardship. I would like to see all Christian organizations match and surpass this organization's example.

It is suggested that all leaders take similar action to state in writing their organizations' commitments to the biblical principles of transforming hearts to be rich toward God. Basing such statements on the spiritual discipline of simplicity and frugality, the biblical principles of sacrificial giving and stewardship, and the ministry's commitments to proclamation, invitation, and conversion would ensure their relevance to any Christian mission (see Adam Morris's chapter).

In *Stewards in the Kingdom*, R. Scott Rodin outlines five principles that should be incorporated into a Christian organization's policy: first, the need for people to be freed from money; second, the expectation of God's rewards; third, the acknowledgment of the Holy Spirit as prime motivator; fourth, the centrality of constituents' relationship with God; and lastly, a deep understanding of fundraising as a ministry of the gospel.[15]

One aspect of setting policy, for example, is defining the criteria for establishing fundraising goals in an organization that is concerned about heart transformation and following God's leading. Setting policy in this area would need to take into account the principles that it is the Holy Spirit, not fundraisers, who motivates people to give; that a constituent's relationship to God is ultimately more important than achieving a specified dollar amount; and that fundraising is a ministry of the gospel as much as the other ministries of the organization it supports.

When leaders are committed to following God's leading by pursuing heart transformation, complete provision will be found. Rodin continues, "Imagine a program whose objectives were built around the desire to encourage and challenge donors to a greater and deeper walk with Jesus Christ, to a more committed level of discipleship and a lifestyle that reflected the ethics of the kingdom of God."[16] Similarly, Romans 12:4–8 shows that, just as there is complete order, proportion, and sufficiency in the Spirit's gifts when the diverse members of a Christian organization are full of the Holy Spirit, there is also complete provision ordained by God for every vision that is His. If ministry leaders and organizations and the givers whom the Holy Spirit moves to give to the ministry are all obedient, then they all experience what the disciples and multitude experienced when Jesus broke the loaves and fishes. Therefore, goals should be based on the costs of full ministry, with individual givers challenged to give sacrificially to God in response to the Spirit's direction.

Direct Hiring

How does the CEO ensure that biblical stewardship and transformation are a significant concern throughout the organization? One of the best ways to assure implementation of these values across the organization is to hire people who share them. Jeavons and Basinger suggest that Christian organizations need to hire employees who "affirm [the organization's] theological tradition,"[17] sharing the vision and values of the organization. To accomplish this, you should develop questions for the hiring process that intentionally reveal prospective employees' biblical stewardship values, and make them a significant part of deciding whom to hire (see Adam Morris's and Rebekah Basinger's chapters).

Educate Employees

As a leader, the CEO has a responsibility to teach and model generosity and other godly characteristics to those he or she leads. Paul instructed Timothy:

Instruct those who are rich in this present world not to be conceited or to fix their hope on the uncertainty of riches, but on God, who richly

317

supplies us with all things to enjoy. Instruct them to do good, to be rich in good works, to be generous and ready to share, storing up for themselves the treasure of a good foundation for the future, so that they may take hold of that which is life indeed.[18]

Dallas Willard agrees that leaders today should continue to follow Paul's instructions, stating, "Churches must become schools of spiritual discipline where Christians are taught how to own without treasuring; how to possess without, like the "rich young ruler," being possessed; how to live simply, even frugally, though controlling great wealth and power."[19] Ministry leaders should instruct people in the way they should handle their riches. The ongoing education of employees might include intentionally structured workshops, talks, small group discussion, and appropriate materials. Having Crown Financial Ministries or Good $ense Ministries come to your organization might be one helpful resource. Until key employees adopt this value of growing givers' hearts, change within the organization will be slow.

Guide the Board

The CEO should be an active encourager, servant, educator, and guide for the board in this area of facilitating the growth of givers' hearts. Once the board adopts as policy the Biblical Principles for Stewardship and Fundraising (see Joyce Brooks's chapter), the CEO will need to continue to educate and encourage the board to adhere to these values in both word and deed. Rebekah Basinger's chapter provides an expanded discussion on the board's role in growing givers' hearts.

5. EDUCATING YOUR CONSTITUENCY

The final step (after you have dealt with your own heart and influenced the internal organization you lead) is to influence the constituents you serve by providing an ongoing program of education and activities that furthers the goal of growing givers' hearts to be rich toward God. This should include your communication through direct mail, publications, fundraising, and events (see Gary Hoag's and Adam Morris's chapters for suggestions).

A change of heart effected by the ministry of fundraising demands the renewing of one's mind (Rom. 12:2). Organizations should offer a message about the will of God that intersects with givers' spiritual journeys in a way that alters their actions. The information connects with their spirits, deepening their awareness and inspiring a response in mind, heart, and hands. As the teaching and learning process deepens givers' knowledge and commitment, their hearts become one with those to whom and with whom they minister. Even more importantly, their hearts have grown closer to God's heart as they imitate God's Son in His love, obedience, and generosity.

The organization can lay the foundation for educating constituents in stewardship and generosity by expressing its commitment to biblical principles of stewardship, giving, and asking in its vision statements, catalogues, and other published materials. This states up front that the organization believes its constituents' (and its own) relationship to money is important, and provides the grounding for all future discussions of finance and giving (see Adam Morris's chapter).

Your written theology of possessions and the importance of stewardship in spiritual transformation should be made available to your constituents. It should explain in greater depth the organization's commitment to these principles and the reasons for that commitment, inviting constituents to learn and understand further what the Bible teaches about stewardship and its role in their overall growth in following Christ. One example is Biola University, which lists these beliefs on its website and has a brochure to explain these principles.[20]

Heart-changing teaching through fundraising ministry often begins with storytelling. Real accounts of need, godly courage, and the transformation of hearts invite your constituents to enter such stories with their own prayerful engagement. In time, as their hearts are truly transformed, engaged giv-ers become engaged storytellers—or teachers—who deepen communion with God and broaden public awareness of how God grows givers' hearts and expands organizations.

A change of heart sometimes requires an earnest urging to do the right thing. Exhortation is the organizational quality most likely to relate to trans-forming hearts through reproof. The president of a Christian community development organization tells a familiar story. A longtime board member and donor to the ministry sold his business for a substantial gain. Soon, he was invited to consider board service at the two highly regarded Christian colleges his children had attended. When one of them also offered an hon-orary doctorate, this very bright man who was embarrassed by his lack of a college degree concluded that he would make a major gift to that institu-tion and then join its board. Since the meeting dates conflicted with those of the community development organization, he informed his old friend there of the "difficult but prayerful" decision to leave the CDC's board and join the college's. The CDC leader took his friend aside and lovingly but firmly challenged his motives. The reproof reached his friend's heart, leading to a decision to remain on the CDC board and share his increased giving evenly between the college and the CDC.

Service can be thought of as the strategies we employ to realize the vision and mission. Fraser suggests that the strategies of a transformed ministry express the organization's fundamental aspiration and commitment to a single governing principle, "Thy will be done on earth as it is in heaven" (Luke 11:2 KJV). As such, strategies become a set of choices we make to per-form activities differently, to design and run systems in distinct ways, to relate to one another and our constituents according to a pattern that we believe is pleasing to God. Service as implemented strategies is an expression of faith that God will graciously bring about the enduring results that He wills. It expresses an understanding of His will and our own willingness to be accountable agents thereof through decisive action. It communicates our obligation to others who are committed to the same vision and mission. It engages in certain actions and processes (and *not* others) that are based on a godly framework for personnel decisions, program development, and allocation of resources. It arranges and honors accountability and reward patterns that are just, ensuring that agreements are kept and that processes conform to the will of God as expressed in Scripture. How revolutionary it would be if we could influence our organizations and constituents to implement biblical stewardship themes with these strategies that would result in transformed stewards who are rich toward God. Without doubt, if the majority of Christian organizations were to do this, there would be a revolution in generosity.

DAVID R. BLACK (Ph.D., Ohio University) has served as president of Eastern University since 1997. During that time, Eastern has added four innovative schools to its existing undergraduate and graduate colleges. In 2002, Black led the university's union with Eastern Baptist Theological Seminary (now Palmer Theological Seminary), which is distinctive among American seminaries because of its preparation of pastors for urban, Appalachian, and Third World communities confronted by economic hardship. Dr. Black speaks and writes frequently on social and education issues and serves on a number of boards.

1. Randy Alcorn, *Money, Possessions and Eternity,* rev. ed. (Wheaton: Tyndale House, 2003), xii.
2. Cf. Hebrews 13:5; 1 Timothy 3:2–3; 6:6–9; Titus 1:11; 1 Peter 5:2; Philippians 4:11–13.
3. See Adam Morris's chapter, "Organizing Fundraising to Transform Stewards to Be Rich toward God."
4. Wesley K. Willmer, *God & Your Stuff: The Vital Link between Your Possessions and Your Soul* (Colorado Springs: NavPress, 2002), 107–9.
5. Cf. 1 Timothy 6:17–19; James 1:17.
6. Cf. Malachi 3:10.
7. Henri Nouwen, *The Spirituality of Fundraising* (Nashville: Upper Room, 2004), 6, 23, 25.
8. Ibid.
9. Thomas Jeavons and Rebekah Basinger, *Growing Givers' Hearts: Treating Fundraising as Ministry* (San Francisco: Jossey-Bass, 2000), 100.
10. Ibid.
11. Biblical Principles for Stewardship and Fundraising can be found at www.stewardship.org.

12. Adam J. Morris, "The fund-raising techniques of evangelical parachurch organizations and God's view of money and possessions" (Unpublished dissertation, Biola University, 2002).

13. R. Scott Rodin, *Stewards in the Kingdom* (Downers Grove, Il.: InterVarsity, 2000), 129.

14. Ibid.

15. Ibid.

16. Ibid.

17. Jeavons and Basinger, *Growing Givers' Hearts*, 103.

18. In 1 Timothy 6:17–19 (NASB), this charge leads the reader to inquire as to who is rich. Visit www.globalrichlist.com to be surprised as to how your annual salary compares to salaries around the globe.

19. Dallas Willard, *The Spirit of the Disciplines* (San Francisco: Harper, 1991), 214–15.

20. See http://www.biola.edu/admin/donations/principles.cfm.

Chapter

THE CHRISTIAN CONSULTANT
AS A FACILITATOR OF HEART TRANSFORMATION

BY JOHN R. FRANK,
President, The Frank Group

A commonly held secular worldview is that people give when they are manipulated by guilt, persuaded by the benefits offered, or influenced through a wide variety of marketing/transactional mechanisms. The accompanying perception of consultants is that they carry a bag of tricks to facilitate these transactions. Contrary to this worldview, the premise of this book is that generosity results from a spiritual transformation as the giver's heart conforms to the image of Christ. This perspective suggests that the focus when dealing with believers and their giving should be primarily on growing givers' hearts,[1] or raising up stewards to be rich toward God, and not simply getting money using any technique that works.

This book builds a case explaining how God views money and how God expects us to give, creating a model for how churches and other Christian organizations seek money, with the purpose that people will give generously from hearts conformed to Christ and organizations will be funded through a God-honoring practice. This chapter focuses on applying this Christian worldview of God, money, giving, and asking to the work of the Christian consultant in an attempt to answer the question: How can a Christian consultant facilitate heart transformation within his or her sphere of influence?

The primary purpose of a Christian consultant should be to further God's eternal Kingdom, not to build a consulting business. The role of a Christian consultant is to influence a Christian organization's policies and practices so that their primary purpose in raising money from their constituents is to raise up givers' hearts to be rich toward God (see Richard Haynie's chapter). When this is accomplished, constituents' hearts are transformed by becoming conformed to Christ and giving generously, the organization reaps financial gain, and the consultant experiences the joy of contributing to the work of God in the world. Mark Powell captures this concept beautifully when he writes: "There is a strong connection between *love* and *giving*. Most of us know what it is like to love someone so much that we want to give them things. The motivation for such gifts is not primarily obligation but desire—we give not because it is something we *should* do but because it is something we *want* to do."[2]

While this is a perspective that goes against common practice, there are some organizations that operate out of this worldview. I have personally watched one such organization be transformed to this distinctively Christian way of thinking and acting. The ministry's entire team—including board, staff, and campaign workers—began to embrace the concept of development as ministry and to look at their donors as stewards. The leadership of the organization went through training in a biblical philosophy of stewardship and began implementing asking strategies in line with growing stewards to be rich toward God. They prayed for givers and invited them to become involved in the campaign through a prayer support committee and prayer walk, in addition to offering giving opportunities. The campaign process took longer than was originally expected, and there were many problems, but in the end (although the feasibility study had shown that no one had raised more than one million dollars for a building project in that community), the transformed organization raised over $2.2 million and built a new rescue mission. Today, other organizations in that community are following this ministry's example of transforming hearts through their fundraising campaigns.

In order to understand and enable consultants to lead clients down this road, this chapter will (1) make the case for the Christian consultant as an agent of heart transformation, (2) demonstrate that the process starts with the consultant's personal values, (3) outline a distinctively Christian approach to consulting, (4) discuss how the Christian consultant can infuse biblical values into his or her work across an organization, (5) point out pitfalls to avoid, and (6) suggest the potential of a transformed Christian consultant.

1. WHY THE CHRISTIAN CONSULTANT IS AN AGENT OF HEART TRANSFORMATION

A Christian consultant can be a catalyst in facilitating the spiritual growth and heart transformation of many people within the constituency of the organizations that they serve. A Christian consultant must see this process clearly to become an agent of heart transformation. Figure 17-1 provides an outline of this process to show the link between the consultant's values, the policies and practices of the organization, and the potential to transform the hearts of the constituents to become generous.

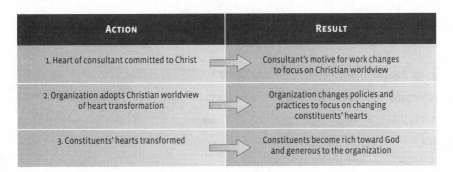

Figure 17-1: Three-Step Process[3]

The process begins in the heart of the individual consultant, when he or she begins to follow Jesus Christ and is transformed into a new creature in Christ. The consultant's worldview—including his or her life purpose, motives for work, and a consulting career, as well as priorities in working professionally with organizations—is transformed by his or her commitment to Jesus Christ. This transformation spreads outward to influence the organization, and through them, the constituents the organization serves. Figure 17-2 graphically demonstrates how this process works so that the consultant's influence through the organization's practices transforms the hearts of constituents.

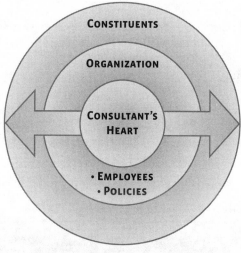

Figure 17–2

2. IT STARTS WITH THE CONSULTANT'S HEART

An initial decision and change of heart, which comes about through the work of the Holy Spirit, is the beginning of a Christian worldview that will develop and mature with the Christian steward over his or her lifetime. As Michael Wilkins writes, "The only appropriate response for that gift was to give myself back to God in gratitude for Him to use in whatever way He wanted. I could give to God every area of my life because His grace had made me a very different sort of person from what I was before."[4] As each Christian consultant looks at his or her own life and walk with Christ, as well as personal and professional goals, he or she considers his or her own values with respect to money, giving, and stewardship and understands that this transformation process is not a strategy but brought about by conforming his or her heart to the image of Christ. Then, and only then, can they be role models and teachers of biblical stewardship. Following are some questions a Christian consultant should ask him or herself in this area:

- Have I accepted Christ into my heart, and does that relationship make a difference in my life?
- Are my personal finances and giving in order from a biblical perspective?
- Do I seek to "excel in the grace of giving" (2 Cor. 8:7)[5] in my personal life?
- Do I sense a calling from God to be a consultant?
- Do I seek to accumulate treasures in this lifetime through my income as a consultant?
- Am I known as a person who is generous with my time, my talents, and my resources?
- When I teach a client about stewardship/development/fundraising strategies, do I emphasize the spiritual growth of the steward as the end goal?

Seeing the role of a consultant as a calling instead of merely a business career is a necessary paradigm shift. For a Christian, work is ministry and an extension of his or her faith and values. As a consultant works with various ministries, there will be opportunities to teach, pastor, counsel, and challenge individuals and groups of people. To be a disciple of Christ and to disciple other followers of Christ in stewardship are high callings. When we are good stewards, we represent Christ to the world to consider who God is and what is the true nature of His gospel. Transformational stewardship is key to Christian maturity, to following Christ and living the gospel on a daily basis.

My journey in transformation first began when I had to raise support to travel with a music ministry. The church in which I had grown up had never sent missionaries or raised support. It was all done through the church administration and structure. I had heard teaching on giving and tithing and their connection to following Christ. But I had never experienced it personally. It was then that I "tried" this step of faith idea. Could I really give first and then watch God provide my needs? I sent in a $225 deposit for this ministry adventure out of my $610 salary as a high school music teacher. The result was that God provided everything I needed that month. Every bill was paid, although I could not have planned it that way. God showed me that He was my source and I could depend on Him; my responsibility was simply to be a good steward of all that He entrusted to me.

It is based upon this foundation, as a Christian whose heart has been transformed, that I work with churches and parachurch organizations to help them experience the same type of transformation. I have been transformed not only by my personal experience in giving, but also by seeing God lead organizations, development staff, and constituents into a transformational experience.

3. A DISTINCTIVELY CHRISTIAN APPROACH TO CONSULTING

As a result of the change in the Christian consultant's heart, he or she starts to realize that Christian values should permeate his or her business. It becomes apparent that there is a significant difference between a Christian and a non-Christian approach to consulting. Figure 17–3 presents a comparison between a consultant who holds a Christian worldview of biblical stewardship and one who does not.

	CHRISTIAN WORLDVIEW	NON-CHRISTIAN WORLDVIEW
1. Purpose in life	Follow Christ, lead others to Christ	Enjoy life, accumulate earthly rewards
2. Ownership of money	God owns all	I own all
3. Goal of work	Raise up stewards to be rich toward God	Earn lots of money
4. Practice	Disciple believers / organizations, fulfill Great Commission	Clever marketing moves
5. Focus	Grow in faith and release resources to God's work	Earthly success
6. Rewards	Are in heaven	Wealthy lifestyle on earth
7. Long-term results	Eternal rewards in heaven	Present rewards will evaporate
8. Calling	Holy unto God's Kingdom	Recognition/status on earth
9. Priority	Clients' and constituents' spiritual growth	Clients' earthly net $ success
10. Generosity comes from	Transformation of heart to be rich toward God	Transaction—response to marketing techniques
11. Motivation	Biblical worldview	Personal freedom
12. Source of truth	God's Word	Relativism, Deism, other religious texts, etc.
13. Giving motivated by	Building God's Kingdom/ growing eternal rewards	Tax benefits, personal recognition on earth
14. Concern for person	Whole life, eternal soul	Financial aspect only
15. Source of power to change	Holy Spirit changes hearts	Personal persuasion, individual actions
16. Comfort/peace of mind	Knowing one is living life in obedience to God/contentment	Personal earthly success

**Figure 17-3: The Differences between a Christian
and a Non-Christian Worldview of Consulting**

As Figure 17–3 implies, a Christian's approach to consulting will incorporate many different components. A specific order cannot be dictated for every consultant, but the following are suggested as important professional and spiritual aspects of a Christian consultant's practice.

Prayer

Prayer should play an integral role in the Christian consultant's personal life, consulting practice, and counsel to their clients. Consultants should take advantage of the opportunity to remind their clients that prayer, relationship with God, and ministry are closely intertwined. One way of establishing prayer with clients is to suggest that they form a prayer support committee as a part of their capital campaign organization.

Personal/Company Commitment to Generosity

The Christian consultant is a member of the leadership of his or her client's campaign; as a leader, the consultant should seek to be a teacher not through words alone but by example as well. One way to exemplify this generosity is for the consultant, personally and/or professionally, to contribute financially to each capital campaign of which he or she is a part. Such a practice demonstrates the generosity that the consultant is working to help his or her clients grow in their own hearts and in their constituents.

Teaching Scripture

The Christian consultant should be able to convey key scriptural truths relating to the transformation of the steward and raising up givers to be rich toward God (see section one of this book). The consultant should have a thorough understanding of the theology of stewardship, one that has penetrated and transformed his or her own heart to be rich toward God. The consultant can then teach clients the scriptural basis for prioritizing the transformation of givers' hearts and demonstrate that the process works.

High Standards of Commitment

The consultant should have high standards of ethics, integrity, communication, and responsibility (see Paul Nelson's chapter). The Christian consultant needs to build trust and earn the right to speak to the client through his or her own personal and professional commitment to high, biblical standards.

Adjusting Roles during the Relationship, with the Goal of Independence

In the beginning, the client may need strong leadership; as the client learns and grows, the consultant's role transitions into instruction, then coaching and training for the long-term. Later, the consultant primarily advises and encourages the client as they implement their Christian worldview. The consultant should be attuned and responsive to the changing needs of the ministry as it grows in its understanding and implementation of the transformational worldview.

A Christian consultant who sees the world and his or her job in light of a biblical philosophy of stewardship senses a calling to be an agent used to transform organizations. Consultants should integrate their Christian identity and commitment into their work, openly pursuing an agenda of teaching and facilitating each organization to connect their constituents to the ministry in a way that furthers each individual's growth as a steward who is rich toward God.

4. HOW THE CHRISTIAN CONSULTANT CAN INFUSE TRANS-FORMATIONAL VALUES ACROSS AN ORGANIZATION

A ministry that hires a consultant probably has a fairly complex organization. The consultant will generally be most effective in helping an organization as a whole to adopt a biblical worldview of stewardship if he or she works directly with the people that make up each layer of the organization and facilitates their communication with one another. Figure 17–4 depicts the wide spectrum of openness to a message of spiritual transformation—from welcome to hostility—that a consultant will encounter within client organizations. Further, it suggests approaches for the Christian consultant to take to each of these three leadership groups depending on their organization's attitude to transformation.

	Highly Transactional— Hostile Toward Faith Issues	Transactional System— Open to Change	Working to Transform Organization	Transformational Model Completely in Place
Board of Directors	Show proven results of the transformational model	Explain their role in the organization's transformation	Encourage and assist in refining strategy	Help them maintain the momentum
CEO	Work quickly to establish trust	Share success stories; challenge them with their spiritual responsibility	Immerse them in the process of growing givers' hearts.	Help the CEO continue involvement with stewards
Director of Development	Show examples of the process and results of growing givers' hearts	Bring proven strategies of design, communication, and results	Train in actual strategies	Continue to encourage and counsel in reporting success

Figure 17–4: Spectrum of Openness to the Message of Spiritual Transformation

The Board

When a board is hostile toward a transformational model, the consultant can show them proven results from an organization the board may respect. If they are open to change, the consultant can begin training and show them their role in transforming the organization. If the board is already moving toward a transformational model, encouragement and assistance in refining strategy may be the best role for the consultant. Once they realize the results of fundraising as ministry, the consultant can help them maintain the momentum by advising the board to keep up with proper reporting of transformational giving, sharing stewards' testimonies, and introducing transformational giving and asking to new board members.

No matter where the board falls on the above figure, the consultant can challenge and encourage them to be rich toward God. There should be ongoing training to keep board members aware of stewardship trends, policy revisions, and educational opportunities regarding facilitating transformation through seeking resources (see Rebekah Basinger's chapter). The consultant can be a valuable resource when considering policies such as gift acceptance, development goals, acceptable strategies, and donor relations' policies. It is important to demonstrate to board members that bottom line numbers are not the only item worthy of reporting. The consultant can give examples of development reports that keep the focus on transformation by combining givers' stories of growth with the financial reports.

The CEO

If the CEO is hostile to this change, the consultant will need to work quickly to establish trust, sharing success stories and references, while challenging the CEO with his or her spiritual responsibility for the leadership of the ministry. Trust will be established when the consultant prays sincerely with the CEO, when the consultant allows the CEO to share his or her concerns and weaknesses without trying to "fix" everything, and when the consultant can dissent constructively from the CEO while sharing the same vision for the ministry. The consultant can coach and train the CEO in this process, especially by encouraging him or her to meet those who give to the organization the CEO leads. Once a good leader meets and listens to a transformed steward's reasons for giving to ministry, their personal view of givers changes.

If the CEO is open to personal and organizational transformation in stewardship, then the consultant should begin immediately to immerse him or her in the training and donor relations aspects of the development program. If he or she is already on the way, consider how to help the CEO continue being involved with stewards and overall strategy approval through reporting and ongoing training.

The Director of Development

If the director of development is hostile to changing to a transformational paradigm, the consultant should walk alongside him or her and show examples of the process and results of conforming to a biblical worldview of giving and asking. The consultant must bring proven strategies of design, communication, systems, and results to the director of development. A development program that focuses on the growth of givers' hearts by helping them be conformed to the image of Christ involves much more than merely inserting Scripture into fundraising appeals. It is a complete philosophy with proven strategies that build relationships with stewards (see Adam Morris's chapter) and connect them to God's work. The consultant should help the director of development understand the biblical worldview of stewardship that teaches that God, the owner of all things, always provides the resources ministries need to accomplish His work in the world, and wants to use those who ask to conform givers to the image of His Son and grow them in generosity.

The relationship between the consultant and the director of development is an ongoing process involving leadership, teaching, and advising. In the beginning, the consultant may lead the director in stewardship strategies and even prioritization. Depending on the director's experience, the consultant may lead the director in choosing communication strategies, how to communicate with constituents (see Gary Hoag's chapter), and how to communicate with the CEO and the board. After this the consultant should move into training, in areas such as working with major donors or planned giving, as well as new staff. As the director of development becomes more confident in his or her understanding of stewardship issues and strategies, the consultant can respond as an advisor when questions about particular situations arise.

All of the consultant's suggestions can only be implemented carefully and with prayerful buy-in from the ministry board and staff. The consultant's role is twofold. First, he or she communicates the vision—individual believers being conformed to the image of Christ, resulting in generosity—in order to fuel the process of transforming the organization's giving and asking paradigm and practices. Second, the consultant helps implement strategies to sustain transformational ministry for the life of the organization.

5. PITFALLS TO AVOID

Since consulting is such a complex process, involving multiple and changing roles for the consultant, there are many ways to stray from the path and lose effectiveness. In order to establish and sustain a strong ministry as a consultant, you will want to avoid these subtle pitfalls.

Thinking it is your influence, not the work of the Holy Spirit, that changes people. Recognizing that the changes that occur in clients' hearts through the teaching of biblical stewardship can only be the result of God's work can help the consultant to remember that he or she is in the business to be used as God chooses and to give glory to God for the work He does.

Failing to pray. A consultant must be personally prayerful to be reminded that God is the source of all knowledge and wisdom. Setting up prayer in board meetings, major donor meetings, and campaign steering committee meetings is not just a show of spirituality. It is a demonstration of what sets Christians apart from every other fundraising effort.

Putting your financial gain before God's priority of raising up stewards to be rich toward Him. Choosing clients can be a test of the consultant's priorities. When the consultant needs a new client financially, it is tempting to look at the money alone rather than at the relationship he or she is establishing. The Christian consultant's prayer should be in this spirit: "Lord, connect me with the clients that You want me to counsel and that desire a relationship with me for their ministry." Having accepted a client, the consultant is often under the pressure to earn the right to be heard by raising money first. It is critical to address the issue of transformational asking versus transactional fundraising from the beginning of the relationship with the client, and work out at the start how the consultant will help the client accomplish both short- and long-term goals.

Failing to lead clients toward a Christian worldview and faith. If we fail to challenge a ministry to move to a transformational philosophy and just continue consulting with them through transactional strategies, we are merely fundraising tacticians. Our responsibility in the use of our skills and talents as a consultant in stewardship is to teach the truth and assist ministries in the implementation of this truth.

Measuring outcomes transactionally. Where the larger business community asks about the return on their investments, stewards should be asking ministries the same question: What is this ministry doing with the money I have invested in its work? The ministry's response to this inquiry should include: How God is using givers' resources through the work of the ministry, the balance of giving and spending, how those related to the ministry are growing in their relationship with Christ, and the organization's witness before the world.

Transactional methods. We should avoid fundraising methods that emphasize a transaction in place of transformation. This includes premium offers that promise a return for a certain sized gift, appeals that are detached from the spiritual basis of the organization, and all deceptive or emotional asking practices that are used to produce guilt.

Jeopardizing relationship with givers. If fundraising is about raising up stewards to be rich toward God, then bringing stewards alongside as partners in ministry must be a priority. We should take care in all communication with givers, never making use of impersonal fundraising language. Any fundraising that robs givers of the joy of giving or leaves them feeling like a "means to an end" should be avoided. It goes without saying that we must respect the giver's privacy. Further, when we value transformed hearts rather than transactions, we will not make class distinctions based on the amount of money given.[6]

The consultant's responsibility as a leader and teacher is to guide the ministry toward a transformational stewardship approach possessing great potential for God's Kingdom.

6. THE POTENTIAL OF A TRANSFORMED CHRISTIAN CONSULTANT

Believers Grow

The consultant can be a teacher, trainer, and personal example of the process of transformation. The consultant's goal is for each ministry to exemplify and practice biblical stewardship in such a way that each of their givers is connected to the work of the ministry, growing in his or her faith and being transformed by the God who owns it all.

Organizations Become Models of Christ to the World

In an organization that has been transformed to see generosity through a biblical worldview, the leadership creates an atmosphere in which learning and cultivating transformation are the foundation of the ministry. Every issue is discussed from the presupposition that God owns the ministry and cares about the spiritual growth of each giver.

Many May Come to Christ as Resources Are Freed Up for Kingdom Purposes

When hearts are transformed to be rich toward God, both people and resources are freed to spread the good news of the Kingdom of God. When we are generous, God is faithful to take care of our every need and multiply our stewardship investments in His kingdom. A revolution in generosity flowing from hearts conformed to the image of Christ will result in abundance.

7. CONCLUDING THOUGHTS

Consultants play a vital part in the ministry of stewardship. As they understand from a biblical perspective the difference that transformational stewardship can make, their business becomes ministry, and their motivation is eternal. As people who teach biblical stewardship, lead leaders into a transformation, and guide the execution of transformational stewardship strategies, consultants impact ministries and, through them, the world.

The consultant can be a teacher, trainer, and personal example of the process of becoming a generous steward. It is not the fees or success that defines a Christian consultant. It is about helping ministries become good stewards and facilitate transformation. "It was he who gave . . . some to be pastors and teachers, to prepare God's people for works of service, so that the body of Christ may be built up until we all reach unity in the faith and in the knowledge of the Son of God and become mature, attaining to the whole measure of the fullness of Christ" (Eph. 4:11–13). The goal is for each ministry to exemplify and practice biblical stewardship in such a way that each of its givers is connected to the ministry, growing in their faith and being transformed by the God who owns it all.

John R. Frank (D.Min. candidate, George Fox Evangelical Seminary) is founder and president of the Frank Group and a Certified Fund Raising Executive (CFRE) who speaks and consults extensively on the ministry of development. He has an MA in philanthropy and development and is working toward a D.Min. in leadership with a focus on stewardship education. He authored *The Ministry of Development* and *The Monthly Partner.* John can be reached at JohnRFrank@TheFrankGroup.us.

1. Thomas H. Jeavons and Rebekah B. Basinger, *Growing Givers' Hearts: Treating Fundraising as Ministry* (San Francisco: Jossey-Bass, 2000).

2. Mark Allan Powell, *Giving to God: The Bible's Good News about Living a Generous Life* (Cambridge: Eerdmans, 2006) 15.

3. The charts in this chapter are the result of collaboration with Wesley Willmer.

4. Michael J. Wilkins, "Because God Is Generous," *Moody* (March/April 2001): 17.

5. All Scripture quotations, unless otherwise indicated, are taken from the New International Version.

6. Wesley K. Willmer, *God & Your Stuff: The Vital Link between Your Possessions and Your Soul* (Colorado Springs: NavPress, 2002), 109.

Chapter

THE FINANCIAL ADVISOR
AS AN **AGENT** OF **HEART**
TRANSFORMATION

BY RON BLUE,
President of Kingdom Advisors

O ne of my early clients was a heart surgeon. Like many in his profession, he worked long hours saving lives and invested the dividends in a nice home for his family. As a Christian, he attended church regularly but was not particularly involved. A little while after we began working together on his financial situation, he inquired, "Is it okay for a Christian to live in a million-dollar home?" My response was, "What do you think God would have you do?" and after his indication that he did not know what God would have him do, I was able to encourage him to spend time in the Scriptures every day, addressing his question to God instead of asking me. Over the next twenty-five years, God so transformed this surgeon that now he is a leading Christian layman, serving on many significant evangelical boards, giving large sums of money away, and using his position and his home to influence others for the cause of Christ. Prior to our working together, he was leading a segmented life. His spiritual life, his professional life, and his family life operated independently, causing strain. Through the work of the Holy Spirit, God transformed his heart to conform to the image of Christ, and he learned to view life holistically, looking at every financial decision as a spiritual decision. The result was a revolution of character and generosity.

Over forty years of experience in the financial world has taught me many things. One of the most significant is that all good advice ultimately has its root in biblical wisdom, and as a result there is tremendous potential for financial advisors to have a life-changing impact on their clients' spiritual health. As Christian financial advisors, we have the ability to be used by the Holy Spirit to lead people in being conformed to the image of Christ, resulting in peace, contentment, and eternal rewards well beyond financial security here on earth.

I founded Kingdom Advisors because I would like to see stories of transformed lives, like that of my surgeon friend, multiplied a hundredfold as a result of the work of Christian financial advisors. All financial decisions are ultimately spiritual decisions; therefore, the Christian financial advisor gains unique insight into the heart issues of his or her clients. Heart issues are often revealed materially in an individual's checkbook, tax returns, and other financial records. Randy Alcorn, in *The Treasure Principle*, points out that our money is the only area of modern life that cannot be faked, and also the one that we are least likely to share with others.[1] I would like to challenge the Christian financial advisors of the world to turn this around by seeing their work as agents of heart transformation, to radically change their clients and the world for Christ. This work of transformation starts by understanding four key concepts:

1. If you have accepted Christ and been born again, then you are to be conformed to the image of Christ (Rom. 8:29)—a new creature in Christ (2 Cor. 5:17). Dallas Willard, in *Revolution of Character*, describes the process like this: "The water of heaven flows through our being until we are fully changed people. We wake each morning breathing the air of this new world; we experience a new consciousness and our character is transformed."[2]

2. As an apprentice of Christ who is being conformed to His image, the priorities, motives, and methods of your financial services become an extension of your faith and the Great Commission to make followers of Christ throughout the world. George Barna writes of "complete dedication to being thoroughly Christian by viewing every moment of life through a spiritual lens and making every decision in light of biblical principles. These are individuals who are determined to glorify God every day through every thought, word and deed in their lives."[3]

3. Your primary purpose and priority as a Christian financial advisor is to assist your clients to be eternally rich toward God, not merely financially wealthy by the world's standards. Luke 12 explains why in the parable of the rich fool, concluding in verses 20–21: "'Fool! This night your soul is required of you, and the things you have prepared, whose will they be?' So is the one who lays up treasure for himself and is not rich toward God."[4]

4. As you conform to the image of Christ and as your own finances and financial advice become an extension of your faith, you will grow spiritually, be used by God, and see eternal fruit in your clients. God's eternal Kingdom will advance as your clients become generous givers. Chapter 4 of John's gospel paints the picture of a field ripe for harvest, and Jesus comments in verse 36, "Already the one who reaps is receiving wages and gathering fruit for eternal life, so that sower and reaper may rejoice together."

If you need further explanation of these key concepts, you may refer back to chapter one. In the pages that follow I want to provide you with a practical guide to applying these concepts by:

1. Highlighting the differences between a Christian worldview and a non-Christian view of financial services
2. Identifying why you must start with yourself
3. Explaining how financial services is ministry
4. Outlining the learning process

5. Providing some tools for discerning your clients' spiritual position and tips for encouraging them in the process of growth

6. Describing how the three roles of financial planning can help clients be rich toward God

7. Pointing out pitfalls to avoid

8. Illustrating the potential for Kingdom impact

It is my prayer that as a result of this application of biblical principles your life and work will be transformed, such that both you and your clients grow closer to Christ.

1. SET APART: WHAT MAKES CHRISTIAN FINANCIAL ADVISORS DISTINCT

Figure 18–1 highlights the distinctives that set Christian financial advisors apart from their non-Christian counterparts. While many of the professional processes are similar, recognizing the underlying differences is key to our self-identity and decision making in difficult situations.

Second Corinthians 5:17 advises us that "if anyone is in Christ, he is a new creation. The old has passed away; behold, the new has come."[5] While the details of this transformation are unique to each individual, the shift in priorities from the temporal to the eternal should be universal. A concrete example of this shift is our definition of success. All financial advisors want to serve their clients by maximizing returns, but a Christian financial advisor includes the glory given to God in their definition of return and evaluates transactions in a holistic manner. We are called to be conformed to the image of Christ, and as we are, His presence in our lives will infiltrate every aspect of who we are, including our work, and help us appreciate its value for ministering His love to those around us (Rom. 12:2).

	NON-CHRISTIAN FINANCIAL ADVISOR	CHRISTIAN FINANCIAL ADVISOR
1. Purpose in life	Enjoy earth, accumulate earthly wealth	Follow Christ, win others to Him
2. Goal of work	Become wealthy by human standards	Raise up stewards rich toward God
3. Ownership of money	Self	God
4. Practice	Clever financial moves	Disciple believers, fulfill Great Commission
5. Focus	Accumulation of wealth on earth	Growth in faith and release of resources to God's work
6. Rewards	Wealthy lifestyle now	Crown in heaven
7. Result	Fleeting/will evaporate	Eternal
8. Calling	Make/accumulate money	Holy unto God
9. Priority	Earthly net worth	Spiritual growth is more important than accumulated wealth
10. Generosity comes from	Transaction—response to what you get out of it (recognition, tax savings, etc.)	Conformity of heart toward God
11. Motivation	Personal freedom	Pleasing Christ
12. Source of truth	Whatever you like	God's Word
13. Why be generous	Tax benefits, personal recognition	Reflect the image of Christ
14. Concern for person	Financial aspect only	Whole life, eternal soul
15. Source of power to change	Personal persuasion, individual actions	Holy Spirit
16. Comfort/peace of mind	Earthly wealth	Knowing you are in God's will / contentment

Figure 18–1: The Differences between a
Non-Christian and a Christian Financial Advisor

2. IT STARTS WITH YOU

It is almost impossible for a financial advisor to lead someone where they have not personally traveled. We must allow for spiritual growth in conformity to Christ in our own lives, before we attempt to lead our clients. One way we reflect the image of Christ in our own lives is by being generous, as Christ is generous. Until we adopt these values and act upon them in our lives, we will not be genuine with our clients.

There are seven hard questions that I use to evaluate my effectiveness as a Christian financial advisor (see figure 18-2). They lead me through a process of growth with the help of the Spirit, which I can then adapt for use with my clients.

1. Is my practice His practice and His calling?
2. Does my personal mission statement clearly reflect that God owns my business?
3. Do my clients know that I am a Christian?
4. How is my advice different as a Christian?
5. How would my staff evaluate my faith?
6. How would my family evaluate my faith?
7. Are my clients more conformed to and reflective of the image of Christ as a result of working with me?
8. What eternal heart growth have I observed in my clients as a result of their relationship with me?

Figure 18–2: Hard Questions

The order of the questions is important. There is a progression that starts with my internal heart attitude and ends with the eternal fruit of faithfulness. The first question addresses foundational issues. Who is really in control, am I where I need to be, and is the work I am doing dedicated to God's glory or my own? Questions two and three refer to my external witness. They press me on my willingness to confess Christ's lordship before others in my workplace. Then question four forces more internal analysis to ensure that I am not simply yet another financial advisor doing the same thing as my secular counterparts, with a Christian label plastered on top. Five and six encourage me to examine my witness to others who know me well and would be likely to recognize areas where I need work. Questions seven and eight are the reward. Look back at the last months or years of effort and realize that God has worked mightily in, through, and sometimes despite you, to bring people (like the surgeon mentioned at the outset) into His Kingdom and to have them mature in Christ. The return on investment becomes satisfying indeed!

3. FINANCIAL SERVICES IS MINISTRY

It is common in Christian circles to hear a dichotomy between "work" and "ministry," with those who choose the life of a pastor or other "full-time minister" receiving commendations for *really* serving God. However, this separation lacks scriptural backing, and a review of relevant texts demonstrates the opposite: all work should be done for the glory of God, and our attitude toward the task at hand matters more than the *type* of work being performed. As Ken Boa suggests, "secular" work becomes spiritual when done to the glory of God, and "spiritual" work becomes secular when done to please and impress men.[6]

For a Christian financial advisor, work is ministry. It is, and ought to be viewed as, an extension of our faith and values, because work is normative, part of the "all things" we are to do for the glory of God, and a consistent opportunity for building others up that should be embraced, not overlooked.

In Genesis 1, God blessed Adam and outlined the first job description: "Be fruitful and multiply, and fill the earth and subdue it and have dominion over the fish of the sea and over the birds of the heavens and over every living thing that moves on the earth."[7] Humankind was called to work long before the curse, which implies that working itself is normative and should be embraced with a sense of satisfaction and enjoyment, not resisted with disdain as drudgery. Further, there is no escape clause in 1 Corinthians 10:31, where we are commanded to do "*all* to the glory of God." All things for Christian financial advisors include both keeping our own assets in order as good stewards so we can be give generously, and assisting others to do the same.

The link between possessions and the soul explains why financial services provides opportunities for ministering to clients, but that is only the beginning.

Our work is also ministry to the extent that our relationships with co-workers and staff can demonstrate Kingdom commitments.

When we are saved, our ideas of success change, and so does the way we view other people. As Christians, we minister not only to our clients but to everyone around us—every interaction matters. The way we do our work—excellently, with care and attention to quality—and the character we demonstrate in everyday interactions can speak volumes.

It is my observation that the financial advisor has more opportunities to help a client change their belief system than almost anyone else—including their pastor—because we have access to clear evidence of the client's priorities. Matthew 6:19-21 exhorts, "Do not lay up for yourselves treasures on earth, where moth and rust destroy and where thieves break in and steal, but lay up for yourselves treasures in heaven, where neither moth nor rust destroys and where thieves do not break in and steal. For where your treasure is, there your heart will be also." In other words, our souls and our possessions are intimately connected; financial decisions both affect current and direct future spiritual growth. While a personal balance sheet may not tell the whole story, in the modern world it is a good indication of an individual's priorities and passions.

Few individuals have a rationale or motivation for sharing their intimate financial details with their pastor or other leaders, so frequently financial advisors are the only people with access to this personal information. This exclusivity implies that financial advisors bear even more responsibility for what they do with the information. The Christian financial advisor has a unique, powerful opportunity for influencing heart-shaping decisions. This kind of discipling is not easy but, as the story of the surgeon demonstrates, it can be very rewarding.

Conforming to Christ does not happen overnight. It is a steady process of purification, renewal, and growth that is best learned alongside a veteran from the field. Understanding the steps in the learning process can help financial advisors encourage their clients along the road to spiritual maturity.

4. THE LEARNING PROCESS

Figure 18–3 helps visualize the process individuals go through as we engage new ideas and incorporate them into our daily lives. Perhaps the most perplexing part of this process is the time it takes to transform our thought patterns. Holistic change requires immense investments of time and energy. In learning any new system of thought, we start with the theory—considering the way things

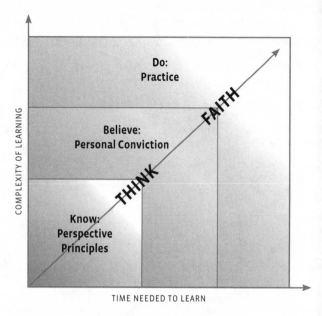

Figure 18–3: The Learning Process

ought to be. The bottom left corner represents that step. The next step is a bit more challenging, because it involves beliefs, which cannot be accessed directly by our minds but still must be influenced if our actions are to be transformed. Often we require stories or a series of personal experiences to "drive the point home" and move us out of the realm of intellectual assent into actual belief and personal conviction. The final step, acting on these ideas, requires an exercise of faith because it is the test of newly adopted ideas.

5. THE SPECTRUM OF FAITH: DISCERNING WHERE YOUR CLIENTS ARE SPIRITUALLY

Few people know the power of possessions better than financial advisors, and as Paul so eloquently states, the end goal of work (ministry) is to present every person complete in Christ (Col. 1:28–29), which of course includes his or her use of what has been entrusted to them. Elsewhere, Paul uses the language of conforming to the image of Christ to describe that same process of transformation (Rom. 8:29). Practically, people tend to move along a spectrum of faith, and discerning where they fall in that spectrum can be very useful in our attempts to minister to them (see figure 18–4).

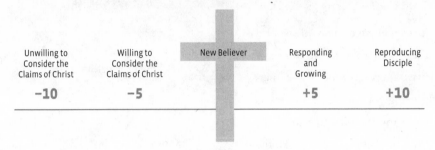

Unwilling to Consider the Claims of Christ	Willing to Consider the Claims of Christ	New Believer	Responding and Growing	Reproducing Disciple
−10	−5		+5	+10

Figure 18–4: The Spectrum of Faith

Those at -10 are opposed to the claims of Christ and critical of His church and its role in the world, although they do not necessarily reject all forms of personal belief outright. They will probably comprise the smallest segment of your customers, if only because your faith is likely to be evident enough to dissuade them from employing your services. Those around -5 are willing to consider the claims of Christ and may have friends who believe, but have not yet embraced those beliefs as true. With these individuals, it is often fruitful to discuss matters of contentment and challenge them to consider how much money is enough. Be prepared for the discussion to turn toward things eternal, but do not be terribly disappointed if the process is a slow one.

New believers are exciting and challenging to shepherd. Their world is turning on its head, and that transition can lead to a bumpy ride as they attempt to place Christ at the helm in every area. Our goal with new believers is to help them think through how to submit their financial life to Christ and assist them as they organize their possessions as stewards who are learning to be rich toward God and generous to His work. Clients who fall somewhere between new believer and +5 recognize Christianity is important and ought to be the foundation of every decision they make but sometimes get hung up on the mechanics. When challenged, they will frequently respond positively, but with varying levels of actual compliance. Our goal in working with them is to cast a vision of the way the world could be and challenge them to be an active part of the transformation process through godly stewardship and generous giving.

The reproducing disciple may challenge you as frequently as you do them. A vibrant picture of growth in Christ, these individuals look forward to every day as a chance to reach others with the good news. They still need our help in keeping their finances straight and looking at the long-term plan, but the goal here is to build in a sustainable manner; the engine is already running. They will have to watch out for a lot of the same pitfalls that we do.

The way you minister to each group will vary, but your underlying purpose is the same, recognizing that: I am called to be a disciple of Christ, and a discipler of others in my present vocation. The stewardship of my practice is a holy calling requiring intentionality and will have eternal consequences. Intentional heart transformation is a difficult process, and I cannot facilitate it unless I have personally traveled the path I am encouraging others to walk. I am called to be conformed to the image of Christ and imitate His generosity, and as a result of my transformation to assist others.

6. THREE ROLES OF A CHRISTIAN FINANCIAL ADVISOR

The road to spiritual maturity is not easy; it requires overcoming our sinful nature, which makes us self-centered, and allowing instead our understanding of Christ, including His generosity, to pervade our understanding of what it means to be a good person. Financial advisors are key to this process, and we fulfill three roles that overlap depending on where the client is in his or her faith journey, as illustrated in figure 18-5.

A Christian financial advisor acts as a heart transformation agent by being a leader, advisor, and counselor. These roles are not mutually exclusive, but understanding the purpose of each allows us to identify various arenas of ministry and approach clients accordingly.

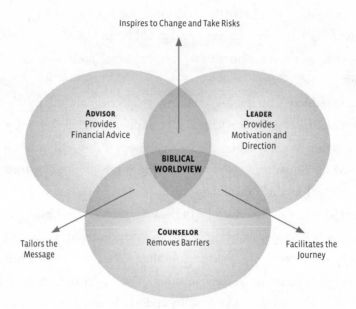

Inspires to Change and Take Risks

ADVISOR
Provides
Financial Advice

LEADER
Provides
Motivation and
Direction

**BIBLICAL
WORLDVIEW**

Tailors the
Message

COUNSELOR
Removes Barriers

Facilitates the
Journey

Figure 18–5: Three Roles

ROLE 1: THE ADVISOR

Financial planning is the continuous predetermined allocation of limited financial resources to unlimited changing alternatives, so our first role is that of a professional financial advisor. While we have the same job titles as our secular counterparts, our goal is the client's peace of mind rather than solely maximizing his or her portfolio. Our responsibility is to facilitate the decision-making process, taking into account where clients fall on the spectrum of spirituality, and encourage implementation, which contributes to the client's peace of mind. Obviously one of the prerequisites for this role is technical competence. Our clients come because they need advice regarding their finances, so the most obvious response is to educate them about their financial options. The difference is that we are able to go beyond professional expertise and integrate biblical principles, even for those who want nothing to do with Christ.

This role overlaps with leadership because we do not simply outline options, but inspire our clients to take action. To do this effectively, we must act as leaders, keeping in mind the acknowledgment of 1 Chronicles 29:11–12: "Yours, O Lord, is the greatness and the power and the glory and the victory and the majesty, for all that is in the heavens and in the earth is yours. Yours is the kingdom, O Lord, and you are exalted as head above all. Both riches and honor come from you, and you rule over all. In your hand are power and might, and in your hand it is to make great and to give strength to all." Through dialogue the advisor is able to lead his clients to acknowledge that God will provide for the work He gives each of us, which allows them to work and plan, not out of worry but out of trusting gratitude to God so that they can give generously.

ROLE 2: THE LEADER

John Maxwell suggests, "Anytime you try to influence someone's behavior, you are engaged in an act of leadership."[8] As financial advisors, we are engaged in such actions all day long by mentoring, encouraging, and in some cases cajoling our clients toward better financial and spiritual health. Broader leadership theory identifies two primary types of leaders: transactional, where the leader and follower simply exchange information, and transformational, where the leader senses and satisfies the higher needs of the follower in a way that transforms both the leader and the follower. Some of the decisions we challenge our clients to make as they seek to become conformed to the image of Christ are difficult ones, and they likely will not walk down those paths without a bit of friendly encouragement and solid examples of mature stewardship and generosity. Our role is to live in such a way as to be able to tell our clients, as Paul told the Corinthian church, "Be imitators of me, as I am of Christ."[9]

In my experience there are five characteristics we must develop to become transformational leaders: deeply abiding character, highly developed competence, clear vision, passionate commitment, and the uncommon wisdom that comes from submitting to God's Word. Most are common sense but still require our devoted attention. This last is particularly important. While any financial advisor can develop the first four, it is only through faith and the Holy Spirit that we access uncommon wisdom. When we view ourselves as God's servants, working in our clients' lives to lead them closer to Him, the example of Moses can be helpful. In Exodus 3 (NASB), Moses asks, "'Who am I, that I should go to Pharaoh, and that I should bring the sons of Israel out of Egypt?' And He said, 'Certainly, I will be with you'"[10] The task may seem like an overwhelming responsibility at times, so it is good to remember that we are not walking this road alone.

ROLE 3: THE COUNSELOR

As a counselor our primary purpose is to remove barriers by engaging our clients in dialogue. This may frequently take the form of Socratic questioning, as my conversation with the heart surgeon illustrates. It overlaps with the role of advisor because it encourages us to speak the language of our client. Viewing ourselves as counselors reminds us that a memorized script is not enough. Individuals understand issues from radically diverse perspectives that reflect their unique experiences, and our job is to adapt our words so that our meaning and care are evident.

While neither easy nor simple, viewing ourselves in all three of these roles results in progress as you, your staff, and your clients become more like Christ. It can increase engagement in Kingdom work because our interests tend to follow our investments. Putting money into and encouraging others to invest generously in instruments with eternal dividends can help us focus on heavenly things. Not only do we experience increased personal investment in God's glory, but the money given, whether supporting the local battered women's shelter or invested in a multinational corporation providing employment in the Third World, can also glorify God externally.

7. PITFALLS TO AVOID

Every ministry has its peculiar pitfalls, and financial services is no exception. The most pervasive and difficult to overcome are attitudinal, but methodology can occasionally get us in trouble as well.

Pride—Because God frequently chooses to use us as instruments of change, it is tempting to look at growth in a client and take the credit for ourselves. While this is as ridiculous as a spatula taking credit for making a pancake, we are likely to fall into this trap unless we watch our step. Clients may feed our delusions with praise and thanks, and a proper understanding of ourselves as God's ambassadors is the only way to avoid the alluring idea that we deserve the credit. It is the Holy Spirit that changes people's hearts, and taking glory from Him for ourselves is nothing short of idolatry. It is helpful to remember that the Holy Spirit is working the same process of transformation in our lives as in our clients'.

Greed—Greed is more straightforward. There will be times when discipling clients will cost you revenue. For one thing, it takes a bit more time investment on your part, and for another, clients who respond by giving generously may reduce the amount of money under your management. Do not let short-term financial pain interfere with the long-range goal of ministry: everyone conforming to the image of Christ. Remember that God owns all the money, and rejoice with your clients when they obey God's call to give generously of what He had entrusted to them to steward. Participate in their act of generosity by not counting it as your loss but as a gift for the work of God. Follow the example of Christ, who set a great example of generosity by giving of Himself, physically, emotionally, and spiritually, to those around Him and everyone who has lived since.

Forgetting to Pray—It is easy to sideline the importance of prayer, but do not let yourself do it! God honors our obedience, and the active submission of our plans to His will is healthy. Prayer keeps our priorities straight and increases our trust in God by reminding us of previous instances where God was faithful.

Neglecting Our Explicitly Christian Faith—In a pluralistic society like ours, it is easier than it used to be to discuss matters of faith generally, but it can still be difficult to transition to specifics. A ministry that merely leads people to believe in transcendent values or a higher power could be worse than a strictly secular practice, because it can result in a false sense of security for the client. Faith in general is not sufficient; faith must be faith in Christ (John 14:6). Transformation is not a general change for the better, but being conformed to the image of Christ (Rom. 8:29).

8. KINGDOM IMPACT: A VISION FOR THE FUTURE

The joy that flows from wise management and generosity is contagious, and it is invigorating to watch it course through families and communities. By encouraging individuals to view their finances as belonging to God for His purposes, we can uniquely equip Kingdom expansion, starting with our clients' own spiritual lives and also including gospel proclamation.

Current gospel growth is exciting, but there remains room for expansion. These field efforts take money, and as Christians living in the United States, we have a unique window of opportunity. Our nation boasts only 2.5 percent of the world's population, but over 40 percent of its wealth. When we consider the evangelical population worldwide, those in the United States control 80 percent of monetary resources. If American Christians' giving increased from 2.5 percent (the current rate) to 10 percent of income (a simple tithe), an additional $150 billion would be available for Kingdom work annually. According to Barna Research, less than 10 percent of the U.S. population who self-identify as born-again Christians tithe, and roughly 23 percent of evangelicals give to their local church.[11]

But church history teaches us that it has not always been this way. Both the Old and the New Testaments provide striking examples of a fully funded church, in which people give joyfully and in some cases have to be told to cease and desist. Exodus 36 narrates: "So Moses gave command, and word was proclaimed throughout the camp, 'Let no man or woman do anything more for the contribution for the sanctuary.' So the people were restrained from bringing, for the material they had was sufficient to do all the work, and more" (Ex. 36:6–7). The people were giving to fund construction of the tabernacle, a symbol of God's glory. They gave out of the abundance of God's blessing, that He might be glorified. Similarly, in the New Testament, we find the early church practicing sacrificial giving in order to glorify God. Acts 4:34–35 explains, "There was not a needy person among them, for as many as were owners of lands or houses sold them and brought the proceeds of what was sold and laid it at the apostles' feet, and it was distributed to each as any had need." In 2 Corinthians 9:8, Paul affirms, "And God is able to make all grace abound to you, so that having all sufficiency in all things at all times, you may abound in every good work," which forestalls any doubts the Corinthians might have about giving to support ministry in other places.

The Barna research I quoted above demonstrates that the task before us is a challenging but possible one. Imagine the impact on the world if the Great Commission were funded in our lifetime. If through your faithful ministry to your clients, and your personal commitment to conform to the image of Christ, the lavish resources we have in this country traversed the globe spreading news of God's love and grace, then communities who currently lack bread could have the church to thank for their ability to irrigate crops, and those 2,286 people groups who currently have no Bible in their language could read it for the first time.[12] Statistically, it can happen. The question is whether we are willing to do what it takes and transform the way we view our business, our clients, and ourselves.

Ronald W. Blue is the founder of Ronald Blue & Co., LLC, and is the current president of Kingdom Advisors. Ron is the author of twelve books on personal finance from a biblical perspective, including the bestseller *Master Your Money*, now in its twenty-ninth printing, and his most recent book, *Wealth to Last*, coauthored with Larry Burkett. Ron has appeared on numerous radio and television programs, including *Focus on the Family*, the *700 Club*, and *Prime Time America*, and is a regular contributor to several national Christian magazines. Ron currently serves on the board of directors of Campus Crusade for Christ, Crown Financial Ministries, Family Research Council, and the National Christian Foundation.

1. Randy Alcorn, *The Treasure Principle: Discover the Secret of Joyful Giving* (Sisters, OR: Multnomah, 2001).
2. Dallas Willard and Don Simpson, *Revolution of Character* (Colorado Springs, Navpress, 2005), 10.
3. George Barna, *Revolution* (Ventura, CA: BarnaBooks, 2007), 8.
4. All Bible quotations are taken from the English Standard Version, unless otherwise noted.
5. 2 Corinthians 5:17.
6. Ken Boa, *Conformed to His Image* (Grand Rapids: Zondervan, 2001).
7. Genesis 1:28.
8. John C. Maxwell, *21 Irrefutable Laws of Leadership* (Nashville: Thomas Nelson, 1998), 11.
9. 1 Corinthians 11:1.
10. Exodus 3:11–12.
11. "Stewardship," Barna Research Group, http://www.barna.org/FlexPage.aspx?Page=Topic&TopicID=36.
12. "Statistics," Wycliffe Bible Translators, www.wycliffe.org.

V.

Pitfalls and Potential of Revlutionary
GENEROSITY

*The biblical model of transformational stewardship
has revolutionary potential, but there are many pitfalls to
avoid along the way. This section offers suggestions for staying
within the bounds of integrity, collaborating with other
ministries, and persevering on the road to generosity.*

Chapter

LESSONS LEARNED FROM THE UNDERBELLY:
How to RAISE RESOURCES
with INTEGRITY

By Paul D. Nelson, *President of the Evangelical Council
for Financial Accountability (ECFA) from 1994 to 2006*

I n an ideal world, both Christian faith and witness are in alignment—for both believers and Christian organizations. While most Christian organizations are ethical and stand with integrity, there are those that allow themselves to become ensnared in compromising situations. This minority often brings shame to the broader witness of Christ and can become an obstacle for organizations seeking to raise resources by growing givers' hearts to be rich toward God. For these reasons, it is essential for all Christian organizations to work together to do right in the sight of God, to maintain a credible witness that encourages constituents to conform to the image of Christ and be generous as Christ is generous.

I write this chapter from my twelve-year experience as president of the Evangelical Council for Financial Accountability (ECFA). During this time I met many wonderful people and saw the fruits of many successful ministries. But the nature of ECFA also requires us to examine in detail the compliance of organizations in which ethical irregularities are suspected. I have thus been involved with the inner workings or "underbelly" of many evangelical organizations in countless audits and detailed studies of financial practice, governance issues, conflicts of interest, and questionable fundraising practices. I believe most of these "underbelly" problems could have been avoided with policies and organizational structures that provide appropriate accountability.

What follows is an outline of four lessons I learned; these are issues that I wish organizations were aware of and are essential to preserving the work of a ministry and not defaming the name of Christ. But first, I would like to take a look at the pressures that drive leadership to these pitfalls in the first place, the heart transformation that pulls us back to integrity, and the importance of accountability in accomplishing a ministry's mission with excellence.

THE LEADERSHIP PRESSURE

One of the heaviest weights carried by the CEO of any ministry is leading the never-ending process of raising resources. Most CEOs of Christian organizations do not publicly acknowledge the level of stress they bear. They must put on a happy face and be discreet in conversation with outsiders and insiders alike. The pressure is never ending, because it is assumed if you have a good year or a successful fundraising event, another and another must follow it.

Once the fundraising goal has been met (with very little acknowledgment of the blood, sweat, and tears that went into achieving the success), decisions are quickly made to increase the fundraising goal, and the cycle repeats itself. This cycle brings with it a host of temptations to ethical pitfalls. Time constraints, internal pressures, high expectations—these and more add a level of stress that tempts us to forgo our integrity. So how is it that Christians abandon the transformational message of Christ when it comes to raising the funds to proclaim that very message?

The very core of this book—encouraging a revolution in generosity by transforming stewards to be rich toward God—is compromised when Christian organizations fail to operate with integrity.

This transforming work of the Holy Spirit to create generosity is best facilitated in individuals when organizations are accountable, ethical, and do business with integrity and Christ-honoring character. *Integrity* means wholeness or completeness. It comes from the same root as *integer*, which is a whole number. Leaders who are not whole become double minded; they are fractions of what they could be and will always fall short of God's calling on their lives and the actions of the organization they serve.

Integrity has a direct link with transformation of the heart. God's transforming power in the life of a Christian should revolutionize every aspect of his or her being. Though transformation manifests itself externally, if one's very heart and mind are not being changed internally, then there is no transformation.

When we are transformed, our double-mindedness is replaced by truth and wholeness—in other words, with integrity—and we do the right thing whether or not anyone else is watching. If true transformation brings wholeness, then integrity is a natural and necessary characteristic of a Christian—both at home and at work. Allow the transforming power of Christ to bring integrity to all you are and do, including Christian fundraising ministry. This is the power behind integrity. Now we will look at the practice of it.

ACCOUNTABILITY ENCOURAGES INTEGRITY

Do Christians do a better job when someone is checking their work? You bet. The truth is that we are weak. Accountability is the system of internal controls and checks and balances necessary to any well-run organization or personal life. By humbly submitting our business practices to outside eyes, we acknowledge that integrity is not easy and that we need help. When we know that what we are going to do may be reviewed by others, the motivation to act with integrity is strengthened. Finally, accountability can establish trust within an organization and between organizations. Wherever truth, integrity, and humility are, success is more likely.

People do a better job when accountability is real. That is the principle behind ECFA. My hat is off to over 1,200 organizations that voluntarily submit to a group of their peers. Even with an understanding of the stress, the role of whole-life transformation, and the role of integrity and accountability, challenges remain that require special diligence. What follows are four lessons learned from the underbelly that I hope will assist leaders in acting with integrity and avoiding pitfalls, so that Christian organizations can be all God wants them to be in growing givers' hearts and transforming stewards to be rich toward God.

LESSON 1: THE DANGER OF RATIONALIZATION

The first lesson is the danger of rationalization: the temptation we face to make an ethically hazy choice and justify it. It is amazing how something as commendable as wanting to do more and do it better can place us on the wrong track of justifying our strategy and actions. It is the familiar "The ends justify the means."

The problem occurs when good people who want to do the right thing get caught up in the tyranny of the urgent. Some just need technical guidance to be sure they are in compliance with the law and appropriate standards.[1] Others, however, eschew guidance and allow their own effectiveness to cloud their perspective. They conclude, "If it works, it must be God." They begin operating in their own strength and unwittingly adopt the notion that everything is variable, including ethics. This has become a prevailing thought, especially in fundraising. For that reason, every ministry should develop a philosophy of fundraising resulting in firm policies (see Adam Morris's chapter), and every event or initiative related to fundraising should pass through these policies for approval.[2]

I discovered two concerns that are often rationalized: (1) gimmicks and (2) thinking that because something is legal it is ethical.

Avoid Gimmicks and Deception

A major issue in fundraising is the use of inappropriate "gimmicks." A number of people find some gimmicks acceptable. But what about provocative wording on the envelope of an appeal letter, or handwritten postscripts or notes in margins giving the impression that letters are personalized, when, in fact, they have been prepared by a computer? Or what about emotionally charged appeals with an urgent tone, or signatures of CEOs on letters they didn't write, read, or approve? These misleading tactics skew the motivation for giving by implying you will get something in return; this does not facilitate the growth of givers' hearts.

Some individuals and organizations truly are creative in making their case for giver support; however, without even seeming extreme, the gimmick approach crosses the line of truthfulness. Is it really truthful to send fundraising appeals that look like express mail or Federal Express packages when they are actually sent third-class bulk mail?

Another problematic gimmick is the misuse of testimonials. Testimonials are a powerful way of communicating the effectiveness of a ministry. But what happens when certain elements of testimonials are omitted? Or what if the testimony describes an event that did not happen at the ministry that is raising the funds, even though there is a clear implication that it did? What if there is no time reference and the testimony is five or ten years old?

Consider the charity that asked for gifts to its homeless shelter so it could serve thousands of meals during the holidays. Such an appeal has historically been very effective. A missing element in the communication was that local supermarkets donated 95 percent of the food to the homeless shelters—the charity only needed about 5 percent more. This meant that the funds that came in were far in excess of what was needed to supplement the total food requirement. The rationalization was that these excess funds were used for the ongoing operation of the organization throughout the year, but the giver was led to believe the money was for something else entirely. Complete truthfulness is the only way to be ethical and lay a foundation for growing givers' hearts.

Legality

Another example of variable ethics is rationalizing that if a certain action or practice is legal, then it must be ethical. Certainly, ministries must operate within the law, but legality should not be confused with ethics or morality. Identical practices may be legal in one state and illegal in the next. Abortion, pornography, and gambling are all legal. But in ministry, our call to the Lord's work requires a higher standard.[3]

For example, it may be perfectly legal to redefine certain terms in a way that may not be fully understood by a giver. In practice, there are different—sometimes interchangeable—definitions for matching gifts and challenge gifts. One is "at risk" while the other merely "challenges" others to give. Great care should always be taken to avoid confusion for the giver.[4] The focus is to use ethical practices that help givers conform to the image of Christ.

LESSON 2: REPORTING FUNDRAISING COST

A second lesson is related to the reporting of fundraising cost percentages. A newspaper headline featuring an attorney general investigation's finding that of the money raised by a particular charity, 95 percent had gone to fundraisers' costs and only 5 percent reached the charitable cause, substantially wounding fundraising for all charitable causes. Because of the media attention drawn to the excesses of a few, state attorneys general and Internet rating organizations have placed a disproportionate emphasis on the percentages in fundraising costs.[5] The giver has been educated to ask, "How much of my dollar is going for the charitable cause?" That is a fair question, especially when givers think only pennies wind up going to the cause. It is less than great, however, when these percentages are used to compare the worthiness of one organization to another.

There are many legitimate reasons why percentages of fundraising costs and overhead differ among charities. The type, size, and visibility of the ministry can make a huge difference in results. For example, front-page coverage of natural disasters drives donations to relief organizations during a crisis. The "free" exposure makes their fundraising percentage look good. Other examples include the type of contribution (all cash versus part cash and part gift-in-kind), the maturity of the ministry, and even special fundraising initiatives such as capital campaigns. All these considerations impact the numbers though they have little to do with whether one organization is more worthy of support than another.

This attention to fundraising percentage sets up an obvious temptation. Every ministry leader is responsible for making sure that both allocations and the calculation of the fundraising cost percentage are prepared and communicated accurately. Because accounting rules allow for some room for judgment or shifting allocation of expenses, organizations may feel pressured to push the limits of what an auditor might allow. This is where the responsibility of reporting with integrity supersedes the possibility of an unfair comparison with others less diligent in making sure the numbers are right. This also highlights the need as never before for organizations to communicate results. It boils down to this: report your numbers truly and specifically, talking as much about what you did with the last dollar as what you are going to do with the next.

LESSON 3: USE OF DESIGNATED GIVING

If there is any one pitfall that crosses the line in all nonprofit work, both ethically and legally, it is raising money for one thing and then spending it on another. This issue was dragged before the public eye following the 9/11 attack on the World Trade Center and again after Hurricane Katrina. The suggestion that the money given for the disaster victims might be used for future disasters or research or any other purpose, no matter how noble or even logical, brought down the scorn of government regulators, private watchdogs, the media, and the general public.

Although the giver can designate restrictions at the time of the gift on how a charity may spend the contribution, more often restrictions are set by how the charity frames the solicitation. Professional fundraisers advise that the more restrictive the gift, the better the response. But the more restrictive the gift means just that—the money is restricted to the purpose for which it was raised. When reviewing a solicitation in any form, a good rule of thumb is to ask: "What does the giver think is going to happen with the donation when she or he is writing the check?"

What happens when money is really tight? An unfortunate but common practice in the ministry community is borrowing against restricted funds. If ever there were a red flag for board members or CEOs, this is it. But what is an organization to do if it is faced with meeting a Friday payroll and the only liquid funds it has are in an account restricted for a designated purpose? It is legal in the United States (but not in Canada) to borrow funds from one account for another, but there must be a plan for repayment. These borrowings are clear indicators that an organization needs to change course or risk an embarrassment or failure of its mission.

In 2005, Zogby International, a polling firm, was commissioned by the plaintiffs of what may be the largest "donor intent" lawsuit in U.S. history. According to their nationwide survey, 97 percent of the respondents said they consider it a very or somewhat serious matter if charities spend money for other than their intended purpose.[6] While it may seem obvious, the conclusion is that givers should never be taken for granted and they must be respected on many levels, not the least of which is honoring their intent.

LESSON 4: RESPECT FOR THE GIVER

By respecting givers, we are exhibiting the integrity that is a result of a transformed life and ministry. A common characteristic of successful organizations is a track record of trust with their givers who form long-term relationships with the organization. Treating givers with respect is not only something that should be expected from a Christian organization; it is also flat-out good business.

Sometimes a giver becomes disillusioned because he or she cannot meet the needs of a ministry. For example, suppose a new giver pledges $20 a month. After a short time, the giver receives a letter explaining how much more could be accomplished if the giver gave $40. The giver believes so much in the ministry that she or he digs deeper into the grocery budget and comes up with $40 as requested. But alas, a software program targets this same giver to be encouraged to give $80 the next time. This process eventually burns out givers, causing them to drop off. The cycle begins again as the ministry increases its prospecting for new names, which is by far the most expensive method of fundraising.

Ministries also foster an unfavorable image when givers learn that a prospecting mailing list will initially net only 10 to 20 percent back to the program. As much as 80 to 90 percent of what is raised as a result of the first mailing is consumed by the cost of the mailing. Regular contributors are the lifeblood of the organization, yet the return on the investment of obtaining those names is only realized over time. It is rarely beneficial with the first mailing.

Given these circumstances, it is always better to use previously received, *unrestricted* funds for sending a prospective appeal, especially if the appeal is for a restricted purpose. Small organizations do not always have such a reserve, though, and many givers would be upset if they knew that a large percentage of their first contribution was going to pay for the fundraising costs of the mailing. In those cases, great care should be taken to not make the appeal unrealistic by claiming the money will go for a specific project when, in fact, most of it will be consumed by the cost of the mailing.

A number of recent trends irritate givers rather than respect them. For example, most people profess to be disturbed by telemarketing. There is some evidence to suggest that even those who love a ministry and respond to a tele-marketing call still do not like it. Each organization has to make decisions regarding how they will fund their mission and how they will treat their givers. The two should not be on separate tracks.

Another technique that irritates givers is the frequency of mail or contact. Many givers interpret repeated mailings as wasting their investment in the ministry, even though more frequent contact usually results in more money, albeit on a diminishing return. "I can't get off the mailing list!" is a common complaint. Organizations should take care to purge the names of those who have made it clear that they do not wish to receive further solicitations.

Furthermore, privacy policies should be made known to givers, especially as regards selling or renting their names. Give them the opportunity to either opt in to receive information or opt out of further solicitations. Givers should not be subjected to crisis letters or stories that induce guilt trips. There is no question that these approaches raise money in the short-term, but neither do they grow givers' hearts to be rich toward God.

CONCLUSION

This chapter outlines what happens when there is a divergence between the values that characterize the Christian experience, and fundraising practices. The sheer stress of fundraising sometimes leads to rationalizing decisions to use questionable methods that denigrate the giver and ultimately dishonor Christ. Ministry leaders must honor Christ above everything else in *all* of their activities. They live their lives and lead their organizations with a commitment to never do anything to undermine the witness of the Christ we serve, and this must include fundraising practices.

A good policy is this: if there is any question about the propriety of a fundraising appeal or any transaction, rethink it and discuss it with trusted advisors. If questions persist, then do something different. Just as a tornado can swiftly decimate a long-standing structure, so integrity and trust built over time can be lost in the blink of an eye.

I believe it was D. L. Moody who said, "When God is your partner, plan big." Big visions produce big results, but big visionaries must be true statesmen. In an age when our elected leaders, corporate executives, Hollywood elite, and sports heroes are falling woefully short of exhibiting statesmanship, the public desperately needs ministry leaders whose walk with the Lord unmistakably reflects integrity in every aspect of the ministry. More importantly, God desires this same thing from us—He has entrusted us with much, and He wants us to use it with integrity so we are growing givers to conform to the image of Christ.

The essence of integrity is captured in a verse written by Elaine Nelson. With no intent to impugn the beautiful words of the apostle Paul, she offers the following:

> Though we speak with great charismatic oratory about the need for accountability and have not integrity, we are as sounding brass and tinkling cymbals.
>
> Though our ministry swells with pride as we display our showy programs of reaching out to the poor and needy and have not integrity, we are nothing. And though we burn with great zeal for the lost at the expense of our integrity, it profits us nothing.
>
> Integrity manifests itself best when no one is looking. It labors long, knowing that financial and ethical excellence do matter to God. It seeks not its own glory but only the glory of the Kingdom. It does not deem meticulous stewardship as non-essential to its cause.
>
> Integrity does not fail even though there be ministry abuse of every sort. Eventually, those abuses will cease under God's control even though there be a famine of Christian ethics. For that too will vanish away and be forgotten.
>
> Now we often see through a glass darkly as imperfect vessels. But when inward integrity, through His Spirit, comes to rule in our lives, then that which is self-seeking and slipshod will be done away.

And now abide accountability, zeal and integrity. But the greatest of these is
integrity . . . in the heart of man.[7]

PAUL D. NELSON was president of the Evangelical Council for Financial Accountability (ECFA) from 1994 to 2006. The organization, founded in 1979, is an accreditation agency for over 1,200 Christian ministries. Prior to his appointment to ECFA, he was executive vice president and chief operating officer of Focus on the Family from 1985 to 1994. Paul can be reached at candleberryhill@aol.com.

1. Paul Nelson, *Focus on Accountability* (ECFA, 4th quarter 2005).
2. Sample policies are available through ECFA.
3. Paul Nelson, "Ethics, Integrity, and Stewardship," *NRB* magazine, Feb–Mar 2006.
4. Dan Busby, *Focus on Accountability* (ECFA, 4th quarter 2005).
5. Paul Nelson, "Useful, but Limited," *Philanthropy Magazine*, Jan–Feb 2004.
6. "Ignore Donor Intent at Your Peril," *Fundraising News* (Association of Fundraising Professionals, 2006), http://www.nsfre.org/ka/ka-.cfm?content_item_id=23175&folder_id=2545.
7. Elaine Nelson, 1996.

Chapter

No COMPETITION
in the KINGDOM

By SHELLY A. COCHRANE, *Executive Director of*
Ministry Advancement, The Evangelical Alliance Mission

C ompetition is woven into the very fabric of Western society: healthy competition is said to produce excellence. Parents and teachers introduce children to competition at an early age, and churches join in too, with everything from Sunday school contests for best attendance to challenges for Scripture memorization or Bible quizzing. Competition is believed to improve performance and increase motivation. How should followers of Christ view competition? The purpose of this chapter is to examine whether competition among ministries advances or hinders efforts to transform givers' hearts to be rich toward God through their giving. We will first look at how competition has saturated Christian ministries, and the resulting effects. Next, we will examine the role of competition in the two fundamentally different fundraising models: the human-centric model and the God-centric model. Finally, we will see what comes of competition and its side effects when we apply the God-centric model to a Christian ministry.

WHAT DOES COMPETITION LOOK LIKE IN MINISTRIES?
Competition within Organizations

Ministries compete against other Christian organizations for material and human resources, and *within themselves* as well. Stories abound of supported workers hiding the personal identities of their giving partners from their organizational coworkers so that they maintain an exclusive, proprietary relationship with their supporters. One ministry reported having to reprimand a few of its supported staff for writing to supporters to redirect their contributions directly to a bank account rather than send them through the ministry. The staff members did not want the ministry to take the administrative fee on the donations, a fee that offset the actual expenses incurred to communicate the staff members' special need for funds.

Another ministry had to resolve issues that resulted from a key development officer leaving to go work for another ministry. The staff member took a copy of the whole donor file from the ministry he left and began contacting the givers to start contributing to the ministry that had newly hired him. The ministry where he previously worked contacted him to discuss the matter. Tensions left the situation awkward and strained.

Competition with Other Organizations

Some ministries compete against their peer ministries. Relief organizations each target the demographic of people known to give generously after natural disasters. Mission agencies compete against their counterparts at multiagency conferences and events. Christian schools, colleges, seminaries, mission agencies, relief organizations, rescue missions, camps, and radio stations utilize every available marketing method to woo givers into a preferred relationship with their ministry ahead of the myriad other charities that also need funding. They work desperately to distinguish themselves from the others so they can draw every possible resource to their own cause. Parachurch ministries and churches compete for funds from the same individuals.

Most ministries use marketing tools, media, and technology—everything they can find—to get and keep "market share." One common ploy is luring the giver by offering incentives and premiums of all kinds. They engrave bricks, publish an honor roll, mount brass plaques on new furniture, and erect signs along sidewalks. They give perks and create VIPs out of people who give large gifts, relegating modest givers to nonpreferential treatment.

The development officer sees his or her job as attempting to endear a giver more successfully than the development officer down the street. The ministry that "wins" gets the resources to survive another day; the ministry that "loses," has one less option for sustainability. It would appear that organizations perceive their future viability to depend first and foremost on successfully securing as many givers as possible for their own cause. Competition breeds an ethos that is more about impressing the giver than inviting that steward to have a generous heart that is rich toward God. It becomes more about growing the organization than growing givers' hearts in the Kingdom of God.

More Serious than It Seems

In reality, the issue of competition is only a symptom of a much greater problem. Competition in the Kingdom exposes the fact that Christians falsely believe that resources are finite and inherently limited. Society operates on the assumption that the world is a closed system of limited goods, making competition for resources mandatory to survival. Christians engage in competition without noticing that it fundamentally contradicts the nature of God and the example of Jesus Christ. Competition in the Kingdom exposes a human-centric worldview that contradicts Scripture; it is evidence of a focus on monetary transactions versus the transformation of hearts to be rich toward God. Consideration of a God-centric worldview demands that competition be challenged.

THE HUMAN-CENTRIC MODEL

The human-centric model combines Christian principles with existing cultural values to create a hybrid that is tolerable to Christianity. Christian leaders screen Western management methods to filter out unethical traits and add Christian teaching, and the combination is a profitable business endeavor that passes as compatible with the Christian faith. The premise is that the prevailing social system, combined with upright Christian practices, produces a successful result.

Christian fundraisers are taught to make competition work for the benefit of their ministry. Development officers utilize market research to analyze the Christian market and gain an advantage over other ministries. They work on developing their organization's brand. They identify their competitors and emphasize their own ministry distinctives in order to capture market share. The fundraiser is expected to develop personal skills in marketing and sales. He or she must be able to influence people and develop networks of personal relationships, convincing stewards that his or her ministry is indispensable to the Kingdom and that it merits funding—perhaps even more than other ministries. The role of the fundraiser is to get the money in the door. Every advantage is important because the marketplace is "saturated."

The relevant question is not whether Christian ministries functioning according to this human-centric model are generating adequate resources. We must ask what God's perspective is toward a system that is essentially a human means to a human end. The human-centric model is built on Christians employing skill and effort stemming from their own abilities and knowledge. What would an alternative model, centered on the intervention of God, look like?

A GOD-CENTRIC MODEL

There is no evidence in God's Word to indicate that God encourages competition to improve performance and motivation in the Kingdom of God.

A God-centric model is not based on a finite, closed system that encourages competition but rather on the infinite nature of God Himself. God is never confined to limitations of time and space. As Creator, God presides over the ultimate open system.

The account of the widow of Zarephath (1 Kings 17:8–16) demonstrates God's abundant supply. Elijah asked the woman to bring him a drink of water and a bite of bread. The woman explained that she had only a handful of flour left in the jar and a little cooking oil left in the bottom of the jug—enough for one last meal for herself and her son. Elijah told her, "This is what the Lord, the God of Israel says: There will always be plenty of flour and oil left in your containers until the time when the Lord sends rain and the crops grow again!" So she did as Elijah said, and she and Elijah and her son continued to eat from her supply of flour and oil for many days. No matter how much they used, there was always enough left in the containers, just as the Lord had promised through Elijah. God's abundance toward the widow and her son was proven by the continuous provision of flour and oil that flowed for as long as they needed it.

Another example of God's open system of resources is illustrated in Mark chapter 8, where Jesus feeds four thousand people with the food of a single boy. In this account, abundance is evident in the overwhelming quantity of food that God provided the hungry followers. Multiple basketfuls still remained after everyone had eaten as much as they wanted, proving God's ability to provide more resources than was possibly needed.

True to His nature, God introduces whatever new or additional resources are needed in any given situation, to accomplish His purposes. God supplied new resources that were not part of the known equation when He created manna for the children of Israel. The wanderers were not required to compete over a preexisting quantity, because God introduced each day's provision in abundance. Even as the head count of Israelites varied from year to year, God's bounty for the hungry travelers exceeded whatever could be consumed.

Competition played no role in the Israelites' efforts to secure sufficient food for their families.

The foundation of the God-centric model presupposes an infinite God who is actively involved with His finite creation. God has not destined humans to live in a closed system, comprised of barely sufficient resources that they must compete for in order to survive. Throughout history God has demonstrated repeatedly that He creates and renews resources more abundant than men require. Competition is entirely irrelevant and superfluous since God's provision exceeds every possible demand.

The Human Element: Faith in God's Supply

Does that imply that human effort is not involved in obtaining God's provision? Do human actions influence God's response? Scripture shows that God has accomplished His plan down through the ages through both conventional and extraordinary means according to His sovereign purposes. God created people with the ability to learn and think and act. Very often God accomplishes His will by enabling men and women to exercise their gifts and abilities to produce good results.

God enabled Joseph to become an accomplished businessman in Egypt and steered his efforts to spare the Israelites from famine. While training to learn the language and culture of Babylon, God gave Daniel and his three friends the intellectual capacity to learn everything they needed to know to be chosen for the king's service. The very ability to gain knowledge and acquire expertise comes from God. The very ability to master marketing and fundraising techniques and use them successfully comes from God's enabling grace.

Though God often uses and molds people's natural abilities, He also makes a habit of utilizing entirely counterintuitive solutions. God gave Gideon victory through trumpets and broken pots, not through an expanded army. His people must have faith as they follow a God-centric model.

Whether God shapes common events or precipitates something entirely radical, He is the one who initiates a plan and supplies the resources in order to fulfill His purposes. There is a vast difference between the God-centric examples of God working through conventional wisdom for His purposes and the human-centric model that uses solely human means to human ends. The God-centric model relies on the catalytic nature of God from start to finish, regardless of the means through which He intervenes in the world. God determines whether the conventional or the radical will accomplish His plan, and He engages people to participate with Him in carrying it out. Through faith, believers respond to God's invitation to join with Him. Jesus declared, "I tell you the truth, anyone who has faith in me will do what I have been doing. He will do even greater things than these, because I am going to the Father. And I will do whatever you ask in my name, so that the Son may bring glory to the Father. You may ask me for anything in my name, and I will do it" (John 14:12–14).[1] "Everything is possible for him who believes" (Mark 9:23). Paul wrote, "And my God will meet all your needs according to His glorious riches in Christ Jesus" (Phil. 4:19).

Faith displaces the prevailing human-centered values of society. John declares, "Everyone born of God overcomes the world. This is the victory that has overcome the world, even our faith" (1 John 5:4). God expects His chosen ones to live out their rock-solid confidence in who He is and how He acts, responding in obedience to His bidding, however counterintuitive that may be. In a critical moment when resources are needed, God's servants act in faith, not succumbing to the pragmatic attitudes and competitive practices of the culture around them. God acts in ways that prove that He is the One who gives victory. "God chose the weak things of the world to shame the strong. He chose the lowly things of this world and the despised things—and the things that are not—to nullify the things that are, so that no one may boast before him" (1 Cor. 1:27–29). Faith means that people trust God to utilize the methods He ordains to accomplish the outcomes He intends. The believer's role is to follow God's lead and carry out His instructions in obedience.

SO WHAT DOES BIBLICAL STEWARDSHIP LOOK LIKE IN A GOD-CENTRIC MODEL?

How does Christian fundraising work if competition has no part in it? How does faith play out in practicality? Victor Matthews gives three facets: "The first is that of submission to God and His Word. The second is the practice of obedience. Genuine faith is a correct response to God and this is always inseparable from obedience in daily life. The third characteristic of faith is that of trust."[2]

Submission

Christian leaders and fundraisers must concentrate on desiring God's will for their organizations—nothing less, nothing more. God resources what He initiates, and great care must be given to discerning the mind of Christ before creating an agenda that requires funding. Leaders must constantly come before God with open hands, willing to have Him wipe away or change any and every part of the organization or program that He sees fit. No one dare ask God for resources without first offering Him free reign to change or discontinue the ministry. If withholding resources is one of God's ways of giving direction, then leaders need to embrace that and ask God for new marching orders. Submission to God overrides the fear of failure or worry about being out of a job. Self-preservation is not compatible with faith.

Obedience

Obedience calls ministry leaders and fundraisers to step out in faith regardless of looking foolish. Noah committed to following God's plan and bore the scorn of society for years. Obedience means following God even when His ways are not respected in the human realm. To obey God means that believers must repent from having substituted human strategy for God's centrality. When Christians feel that staking their ministries' viability on the intervention of God is too risky, they resort to their own scheming for finding what they need.

Trust

Union with God through faith is the supreme goal—even more significant than any ministry activity that succeeds. The greatest work for the Kingdom may, in fact, be demonstrating reckless abandonment to God in a fallen world."[3] Trust is nerve-wracking, and in the lonely hours up against hard financial deadlines, ministry leaders find themselves clutching at anything that will stave off disaster. Somehow in those moments, translating faith in God into money in hand seems to truly be a leap of faith. When the believer crosses the line from fixating on the tangible to relinquishing himself into the hands of a fearsome God—precisely this desperate dependence is the substance of faith. George Barna writes, "The hallmarks of the Church that Jesus died for are clear, based on Scripture: your profession of faith in Christ must be supported by a lifestyle that provides irrefutable evidence of your complete devotion to Jesus."[4]

COLLABORATION, NOT COMPETITION

So what does that mean for the day-to-day life of a ministry leader or fundraiser? How do ministries relate together with one another and with givers in a God-centric world without competition?

Collaboration based on unity and humility in the body of Christ offers a strong testimony to a human-centered society. One example of this happened after the Katrina hurricane devastation. A constituent who had pledged a $200,000 gift to HCJB Global called them after the hurricane disaster to say that he and his wife would be giving to Katrina victims instead of fulfilling their commitment to the radio ministry. Dick Jacquin, the head of development at HCJB, thanked the giver for responding to how the Holy Spirit was leading them. He told them that God would provide for HCJB's ministries and that they should obey His voice. Dick prayed with them over the phone and then hung up, disappointed at the loss of such a large gift but truly believing that God is in control of all things. Two weeks later that same constituent called back. He thanked Dick for his gracious attitude and said that he and his wife had since found a way to fulfill their original pledge to HCJB and give toward hurricane relief as well. The true heart attitude within HCJB was one of faith and obedience to God, not coercing the giver into something when God was prompting him or her to do something else. In the same spirit, both HCJB and Trans World Radio refer givers to each another when a giver can be best served by the other ministry.

In God's economy, all ministries submitted to His leading point toward the same end. Jeavons and Basinger write, "God has no favorite causes. . . . Fundraisers who truly believe that God is enough and that no one ministry is inherently more valuable than another are free to encourage right motives for giving and let donors follow their hearts and feed their souls."[5] Biblical stewardship principles should result in practical collaboration both within and between Christian organizations.

SUGGESTIONS FOR TANGIBLE IMPLEMENTATION OF A GOD-CENTRIC MODEL:

Within a Christian Ministry

Demonstrate an organizational dependence on God with concentrated prayer and fasting prior to rolling out programs and priorities. The Evangelical Alliance Mission (TEAM) leadership, for example, sets aside the first Monday of the month as a time for staff to pray and fast together through the lunch period. Any meeting, consultation, or appointment can be paused at any time by anyone who calls for a time to stop and pray. Grace Brethren International Missions is another organization that values prayer as part of their organizational culture. Mike Taylor reports that it is commonplace to see staff huddled in the hallway praying together at some point during the workday.

Establish spiritual accountability for the ministry as a whole, including the board of directors and senior leaders. Outside accountability can help a ministry stay spiritually sharp or help bring revival. Set up an accountability relationship with an independent person or group who looks for evidence of spiritual health and vitality. The accountability person may ask questions like: How does the board's leadership demonstrate that they "live by faith, not by sight" (2 Cor. 5:7)? In what ways do board members engage in providing spiritual direction for the ministry? How does the board verify/affirm the spiritual health and vitality of the senior leaders? The ministry would do well to have an outside "chaplain" or "shepherd" who is empowered to ask the hard questions and report what he or she finds in a way that can usher in change if necessary.

Make sure that the stewardship personnel are people of faith and dependence on God, who are committed to growing givers' hearts. Development staff should be among the most spiritually mature leaders in the whole ministry. They must exemplify the walk of faith, demonstrating their trust in God by giving generously from a heart conformed to Christ's image, and must be comfortable challenging a giver to walk by faith. They should be devoted to God's work in His people to transform and grow their hearts, more than their own particular ministry.

Make a covenant that organizational longevity and sustainability will never be esteemed above seeking God's will. God will reveal His intent for the duration and scope of a ministry if His followers look to Him for direction. Every ministry must be willing to yield to God's sovereign plan even if His plan does not match the aspirations of the ministry leaders. Blackaby makes a bold statement about interpreting the blessing of God: "Leaders can achieve their goals and yet be out of God's will. Reaching goals is not necessarily a sign of God's blessing."[6]

Consider spiritual maturity and dependence on God as primary qualities when looking for board members and staff, followed secondarily by skills and credentials. Make sure that competition is not rewarded under the guise of celebrating "self-starters" who are "driven to succeed." Appoint people who demonstrate faith, not those who bring in the most money. "The danger is in believing that human reasoning can build the kingdom of God. It cannot. The role of spiritual leaders is not to dream up dreams for God, but to be the vanguard for their people in understanding God's revelation."[7]

Working with Givers

What is the fundraiser's relationship to givers in a God-centric model that affirms that God, not the giver, is the focus of provision? As the fundraiser lives out an active faith in the presence of the giver, he or she receives an opportunity to encourage the giver to emulate that same kind of faith in his or her own life. Strong bonds form through praying together and seeking God's face for the future provision of a ministry that God is empowering.

Invest in ministry partners on the basis of spiritual values and faith more than on giving potential and wealth. Make God the center of the relationship and the recipient of esteem. Willmer states that "giving is primarily a spiritual matter . . . an act of obedient worship. . . the spiritual growth of supporters should be the primary concern of every Christian fundraiser."[8]

Intentionally ask God for new provisions and counterintuitive solutions in addition to engaging conventional marketing and solicitation practices. Utilize conventional wisdom to the best of your ability, but don't settle for that as the primary or only source of funding. Be willing to be God's fool in the eyes of society so that God receives maximum glory. Blackaby makes a pointed statement about leaders claiming God's endorsement to man-made plans:

> Spiritual leaders must continually remind themselves that what God has promised, God will accomplish completely in His time and in His way (Philippians 1:6). The leader's job is to communicate God's promise to the people, not to create the vision and then enlist people to buy in to it.[9]

Genuinely seek God's vision for the ministry and invite givers to seek God's will for their involvement.

COLLABORATING WITH OTHER MINISTRIES

Seek out like-minded ministries who are willing to live by faith even though they run the risk of appearing foolish to the outside world. Share prayer requests and encouragement to take spiritually motivated risks. Pledge to each other that competition will never characterize your organization. Network with ministries in the Christian Stewardship Association who share a kindred spirit of being sold out to God.

Share ideas among ministries. A number of ministries collaborate in a grant-seekers forum that assists ministries in exchanging ideas on how to work with the many foundations that contribute to Christian organizations. Participants share best practices with one another and garner advice from experts who address the group so that they all benefit from foundation funding.

Share relationships with givers. Denise Kuhn shared the joy she experienced after assuming an increased fundraising role with Mastermedia International. Denise met the development officer of a prominent ministry, John, who gave her advice on building relationships to share her vision for what God is doing in the lives of the media community. After talking together, John offered to connect Denise with some of his friends in Texas who are major givers to the ministry. Denise reported that one of those givers made a six-figure gift to Mastermedia subsequent to John's introducing her to them. John's understanding of biblical stewardship allowed him to share his relationships with givers with another ministry without fear that his ministry would fall short if a giver gave elsewhere.

Be a ministry that makes financial gifts to other ministries. Fight off the spirit of entitlement that comes from always being on the receiving end of financial contributions. Give sacrificially according to the Lord's prompting. Being able to give freely shows that you understand that God's resources are infinite and that He is the provider of everything you need. It is the nature of God to give. God gave life. God gave His Son. God gave eternal life. We are created in His image, and when we are like Him, it is our nature to give.

CONCLUSION

Whether the structural competition that has crept into our ministries is accidental or intentional, a choice has to be made. Every single servant of God must choose: Either God is abundantly able to meet every need according to His riches in Christ Jesus or there is a shrinking pie of resources and it is every man for himself in getting a piece before it's gone. Ministry leaders cannot operate in both worlds.[10] The very tolerance of competition in Kingdom work divulges a greater allegiance to the human-centric mentality of natural selection than to the God-centric conviction that faith in God alone unleashes the impossible. The human-centric model that fosters self-preservation and competition contradicts biblical stewardship that is predicated on faith. The God-centric model, emanating from faith, enriches both the fundraiser and the giver, resulting in the generous outpouring of resources to the glory of God.

The most valuable benefit a giver can receive through a close relationship with a Christian fundraiser is to learn what it means to have a heart surrendered and generous toward God. The fundraiser who demonstrates wholesale faith in God rather than competitiveness is most likely to inspire true discipleship in the steward. The steward who is inspired to follow Christ with his or her whole heart is undoubtedly the one who will give most generously! The very competitive advantage meant to give the fundraiser the edge will, ironically, stunt true spiritual growth in the giver, resulting in less giving because of weaker heart commitment to God.

For Christians to experience the outpouring of God's blessings, they first need to repent from their own self-reliant attitudes and behavior. They must cry out to God in humility, renouncing the cultural values that oppose Him.

SHELLEY COCHRANE worked as a TEAM (The Evangelical Alliance Mission) missionary among Yugoslavs in Europe for eleven years. Since 1998 Shelley has served as the director of mobilization for TEAM, developing personnel and material resources and emphasizing prayer support for the vision God has given to TEAM. Shelley oversees the staff, strategy, and budget of the Mobilization division of TEAM, which includes stewardship ministries, partner relations, communications and media, and new member development. She also serves on the board of directors for the Christian Leadership Alliance. She can be reached at scochrane@teamworld.org.

1. All Bible quotations, unless otherwise noted, are from the *New International Version*.

2. Victor M. Matthews, *Growth in Grace* (Grand Rapids: Zondervan, 1970), 114–15.

3. Henry Blackaby, *Experiencing God* (Nashville: Broadman Holman, 1994), 170.

4. George Barna, *Revolution* (Carol Stream, IL: Tyndale House, 2005), 25.

5. Thomas Jeavons and Rebekah Basinger, *Growing Givers' Hearts: Treating Fundraising as Ministry* (San Francisco: Jossey-Bass, 2000), 98.

6. Henry & Richard Blackaby, *Spiritual Leadership* (Nashville, Broadman Holman, 2001), 145.

7. Ibid, 84.

8. Wesley K. Willmer, *God & Your Stuff: The Vital Link between Your Possessions and Your Soul* (Colorado Springs: NavPress, 2002), 95.

9. Blackaby, *Spiritual Leadership*, 72.

10. R. Scott Rodin, *Stewards in the Kingdom: A Theology of Life in All Its Fullness* (Downers Grove, IL.: IVP, 2000), 150.

Chapter

LESSONS LEARNED ON THE
JOURNEY OF GENEROSITY

BY DARYL J. HEALD,
President of Generous Giving

D on't you know that our God is a generous God? Because He is always generous with us, we are generous to Him and to each other." I heard Ruth's words through a translator while I was with a group distributing Operation Christmas Child shoe boxes in the poorest part of Xalapa, Mexico. Ruth had started a ministry feeding and teaching children in the area. She took care of more than a hundred children every day. I cried as I listened to her explain "la generosidad," the Spanish phrase for generosity. As I learned that day, this woman toward whom I had come to be generous understood the origin of generosity far better than I. Generosity flows from a heart that is conformed to the image of Christ. As we grow like Christ, we reflect the generosity He has shown to us. This basic understanding of generosity undergirds all the lessons I've learned along the journey to generous giving.

The road to becoming generous, as you have learned throughout this book, is a process of spiritual growth. It involves learning, growing, and surrendering.

It is part of our sanctification—a dynamic journey of conforming to the image of Christ. It is much more than writing checks for a set percentage of our incomes. It is loving and honoring God by becoming stewards (managers) of *all* the resources God has entrusted to us for His glory.

As with all journeys, we will encounter different kinds of people, roadblocks, and circumstances along the way. In the following pages I will present some experiences and stories of givers (including my own) who are in different places on the road to Christlike generosity. As you read this chapter, it will become evident that I do not lead out of strength but out of weakness. I am a recovering materialist in the midst of God's transforming work. My saving grace is my wife's spiritual gift of giving. She has pried my hands open many times. My hope is that you can benefit from my experiences and receive the joy intended for all of us when we give as generously as God has given to us (2 Cor. 8:9). If a significant number of my fellow Christians accept this charge and become generous as Christ is generous, then we will begin to unleash our great potential to bring God's Kingdom of peace to our lost world. For the purpose of this chapter, I will explain the seven lessons I've learned on my journey. It is my prayer that they will encourage many others to be generous and that askers can use these lessons as they facilitate giving.

LESSON 1: KNOW WHY YOU GIVE

For many Christians, giving is like obeying traffic laws: We follow the "rules of the road" out of the duty to obey the law. I was stuck in this rut for a long time, checking off another box trying to please God. I wanted others to think that I understood generous giving, but in reality, I never saw nor understood the big picture. Thus, I never fully experienced all that God promises. When asked why they give, many answer, "because God commands us to give," or, "because it's part of our tradition, our heritage, and our duty." When I first asked myself why I give, it sounded very rhetorical. It is such an easy answer—it's the Christian thing to do, right?

As Todd Harper mentions in his chapter, this is a great question to raise when asking someone to give, in order to make sure givers comprehend a biblical foundation for giving. Along this line, George Barna conducts a giving survey of the evangelical church every year. He asks a couple of questions; for instance, "What does God require of you in your giving?" Seven out of ten evangelicals answer that God requires 10 percent, or the tithe. Then he asks, "Do you tithe?" and fewer than 3 percent say they do.[1] There is no doubt that God desires us to give, and as Walt Russell's chapter explains, we do not give from an obligated heart but, rather, from a blessed heart reflecting the generosity of Christ. It is in response to and out of gratefulness for the generous sacrifice of Christ that we give. Mark Powell writes, "We give out of glad and generous hearts as an expression of love and devotion to the God who is so good to us. When we do this, we discover the very essence of Christianity: a heartfelt relationship with God in which joy and thanksgiving replace self-interest or guilt."[2]

When we see giving as a reflection of the grace of God in us, we experience joy, freedom, contentment, reward, worship, blessing, and favor. We see this over and over in the Bible: "It is more blessed to give than to receive" (Acts 20:35); "Where your treasure is, there your heart will be also" (Luke 12:34); "You cannot serve both God and Money" (Matt. 6:24). The apostle Paul's words are paraphrased this way: "It's not for my sake that I'm asking; it's for yours" (Phil. 4:17). This journey is not just a rote duty—it's an exciting opportunity to receive God's abundant blessings. The eternal investments are what matter most to God—they are among the most important goals of our giving adventure. Make sure you know why you give.

LESSON 2: UNDERSTAND THAT GOD OWNS ALL

We cannot arrive at the goal of Christlike generosity when we're operating under faulty assumptions. My progress was stalled for some time because I believed that if I gave 10 percent, then I got to keep 90 percent and do with it whatever I wanted. However, biblical generosity is never defined as giving only 10 percent (see Craig Blomberg's and Walt Russell's chapters). It's all God's. As George Barna says, "I surrender 100 percent."[3] We should be ready at any moment to give to any Kingdom opportunity that God brings to our attention.

If we say everything is God's but live as if it's ours, then our decisions about giving have no power. I know many people who have found great freedom once they realized that it wasn't all on their shoulders. When we understand that God is the One orchestrating our lives, then we can relax. Down deep, we know that if everything were dependent on us, there would be reason for fear and anxiety. It is God who gives and God who takes away (Job 1:21).

LESSON 3: REALIZE THAT GIVING IS AN INVESTMENT WITH REWARDS

Everyday financial investments can shed light on how we should approach eternal, Kingdom-focused giving. One day I had the opportunity to get in on a potentially lucrative investment deal. The minimum investment was larger than I had anticipated. But since I viewed this as a money-making opportunity, I was willing to move, shuffle, and unwind other things to meet the minimum.

Soon after, it occurred to me that I never before had viewed a Kingdom investment in the same way. A friend asked me how to decide on an appropriate giving level. I told him it should be commensurate with the opportunity— buy as much as you can—like the investment deal I just made. Then I realized that I was more willing to invest larger amounts in temporal opportunities than eternal ones. This exposed the gap between what I said I believed about giving to the work of the Kingdom and what I actually did with my giving.

The "ah-ha" for me was this: What I invest on earth is soon gone, and what I give to eternal Kingdom causes reaps eternal rewards. Wesley Willmer writes that we "have a choice as to which kingdom [we] will follow, the temporary kingdom here on earth or the eternal kingdom where our soul will dwell forever with God."[4] If you think something is a great opportunity, then you are willing to put a lot of resources into the deal. A savvy investor looks at an opportunity and asks, "How much of it can I buy?" He doesn't think, "What's the least amount I can put into this good deal?" My poor thinking had created an artificial ceiling on my giving. Risk is to the investment world what faith is to the giving world. Any investment deal requires risk, just as every giving opportunity requires faith. We measure the efficacy of the risk by the projected return. But God promises that when we give generously we will reap thirty-, sixty-, and one-hundred-fold returns (Mark 4:8). That's 3,000, 6,000 and 10,000 percent! Like most things in God's Kingdom, what we expect is turned upside down—what I give is never lost, but what I keep I eventually lose.

There was once a man who sold his company and made a very large profit from the sale. He did three major things with the money: He bought a big boat, purchased a jet, and gave a large gift to a youth ministry to build a camp.

Ten years later he visited the leader of this youth ministry, who recounted many stories of how instrumental the camp had been in impacting thousands of children's lives. This youth leader asked what advice the giver would give to someone in his position of success and wealth. The giver replied, "I wish I could do it over again. I don't have the plane or the boat anymore—they were fun for a while, but they're both in junkyards now. After ten years, though, the camp is still a place of ministry, and thousands of kids have come to Christ— this investment has lasted." Randy Alcorn writes, "The money God entrusts to us here on earth is eternal investment capital. Every day is an opportunity to buy up more shares in His kingdom. *You can't take it with you, but you can send it on ahead.*"[5]

Another issue when considering the future is the wise investment of what God has given you when you can no longer use it. I've heard some say that their goal is for their last check to bounce when they die. Good idea, but most of us will leave something behind, and it must go somewhere. If there is no estate plan, it will go to the government. So, if you get hit by the proverbial bus tonight, who will inherit what you have left? Is it your spouse, children, grandchildren, or charities? Whoever receives the funds needs to be prepared. One should never pass on wealth without wisdom.

LESSON 4: BE ACCOUNTABLE

Our giving journeys are not effortless strolls to be taken alone. Left to our own devices, we inevitably will veer off the right path. As we were reminded in Paul Nelson's chapter, we need godly companions to give us direction and tell us when we are lost.

If the church or our spouses don't know what we are giving, this can cause problems. The communal and familial aspects of the Christian life require that there be people who will hold us accountable and challenge us. Jesus also exhorts us, "Let your light shine before men in such a way that they may see your good works, and glorify your Father who is in heaven" (Matt. 5:16 NASB). The writer of Hebrews tells us to "stimulate one another to love and good deeds" (Heb. 10:24 NASB). "Stimulating one another" means encouraging one another to step out in faith and go beyond our comfort levels in areas of obedience such as giving.

Early in our journey of generosity, a friend challenged Cathy and me to give more. We had just finished a Crown Financial Ministries course and decided to increase our giving goal to 20 percent. Each year we would increase that amount by 1 percent. I felt pretty good about that and mentioned it to a friend, hoping he would be impressed with our commitment. After "boldly" sharing, I asked him at what level he and his wife were giving. He told me that they were giving 40 percent of their income and suggested that Cathy and I could do the same. Talk about feeling humbled! At that point in our journey, I didn't know people gave that much. His openness and lack of arrogance or condemnation appropriately challenged me. He was a motivator. His model eventually allowed us to do the same. Cathy and I talked and prayed about this decision. Our conclusion was to set our new goal at 40 percent and by God's grace to increase it every year.

Being held accountable and finding trusted relationships are keys for all of us as we strive to live like Christ. He created us for community. Small groups are a part of the culture within most churches and parachurch ministries, and they encourage groups of men and women to have fellowship together. There, we can share openly about all aspects of life, including work, relationships, and finances. This safe environment helps each participant to live a life of integrity and godliness. It was through a friend's experience in community that I took another life-altering turn. He shared with me:

One morning our weekly small group meeting started out like all the others; however, one of the guys came in and changed the nature of our group forever. He threw onto the table a bunch of papers that looked a lot like financial statements. When we realized what we were looking at, everyone felt awkward. He broke the silence as he told the group, "After all these years, we've played all of our cards except for one. We are willing to talk about almost everything and to hold each other accountable on every issue except in this one area. We are still holding one card, so I'm playing it now.

Here's my net worth, what I made last year, what we live on, and what we gave. Now I want you to hold me accountable in these three decisions: (1) Not to increase our net worth, for we have accumulated more than we need. (2) Not to increase our lifestyle. We want to draw the line and not increase what we spend on ourselves even if we make more income. Our goal is to give this specific dollar amount next year. (3) To give more if we have an increase."

That was the beginning of true transparency. It was shocking at first, but there was an openness and honesty that our group had never experienced until we shared specifically where each of us was in the area of finances and giving. We set goals in order to be held accountable.

After hearing that story, I realized that my small group had never played the money card, so I decided to try it out. I met my accountability friend and began with the usual list of questions. I was a little nervous, but then I went for it. I asked as casually as possible, "So, how much did you make, and how much did you give last year?" After he choked on his food, he replied, "That's awfully personal" (unlike all the things we've talked about before?). I then realized that I had broken protocol and that if this were going to work, I needed to share first. So I gave him details of what we made and what we gave last year. I told him that Cathy and I had decided we didn't want to spend any more than what we planned in our budget. We wanted to give more, and I wanted him to hold us accountable. He thought about it for a while and finally shared the same. Our relationship is now deeper and freer. There is also greater trust—because there are no secrets.

Think about your experiences in small groups or with trusted friends. Have you ever shared these details with anyone? If you are married, do you and your spouse share and plan together? We gladly welcome a good friend to help us to stay focused, guard our hearts, and keep our eyes on God. However, we don't talk about money. It stays close to the vest. Why is this? One reason probably is that money is the idol of today's culture. It's the other "god" that competes with the true God for our affection and attention (Matt. 6:24). I believe that our love of money is the systemic issue holding us back from being all that we have been created to be. Jesus makes it clear that we cannot serve two masters (Luke 16:13). In the American church we think we can love Jesus and our stuff equally. In my foolishness my ideas have sounded more like this: I need just enough of Jesus to be safe, and then I can have a lot of stuff to make me look good. Yet my understanding of what Jesus said refutes that false supposition. He says that either He is my sole master or He is no master at all. We must be progressing either toward Christ or toward money—we cannot go both ways.

LESSON 5: AVOID THE ALLURE OF AFFLUENCE

Along the way there will be many distractions to lure us away from the goal of our journeys. One of the strongest is our desire for affluence—to have the most and the best. When pursued, however, it proves to be a disappointing dead end.

Once, when I was about to leave for a conference, a friend offered to pick me up on his private plane. It didn't take me long to cancel my airline ticket. On the flight over, I found myself thinking, "This is the only way to travel. If I had this jet, I would never ask for anything else. As we sat talking, my friend reached down and handed me the back section of the *Wall Street Journal*. He confessed this was a problem area for him—the want ads, which highlighted luxury cars, planes, and extravagant homes for sale. He felt embarrassed sharing this, but after looking at the advertisements of new jets, he felt like he needed to upgrade.

Finally, I realized the fallacy of my own thinking. I had believed that having a particular car, house, or jet would bring me contentment. However, my friend's honesty helped me to understand that regardless of income level, discontentment pervades our stuff-driven culture. There we were, sitting in a private plane, and it wasn't enough. As Scripture says, "Whoever loves money never has money enough" (Eccl. 5:10 NIV). Similarly, the apostle Paul warns us not to put our hope in wealth, as it so easily fades, nor to be arrogant but, rather, to lay up for ourselves treasures in heaven (1 Tim. 6:17–19).

It is easy to become mired in the need for more new stuff—the more we get, the deeper we sink. There is a built-in obsolescence in consumerism: Fashions, electronics, cars—all of it becomes outdated or useless within a few years. I need discipline to be content with what I have. There is a freedom in not chasing the latest and the best: Less truly is more. Do we possess our things, or do our things possess us?

When industrialist John D. Rockefeller, the wealthiest man in his day, was asked, "How much is enough?" he famously replied, "Just one dollar more."

But we as Christians are called to be content whatever our circumstances, whether in plenty or want. Our hope and security do not lie in how much we possess. Life is dynamic, and there are points when in the eyes of those around us, we are defined by our accumulation. So we get into the habit of having more and more, and many people reach the point of overaccumulation without even realizing it. A very powerful weapon against overaccumulation, then, is to draw an end line and say, "This is all we will ever need, and anything above this number, we will give away." My wife and I had drawn this line when her father informed us that we would be receiving some unexpected money from a family estate. The freeing thing is that we never had to wrestle with what to do with it, because we had already determined that we would give away whatever came in beyond our end line.

William Wilberforce, the great British social reformer of the 1800s, was backed financially by a businessman named John Thornton. Thornton's giving provides a window through which the character of his faith shines. One instance in particular affords a powerful example. While going through the day's correspondence one morning, Thornton opened a letter informing him that one of his ships with valuable cargo had wrecked, a disaster that meant a considerable financial loss for him. The news hit him hard, and he became lost in serious reflection. However, after several moments, he resumed going through his correspondence, opening several letters requesting his aid or support. Remarkably, his mood began to lighten. He took out his checkbook and began to write checks, saying, "Let us try to do a little good while we still have the means to do so."

The so-called "good life" and the lifestyles of the rich and famous are defined not by the wisdom of Scripture but by our culture of consumption. Life filled with material possessions is not the biblical definition of life. Jesus said, "A man's life does not consist in the abundance of his possessions" (Luke 12:15 NIV). We all have to wrestle with this basic question: What is life really about? Is it about accumulating and adding to our treasuries? We must ask ourselves, "Am I about possessing the Kingdom, or are the false assumptions of culture possessing me?" One principle has helped me: The only way to break the power money has on me is to travel lightly by giving it away.

It is hard to give money away. That is why we desperately need God's intervention to conform our hearts to the image of Christ; only then will we be able to be generous as Christ is generous. When we pray for His guidance, the Holy Spirit leads us to let go of wealth's ownership. Mark Powell notes that "the Bible teaches that generosity is a fruit of God's Holy Spirit (Gal. 5:22–23). The way to become generous people, then, involves not quenching God's Spirit (1 Thess. 5:19), but allowing the transforming work of Christ to have its full effect in shaping us to be the people God wants us to be."[6] In this way, prayer guides us onto the course of an eternity-minded agenda for managing wealth. Ironically, when we surrender to the Lord our control over wealth, wealth no longer has control over us. The secret is to put to death the desire to allocate our wealth the way we please. When we accomplish this with the help of the Holy Spirit, we will release vast resources for the advancement of God's Kingdom.

LESSON 6: BE WILLING TO ADMIT NEED

One of the most difficult legs of my giving journey has been one of the most recent. I came to a realization that confession is part of giving. In order to give generously, I must first recognize all that God has given me. Then I must place myself in a position to receive from Him. Why has this been so hard for me? It's vulnerable and humbling. It shows others our incompleteness, that we don't "have it together." It can even mean an admission of failure.

My understanding of this principle started with a simple phone call to a friend to ask a question. As I explained the reason for my call, he stopped me in midsentence and asked, "Are you asking for help?" I stumbled through an explanation about having a logistical problem or something lame like that, and so he asked again, "Do you need help?" I finally replied, "Yes, I guess I do."

He said, "Great, finally you have a need that maybe I can help you with." He went on to say, "OK, here's the deal: You tell me what it is you need, and from this moment on, I don't want you to think about it again. Consider it done, and consider it my privilege to give to you in this way." I was blown away. For one thing, I was impressed with his apparent need to be able to reciprocate in our relationship—reciprocity truly is part of giving. Additionally, I was surprised at his directness in asking me if I had a need. It was revealing to me that my posture wrongly communicates that I'm fine and don't need help. I had been skewing my understanding of generosity on the giving side, believing it's only others who have needs, not I. When I'm not balanced in giving and receiving, I stagnate.

LESSON 7: SET LIFESTYLE AND GIVING GOALS

Every choice in life involves an opportunity cost, and when it comes to money, we stand at a crossroads with four options: spend it, save it, invest it, or give it. What I decide to spend affects my ability to give; all my financial decisions are interdependent. If we truly believe that God's Kingdom is the best place to invest, then we should orient whatever we have been entrusted to maximize our ability to give. How can we start increasing our giving to God's Kingdom? Following are some questions that set a framework for this great change of heart and habit.

Where is your heart?

As I mentioned earlier, generosity is first and foremost a heart issue. You will genuinely reflect Christ's generosity when you are conformed to His image. If your heart isn't right, no budget or lifestyle formula will work because it will be disingenuous. Giving starts spiritually and works outward. Once your heart is right, then you can start organizing the outward expressions of generosity.

What's the appropriate lifestyle budget?

In most cases, we increase our expenses as we increase our incomes. This was our family's scenario until we took the Crown Financial Ministries course and got a handle on our true income and expenses. As I mentioned before, we increased our giving goal, and one of the reasons we could do that was our decision to live on a portion of our income and then give the rest. So we capped our number and budget accordingly. There is no prescription for an exact amount, but if you ask God, He will reveal the appropriate amount for you. This is another discipline that allows us to break the power of money.

What is my annual giving goal?

If you aim at nothing, you'll hit it every time. My wife and I operated for many years without a giving goal. During that time, I was able to check the tithe box, but who knew where the rest went? Goals give clarity and account-ability to our giving. Having an annual giving goal allows us to see our faith in action and gives us the opportunity to celebrate what God does in our giving. There are many excuses for not giving (see Walt Russell's chapter), but with God's work in our hearts, we can overcome all of them as we journey along the road to generosity.

What is my lifetime giving goal?

Ultimately, this is what we are working to see adopted by givers. Ohio busi-nessman Stanley Tam, now in his nineties, had a bold goal of giving $100 mil-lion to world missions. He set that goal in the 1950s and by God's grace has surpassed it. My mentor, John Edmund Haggai, has challenged many believ-ers to attempt something so great for God that it's doomed for failure unless God is behind it. In other words, when setting a lifetime giving goal in faith and prayer, make it a number that is beyond what you deem realistic.

The journey to Christlike generosity is the dynamic daily conforming to the image of Christ. It is long and hard in places, and we never will arrive at perfect conformity or generosity until we are in heaven. I confess that the moment I think that I can operate with an open hand, I find myself wrapping my fingers back around my "stuff." So why even take this journey of giving? Because it is worth it. When we make the choice to invest in the eternal instead of the temporal, then the floodgates of heaven will open on us. We will experience the joy, contentment, reward, favor, blessing, and peace that God intended for us to have. We will get a taste of the life that is truly life. We will arrive at our journeys' goal: the center of God's will and the funding of Jesus Christ's Great Commission.

DARYL J. HEALD is president and cofounder of Generous Giving, a ministry working since 2000 to motivate Christians toward greater biblical generosity. He serves on the boards of Crown Financial Ministries, ProVision Foundation, and the Haggai Institute and is also an elder at Lookout Mountain (Tennessee) Presbyterian Church. He is on the executive committee of the Maclellan Foundation, a fifty-year world leader in Christian grant making. He and his wife, Cathy, live in Lookout Mountain, Georgia, with their five children.

1. George Barna, *Revolution* (Carol Stream, IL: Tyndale House, 2005), 33.
2. Mark Allan Powell, *Giving to God: The Bible's Good News about Living a Generous Life* (Cambridge: Eerdmans, 2006), 5.
3. Barna, *Revolution*, 129.
4. Wesley K. Willmer, *God & Your Stuff* (Colorado Springs: NavPress, 2002), 25.
5. Randy Alcorn, *The Treasure Principle: Unlocking the Secret of Joyful Giving* (Sisters, OR: Multnomah, 2001), 19.
6. Powell, *Giving to God*, 4.

Appendix

Understanding and Applying
BIBLICAL PRINCIPLES FOR
Stewardship and FUNDRAISING

By JOYCE M. BROOKS, *Director of Foundations and*
Major Gift Operations, Biola University

I n 2003, noting that Christian organizations tended to use secular fundraising methods with little consideration of whether those practices were consistent with God's Word, Wesley Willmer convened a national task force under the joint auspices of the Christian Stewardship Association (CSA) and the Evangelical Council for Financial Accountability (ECFA) to address this concern. The task force consisted of twenty-three Christian leaders, including three with experience as seminary presidents.[1]

The task force developed the Biblical Principles for Stewardship and Fundraising, and since then many have asked for additional help to understand how to put these principles into practice. The purpose of this chapter is to provide that assistance.

The principles provide the framework for this chapter and are comprised of ten assertions, an introductory statement, and a conclusion—each of which is printed in bold below. The chapter then seeks to answer two questions about each phrase within the Principles: "What does it mean?" and "How does it apply to raising money?"

BIBLICAL PRINCIPLES FOR STEWARDSHIP AND FUNDRAISING

Christian leaders, including development staff, who believe in the Gospel of Jesus Christ and choose prayerfully to pursue eternal kingdom values (Matt. 6:19–21, 33), will seek to identify the sacred kingdom resources of God's economy within these parameters:

Christian leaders, including development staff who believe in the Gospel of Jesus Christ and choose prayerfully to pursue eternal kingdom values . . .

What does this mean? All leaders who affirm Jesus Christ as Lord—including pastors, teachers, professors, elders, deacons, and members of resource development teams at Christian organizations—all who believe that the gospel of Jesus Christ is the good news that God loves us so much that He sent His Son to pay the penalty for our disobedience so that we might live in communion with Him for eternity. If we believe that is true and have accepted God's gift of salvation, then we will follow the commands of Matthew 6:19–21: "Do not store up for yourselves treasures on earth. . . . But store up for yourselves treasures in heaven. . . . For where your treasure is, there your heart will be also."[2] If we claim that Jesus Christ is Lord of our lives, then our chief priority will be to please God, not ourselves. Rather than focusing our life efforts on accumulating what is of value to us, we should focus on finding out what God values, through prayer and the reading of Scripture.

How does this apply to raising money? Christians who are in leadership positions have the sacred privilege to interact with prospective ministry partners about how God desires them to use the resources entrusted into their care. One who embraces the gospel of Jesus Christ will actively, prayerfully, seek to learn what God wants for one's ministry and for the ministry partners with whom one interacts. One will pursue the transformational raising up of stewards to be rich toward God, which this book espouses. A Christian leader will not covet what others have, but will prayerfully ask God what He desires—both for the leader and for the ministry.

. . . will seek to identify the sacred kingdom resources of God's economy within these parameters . . .

What does this mean? Christian leaders should trust God to provide resources to further the work of His Kingdom.

How does this apply to raising money? There are two major paradigms to explain raising money: (1) a marketing paradigm that considers a gift a transaction between the giver and the charity that results from the persuasion of the fundraiser, and (2) a transformational paradigm that believes one who gives does so out of a heart that God has transformed and that is generous because Christ is generous (see Richard Haynie's and Walt Russell's chapters). The one is human-centered, the other God-centered (see Shelley Cochrane's chapter).

1. God, the creator (Gen. 1) and sustainer of all things (Heb. 1:3; Col. 1:17) and the One "who works within us to accomplish far more than we can ask or imagine" (Eph. 3:20), is a God of infinite abundance (Ps. 24:1; 50:10–12) and grace (2 Cor. 9:8; Phil. 4:19).[3]

God, the creator and sustainer of all things . . .

What does this mean? The Bible teaches that God is the Creator. He created "heaven and earth, the sea, and everything in them" (Ps. 146:6). This is so fundamental to understanding who God is and our relationship with Him that the first verse of the first book of the Bible begins by establishing this fact: "In the beginning God created the heavens and the earth" (Gen. 1:1). Because God is the Creator, He has the right and authority to demand obedience from us. And God is worthy of our worship because He created all things (Ps. 148). Not only did God create the universe; He also holds all things together (Job 38–39; Matt. 6:25–34) and promises to provide for all that His followers need.

How does this apply to raising money? If God has the power to create all things, and if God holds all things together under His authority, then God is sufficient to provide the resources needed to carry out His ministry.

God is the One "who works within us to accomplish far more than we can ask or imagine" . . .

What does this mean? The Holy Spirit will empower us to trust Christ enough to allow Him to live within our hearts (Eph. 3:14–19). Christ's love for us is so great that it is beyond our understanding, and by "being rooted and established in love" (Eph. 3:17) we "may be filled to the measure of all the fullness of God" (Eph. 3:19). Therefore, we will grow in the knowledge of His love and be empowered to trust that God "is able to do immeasurably more than all we ask or imagine" (Eph. 3:20).

How does this apply to raising money? God loves us so much that He will fully provide for us. Furthermore, as believers trust Christ enough to be conformed to His image, God will transform their hearts (see R. Scott Rodin's chapter) so they can rest in the understanding that God is able to provide far beyond what they can even imagine. The more a believer trusts in God's loving provision, the more generous he or she will become.

. . . a God of infinite abundance and grace.

What does this mean? God owns all things, and therefore He is a God of infinite abundance; everything He created ultimately belongs to Him, yet He delights in providing abundantly for His people. As Shelley Cochrane points out in her chapter, there is no limit to God's potential abundance. Blomberg found it significant that God declared the world He had created "good" (Gen. 1),[4] and went on to point out that God's intent was for His people to joyfully benefit from the abundance He created.[5]

Furthermore, God's mere desire to be in relationship with us stems from His grace. Rodin notes: "The movement of God toward us was a movement of grace.... The grace of God revealed in Christ is the hallmark of our faith."[6]

How does this apply to raising money? If God owns all things and delights in providing for His people, then we can rely on God to provide for our ministry organizations. There is no need to trust in manipulative, transactional fundraising practices. We can trust God to provide abundantly through transformed hearts.

2. Acknowledging the primacy of the Gospel (Rom. 1:16) as our chief treasure (Matt. 13:44), Christians are called to lives of stewardship, as managers of all that God has entrusted to them (1 Cor. 4:1–2).[7]

Acknowledging the primacy of the Gospel as our chief treasure . . .

What does this mean? It is Good News that we can live in an intimate relationship with the Creator of the universe because of the death and resurrection of our Lord and Savior Jesus Christ. When viewing our lives from an eternal perspective, nothing else matters. Without the opportunity to be reconciled to God, we would be doomed to live a life of pain and die without hope for relief from eternal suffering. The gospel is fundamental to our well-being: it is the most important thing we possess—it is our chief treasure.[8]

How does this apply to raising money? Nothing but the good news of Jesus Christ is important. Our latest campaign project pales in comparison to the message of the gospel. When development professionals raise funds for buildings, scholarships, salaries, or other projects, they should remember that these are only vehicles to further the cause of God's Kingdom, not ends in themselves.

Christians are called to lives of stewardship, as managers of all that God has entrusted to them.

What does this mean? Because God is the Creator and thus the ultimate owner of all things, everything we claim to possess is not in actuality ours but God's. Everything we have is given to us by God, and He holds us responsible for managing these possessions in a manner that is pleasing to Him. As managers of God's resources, we will be required to account for what we have done with what God has given us. Rodin points out that this managerial responsibility takes place within the context of relationship with God: "We are stewards under the reign of this God who calls us into fellowship with him in Christ Jesus."[9]

How does this apply to raising money? If all things belong to God, then any resources that may be given to a charitable organization in reality belong to God. Development officers may confidently present giving opportunities, recognizing that the ministry is not seeking to take anything away from the ministry partner; rather, the partners are giving from what God has entrusted into their care. When prospective ministry partners consider whether or not to support a cause, they should pray and ask God if it is His will that a gift be given. Similarly, when development professionals present giving opportunities to prospective supporters, they should do so acknowledging that it is the responsibility of the prospective supporter to seek out God's will or call (see Lauren Libby's chapter) regarding His resources.

3. A Christian's attitude toward possessions on earth is important to God

(Matt. 6:24; 1 Tim. 6:6–10), and there is a vital link between how believers utilize earthly possessions (as investments in God's kingdom) and the eternal rewards that believers receive (Phil. 4:17; Matt. 19:27–30; Matt. 25:31–46; 1 Tim. 6:17–19).[10]

A Christian's attitude toward possessions on earth is important to God.

What does this mean? When a rich young man asked how he could receive eternal life, Jesus told him to "sell your possessions and give to the poor, and you will have treasure in heaven. Then come, follow me" (Matt. 19:21). Rather than following through on Jesus' advice, the young man "went away sad, because he had great wealth" (Matt. 19:22).[11]

How does this apply to raising money? Prospective ministry partners should be challenged to trust God to provide for them and to seek to be rich toward God (Luke 12:21). Supporters should be challenged to value God and follow the lead of the Holy Spirit above and beyond all things. Development professionals should also put love for God above everything else; their lives should be examples of godly stewardship, and they should resist the temptation to covet the possessions of the ministry partners with whom they interact (see Adam Morris's chapter).

There is a vital link between how believers utilize earthly possessions (as investments in God's Kingdom) and the eternal rewards that believers receive.

What does this mean? In Matthew 16:26 Jesus asked, "What good will it be for a man if he gains the whole world, yet forfeits his soul?"

God holds us accountable for what we do with the possessions that He has entrusted into our care; we will have to report to God what we did with the resources He gave us. If we have used the resources to glorify God, we will be rewarded; if we fail to use those resources in a way that pleases God, we will not be rewarded.[12] Alcorn proposed what he called "the Treasure Principle: You can't take it with you—but you *can* send it on ahead."[13]

How does this apply to raising money? Giving decisions are spiritual decisions with eternal consequences. Stewardship professionals should focus on what God can do with resources rather than on the resources themselves. A development officer should communicate (see Gary Hoag's chapter) the mission and vision of the organization and challenge prospective ministry partners from an eternal perspective. Development professionals can challenge individuals to consider what they value as stewards (see Todd Harper's chapter) and whether or not they will hear God say, "Come, you who are blessed by my Father; take your inheritance, the kingdom prepared for you since the creation of the world" (Matt. 25:34).

4. God entrusts possessions to Christians and holds them accountable for their use, as a tool to grow God's eternal kingdom, as a test of the believer's faithfulness to God, and as a trademark that their lives reflect Christ's values (Luke 16:1–9).[14]

God entrusts possessions to Christians . . .

What does this mean? God retains the rights of ownership for everything He created, but He entrusts responsibility for looking after His creation to humans: God told Adam and Eve to rule over and work at and take care of what He created (Gen. 1:28; 2:15). When King David dedicated the resources that had been donated for the construction of the temple, he acknowledged to God, "Wealth and honor come from you; you are the ruler of all things. . . . Everything comes from you, and we have given you only what comes from your hand" (1 Chron. 29:12, 14).

How does this apply to raising money? It is the responsibility of resource development professionals to both educate and challenge Christians to think from this perspective, ensuring that believers understand that they in actuality own nothing and are merely the managers and distributors of God's resources. All forms of communication should reinforce this belief system.

. . . and holds [Christians] accountable for their use . . .

What does this mean? As with any owner, God expects His resources to be handled in a way that pleases Him, and there will come a time when God will conduct an audit to determine whether each Christian has glorified God through the use of the possessions that have been entrusted into his or her care. In Matthew 25:14–30, Jesus uses the parable of the talents to teach the principle of using resources in a way consistent with the owner's expectations. Jesus goes on to describe the final judgment (Matt. 25:31–46) where each person will be rewarded or condemned based on whether he or she compassionately provided for those in need. The apostle Paul reiterates this image, saying, "For we must all appear before the judgment seat of Christ, that each one may receive what is due him for things done while in the body, whether good or bad" (2 Cor. 5:10; cf. Matt. 16:27; Rom. 14:10–12).

How does this apply to raising money? Stewardship professionals can challenge Christians to consider whether—at the end of time when they are standing before the judgment seat of Christ—they will feel confident that they have used God's possessions in a manner pleasing to God. Resource development professionals may also intentionally describe how support of a given project or ministry is consistent with God's expectations as described in Scripture.

. . . as a tool to grow God's eternal Kingdom . . .

What does this mean? God has provided us with resources to further His eternal spiritual Kingdom.[15]

How does this apply to raising money? Stewardship professionals can confidently challenge Christians to think of their donations as investments in God's Kingdom. When Christians leverage possessions to bless Christian ministries, the profits reaped from such investments last for eternity.

... as a test of the believer's faithfulness to God ...

What does this mean? Willmer suggested that how we use possessions serves as "a four-part take-home test. The test is to: (1) determine who is master of our life; (2) assess how much responsibility we will be given in heaven; (3) determine how faithful we were in dispensing God's grace; (4) see what honors we will receive at commencement into heaven."[16]

How does this apply to raising money? Stewardship professionals should be more concerned about the eternal spiritual state and growth of their prospective ministry partners than they are about receiving a gift for their particular ministry. If the potential supporter appears to be more focused on the pursuit of wealth and the recognition he or she may receive in exchange for a gift, the development officer would be wise to disciple the person toward an eternal perspective.

... as a trademark that their lives reflect Christ's values.

What does this mean? How we use our possessions demonstrates whether we are members of God's Kingdom. Jesus said, "By this all men will know that you are my disciples, if you love one another" (John 13:35).[17]

Our allegiance to Christ should be so obvious that a stranger could tell based on how we use the resources entrusted to us. When we show love to others by volunteering our time to help at the food pantry or tutor children after school, visiting the sick or those in prison, or supporting the homeless shelter ministry in our neighborhood, then our lives will reflect Christ's values.

How does this apply to raising money? Stewardship professionals should confidently encourage prospective ministry partners to consider whether they are using the resources entrusted into their care in such a way that others would be able to tell that they are believers. When generosity is a reflection of Christ in us, our character changes and people see an outward difference.

5. From God's abounding grace, Christians' giving reflects their gratitude for what God has provided (Lev. 7:11–15; 2 Cor. 9:10–15) and involves growing in an intimate faith relationship with Christ as Lord of their lives (Mark 12:41–44; Luke 12:16–34).[18]

God's abounding grace . . .

What does this mean? Scripture teaches that God gives grace to the righteous. The Old Testament Hebrew word for *grace* can also be translated as "favor, kindness, pleasant, precious" and the New Testament Greek word as "grace, acceptable, benefit, favor, gift, pleasure." Psalm 84:11 declares, "The Lord bestows favor and honor; no good thing does he withhold from those whose walk is blameless." And the apostle Paul reminded the church in Corinth, "For you know the grace of our Lord Jesus Christ, that though he was rich, yet for your sakes he became poor, so that you through his poverty might become rich" (2 Cor. 8:9). Paul goes on to say, "God is able to make all grace abound to you, so that in all things at all times, having all that you need, you will abound in every good work" (2 Cor. 9:8).

How does this apply to raising money? Because God's grace is given to "those whose walk is blameless" (Ps. 84:11), Christians should actively pursue a righteous life—while embracing God's free gift of righteousness, since we "are justified freely by his grace through the redemption that came by Christ Jesus" (Rom. 3:24). Both stewardship professionals and ministry partners can rest in God's promise to provide all we need—and even more. Christian nonprofits can be confident that they will receive the resources to enable them to "abound in every good work" (2 Cor. 9:8). Ministry partners can be confident that if they support ministries, they will still have sufficient to pay the mortgage and feed their families.

Christians' giving reflects their gratitude for what God has provided . . .

What does this mean? Paul taught that the generosity of those who give out of the abundance that God has given them "will result in thanksgiving to God" (2 Cor. 9:11): those who are recipients of generosity will thank God for His provision. Couching God's abundant provision within the framework of "the grace of our Lord Jesus Christ" (2 Cor. 8:9), the apostle goes on to exclaim, "Thanks be to God for his indescribable gift!" (2 Cor. 9:15). The natural response to God's grace is thanksgiving, and one way to express that thanksgiving is by giving generously. This is a voluntary outgrowth of the process of sanctification.[19] The Old Testament sacrificial system assumed that the faithful would present offerings as a means of showing thankfulness to God (Lev. 7:11–15; 22:29; cf. 2 Chron. 29:31; 33:16).

How does this apply to raising money? Generosity results from a life conformed to Christ, because Christ was generous. As stewardship professionals focus on transforming hearts to be rich toward God, the believer will respond with generosity out of gratitude for what God has provided.

Christians' giving involves growing in an intimate faith relationship with Christ as Lord of their lives.

What does this mean? It may feel risky to give away some of the resources God has given to us, but when we do so we are taking concrete steps to demonstrate our trust in God to take care of us. Through giving we also acknowledge Jesus Christ to be the Master of our lives. Rather than making the accumulation of money our priority or relying on our own ability to make a living, we choose to trust and obey our Lord when we give to others. And as we grow in our ability to trust in our Lord, we develop a closer, more intimate relationship with Him.

Alcorn has said, "Gaze upon Christ long enough, and you'll become more of a giver. Give long enough, and you'll become more like Christ."[20] He goes on to say, "Giving jump-starts our relationship with God. It opens our fists so we can receive what God has for us. When we see what it does for others and for us, we open our fists sooner and wider when the next chance comes."[21]

How does this apply to raising money? Stewardship professionals are providing a spiritual ministry when they present giving opportunities to Christians, giving believers the chance to develop a closer relationship with the Lord Jesus Christ. For this reason, those who have been called to ask others for support can do so with confidence, knowing that they are carrying out the work of the church to make disciples (Matt. 28:19–20).

6. Because giving is a worshipful, obedient act of returning to God from what has been provided (1 Chron. 29:10–14), Christian fundraisers should hold a conviction that, in partnership with the church, they have an important role in the spiritual maturation of believers (James 3:1).[22]

Because giving is a worshipful, obedient act of returning to God from what has been provided . . .

What does this mean? Both the Old and New Testaments contain commandments to give back to God by supporting others (Deut. 14:22–29; 1 Cor. 9:14; 16:1–2; Gal. 2:10). At the dedication of the material for the temple, King David worshiped God, saying, "Everything comes from you, and we have given you only what comes from your hand" (1 Chron. 29:14).

How does this apply to raising money? Stewardship professionals can confidently encourage prospective ministry partners to consider making a gift as worship to God because the resources that believers may contribute actually belong to God. Development officers are not trying to take away anyone's money. When a development professional asks a Christian to consider making a gift to his or her ministry, in essence one of God's stewards is simply consulting with another of God's stewards. Furthermore, the stewardship professional is facilitating God's work in the giver by giving a fellow Christian an opportunity to worship God through obediently giving back to God from what God owns already.

. . . Christian fundraisers should hold a conviction that, in partnership with the church, they have an important role in the spiritual maturation of believers.

What does this mean? Jesus warned, "For where your treasure is, there your heart will be also" (Luke 12:34), and, "You cannot serve both God and Money." (Luke 16:13; cf. Matt. 6:24). The apostle Paul wrote, "For the love of money is a root of all kinds of evil" (1 Tim. 6:10). Given these admonitions—along with Jesus' command to "make disciples of all nations . . . teaching them to obey everything I have commanded you" (Matt. 28:19–20)—it is clear that a significant role of the church is to challenge believers to trust and serve God alone. Christian development professionals have the special opportunity to partner with the church in this effort.

How does this apply to raising money? Because giving is a spiritual decision, and believers become generous as they are conformed to the image of Christ, Christian stewardship professionals are involved in facilitating the spiritual maturation of believers so they become generous. As they interact with prospective ministry partners, stewardship professionals often get a glimpse of both the financial situation and value system of these fellow believers. This gives development officers the opportunity to encourage and challenge fellow Christians to put their trust in God and to become generous as Christ is generous.

7. The primary role of a Christian fundraiser is to advance and facilitate a believer's faith in and worship of God through a Christ-centered understanding of stewardship that is solidly grounded on Scripture (2 Tim. 3:16–17).[23]

The primary role of a Christian fundraiser is to advance and facilitate a believer's faith in and worship of God...

What does this mean? The primary role of a Christian development officer is to encourage prospective supporters to grow in their relationship with Christ. Believers will become generous as they are conformed to the image of Christ. Development professionals are called to educate ministry partners regarding the biblical perspective of giving, to challenge believers who are trusting in their net worth rather than in God, and to provide a vehicle with which to worship God by facilitating and receiving charitable giving.

How does this apply to raising money? Advancing a believer's faith, as suggested throughout this book, means the organization's focus is on transforming hearts to be rich toward God. Rather than holding development officers accountable solely for the amount of donations raised, performance will also take into account their heart-to-heart discussions with prospective ministry partners. The nature of the face-to-face visit will change from that of begging or manipulating to communicating ministry needs and discerning spiritual readiness. Ministries' publications should be intentional in educating their constituency regarding the biblical view of possessions and the stewardship responsibility of every believer. Direct mail appeals should reflect the scriptural basis for supporting the ministry.

. . . through a Christ-centered understanding of stewardship that is solidly grounded on Scripture.

415

What does this mean? Christian fundraisers are called to use all relevant Scripture to educate their constituency regarding the biblical understanding of possessions and giving. Believers need to be taught that God is the ultimate owner of all things (Gen. 1:28; Ps. 24:1; 1 Chron. 29:11–16), we are the managers of God's resources, and He will hold us accountable for what we do with what we have been given (Matt. 25:14–46). Christians must learn to trust in God rather than money (Luke 12:15–21) and understand that giving is an expression of worship to God (Lev. 7:11–15; 22:29; cf. 2 Chron. 29:31; 33:16).

How does this apply to raising money? Christian development officers must accept the responsibility to educate believers regarding biblical stewardship principles. Stewardship professionals can offer seminars on stewardship at local churches, assist pastors by preaching sermons on giving, publish articles about the biblical perspective of possessions in their ministry publications, and ensure that those within their direct realm of influence (i.e., employees, students, alumni, clients, parishioners, supporters) receive stewardship training.

8. Recognizing it is the work of the Holy Spirit that prompts Christians to give (Isa. 32:15–17; 34:16; John 6:63; 14:15–21; 15:4–5, 16–17, 26; 16:13–14; Rom. 12:4–8; 1 Thess. 1:2–6; 2:13; Gal. 5:16–25; 1 Peter 1:2) (often through fundraising techniques) (Neh. 1:4–2:8; 2 Cor. 9:5–7), fundraisers and/or organizations must never manipulate or violate their sacred trust with ministry partners.[24]

. . . it is the work of the Holy Spirit that prompts Christians to give . . .

What does this mean? Giving is contrary to our sin nature. Jesus cautioned His followers to "be on your guard against all kinds of greed" (Luke 12:15) and counseled them to "not store up for yourselves treasures on earth" (Matt. 6:19). The apostle Paul warned against "the love of money" (1 Tim.

6:10) and listed envy as one of "the acts of the sinful nature" (Gal. 5:19). Paul instead admonished Christians to "live by the Spirit, and you will not gratify the desires of the sinful nature" (Gal. 5:16), and the apostle Peter noted that "God's elect . . . [had] been chosen according to the foreknowledge of God the Father, through the sanctifying work of the Spirit, for obedience to Jesus Christ" (1 Peter 1:1–2). Jesus promised that He would send "the Spirit of truth [who would] guide you into all truth" (John 16:13).[25]

How does this apply to raising money? It is not the responsibility of the development officer to convince prospective supporters to give; rather, it is God at work within the hearts of Christians that will bring about gifts. Rodin says,

> This should be a liberating and empowering realization. Only within this understanding can we go about our work in the highest professional manner. . . . Only in this context can we really have interactions with our donors that are not all tied to a solicitation and truly be at ease. We all know that successful fundraising is based on the building of good, solid, long-term relationships. This understanding of the Holy Spirit as the motivator of gifts frees us to do that job to its utmost.[26]

Therefore, development officers should pray, trust God, and rest in Him when going about their business. Rodin notes that development officers will still ask for gifts, but, "We will ask simply, honestly and confidently, and then we will sit back and watch God do great things through his people."[27]

. . . often through fundraising techniques . . .

What does this mean? While it is the Holy Spirit who prompts Christians to give, God often uses fellow believers involved in raising funds to facilitate the process. God instructed Moses to "tell the Israelites to bring me an offering" (Ex. 25:1) for materials to construct the tabernacle. King David challenged the leaders of Israel to donate toward the construction of the temple (1 Chron. 29:1-9). Nehemiah was bold to ask King Artaxerxes for the resources to rebuild the walls of Jerusalem (Neh. 1:4-2:8). And the apostle Paul wrote an appeal letter to the church in Corinth requesting donations for the poor in the church in Jerusalem (2 Cor. 8-9).

How does this apply to raising money? It is a balance between prayer and work. While praying for God's provision should be a part of every Christian fundraiser's daily life and work, God uses the process of relationship building, education, and mentoring to bring stewards' resources into the Kingdom. God tends to work through individuals to carry out His work, and the Holy Spirit may well use an appeal letter, ministry update, or personal visit (with the appropriate biblical perspective) to challenge a believer to make a gift.

. . . fundraisers and/or organizations must never manipulate or violate their sacred trust with ministry partners.

What does this mean? Christian organizations work in partnership with their supporters to carry out the work of God's Kingdom. Ministry partners trust the nonprofit to use their gifts for God's glory.

How does this apply to raising money? Resource development professionals should always be honest with their ministry partners. It is never acceptable to claim that there is a financial crisis when one does not exist. Neither is it appropriate to use guilt as a motivation for generating gifts. Any donations a nonprofit receives should be used for precisely what the giver intends. Furthermore, ministries should be wise and discreet with the gifts entrusted to them; it is inappropriate for nonprofit leaders to use donations to fund lavish lifestyles.

9. An eternal, God-centered worldview promotes cooperation, rather than competition, among organizations, and places the giver's relation-

ship to God above the ministry's agenda (1 Cor. 3:1–9; 2 Cor. 4:16–18; Gal. 5:13–25; Phil. 4:17).[28]

An eternal, God-centered worldview . . .

What does this mean? God has always existed and will always exist. "'I am the Alpha and the Omega,' says the Lord God, 'who is, and who was, and who is to come, the Almighty'" (Rev. 1:8). Therefore God is not limited by time. God's perspective is eternal; as the psalmist said, "Before the mountains were born or you brought forth the earth and the world, from everlasting to everlasting, you are God. . . . For a thousand years in your sight are like a day that has just gone by, or like a watch in the night" (Ps. 90:2, 4).

If we are to have a God-centered worldview, we will seek to view the world through God's eternal perspective rather than focusing just on what we see before us at this present time. As the apostle Paul wrote to the church in Corinth, "So we fix our eyes not on what is seen, but on what is unseen. For what is seen is temporary, but what is unseen is eternal" (2 Cor. 4:18). Furthermore, we will focus on God's priorities, not our organization's priorities. As the apostle Paul exhorted the Christians in Colossae, "set your hearts on things above, where Christ is seated at the right hand of God. Set your minds on things above, not on earthly things" (Col. 3:1–2).

How does that apply to raising money? Our individual ministries are just one small segment of God's eternal plan. While God may have called a stewardship professional to serve Him through a given nonprofit, God is much bigger than that one ministry organization. God works out His will through myriads of people and organizations, and all nonprofit ministries that have been established by God have a part in furthering God's Kingdom. The stewardship professional should interact with people from the worldview that God is working to further His Kingdom, and the priority is God's eternal Kingdom, not the organization.

. . . promotes cooperation, rather than competition, among organizations . . .

What does this mean? Jesus called us to be united as a body of Christ. The night before His crucifixion, Jesus gave His disciples a commandment: "Love each other as I have loved you" (John 15:12). He went on to pray that His disciples "may be one as we are one" (John 17:11) and that "those who will believe in me through their message, that all of them may be one, Father, just as you are in me and I am in you" (John 17:20–21). As Rodin has said, "We are now called to live as people who are one in Christ. Not 'as if' we were, but because we *actually are!*"[29] If we are one in Christ and if we are all carrying out the work God has called us to do, then we are working together to further God's Kingdom rather than competing with one another for market share or donations.

How does that apply to raising money? Stewardship professionals should shift the way they think about other Christian nonprofits (see Shelley Cochrane's chapter). Rather than viewing other organizations as "the competition," they should embrace them as other avenues for God to carry out His work. Furthermore, if a prospective ministry partner chooses to support a different charity rather than the one a given development officer represents, the response should be one of joy that the individual is giving to God's work, and that supporter should be commended for carrying out his or her stewardship responsibilities.

. . . and places the giver's relationship to God above the ministry's agenda.

What does this mean? From an eternal perspective, it is much more important to encourage others to take concrete steps to submit every aspect of their lives to the will of God than it is to raise donations for a given nonprofit organization. Jesus' final instructions to His followers before His ascension was to carry out the Great Commission (Matt. 28:16–20), which demonstrates the importance of God's relationship to each individual.

Rodin counsels Christian development professionals to be less concerned about how much ministry partners give and more concerned with "how they give and why they give."[30] He goes on to say that "the spiritual growth of our donors should be the primary concern of every Christian fundraiser! It is in this context that we should be planning our annual program of visitations, letters, phone calls, mailings, publications, and solicitations."[31]

How does that apply to raising money? Stewardship professionals should encourage and commend a giver for supporting God's work—regardless of which ministry is receiving the benefit—rather than seeking to discourage gifts to another nonprofit.

10. In our materialistic, self-centered culture, Christian leaders should acknowledge that there is a great deal of unclear thinking about possessions, even among believers, and that an eternal kingdom perspective will often seem like foolish nonsense (1 Cor. 2:14) to those who rely on earthly kingdom worldview techniques (1 Cor. 2:1–5).[32]

In our materialistic, self-centered culture, Christian leaders should acknowledge that there is a great deal of unclear thinking about possessions, even among believers . . .

What does this mean? Our society values the accumulation of wealth and focuses its attention on pleasing self rather than focusing on God and adopting His value system. One cannot love the world and love God at the same time (1 John 2:15). The world's value system consists of "the cravings of sinful man, the lust of his eyes and the boasting of what he has and does" (1 John 2:16), and these are inconsistent with God's value system. Jesus said that what was most important was to "love the Lord your God with all your heart and with all your soul and with all your mind . . . [and to] . . . love your neighbor as yourself" (Matt. 22:37–39). As Christians who live in a culture steeped in the selfish desire to accumulate wealth, our challenge is to intentionally adopt

God's value system rather than let the world's priorities rule their lives.

How does this apply to raising money? Stewardship professionals must seek a heart transformation within their own lives so they strive for what God desires. This transformation of the heart to a countercultural position will affect both their personal lives and their ministry. As Christian leaders are actively seeking to adopt God's value system, they are called to challenge the believers with whom they interact to undergo a heart transformation as well, so that the ministry partners likewise focus their priorities on pleasing God rather than succumbing to a life of selfish materialism.

. . . an eternal kingdom perspective will often seem like foolish nonsense to those who rely on earthly kingdom worldview techniques.

What does this mean? This approach seems naïve and impossible to someone who does not believe that God provides every need and transforms hearts. Direct marketing experts may insist that one must offer a premium to ensure a strong response in direct mail fundraising, or fundraising professionals may expound on the importance of using prestige as a motivator for joining a giving club; but Christian leaders are called to trust God's wisdom, rather than man's wisdom. From an eternal Kingdom perspective, charitable giving is not a transaction; it is an act of worship as the heart is transformed.

How does this apply to raising money? If God has called a charity to fulfill a particular mission, God will provide the resources to carry out that responsibility. There is no need to rely on fundraising techniques that use sinful desires to manipulate individuals to make a gift. Rather, Christians who undergo a transformation of the heart will become like Christ; because Christ was generous, they too will be generous. Trust God and follow His way.

When these principles are implemented, which rely on God changing hearts more than on human methods, the resulting joy-filled generosity

of believers will fully fund God's work here on earth (Ex. 36:6–7).[33]

What does this mean? When resource development professionals determine to carry out their work from God's eternal Kingdom perspective rather than being motivated by the value system of this world, they and the ministry partners with whom they work will undergo a personal life transformation in Christ. As a result of this transformation, they will reflect Christ's character, demonstrating a life of love, sacrifice, joy, and generosity. Because of their joyful generosity, God will provide all that Christian nonprofits need to carry out the work of His eternal Kingdom.

How does this apply to raising money? Be faithful to God's ways, and the resources will follow. These biblical principles serve as a guide to stewardship professionals as they seek to raise the resources required to carry out God's work. Rather than relying on the advice of secular fundraising experts, Christian resource development officers are called to rely on God and His wisdom and in so doing to receive from God all that is needed when He creates a revolution in generosity.

JOYCE M. BROOKS (Ph.D., Biola University) is the director of Foundations and Major Gift Operations at Biola University in La Mirada, California. She has been a development professional since 1983, and her experience spans all aspects of development, including annual giving, major donor research, development services, capital campaigns, events, major gifts, and foundation relations. Her dissertation title was: "A Study of the Motivations and Preferences for Charitable Giving among Women and Men Who Support Evangelical Christian Higher Education." Joyce is a published author and has presented scholarly papers at Evangelical Theological Society conferences. She can be reached at Joyce.Brooks@biola.edu.

1. The members of the joint CSA/ECFA Task Force that developed the Biblical Principles for Stewardship and Fundraising (with titles as of the time of committee service) were: Randy Alcorn (Founder and Director, Eternal Perspectives Ministries), Rebekah Burch Basinger (Consultant for Fundraising and Board Education), Ron Blue (Managing Partner, Ronald Blue & Co.), Howard Dayton (CEO, Crown Financial Ministries), Lu Dunbar (President, Royal Treasure), Daryl J. Heald (President, Generous Giving), Thomas Jeavons (General Secretary, Philadelphia Yearly Meeting of the Religious Society of Friends), Brian Kluth (Senior Pastor, First Evangelical Free Church, Colorado Springs, CO), Lauren Libby (Vice President and COO, The Navigators), Tom McCabe (President, KMA), Thomas H. McCallie III (Attorney, Maclellan Foundation), David L. McKenna (Chairman of the Board of Trustees, Spring Arbor College; Former President: Spring Arbor College, Seattle Pacific University, and Asbury Theological Seminary), Adam Morris (Committee Vice Chair, and Senior Director of Stewardship and Resource Development, Biola University), Richard J. Mouw (President and Professor, Fuller Theological Seminary), Paul D. Nelson (President, Evangelical Council for Financial Accountability), John Pearson (CEO, Christian Management Association), Scott Preissler (President and CEO, Christian Stewardship Association), R. Scott Rodin (Consultant; Former President: Eastern Baptist Theological Seminary), J. David Schmidt (President, J. David Schmidt & Associates), Janet Stump (Director of Development, Association of Christian Schools International), Rollin Van Broekhoven (Federal Judge, Washington, D.C.), Mark Vincent (President and Lead Partner, Design for Ministry, Mennonite Church), Wesley K. Willmer (Committee Chair, and Vice President of University Advancement and Professor, Biola University).
2. All Bible quotations are from the *New International Version*.
3. Additional Reference: John 1:14.
4. Craig L. Blomberg, *Neither Poverty nor Riches: A Biblical Theology of Material Possessions,* New Studies in Biblical Theology (Grand Rapids: Eerdmans, 1999), 243–44.
5. Ibid.
6. R. Scott Rodin, *Stewards in the Kingdom: A Theology of Life in All Its Fullness* (Downers Grove, IL: InterVarsity, 2000), 42.
7. See also Gen. 1:26–30; Matt. 25:14–46; 28:18–20; 1 Cor. 1:18, 23–24; 9:23; Phil. 3:8–11; 1 Peter 4:10.
8. Rodin, *Stewards in the Kingdom*, 60.
9. Ibid., 56.
10. See also Matt. 22:37; Luke 14:12–14; 1 Cor. 3; 2 Cor. 5:10; Eph. 2:10.
11. Randy Alcorn, *The Treasure Principle: Discovering the Secret of Joyful Giving* (Sisters, OR: Multnomah, 2001), 11.
12. Wesley K. Willmer, *God & Your Stuff: The Vital Link between Your Possessions and Your Soul* (Colorado Springs: NavPress, 2002), 29.
13. Alcorn, *The Treasure Principle*, 17–18.
14. See also Lev. 19:9–10; Deut. 14:22–29; 24:19–22; Isa. 58:6–7; Mal. 3:10; Matt. 6:24–33; 22:34–40; 25:14–46; Luke 12:15–34; John 13:34–35; 15:8–17; Rom. 1:1; 1 Cor. 9:14; 16:1–2 Cor. 8–9; Gal. 2:10; 6:10; Eph. 2:10; Col. 3:17; 1 Tim. 6:17–19; James 2:15–16; Heb. 13:15–16.
15. Willmer, *God & Your Stuff*, 15.
16. Ibid., 15–16.
17. Ibid., 20.
18. See also Gen. 14:20; Ezra 2:69; Luke 7:36–50.
19. Craig L. Blomberg, *Heart, Soul, and Money: A Christian View of Possessions* (Joplin, MO: College Press, 2000), 86.
20. Alcorn, *The Treasure Principle*, 31.
21. Ibid, 32.
22. See also Rom. 12:1.
23. See also Ex. 34:32; 35:21.
24. See also 1 Chron. 28:6; 29:9; Prov. 21:1; Isa. 55:8–11; 2 Cor. 3:5.
25. Blomberg, *Heart, Soul, and Money*, 107.
26. Rodin, *Stewards in the Kingdom*, 210.
27. Ibid.
28. See also Ps. 90:1–12.
29. Rodin, *Stewards in the Kingdom*, 47.
30. Ibid., 212.
31. Ibid.
32. See also 1 Cor. 1:17–31.
33. See also Matt. 6:10; 2 Cor. 9:8–12.